THE PERSONALITY CONTINUUM AND CONSUMER BEHAVIOR

The Personality Continuum and Consumer Behavior

Paul J. Albanese

Q

QUORUM BOOKS
Westport, Connecticut • London

Library of Congress Cataloging-in-Publication Data

Albanese, Paul J.
The personality continuum and consumer behavior / Paul J. Albanese.
p. cm.
Includes bibliographical references and index.
ISBN 1–56720–558–5 (alk. paper)
1. Economics—Psychological aspects. 2. Economic man. 3. Self-interest. 4. Self-control. 5. Personality. 6. Consumer behavior. I. Title.
HB72.P8A495 2002
330'.01'9—dc21 2002069692

British Library Cataloguing in Publication Data is available.

Library of Congress Catalog Card Number: 2002069692
ISBN: 1–56720–558–5

First published in 2002

Quorum Books, 88 Post Road West, Westport, CT 06881
An imprint of Greenwood Publishing Group, Inc.
www.quorumbooks.com

Printed in the United States of America

The paper used in this book complies with the Permanent Paper Standard issued by the National Information Standards Organization (Z39.8–1984).

10 9 8 7 6 5 4 3 2 1

Copyright Acknowledgments

To George W. Goethals, who taught me about the psychology of the human life cycle,
to Robert O. Kirkhart, who taught me about the value of one human life cycle,
to Harvey Leibenstein, whose life cycle was cut tragically short,
and to my father, whose promise I hope one day to have fulfilled.

Contents

FIGURES

ACKNOWLEDGMENTS

I would like to gratefully acknowledge the invaluable assistance of just three people. Morris B. Holbrook, Columbia University, reviewed an early version of the manuscript and made many useful suggestions that I have tried my best to incorporate into the book. For those ideas that went over my head, thank you for the illumination, and for supporting my research over the last decade. To my assiduous graduate research assistant, Amalia Munteanu, who patiently worked through many drafts of the manuscript and carefully prepared all of the quotations for copyright permissions, thank you for your two years of dedication. Finally, I would like to thank Cara Willaman, of the Copyright Clearance Services at Kent State University, who for more than six months worked with diligence, persistence, and patience in the complicated process of clearing the copyright permissions for this book.

Preface

The Personality Continuum is the heart of this book. You may want to take a look at it now to see just what this book is all about. The Personality Continuum is presented as a four-page figure immediately following the Preface of the book.

Everything depends on the level of personality development along the Personality Continuum. The Personality Continuum is divided into four discrete ranges—Normal, Neurotic, Primitive, and Psychotic. Each range of the Personality Continuum represents a qualitatively different level of personality development.

Everything is systematically related to everything else along the Personality Continuum. Each heading across the top of the Personality Continuum represents a different dimension of the personality. The first series of panels represents an object relations theory of the personality—Interpersonal Achievement in Personality Development, Internal Object Relations, Intrapsychic Structural Formation, Predominant Defenses, Intimacy, Preferred Patterning of Sexual Behavior, and the culmination in the Human Capacity. The focus then shifts to behavior—General Pattern of Human Behavior, Pattern of Consumer Behavior, a more specific Pattern of Consumption Behavior, the Individual Pursuit of Self-Interest, and Predictability. The last panel presents a relative ranking of the particular Personality Organizations that occupy each range of the Personality Continuum.

The Personality Continuum provides an integrative framework that brings together contributions from many disciplines for the study of human behavior, including economics, sociology, anthropology, and psychology. The Personality Continuum provides the grand template for a human understanding of consumer behavior.

PERSONALITY

RANGES	INTERPERSONAL ACHIEVEMENT IN PERSONALITY DEVELOPMENT	INTERNAL OBJECT RELATIONS	INTRAPSYCHIC STRUCTURAL FORMATION
NORMAL	Sexual orgasm and the subjective experience of transcendence in an intimate interpersonal relationship forms a new common social boundary around the couple connecting past, present, and future Full integration of satisfying genital sexual activity into an interpersonal relationship by successfully resolving the oedipal situation	Internalization of a value system Depersonification, individuation, reshaping to resemble real person	Protective superego Continuous internalization of more realistic interpersonal relationships through selective, partial, sublimatory identifications, including a complementary sexual identification in harmony with individual identity formation
NEUROTIC	Accept another person, and oneself, as both good and bad and, therefore, a whole and more realistic person	Integration of whole object relations	Ego identity and prohibitive superego
PRIMITIVE	Recognize oneself as separate from other	Self differentiated from object, internalization of the role aspects of interpersonal relationships, modified and more diversified affect	Multiple good and bad selves and objects internalized through identification, part-object relations Punitive superego
PSYCHOTIC	Oneself same as other	Self undifferentiated from object, intense and overwhelming positive and negative affect	Separate all-good and all-bad objects internalized through introjection

CONTINUUM

PREDOMINANT DEFENSES	INTIMACY	PREFERRED PATTERNING OF SEXUAL BEHAVIOR	HUMAN CAPACITY
A range of mature defenses, humor, sublimation, altruism, anticipation, and suppression	Second precondition for intimacy	Passion in an intimate interpersonal relationship; intimacy makes sexual relations satisfying	Capacity for commitment to a value system shared with another person Self-reliance, the capacity for foresight and to plan for the future, a future orientation, the capacity for genuine insight and the urge to change in meaningful ways, the capacity to remain in love and form intimate interpersonal relationships
Repression, intellectualization (isolation, obsessive behavior, undoing, rationalization), reaction formation, displacement (conversion, phobias, wit), dissociation (neurotic denial)	First precondition for intimacy	Failure to achieve preferred pattern of genital sexual activity is an all-absorbing and all-frustrating preoccupation	The capacity to fall in love, the capacity for concern for another person and oneself, and the capacity for experiencing guilt for violating the more realistic parental prohibitions and demands internalized in the prohibitive superego
Splitting, denial, projection (projective identification), fantasy (schizoid withdrawal, denial through fantasy) hypochondriasis, passive-aggressive behavior, acting out		Polymorphous perverse sexual behavior, predatory sexual behavior, intense infatuations, mainly with body parts, not whole person	The capacity for rage, envy, jealousy, possessiveness, the ruthless exploitation of others, varying degrees of immature dependence, and the incapacity to depend on another person
Denial of external reality, distortion, delusional projection			Absence of capacity for reality testing

PERSONALITY

RANGES	GENERAL PATTERN OF HUMAN BEHAVIOR	PATTERN OF CONSUMER BEHAVIOR	PATTERN OF CONSUMPTION BEHAVIOR
NORMAL	Stable and consistent	Rational economic consumer	Dynamic consumption behavior that can be modeled over time Self-control, delay of gratification, everything in moderation, prudent planning of consumption activities
NEUROTIC	Consistent under ordinary functioning, but lacking stability under extraordinary functioning	Neurotic consumer, indecisive, ambivalent, inhibited by feelings of guilt, cognitive dissonance	Striving for consistent self-control, use of precommitment devices to control behavior
PRIMITIVE	Chaotic pattern of alternating and contradictory behavior	Compulsive and more extreme addictive consumer behavior, the dark side of consumer behavior	Struggle with self- control, selective lack of impulse control, crude gratification of impulses, greed, backsliding, ultimately self- destructive, myopic consumption behavior
PSYCHOTIC	Changing and capricious	Irrational economic consumer	

CONTINUUM

INDIVIDUAL PURSUIT OF SELF-INTEREST	PREDICTABILITY	PERSONALITY ORGANIZATIONS
The individual pursuit of self-interest informed by a value system	Predictable	Optimally adjusted
The individual pursuit of self-interest with the capacity for sympathy and within the moral system of society	Predictable under ordinary functioning, regression to earlier patterns of behavior under extraordinary functioning	Depressive Avoidant Obsessive Hysterical Paranoid
The selfish pursuit of individual self-interest	Depending on the situation, oscillating, either/or behavior, as if the person had two selves	Borderline Infantile Narcissistic Antisocial Schizoid
The irrational pursuit of individual self-interest	Unpredictable	Manic-depressive Schizophrenic

The Personality Continuum is an integrative framework and something is lost by disintegrating it into four pages. The whole Personality Continuum can be obtained at **PersonalityContinuum.com**.

PART I

INSIDE ECONOMIC MAN

Introduction: Why?

Why do consumers behave as they do? Why does one consumer behave compulsively or, in the more extreme case, addictively, with regard to a particular consumption activity and in a given situation, while another consumer, in the same situation and with regard to the same consumption activity, is able to delay gratification and exercise self-control? Why are some people alcoholics while others can drink socially? Why is it that some people who turned on, tuned in, and dropped out in the late 1960s were able to go on to lead active and productive lives, while others were left behind in a purple haze? How is it that a person can be a compulsive shopper or addicted to an activity like work or exercise rather than a chemical substance? How is it that a professional athlete with a multiyear contract worth millions of dollars can self-destruct from a huge cocaine habit in front of millions of fans? How is it that the president of the United States can succumb to the charms of an intern less than half his age in the Oval Office of the White House and create a sordid scandal? Why do fools fall in love so easily?

It would be easy to say, "Well, they just lack self-control." But that merely begs the question: Why does one person lack self-control and another not? It is not the situation, because the specific circumstances of the situation can be controlled for, at least to varying degrees.

What does a person bring to a situation? A personality. A person brings his or her own personality to the situation. Everywhere you go, there *you* are.

The person who lingers too long at the bar, has too many drinks, and does not foresee the consequences of driving while drunk is different in a fundamental way from a person who exercises self-control, drinks in moderation, and drives responsibly. But an alcoholic is in some ways similar to a person who smokes marijuana habitually, a truly compulsive shopper who hides away purchases, or a fool who falls in love too easily.

What these people share in common is the same *level of personality development.* A person who is able to delay gratification and exercise self-control is at a higher level of personality development than a person who behaves compulsively or, in the more extreme case, addictively. These variations in patterns of consumer behavior are determined primarily by differences in the level of personality development that has been achieved by the person.

THE PERSONALITY CONTINUUM

Personalities at different levels of development can be arrayed along a continuum of personality development. The Personality Continuum is divided into four discrete ranges that are hierarchically arranged from higher to lower levels of development: (1) normal, (2) neurotic, (3) primitive, and (4) psychotic. The Personality Continuum is presented as a four-page figure following the Preface of the book. You may want to turn to it now and follow along.

Each range of the Personality Continuum—normal, neurotic, primitive, and psychotic—represents a *qualitatively different level of personality development.* The importance of the level of personality development for the study of consumer behavior is that each range of the Personality Continuum is reflected in a qualitatively different pattern of behavior. Personalities within a given range of the Personality Continuum have the same general pattern of behavior. In comparison, personalities at the other levels of development in the other ranges of the Personality Continuum have qualitatively different patterns of behavior. Everything depends on the level of personality development.

The general pattern of human behavior of a normal person at the normal level of personality development in the normal range of the Personality Continuum is stable and consistent. A normal person would be a normal consumer with a stable and consistent pattern of consumption behavior. The consumption behavior of a normal consumer would be quite predictable at one point in time with respect to a specific consumption activity in a given situation. At the highest reaches of the normal range of the Personality Continuum, a person has the capacity to make a commitment, and a commitment by definition is made for the future; therefore, the pattern of consumption behavior of the normal consumer is predictable over time and can be modeled dynamically, as the term is used in economics.

Individuals who have failed to achieve the normal level of personality development occupy lower ranges of the Personality Continuum that result in qualitatively different patterns of behavior (i.e., the neurotic, primitive, and psychotic ranges). The alcoholic, the head with the marijuana habit, and the truly compulsive shopper are at the same level of personality development and occupy the primitive range of the Personality Continuum. In general, they share a chaotic pattern of alternating and contradictory behavior. The alcoholic, the habitual marijuana smoker, and the compulsive shopper, however, do not necessarily have the same personality, since several types of personalities can be at the same level of development and occupy the same range of the Personality Continuum. The dark side of consumer behavior is explored in great depth in this book.

The classification of an individual into the appropriate range of the Personality Continuum opens the way for the researcher to draw on a wealth of general observations about behavior that apply to all personalities at that same level of development. To the extent that an individual's particular personality can be identified, a more specific pattern of behavior can be described and more precise inferences can be drawn about his or her consumer behavior.

The personality organization represents an *organizational framework*. The Personality Continuum provides an *integrative framework* that brings together contributions from many disciplines for the study of human behavior, including economics, sociology, anthropology, and psychology. The integrative framework provided by the Personality Continuum is the grand template for the human study of consumer behavior.

I will endeavor to explain each panel of the Personality Continuum. The panels are the columns, each with its own heading across the top of the Personality Continuum. Each panel of the Personality Continuum represents a different dimension of the personality. The first panel represents the four discrete ranges of the Personality Continuum representing the four qualitatively different levels of personality development: normal, neurotic, primitive, and psychotic. The next six panels represent an object relations theory of personality development: Interpersonal Achievement in Personality Development, Internal Object Relations, Intrapsychic Structural Formation, Predominant Defenses, Intimacy, and Preferred Patterning of Sexual Behavior. The Human Capacity panel in the middle of the Personality Continuum represents the culmination of whatever has been achieved as a human being at each level of personality development. The next five panels primarily represent the behavioral dimensions of the different levels of personality development: General Pattern of Human Behavior, Pattern of Consumer Behavior, Pattern of Consumption Behavior, Individual Pursuit of Self-Interest, and Predictability. The last panel, Personality Organizations, presents a relative ranking of the particular personality organizations, or types of personalities, that occupy each range of the Personality Continuum.

Each panel of the Personality Continuum is divided horizontally into four discrete ranges, representing the qualitatively different levels of personality development. For example, if you want to know how a person at the normal level of personality development would behave in general, locate the Normal Range of the Personality Continuum on the left and then follow across horizontally until you reach the panel with the heading General Pattern of Human Behavior; there the general pattern of behavior is described as being stable and consistent. Alternatively, if you observe a person behaving in contradictory ways that seem to alternate chaotically, you can peruse the Personality Continuum until you find that description of behavior in the General Pattern of Human Behavior panel and follow it back to the Primitive Range of the Personality Continuum. A chaotic pattern of alternating and contradictory behavior characterizes all of the personality organizations in the Primitive Range of the Personality Continuum. The final panel provides the Personality Organizations that occupy the Primitive Range of the Personality Continuum: Borderline, Infantile, Narcissistic, Antisocial, and Schizoid. The rankings of particular personality organizations within the neurotic, primitive, and psychotic ranges of the Personality Continuum are relative, more-or-less, ordinal rankings.

It does not matter where you begin on the Personality Continuum because everything is systematically related to everything else. One can start with an observable pattern of behavior or a diagnostic personality label or a theoretical construct of personality. Everything is systematically related to everything else using the integrative framework of the Personality Continuum.

THE PERSONALITY ORGANIZATION: THE ORGANIZATIONAL FRAMEWORK

The personality organization provides the organizational framework for relating the personality to consumer behavior. The personality organization is the central analytical construct of psychoanalytic object relations theory. Psychoanalytic object relations theory is also called American object relations theory to differentiate it from the earlier British object relations theory.

An object relationship is an interpersonal relationship, and object relations theory is an interpersonal theory of personality development. The personality organization is defined by the level of intrapsychic structural formation and the predominant defense used against severe anxiety in interpersonal relationships (Kernberg 1984A, 1985A, 1985B). Personality organizations with the same intrapsychic structure and predominant defense against severe anxiety occupy the same *range* of the Personality Continuum and represent the same *level* of personality development (Albanese 1990).

Object relations theory of the personality is derived from the intense scrutiny of individual behavior in the clinical situation. Based on the observation of individual behavior in the clinical situation, the psychoanalyst provides interpretations to the person, who is an active participant in the process. Through this active collaboration, the psychoanalyst provides insight that helps the person work through his or her problems realistically. It is the intense scrutiny of individual behavior in the clinical situation that makes object relations theory useful for the study of consumer behavior.

Although object relations theory is primarily a clinical methodology used to diagnose personality problems and prescribe therapy, out of helping a small group of people with problems, the process of normal personality development has been elaborated. To see what it means to be a normal person, simply read across the Normal Range of the Personality Continuum.

The classification of a particular personality organization focuses the analysis more precisely and facilitates the deepening of the analysis of individual behavior. A clinical diagnostic label placed on a person's particular personality organization by a trained and experienced clinician allows the analyst to delve more deeply into understanding the meaning of individual behavior. An important objective of this book is to provide more realistic portraits of behavior to enliven the descriptions of particular personality organizations.

The classification of a particular personality organization represents a point of departure from the Personality Continuum for expanding the analysis into a vast wealth of case literature. In this way, the classification of a particular personality organization goes beyond the Personality Continuum. The precise diagnosis of a person's particular personality organization opens the way to an exploration of the individual's personal history in greater depth and shows how far one can go, or how close one can come, to describing a real person, or oneself, in exquisite, if not excruciating, detail.

THE INTRAPSYCHIC STRUCTURE OF THE PERSONALITY: FREUD'S CRYSTAL

Object relations theory concentrates on the internalization of interpersonal relationships and the formation of the intrapsychic structure of the personality organization. The intrapsychic structure is the enduring part of the personality organization. Interpersonal relationships are relatively enduring; the intrapsychic structure of the personality organization is enduring. Therefore, what the person brings to the situation is the intrapsychic structure of the personality.

The intrapsychic structure of the personality organization constitutes the psychological foundation for the exploration of consumer behavior. When we ask the basic question, "Why do consumers behave as they do?" the answer lies within, with the intrapsychic structure of the personality, the part of the personality organization that is inside the person's head.

The whole edifice of psychoanalytic theory came out of the head of one man, Sigmund Freud. Object relations theory of the personality grew out of Freud's illuminating conception of the superego. In Freud's conception, the superego represented the internalization of an aspect of the interpersonal relationship with one's parents. Object relations theory of the personality represents the refinement of Freud's most fundamental insights after more than a century of elaboration. I am using Freud as a stepping-stone into object relations theory. Nowadays, more often than not, Freud is set up as a straw man. Critics seldom cite the vast literature of object relations theory, a telltale sign of ignoring the refinement of Freud's structural model. Object relations theory is so much more than Freud. Freud remains a frightening figure to many researchers more than half a century after his death on September 23, 1939, and more than a century after the publication of *The Interpretation of Dreams* in 1900.[1]

In his unfinished masterpiece, the famous Lecture XXXI, "The Dissection of the Psychical Personality," Freud used the metaphor of a crystal to enunciate his structural model of the id, ego, and superego: "If we throw a crystal to the floor, it breaks; but not into haphazard pieces. It comes apart along its lines of cleavage into fragments whose boundaries, though they were invisible, were predetermined by the crystal's structure" (Freud 1933, p. 59).[2] The id, ego, and superego each represent a "realm, region, or province" of Freud's structural model of the personality (p. 72).

Freud's crystal is the intrapsychic structure of the personality in the terminology of object relations theory. The substance of psychoanalytic object relations theory is the systematic study of the processes of the internalization of interpersonal relationships and the formation of the intrapsychic structure of the personality.[3] The intrapsychic structure of the personality is the psychological foundation of consumer behavior. An elaboration of the formation of the intrapsychic structure of the personality is an exploration of the psychological foundations of consumer behavior.

OTTO F. KERNBERG AND AMERICAN OBJECT RELATIONS THEORY

I regard Otto F. Kernberg as the leading authority on object relations theory. I rely heavily on his work, especially the essays collected in *Object-Relations Theory and Clinical Psychoanalysis* (1984A) and the case materials in *Borderline Conditions and Pathological Narcissism* (1985A). Perhaps most important, I have been inspired by Kernberg's three brilliant essays on intimacy in interpersonal relationships: "Barriers to Falling and Remaining in Love" (1974A), "Mature Love: Prerequisites and Characteristics" (1974B), and "Boundaries and Structure in Love Relations" (1977).[4] Kernberg's "Structural Derivatives of Object Relations," first published in 1966 and reprinted as the first chapter of Object-Relations Theory and Clinical Psychoanalysis (1984A), provides a gauge of the striking progress that had been made in the formulation of psychoanalytic theory since the publication in 1933 of Freud's unfinished masterpiece, "The Dissection of the Psychical Personality;" and now there has been more than three decades of progress since the publication of Kernberg's 1966 article.

In a book on consumer behavior aimed at an interdisciplinary audience, I felt it absolutely essential to provide Kernberg's words to allow researchers from other disciplines to reach their own interpretations. I quote rather freely because I believe that it is important to support my interpretations of behavior by providing the observations, inscriptions, interpretations, and thick descriptions of those upon whose shoulders I stand; however, I do not wish to be accused of committing the fallacy of arguing from authority, *argumentum ad verecundiam.* I am building my interpretations of behavior on the interpretations of others so that I can delve more deeply into the subject. This is stated succinctly by the anthropologist Clifford Geertz (1973): "Studies do build on other studies, not in the sense that they take up where the others leave off, but in the sense that, better informed and better conceptualized, they plunge more deeply into the same things" (p. 25).[5]

INTERPERSONAL NATURE OF PROBLEMS OF PERSONALITY

That problems of personality are primarily interpersonal is a central tenet of object relations theory of the personality. W.R.D. Fairbairn, the founder of British object relations theory, argued persuasively for the movement of psychoanalytic theory toward a theory of personality development based on the significance of interpersonal relationships: "It is to disturbances in the object-relationships of the developing ego that we must look for the ultimate origin of all psychopathological conditions" (1952, p. 82).

At the most fundamental level, according to Fairbairn, this involves the "explicit recognition of the general principle that problems of personality can only be adequately understood at a personal level and in terms of personal relationships" (1954, p. 106). Fairbairn was thereby led to the formulation of what he described as "a theory of the development of object-relationships based on the quality of dependence upon the object" (1952, p. 34). This is also a central tenet of Harry Stack Sullivan's interpersonal theory of personality development.

The heart of Fairbairn's contributions to British object relations theory is the explicit recognition that personality development depends on the quality of dependence in significant interpersonal relationships (1952, p. 40). Fairbairn's "Schizoid Factors in the Personality," written in 1940, but published for the first time as the opening chapter of his brilliant collection of essays, *Psychoanalytic Studies of the Personality* (1952), stands as a stepping stone between Freud's "The Dissection of the Psychical Personality" (1933) and Kernberg's "Structural Derivatives of Object Relations" (1966).[6]

SULLIVAN'S INTERPERSONAL DEFINITION OF PERSONALITY

Harry Stack Sullivan (1953) has formulated a crisp, operational interpersonal definition of personality: *"Personality is the relatively enduring pattern of recurrent interpersonal situations which characterize a human life"* (pp. 110–111).[7] Sullivan's interpersonal theory of personality, most importantly, his posthumously transcribed masterpiece *The Interpersonal Theory of Psychiatry* (1953), will be cited extensively throughout this book and should be used far more extensively in the social sciences.

In Sullivan's interpersonal theory of personality development, the interpersonal situation is the primary unit of observation: "The concept of *interpersonal situation* necessary for the occurrence of activity in the satisfaction of a need is of fundamental importance" (Sullivan 1953, p. 111). In this way, Sullivan's interpersonal approach to personality is comparable to Fairbairn's emphasis on the fundamental quality of dependence in object relations.

The quality of dependence in interpersonal relationships is the foundation of both Sullivan's interpersonal theory and Fairbairn's British object relations theory of personality development (Fairbairn 1952, p. 34). Kernberg (1985A), in turn, has built American object relations theory on this same foundation and has concentrated on the quality of internal object relations: "The two major prognostic factors that stand out as prognostically significant are the quality of object relationships and the integrity and depth of the value systems and superego functioning. It needs to be stressed again that I use the concept 'quality of object relations' to refer more to the quality of internalized object relations, i.e., the depth in the patient's internal relationships to others, rather than to the extent to which he is involved in social interactions" (pp. 307–308). The theoretical connection to Kernberg and American object relations theory is equally direct: The qualitatively different levels of personality development are primarily determined by the quality of dependence in the relatively enduring pattern of recurrent interpersonal situations that characterize a human life (primarily, because this is not true for psychotic personality organizations).

SULLIVAN'S HEURISTIC STAGES OF PERSONALITY DEVELOPMENT

Sullivan has formulated a set of heuristic stages of personality development based upon his interpersonal definition of personality: infancy, childhood, the juvenile era, preadolescence, early adolescence, and late adolescence. Each stage is defined by the significant interpersonal relationships that characterize a person's life at that point of personality development. For example, the juvenile era begins when a person enters the school system (Sullivan 1953, p. 227).[8] Sullivan's heuristic stages will be elaborated at the appropriate point in personality development through the lens of object relations theory.

Sullivan's interpersonal definition of personality will prove invaluable in transcending the overwhelmingly individual orientation of economic theory: Since the personality develops within the relatively enduring pattern of recurrent interpersonal situations that characterize a person's life, the individual orientation of economic analysis is automatically overcome by simply focusing on the series of significant interpersonal relationships that constitute the wider social system of the individual.

What is not so simple, of course, is forging a theoretical relationship between the economic conception of the consumer, from ordinal utility theory, and the personality organization of psychoanalytic object relations theory. This task entails the definition of a common ground of analysis and the establishment of an integrative framework, central concerns that will be dealt with conceptually and substantively in this book.

A COMPARATIVE ANALYSIS OF PERSONALITY ORGANIZATIONS

The personality organization, defined by the level of intrapsychic structural formation and the predominant defense against severe anxiety in interpersonal relationships, has provided the organizational framework. *Differences in general patterns of behavior vary qualitatively with the level of personality development.* At this more general level, the psychological foundations have been established for the analysis of compulsive and, in the more extreme case, addictive consumer behavior. Personality organizations in the primitive range of the Personality Continuum are characterized by a selective lack of impulse control that is manifested in compulsive and addictive consumer behavior.

To explore compulsive and the more extreme addictive consumer behavior in greater depth, a contrast will be made between personality organizations within the primitive range of the Personality Continuum, and a comparison will be made among personality organizations in the other ranges of the Personality Continuum. In this way, the Personality Continuum facilitates the comparative analysis of personality organizations, as contrasts are made between personality organizations at the same level of development and in the same range of the Personality Continuum, and comparisons are made among personality organizations at the qualitatively different levels of personality development in the other ranges of the Personality Continuum.

The analysis of compulsive and more extreme addictive consumer behavior will concentrate on the borderline and narcissistic personality organizations in the primitive range of the Personality Continuum. Contrasts will be made with other primitive personality organizations, including the schizoid, antisocial, and infantile personality organizations, and comparisons will be made with personality organizations at the neurotic and normal level of personality development.

The Personality Continuum provides the integrative framework that facilitates the comparative analysis of personality organizations. The comparative analysis of personality organizations adds greater depth and detail to the portraits of particular personality organizations. The portrait is not just a pattern of behavior, but a holistic conception of the person. The personality organization provides the organizational framework, and the analysis begins to approach a true thick description. In this way, the comparative analysis of personality organizations goes boldly beyond the Personality Continuum.

CLASSIFICATION OF PERSONALITY ORGANIZATIONS ALONG THE PERSONALITY CONTINUUM

Jung (1924) felt compelled to express incredulity over the existence of personality types, let alone a Personality Continuum, because of the complexity of human personality: "One is even inclined to deny the existence of types in general and to believe only in individual differences" (p. 10). Sullivan, the quintessential interpersonal theorist, was not daunted. His profound view of human nature was codified in the one-genus postulate: "We shall assume that *everyone is much more simply human than otherwise*" (1953, p. 32). Thus we have more in common as human beings than our individual differences would seem to indicate. Sullivan attributed individual differences to differences in relative maturity of the person, and he concluded his exposition of the one-genus postulate by saying, as it were (lest we forget that these are transcribed lectures), "In other words, I try to study the degrees and patterns of things which I assume to be ubiquitously human" (p. 33).

The degrees of human personality are reflected in the continuous and quantitative variations among personality organizations within each range of the Personality Continuum. The patterns of human personality are the qualitatively different levels of personality development represented by the discrete ranges of the Personality Continuum. In this way, the personality organization provides the organizational framework and the Personality Continuum provides the integrative framework for the study of human behavior.

THE CHARACTER CONSTELLATION AND DESCRIPTIVE DIFFERENTIAL DIAGNOSIS

The conception of the basic character constellation represents the observable behavior that is the basis for descriptive differential diagnosis. The character constellation consists of the presenting symptoms of the patient in an institutional or clinical setting. A descriptive differential diagnosis of a particular personality organization is a matter of matching the patterns of observable behavior of the person with the particular character constellation that provides the presumptive prognostic indicators. The result is the classification of the person's particular personality organization along the Personality Continuum.

For a person with a personality organization at the primitive level of personality development, the conception of the character constellation captures the complexity of the human personality. To put it plainly, complexity has a distinctly negative connotation, particularly when development is pathological. In addressing personality organizations at the primitive level of development, Kernberg (1985A) poses the essential question underlying the classification of personality organizations along a personality continuum: "Is it possible to make clear-cut descriptive differential diagnoses among all these character constellations?" (p. 18). Kernberg (1985A) responded "affirmatively, suggesting that descriptive differential diagnosis is possible within the usual limitations of descriptive diagnosis in clinical psychiatry" (p. 18). One limitation is the spectrum of variation in a particular personality organization: "The fact is that within any form of character organization there tends to be much fluctuation" (p. 18).

Kernberg (1985A) concluded that a descriptive differential diagnosis can classify a person's personality organization along a continuum of character pathology: "Nevertheless, I have gradually come to the conclusion that when the descriptive diagnosis is well founded and any particular features of the individual case which appear to go beyond the descriptive diagnosis are carefully recorded, it is indeed possible to place the patient tentatively along a continuum of severity of character pathology" (p. 18). Again, in an equally explicit statement, Kernberg

(1985A) recognized "the fact that an individual patient presenting any of the particular character constellations . . . might be placed at any point along the entire continuum of character pathology" (p. 18).

Kernberg (1985A) offered two caveats on the classification of character constellations along a continuum of character pathology: First, he expressed concern that an attempt to pinpoint character pathology along a continuum implied a dangerous rigidity (p. 18). Second, "a continuum of 'high level' and 'low level' character pathology is not meant as a simple ordering of diagnostic labels, and requires specialized descriptive, but also dynamic and structural, clinical judgments" (p. 21).

A differential diagnosis of a person's particular personality organization requires that the clinician make judgments based on an analysis of descriptive, structural, and dynamic factors. Here the term *dynamic* is used to mean the relatively enduring pattern of recurrent interpersonal situations that characterize a human life (Sullivan 1953, pp. 111–112). Previously the term *dynamic* was used as it is in economics, a pattern of consumption behavior over time, as opposed to static analysis at one point in time.

A descriptive differential diagnosis is presumptive; an analysis of the intrapsychic structure of the personality organization is definitive. Although Kernberg (1985A) is referring specifically to the borderline personality organization, the principle applies for the classification of all personality organizations: "In summary, to focus on the descriptive aspects of psychopathology makes it possible, if present in sufficient intensity, to warrant the presumptive diagnostic conclusion of a borderline personality organization. The definite conclusion in regard to this diagnosis, though, has to depend on the structural analysis of these cases" (p. 21).

A presumptive differential diagnosis of a person's particular personality organization can be made based on the descriptive aspects of the person's observable behavior; however, a conclusive diagnosis requires a dynamic and structural analysis based on clinical judgments (Kernberg 1985A, p. 21). The intense scrutiny of a person's behavior in the clinical setting by a trained clinician on a relatively enduring basis is required for a conclusive diagnosis.

THE PERSONALITY ORGANIZATION AND A PATTERN OF BEHAVIOR

The observation of a person's behavior is the basis for a descriptive differential diagnosis. The equation of a precise pattern of behavior with a particular personality organization facilitates the analysis of variations in patterns of consumer behavior and, ultimately, the specific aspects of individual consumption behavior. Thus the observation of the specific aspects of consumption behavior, the pattern of overall consumer behavior, and a person's general pattern of behavior can be used to draw inferences about the person's particular personality organization.

The personality organization is a package that contains a general pattern of behavior; that is, the personality organization is reflected in a particular pattern of behavior. The personality organization provides the organizational framework for the analysis of individual behavior. To the extent that the person's actual personality organization can be identified, a more specific pattern of behavior can be described and more precise inferences can be drawn about the meaning of the individual's behavior as a consumer.

An individual may have many features and manifest many tendencies in his or her behavior, which are all part of the person's character constellation and particular personality organization. A person may have, say, schizoid features or tendencies in his or her personality and not have a schizoid personality organization. This contributes to the complexity of the classification of the personality organization. The conception of the personality organization as a package becomes especially useful because these features and tendencies are related aspects of the personality organization. This is the basis for an individual-difference or trait-measure approach to personality, identifying and quantifying relatively enduring characteristics of a person; however, this is also one of the major drawbacks of individual-difference or trait measures. The personality organization provides an organizational framework that systematically incorporates these features and tendencies.

SPECTRUM OF VARIATION OF A PARTICULAR PERSONALITY ORGANIZATION

A spectrum of variation exists for each personality organization. A personality organization occupies a relative position within a range of the Personality Continuum, but does not represent a precise point because of the spectrum of variation for each personality organization. This adds to the complexity of personality classification and requires a further refinement of the diagnosis even after the clinician has decided on the diagnostic label for a particular personality organization.

How are the concepts of the character constellation and the spectrum of variation in a particular personality organization related? The concept of the character constellation pertains to the observable patterns of behavior that are the basis for making a presumptive descriptive differential diagnosis of a person's personality organization. The spectrum of a particular personality organization represents the variations on the theoretical construct of that personality organization. The spectrum of variation is an attempt to capture theoretically the complexity of a particular personality organization. The entire spectrum of variation of a particular personality organization represents the same level of development and occupies the same relative position within a range of the Personality Continuum; the variations for each personality organization represent more precise points along the range.

ORDINARY VERSUS EXTRAORDINARY FUNCTIONING

Descriptive differential diagnosis is further complicated by the distinction between ordinary, extraordinary, and high functioning. Under the ordinary conditions of everyday life, a person should function at the basic level of personality development that has been achieved—normal, neurotic, primitive, or psychotic—and that level of personality development forms a baseline of ordinary functioning for the person. Once a person has achieved a given level of personality development, there is no guarantee that that person will stay at that level permanently. The personality organization is defined by the level of intrapsychic structural formation and the predominant defense used by the individual against severe anxiety in interpersonal situations. According to Kernberg (1984A): "Anxiety constitutes a basic motive for defensive operations of the ego at all levels of development" (p. 40).

Sullivan (1953) has provided an interpersonal definition of anxiety: "Anxiety, as a phenomenon of relatively adult life, can often be explained plausibly as anticipated unfavorable appraisal of one's current activities by someone whose opinion is significant" (p. 113). In "The Meaning of Anxiety in Psychiatry and Life," Sullivan (1964) argued that "the exclusively interpersonal origin of every instance of its manifestations is the unique characteristic of anxiety" (p. 238).

Extraordinary functioning represents an interpersonal situation fraught with severe anxiety. Under extraordinary functioning, the predominant defense used against severe anxiety in interpersonal relationships has a tendency to break down. As a result, the person *regresses* to a lower level of personality development and returns to earlier patterns of behavior. A person under extraordinary functioning, therefore, is functioning at a level of personality development lower than his or her ordinary functioning. Regression to a lower level of personality development and a return to earlier patterns of behavior is the essence of a mental breakdown.

The interpersonal situation and regression go together because the origin of the severe anxiety that breaks down the predominant defense is the interpersonal situation. The critical distinctions between *earlier* and *later* achievements in personality development and *lower* and *higher* levels of structural formation and personality development can be clarified here. The essence of a "mental breakdown" or a "mental disorder" is a regression to earlier stages of personality development, the manifestation of earlier patterns of behavior, and the reactivation of earlier internal object relations.

FAIRBAIRN'S HYPOTHESIS AND THE COMPLEXITY OF PERSONALITY CLASSIFICATION

A person with a primitive personality organization can use a variety of neurotic defenses against severe anxiety in interpersonal relationships. As long as the neurotic defenses are securely in place, a person with a primitive personality organization can function at the higher neurotic level of personality development and will essentially appear neurotic from his or her observable behavior. This is Fairbairn's hypothesis: A person with a personality organization at the primitive level of personality development can use higher neurotic-level defenses under ordinary functioning. Fairbairn's hypothesis can be generalized to the use of higher-level defenses against anxiety in significant interpersonal relations by a person with a lower level of personality development; this represents a higher level of functioning for that person relative to the baseline of ordinary functioning.

A person with a primitive personality organization can function at a higher neurotic level of personality development, and this represents high functioning relative to his or her ordinary functioning. In interpersonal situations fraught with severe anxiety, the primitive defense of splitting breaks down, resulting in regression to the lower, psychotic level of personality development and a return to earlier patterns of behavior; this represents extraordinary functioning relative to his or her ordinary functioning. Thus three levels of functioning can be distinguished for a person with a primitive personality organization: Ordinary functioning with the defense of splitting intact; high functioning at the neurotic level with neurotic defenses intact; and extraordinary functioning at a lower level, and in extreme circumstances, at the psychotic level of personality development, when the defense of splitting has broken down. The specific circumstances of the relatively enduring pattern of recurrent interpersonal situations that characterize a person's life determine the level of functioning—ordinary, extraordinary, or high.

The use of neurotic defenses by a primitive personality organization under high functioning makes it difficult to differentiate a true neurotic from a primitive personality organization. Fairbairn's hypothesis presents specific challenges to the differential diagnosis and correct classification of neurotic and primitive personality organizations and contributes further to the complexity of the classification of a person's personality organization.

THEMATIC ANALYSIS: VARIATIONS ON A THEME ACROSS PERSONALITY ORGANIZATIONS

The investigation of variations on a theme across particular personality organizations will be used to elaborate on the comparative analysis of personality organizations. The theme of the subjective experience of emptiness will be used to go deeper into the analysis of compulsive and more extreme addictive consumer behavior. Emptiness is particularly characteristic of the narcissistic personality organizations, and narcissistic personality organizations are particularly prone to addiction; therefore, an investigation of variations on the theme of the subjective experience of emptiness across particular personality organizations will be useful in understanding addictive behavior.

PORTRAITS OF PARTICULAR PERSONALITY ORGANIZATIONS

I intend to hew to a theoretical line in presenting the conceptions of particular personality organizations, using object relations theory of the personality as the organizational framework. In the initial presentation of the portrait of the schizoid personality organization, at the foundation of British object relations theory, the presentation will take on the precise theoretical conception of W.R.D. Fairbairn. Progressing in the history of development of object relations theory to the portrait of the borderline personality organization, at the foundation of American object relations theory, the presentation will take on the densely worded character of Otto F. Kernberg.

I shall endeavor to enliven the theoretical conception of a particular personality organization with detailed descriptions of observable behavior and thereby provide a more elaborate portrait of behavior rather than a crude caricature. The intention to hew to a primarily theoretical line places limits on the amount of elaboration I can provide for any particular personality organization. I shall leave the embellishment to the clinical literature and the reader's expertise and experience.

For fuller portraits of particular personality organizations, one can resort to a variety of related resources that can be easily integrated into the analysis provided here. First, and perhaps foremost, as a general reference source, refer to the *Diagnostic and Statistical Manual of Mental Disorders* (1994) of the American Psychiatric Association, known as the DSM-IV. As direct extensions of the DSM-III, to fill the void on personality disorders, see the still vital Theodore Millon, *Disorders of Personality: DSM-III: Axis II* (1981), James P. Choca, Luke A. Shanley, and Eric Van Denburg, *Interpretative Guide to the Millon Clinical Multiaxial Inventory* (1992), and Robert J. Craig, editor, *The Millon Clinical Multiaxial Inventory: A Clinical Research Information Synthesis* (1993).

Using the personality organization as the basis for analysis, numerous penetrating clinical studies can be integrated, for example, David Shapiro's, *Neurotic Styles* (1965). Brilliant explorations of particular personality organizations can contribute to the depth of the analysis, for example, on the narcissistic personality organization, the incisive work of Marie-Louise von Franz, *Puer Aeternus*, 2nd edition (1981), and on into a myriad of popular literature on particular personality organizations, for example, Christopher Lasch, *The Culture of Narcissism: American Life in an Age of Diminishing Expectations* (1978), on the prevalence of the narcissistic personality organization in America.

The Personality Continuum provides the integrative framework to elaborate with one's own professional experience as a clinician, researcher, or scholar and to embellish, so to speak, with one's own personal experience. The opportunity is provided to examine the meaning of one's own life, thereby facilitating a deeper understanding of oneself as a human being.

SEX AS AN ILLUSTRATION OF PROBLEMS IN INTERPERSONAL RELATIONSHIPS

Since problems of personality are primarily interpersonal, genital sexual activity in an interpersonal relationship tends to illustrate any problems in personality. Harry Stack Sullivan's (1953) views on genital sexual activity in an interpersonal relationship are relevant here: "When I say that the psychiatrist must usually pay attention to this, I do not mean that problems in living are primarily or chiefly concerned with genital activity. But I am saying, of people in this culture who are chronologically adult, that their problems in interpersonal relations quite certainly will be either very conspicuous in, or exceedingly well illustrated by, the particular circumstances governing their handling the emotion of lust" (p. 295). Stated quite simply by Sullivan (1956), "Sex, of course, traditionally reflects all personality problems" (p. 243).

Thus sex illustrates more fundamental interpersonal problems: "Quite frequently it is no trick at all to find something very much more serious than the sexual difficulty; and quite often sexual difficulty is remedied in the process of dealing with other [interpersonal] problems" (Sullivan 1953, p. 296). Sullivan concluded that knowing about a person's sex life does provide useful information: "Since lust cannot be eliminated from personality any more than hunger can, data on personality warp as seen in a person's sexual behavior is bound to be useful to the psychiatrist" (p. 295). However, Sullivan also concluded that it would be a mistake to think that more fundamental interpersonal problems in personality can be resolved by fixing a person's sex life: "But to think that one can remedy personality warp by tinkering with the sex life is a mistake, even though it is a very convenient doctrine for psychiatrists who are chronically juveniles" (p. 295).

THE PATIENT AND A CAVEAT ON THERAPEUTIC APPROACHES

In what follows, do not be put off by the use of the term *patient*, because it designates the universe of persons who have sought treatment for problems of personality and have chosen to examine their own lives, and, therefore, have been scrutinized in a clinical setting. I would prefer to say something like "a person with a narcissistic personality organization" and will do so whenever appropriate; nevertheless, the term *patient* will be used in a very deliberate way to designate a clinical observation.

In the clinical setting, an accurate diagnosis of a client's personality organization is crucial for the clinician to prescribe appropriate therapy. An accurate diagnosis of a person's particular personality organization facilitates the prescription of an appropriate course of therapeutic treatment, that is, what to do about a problem once it has been diagnosed. I draw the line at prescribing therapeutic approaches. The course of therapeutic treatment is for a trained and experienced clinician to determine. It is the classification of a person's level of personality development and, more precisely, the classification of a person's particular personality organization that facilitates the study of consumer behavior.

A NOTE ON THE USEFULNESS OF THE TERM *OBJECT*

The term *object* may be somewhat perplexing. Why not just say *person*? "The term 'object' in object-relations theory should more properly be 'human object,' " according to Kernberg (1984A, p. 58). While this may be of some help, it may also not be very useful: To see someone else as a whole person is an achievement in personality development. The early infant does not see the mother as a whole person; in fact, the early infant does not even see the mother as a separate person. For this reason, the early infant's interpersonal experiences are referred to as "part-object relations" to distinguish them from later "whole-object relations," when the person is whole. The term *object* is necessary, and indeed, its usefulness will be borne out by our subsequent elaboration of an object relations theory of personality development.

WHY RATIONAL ECONOMIC MAN?

Where do we go for a model of consumer behavior? To economics, and the economic theory of consumer behavior, ordinal utility theory, which has a central conception of the consumer, the rational economic man, *homo economicus*. The rational consumer has a transitive preference ordering. Transitivity is a mathematical property of the individual consumer's preference ordering. If a consumer prefers commodity A to B, and B to C, then he or she must prefer A to C to have a transitive preference ordering. If so, then he (or she) is proudly pronounced a rational consumer with great profundity.

In terms of observable behavior, a rational consumer makes consistent choices. Consistency places definite limitations on the shape of the demand curve (Samuelson 1947). As we shall see when we investigate the psychological foundations of consistent behavior, consistency is a surprisingly powerful behavioral postulate; however, more often than not, the lofty concept of rationality is simply a disguise for a lack of a deeper understanding of what it means. Amartya K. Sen (1977) put it rather colorfully in "Rational Fools: A Critique of the Behavioral Foundations of Economic Theory": "But if you are consistent, then no matter whether you are a single-minded egoist or a raving altruist or a class conscious militant, you will appear to be maximizing your own utility in this enchanted world of definitions" (p. 323).

Homo economicus, the rational economic man, however, does not represent the pinnacle of personality development. But after the necessary changes have been made, the economic conception of a rational consumer will prove to be very useful in defining a pattern of normal consumption behavior. This will be elaborated in the chapter "The Normal Consumer." For now, see the Pattern of Consumption Behavior panel for the normal range of the Personality Continuum.

WHY ASK WHY?

Why consumers behave as they do is a question of motivation. What motivates the consumer is the critical question surrounding consumer behavior. Motivation can be defined as the driving force within individuals, both conscious and unconscious, that impels them to action or moves them to behave in certain ways. Motivation is inseparable from the behavior; thinking is procrastinating (Freud 1933, p. 76).

The economic motivation for upward social mobility, to better one's lot in life, is the most powerful economic motivation. It will be analyzed at critical junctures throughout this book. A true understanding of the economic motivation for upward social mobility will require a combination of psychoanalytic, social, and cultural, as well as economic, approaches.

Why not just ask a person what motivated his or her consumer behavior? The typical response is most likely to be, "I don't know." Why do you use the brand of toothpaste you use? When a consumer professes to know his or her motivation, the next day, after sleeping on it, he or she will probably change or amend what was said the day before. Why? Because motivation is in part, at least, unconscious.

Understanding the unconscious, not just the unconscious motivation for behavior, is critical for a thorough understanding of consumer behavior. Sigmund Freud believed that his discovery of the unconscious was his most important contribution to psychology. It became part of his topographical model of the conscious, preconscious, and unconscious, as opposed to his later structural model of the id, ego, and superego. Freudian psychoanalytic theory, not just psychoanalytic object relations theory, is an enormous source of insight into the motivation for behavior.

Some disciplines, like marketing, that profess to know something about consumer behavior hardly mention the unconscious in textbooks on consumer behavior and, as a consequence, fail to recognize the importance of the unconscious processing of information. This is surprising given the early exploration of the unconscious aspects of motivation in the shopping-list studies of Mason Haire (1950) and the motivation research of Ernest Dichter (1960, 1971). More recently the role of the unconscious has been explored from a psychoanalytic perspective by Morris B. Holbrook (1988, 1995).

The consumer in marketing is a peculiarly lopsided being who only processes information consciously. The absence of an understanding, or even an appreciation, for the role of the unconscious in motivation in marketing is a handicap to the analysis of consumer behavior. As a result, marketers appear to be oblivious to the increasingly blatant use of subliminal stimuli in advertising, while being openly mocked by editorials in *Advertising Age* by the very advertisers who resort to this technique. While between 74.3% and 81% of the public believes that advertisers use subliminal embeds, only 7.8% of practitioners profess to the use of subliminal stimuli in advertising (Rogers and Seiler 1994; Zanot, Pincus, and Lamp 1983; Rogers and Smith 1993). At the same time, the literature on subliminal stimuli is burgeoning in psychology. Subliminal stimuli will be used as a vehicle to understand the unconscious processing of information.

KNOW THY PREFERENCES

Why should the consumer's preferences be transitive, or behaviorally, why should a consumer make consistent choices? This assumption is necessary for the mathematical models to work, but is it a good description of actual buyer behavior? Are consumers always consistent in their choices?

There is no harm in making this assumption provided that the nature of the consumer's preferences is known from the observation of actual market behavior. An application of ordinal utility theory would be appropriate if the preferences revealed in the market are transitive. However, if the consumer's observable pattern of consumption behavior does not fit the structure of preferences of the economic conception of the rational consumer, then conventional ordinal utility theory is not appropriate and should not be applied. This understanding contributes to a clarification of the limits of applicability of the ordinal utility theory.

Presumably, a consumer's scale of preferences is known from the observation of actual market behavior. This was the promise of revealed-preference theory (Samuelson 1947); however, this approach has not been widely practiced by economists.[9] The failure to observe the actual market behavior of the consumer has constricted the scope of the superficial conception of the consumer even further by the easy assumption that the scale of preferences is given. This is a scandalous assumption and immediately calls into question the nature of the consumer's preferences that are being held constant by assumption.

The outstanding exception is the growing movement of behavioral economics. If we are going to have a more realistic conception of economic man, we must begin with the interpretation of observable patterns of behavior to broaden the behavioral foundations of economic analysis, not by adding more assumptions to economic theory.

DON'T ASK WHY!

Ordinal utility theory is a good, albeit weak, theory of choice and will prove to be a useful, but limited, theoretical framework for the analysis of consumer behavior.[10] One limitation is that it is a static model that begins with the assumption of a consumer with a given scale of preferences. It becomes circular when the most important question of consumer behavior is asked, "Why does the consumer prefer one bundle of commodities over another?" Economists can only beg the question by going back to where they started, with the consumer's given scale of preferences, and say, "Because the consumer liked that bundle better than the other."

Economics cannot help us with the "why" question. As important as the conception of the rational consumer is to an understanding of behavior, economics as a discipline has little to do with behavior. Economics has become a branch of applied mathematics and should no longer be considered a social science. A standard textbook definition of economics goes something like this: Economics is a social science concerned with the allocation of society's scarce resources among alternative uses for the satisfaction of human needs. The allocation of society's scarce resources involves the working of markets, and that is the métier of economics.

A WARNING ON ECONOMIC MAN

Economic man refers specifically to the theoretical construct of the consumer from ordinal utility theory; thus terms like *rational economic man* are meant to apply equally to men and women. My elaboration of object relations theory also applies equally to men and women. When I do discuss men or male behavior as opposed to women or female behavior, I will clarify the meaning. For an application of object relations theory directly to women, I refer the reader to the superb work of Carol Gilligan, *In a Different Voice: Psychological Theory and Women's Development* (1982), and Nancy Chodorow, *The Reproduction of Mothering: Psychoanalysis and the Sociology of Gender* (1978).

The reader will find some similarities in the substance of this book to the work of Gilligan and Chodorow. That is because we had a common mentor in George W. Goethals, a brilliant teacher and lecturer in the Department of Psychology and Social Relations at Harvard University. I was wandering in the wilderness of Harvard University when I fortuitously found Goethals teaching a yearlong lecture course on the psychology of the human life cycle. He turned me on to the interpersonal theory of Harry Stack Sullivan and the British object relations theory of W.R.D. Fairbairn. Thereafter I was a member of Goethals's seminar "Psychoanalytic Approaches to Personality" and learned about the psychoanalytic or American object relations theory of Otto F. Kernberg.

While I was wandering, I was not lost. I was a student of Harvey Leibenstein, a brilliant economist at Harvard University. Leibenstein was a brilliant behavioral economist, arguably the most influential behavioral economist of the twentieth century. He undoubtedly would have been a primary candidate for Nobel Memorial Prize in economics if his intellectual life had not been tragically cut short by an automobile accident, but his intellectual influence has inspired a generation of behavioral economists. Leibenstein was my mentor in economics, and his influence on my own thinking is profound. I was his research assistant at the time *Beyond Economic Man* (1976) was published. The working title of this book was "Inside Economic Man," a tribute to his influence on my own thought.

SHRINKING ECONOMIC MAN

The movement toward relating the disciplines of economics and psychology must begin with the simple understanding that the consumer is, after all, a person, and not merely a set of assumptions (Albanese 1987; Holbrook 1995). Where do we go from here? Inside economic man, to an exploration of the psychological foundations of consumer behavior. So we shall begin, psychoanalyzing the rational consumer of economic theory—shrinking economic man, so to speak.[11]

The outcome of a successful psychoanalysis is a more realistic conception of oneself and others. The objective here is a more realistic conception of the consumer. Where will we end up? On the Personality

Continuum, an integrative framework that systematically incorporates social, economic, cultural, and psychological factors influencing individual consumer behavior. Along the way, a concerted effort is made to integrate, and not to exclude, the analysis from any discipline that makes a useful contribution to an understanding of consumer behavior.

NOTES

1. I owe the observation that Freud frightens people to Morris B. Holbrook in a personal correspondence dated July 5, 1989.

2. This famous essay, first published in 1933, is commonly known as Freud's Lecture XXXI; however, it is worth noting that Freud never delivered these essays as lectures nor ever intended them to be lectures. In his preface, Freud provided this justification for using the lecture format: "It is only as an artifice of the imagination; it may help me not to forget to bear the reader in mind as I enter more deeply into my subject" (Freud 1933, p. 5). This is particularly apropos of Lecture XXXI, which introduces entirely new material and plunges deeply into a level of theoretical difficulty that was avoided in the previous introductory lectures on psychoanalysis.

3. The structural model has given rise to some horrendous terminology: the psychic apparatus, preferred by Freud, the mental apparatus of Harry Stack Sullivan, the endopsychic structure of W.R.D. Fairbairn, and the intrapsychic structure of the personality organization of Otto F. Kernberg.

4. Throughout this book, I have adopted the convention of providing the page numbers for references to Kernberg's collections of essays (1984A, 1985A, 1985B), but using the original year of publication for his journal articles on intimacy in the text (1974A, 1974B, 1977). I have taken this same tack with other authors, most notably Freud and Michael Balint, as a way to preserve the historical perspective.

5. I am not sure that I agree fully with Geertz that studies do not take up where others leave off. I am always struck by the experience of remembering exactly where I left off when I have had the opportunity to get back to that same point in my research. I feel like I can pick up right where I left off. The deepest vein of research on which I am drawing for this book comes from the summer of 1981, when I read Otto Kernberg's *Borderline Conditions and Pathological Narcissism* first published in 1975, mainly a collection of reprinted clinical articles published between 1965 and 1975, while staying for two months in a cabin on Big Island Pond in Hampstead, New Hampshire. I was actually working on my long-overdue dissertation for my Ph.D. in economics at Harvard University. That summer was the most intellectually productive period of my life up to that time. When I returned to Harvard that fall, I had to backtrack considerably to make object relations theory more palatable to economists, at least to those on my dissertation committee, but I did complete my dissertation

within one year. In the spring of 1988, again living in splendid isolation, this time in Middlebury, Vermont, I had the opportunity to get back to that point once more, when I first began to work on the manuscript for this book. I returned to that intellectual high point in the fall of 1998 while I was on sabbatical from Kent State University, when I began working on this book again after a ten-year hiatus.

6. It may be of interest to note that Fairbairn's influential "Schizoid Factors in the Personality" was published for the first time in *Psychoanalytic Studies of the Personality* (1952), In note 1 of chapter 1, Fairbairn reveals only that "an abbreviated version of this paper was read before the Scottish Branch of the British Psychoanalytic Society on 9th November 1940 (p. 3)." "A Revised Psychopathology of the Psychoses and Psychoneuroses," reprinted as chapter 2 of Fairbairn (1952), was originally published in *The International Journal of Psycho-Analysis* in 1941. In a note at the end of the first sentence, Fairbairn (1952, p. 28) states, "A previous paper entitled 'Schizoid Factors in the Personality' is devoted to this subject, and is included in the present volume."

7. The description of Sullivan's writing as "crisp" and "operational" was made by George W. Goethals in an important article titled "The Evolution of Sexual and Genital Intimacy: A Comparison of the Views of Erik H. Erikson and Harry Stack Sullivan" (1976), p. 540.

8. Sullivan's heuristic stages of personality development and their connection to object relations theory are fully elaborated in Albanese (1982).

9. For a truly unique exploration of the possibilities of revealed-preference theory, see Baumol 1972, pp. 221–232.

10. I have taken this concise characterization of ordinal utility theory as a good, albeit weak, theory of choice from the comments made by Kenneth J. Arrow, Noble laureate in economics, at a historic session of the 1983 ASSA Conference in San Francisco, California, entitled "The Psychological and Sociological Foundations of Economic Behavior." Arrow was a discussant, along with A. Michael Spence and Joseph E. Stiglitz, of papers by Albert O. Hirschman, James S. Coleman, and George A. Ackerlof (reputed organizer of the session); the session was chaired by Gary S. Becker. For me, Arrow's characterization of ordinal utility theory recalled Pareto's challenge to the cardinal utility theorists: "Show me a utility or satisfaction that is, say, three times as great as another" (Schumpeter 1954, p. 1062).

11. "Shrinking Economic Man" was originally suggested to me as a title for this book by my good friend and colleague Shlomo Maital.

Chapter 1

Personality in Behavioral Economics, Marketing, Trait Theory in Psychology, and Organizational Behavior

This chapter is a brief foray into the uses of personality in behavioral economics, marketing, trait theory in psychology, and organizational behavior. The purpose is to establish theoretical linkages that facilitate interdisciplinary research on consumer behavior.

PERSONALITY IN BEHAVIORAL ECONOMICS

While mainstream economics has proceeded in the direction of mathematical modeling, the growing movement of behavioral economics has arisen to redress the balance. For behavioral economists, taking a predominantly psychological approach and using personality as a central analytical construct, Tibor Scitovsky's *The Joyless Economy: An Inquiry into Human Satisfaction and Consumer Dissatisfaction* (1976) is perhaps the most important and influential book in relating psychology and economics. Scitovsky observed, "We [economists] tend to think of people as having different tastes, but in fact they have different types of personalities" (pp. 27–28).

By differences in personality, Scitovsky is referring primarily to differences in physiologically determined average arousal levels. While Scitovsky succeeded in compiling an impressive catalog of psychological contributions relevant to economic theory, he did not satisfactorily provide an integrative framework that could bring together the contributions of economics and psychology in a systematic way (Albanese 1988C).

Personality analysis in economics advanced with Shlomo Maital's *Minds, Markets, and Money: Psychological Foundations of Economic Behavior* (1982). Maital placed great emphasis on the need to investigate personality development: "Giving Economic Man a childhood is, I believe, a natural starting point for integrating economics and psychology" (p. 26). While Maital has provided the most persuasive argument among economists for the need to relate economics and psychology using the personality, he did not adequately address the fundamental question of the common ground of analysis on which the two disciplines can be brought together (Albanese 1988C).

In an effort to collect the various psychological approaches being used in economics, I edited *Psychological Foundations of Economic Behavior* (1988C). The personality of the individual is a central theme for the papers collected in that volume, and particular emphasis is placed on physiological, psychoanalytic, and interpersonal approaches to the personality. Applications are made to an investigation of the behavior of the individual consumer, executive, and entrepreneur, and an effort is made to overcome the individual orientation of the analysis to form a broader social basis for understanding the behavior.

In my own contribution to that volume, "The Intimate Relations of the Consistent Consumer," psychoanalytic object relations theory is applied to an investigation of variations in patterns of consumer behavior. This research was first presented in my doctoral dissertation (1982). Psychoanalytic object relations theory is the principal theoretical approach to be elaborated in this book.

PERSONALITY IN MARKETING

Marketing does not have a central conception of the consumer upon which to base the study of consumer behavior. Surprisingly economics has a better conception of the consumer than marketing. This is surprising since the single most important concept in marketing today is the marketing concept, which dictates that marketers begin with the basic needs of the consumer (Levitt 1960; Webster 1988). The typical consumer behavior textbook is a compendium of contributions from a variety of fields, but lacks an overall organizational framework that would relate these contributions in a meaningful way to provide a better understanding of consumer behavior. For example, a typical consumer behavior textbook contains Abraham Maslow's hierarchy of needs, but that is just one of many contributions cataloged in passing without any effort to integrate it into an overall conception of the consumer (e.g., Blackwell, Miniard, and Engel 2001).

Early efforts to operationalize the personality for research on consumer behavior in marketing have had a somewhat nefarious history. My attempt here is more in the nature of an autopsy rather than a thorough literature review. The most notorious effort was a study by Franklin B. Evans (1959) using the Edwards Personal Preference Schedule to differentiate between the personalities of Ford and Chevrolet owners. According to Holbrook (1992): "Evans (1959) . . . found instead that the prediction was very weak and that simple-minded demographic, socioeconomic, or other 'objective' variables worked just as well or better. This outcome set off a train of controversy that eventually culminated in the conventional wisdom—voiced by Kassarjian 1971—that personality variables work poorly in explaining buyer behavior" (p. 417). Although some effort has been made to reinterpret Evans's (1959) results in a positive way by Jacoby (1969), it is hard to imagine why there should be any difference between Ford and Chevrolet owners in the 1950s (Albanese 1993).

Kassarjian and Sheffet's (1991) influential review of personality and consumer behavior in marketing, while critical of past research, does point to the positive contributions and untapped potential that research on personality may have for the field of consumer behavior: "What is amazing is not that there are many studies that show no correlation between consumer behavior and personality, but rather that there are any studies at all with positive results. That 5 percent or 10 percent or any portion of the variance can be accounted for by personality variables (taken out of context and studied independently of other cognitive or physical variables) . . . is most remarkable indeed" (p. 294)!

In "Personality and Consumer Behavior: Extensions," a critique of efforts to use the concept of personality in marketing, Masao Nakanishi (1972) addressed these same methodological issues: "The low explanatory power of individuals' personality characteristics, doubtlessly a pervasive force in shaping one's behavior, may have stemmed in part from naive conceptualization of the relationships between personality and consumer behavior often held by researchers in the field" (p. 61). Nakanishi concluded with the following observations:

> Although it is a truism that only clear conceptualization of relationships among variables under study helps the researcher determine the data to be obtained and

the analytical techniques to be used, it is also true that we tend to gravitate toward an easy habit of conceptualizing everything in terms of simplistic linear relationships. The more pervasive the effect of personality, the more critical it becomes to clarify the myriad of relationships among many layers of variables interacting with each other since such complex interactions may not reveal themselves as simple linear relationships. In order for us to be able to develop a meaningful theory of personality effects it will be necessary to break out of the mold into which naive conceptualization has forced us. (p. 65)

This challenge has been further clarified by Kassarjian and Sheffet (1981):

We have not yet internalized the conception that the individual must be perceived as a dynamic whole. We ought not to be concerned with rigid connections but rather with temporally extended whole individuals. In short, further traditional research attempting to connect the purchase of canned peas with a personality variable using cross-section data is bound to fail; it does not take into account the effects of the interaction of that personality variable with other personality characteristics, the interaction effects accounted for by needs, motives, moods, memories, attitudes, beliefs, opinions, perceptions, values, and so on, or the effects of the situation or field. (p. 171)

These are the clear challenges, to formulate a dynamically whole conception of the individual personality and clear conceptualizations of the relationship between the personality and consumer behavior, controlling for the situation or field. Kassarjian and Sheffet (1981) followed their clearly stated challenges with a somewhat discouraging lamentation: "Unfortunately no simple methodology for research of this sort has yet emerged. We do not necessarily advocate a return to the extensive study of a single individual such as the psychoanalytic methodology employed by Freud or to the environmental probability of Egon Brunswick. But greater awareness of views espoused by Tolman, Freud, Brunswick, Lewin, and other great minds in the social sciences and philosophy might point out the location of the light at the end of the tunnel" (p. 171).

Why should such a methodology for the study of consumer behavior be simple? Holbrook (1992) has made a contribution to the clarification of the relationship between the personality and consumer behavior in "Patterns, Personalities, and Complex Relationships in the Effects of Self on Mundane Everyday Consumption": "The relationships involved . . . represent complex mediating and moderating effects wherein personality influences the links in a causal chain from product features to purchase intentions in general and shapes the intervening role played by social impressions in particular" (p. 417). "Further issues concern," according to Holbrook, "the complications that arise when we examine the possible moderating and mediating effects wherein personality can intervene in the chain of effects between stimulus properties and preferences or purchase intentions" (pp. 420–421). Holbrook thus provides an important elaboration on the complexity of personality classification in relation to product features, preferences, and purchase intentions.

A clear appraisal of what is meant by an integrative framework has been provided by William D. Wells and Arthur D. Beard in "Personality and Consumer Behavior" (1973): "Behavior is an integrated system, and . . . the parts of the system are interconnected by broad, general underlying dispositions that explain and control its separate parts. This system, the system that unites, integrates, and in some sense produces an individual's behavior, is the domain of the personality theorist" (p. 142).

According to Kassarjian and Sheffet (1991), personality should somehow be tied to "the concept of consistent responses to the world of stimuli surrounding the individual" (p. 281). Although this conception is a good start, it is taken from Hall and Lindzey (1970), a standard textbook in psychology, and does not go anywhere; that is, it is not operationalized in any way. Consistency is a very powerful behavioral postulate; however, Kassarjian and Sheffet (1991) merely pay lip service to it without recognizing the significance of consistent behavior. Object relations theory provides the specific achievements in personality development that are required to become a dynamically whole person. This is depicted in the normal range of the Personality Continuum.

It is worth noting that Kassarjian and Sheffet (1991) make no reference to the vast literature of object relations theory, an enormous source of potential insight into the study of consumer behavior heretofore untapped in marketing. It is unfortunate that the series of articles on "Personality and Consumer Behavior" by Kassarjian (1971) and Kassarjian and Sheffet (1975, 1981, 1991) has been so influential on research on personality and consumer behavior in marketing. I fear that it has stunted the development of the field of marketing and should be relegated to the history of thought. The article, last published in 1991 and subtitled "An Update," has frankly become outdated.[1]

Morris B. Holbrook is one of the few brave souls in marketing with the courage to break out of the fold with "The Psychoanalytic Interpretation of Consumer Behavior: I Am an Animal" (1988) and his innovative *Consumer Research: Introspective Essays on the Study of Consumption* (1995). I have made a preliminary effort to introduce psychoanalytic object relations theory into marketing in a paper titled "The

Paradox of Personality in Marketing: A New Approach to the Problem" (1989). The paradox, stated quite simply, is that we all have a personality, but we do not know how it is systematically related to our consumer behavior. A more elaborate effort was provided in "Personality, Consumer Behavior, and Marketing Research: A New Theoretical and Empirical Approach," which presented the Personality Continuum and an approach to operationalize the personality organization for empirical research (Albanese 1990).

It is my belief that psychoanalytic object relations theory is the location of the light at the end of the tunnel. Psychoanalytic object relations theory offers a theoretical approach for relating the personality organization of the individual to his or her pattern of consumer behavior, and the critical methodological issues of the common ground of analysis and an integrative framework can be addressed using this approach. This is not meant to exclude or depreciate any other approach. The essence of the integrative framework provided by the Personality Continuum is that it brings together the contributions of many theorists and many different theoretical points of view. The Personality Continuum provides the grand template for the study of consumer behavior that Sidney Levy called for in his presidential address to the Association for Consumer Research (Levy 1992).

No comprehensive concept of personality has ever seriously been applied in the field of marketing. At the 1991 conference of the Association for Consumer Research in Chicago, William D. Wells made the following observation with respect to the work of Freud, Abraham, Jung, and Adler: "It seems to me that it is time to go back and take a look at what these seminal thinkers had to say and take them seriously, which we have never really done."[2]

To some extent, attitudes in marketing and preferences in economics are analogous concepts in that both express the consumer's overall evaluation, in marketing with regard to some attitude object, and in economics with regard to a particular bundle of commodities. The similarity ends there, however, since there is no conception of the individual consumer in marketing. An advantage of equating the analogous concepts of attitudes in marketing and preferences in economics is that marketers measure attitudes. Marketers overwhelmingly collect their own primary data and seldom rely on secondary data, as economists most often do. From single-component attitude models that measure attitudes globally to the more sophisticated multiattribute structural models, like the theory of reasoned action (Bagozzi 1992; Fishbein 1963; Miniard and Cohen 1979, 1981, 1983), economists can learn a great deal from marketers about primary data collection, especially in the area of attitudes. In addition, there is a long tradition of observing behavior in marketing, starting with the direct observation of shopping behavior by Wells and Lo Sciuto (1966).

Researchers on consumer behavior in marketing have turned their attention to compulsive buying behavior. Although not a personality approach per se, this research does focus on the dark side of consumer behavior. Empirical research on compulsive buying behavior has been conducted by Faber and O'Guinn (1988), O'Guinn and Faber (1989), Faber, O'Guinn, and Krych (1987), and Rook (1987). These studies represent exploratory research aimed at defining, identifying, and classifying compulsive and impulsive buying behavior as part of a larger pattern of compulsive consumption behavior (O'Guinn and Faber 1989, p. 153). I have investigated the origins of compulsive and addictive consumption behavior, which are related to the borderline and narcissistic personality organizations, respectively (Albanese 1987, 1988C). Hirschman (1991, 1992) has provided a highly personal investigation of addictive behavior.

TRAIT APPROACHES AND THE BIG FIVE-FACTOR MODEL OF PERSONALITY

In practice, personality in marketing has been largely operationalized by trait or individual difference measures, where a *trait* represents the quantification of an identifiable and relatively enduring characteristic of a person, for example, internal and external locus of control or self-monitoring. While some studies have yielded some useful contributions (e.g., Foxall and Goldsmith 1989; Lastovicka and Joachimsthaler 1988), these approaches have largely been unsuccessful in marketing (e.g., Bearden, et al, 1991). How does the trait relate to the overall pattern of behavior of the individual? Knowing a consumer's locus of control, for example, is useful in and of itself, but how is this trait related to the personality of the individual? Most attempts at relating the trait to the personality are merely speculative.

Buss (1989) has argued that individual trait measures can be aggregated into broader patterns of behavior, which in turn can be related to the more comprehensive concept of personality. According to Buss (1989), "Each time one adds a trait, the prediction of behavior becomes more precise, and one moves closer to a major goal of personality trait research: to understand persons as *combinations* of traits" (p. 1385).[3]

The burgeoning contributions of the big five-factor model (FFM) to an understanding of normal personality (e.g., Digman 1990; McCrae and

John 1992; Wiggins and Pincus 1992), and increasingly to personality disorders (Costa and McCrae 1992; Costa and Widiger 1994), represent another important movement in this direction. The big five factors are variously labeled extroversion, neuroticism, openness to experience, agreeableness, and conscientiousness.

This is a promising approach, but has yet to be integrated in a systematic way into the contributions of a categorical classification of personality. Dimensional approaches measure the degree to which a person has a certain personality trait, whereas a categorical approach assesses the likelihood that a person has a certain type of personality. These two approaches to personality are not mutually exclusive, nor can one be subsumed by the other.

The integrative framework provided by the Personality Continuum offers a way to integrate categorical and dimensional approaches to personality, so that no information is lost. Widiger and Frances (1994, p. 20) essentially see a continuum as absent from categorical classifications of personality; however, an assumption is made, usually implicit, that normal and disordered personalities are not qualitatively different, but vary continuously along the same trait dimension. Personality disorders, therefore, represent maladaptive traits that are extreme variants of normal personality traits (Costa and Widiger 1994, p. 8). The argument here is that personality organizations at different levels of development are qualitatively different, and this represents the categorical classification of personality. Each range of the Personality Continuum represents a qualitatively different level of personality development. The importance of the level of personality development is that *differences in the level of personality development determine differential responses on a trait or individual difference measure*. Dimensionality occurs within each range of the Personality Continuum, where personality organizations at the same basic level of development vary *continuously* and quantitatively along the same trait dimension. In general, the pattern of responses on any individual-difference or trait measure will vary qualitatively with the level of personality development along the Personality Continuum. In addition, the pattern of responses will vary in a more precise way with the particular personality organization. The integrative framework of the Personality Continuum, therefore, integrates categorical and dimensional approaches to personality.

Using a trait or individual-difference measure as a proxy for the whole personality treats people as parts. The problem is that a trait is only one part of the person's personality; how that part is related to the whole personality is never specified. This approach is problematical for a number of reasons. First, a single trait may lead to a variety of behaviors. For example, compulsiveness may lead to extremely orderly behavior or extremely disorderly behavior (Wells and Beard 1973). Second, a specific trait may be reflected by more than one personality organization and at different levels of personality development. In general, a pattern of stable and consistent behavior represents a normal level of personality development, but it can be easily mistaken for the rigid behavior and routinized life of a person with a schizoid personality organization at the far lower primitive level of personality development. A trait measure designed to measure consistent behavior in isolation would not be able to distinguish between these two very different levels of personality development. This is an important critique because the implicit assumption in most applications of trait measures is that all subjects have attained a normal level of personality development.

THE BIG FIVE-FACTOR MODEL OF PERSONALITY AND PERSONALITY DISORDERS

A complete synthesis of dimensional and categorical approaches to personality is not possible at this time because of the assumption, usually implicit, that the FFM was developed only on populations of subjects with normal personalities. This is a dubious assumption at best (especially for convenience samples of college students) and begs the essential empirical question of the categorical classification of the subject's personality, which must precede the measurement of dimensionality. Trull and McCrae (1994, p. 59) answer "not yet" to the most obvious question; Is "there good empirical evidence that individuals with different personality disorders can in fact be characterized by distinctive and appropriate personality profiles across the five factors, or dimensions, of the FFM"? Costa and Widiger (1994), however, have made a giant leap in this direction, and the suggested patterns of correlation are reasonably straightforward.

An analysis of the narcissistic personality organization (abbreviated NAR in the following) can demonstrate the potential of integrating the depth of categorical classification and the breadth of dimensional approaches to personality. In addition, it provides an opportunity to explore the chaotic, alternating, and contradictory character of the general behavior pattern of all personality organizations in the primitive range of the Personality Continuum. Trull and McCrae (1994, p. 67) state, "It is also possible to argue that the elements of the NAR—high E (extraversion), low A (agreeableness), low N (neuroticism)—in combination represent a uniquely important configuration of traits." I would agree with this characterization only if the proviso "the NAR under ordinary functioning" is added.

Corbitt (1994) had trouble seeing the narcissistic personality organization (NAR) as a dysfunctional variant of the "normal" personality traits on the FFM: "Narcissistic patients are very vulnerable and self-conscious, but at times express this through a complete denial of any faults or insecurities (Kernberg 1984B). Thus narcissistic patients may deny the existence of their vulnerability, self-consciousness, and hostility" (Corbitt 1994, p. 199). Corbitt's contention is that "narcissistic patients tend to present themselves as psychologically healthy rather than as vulnerable to emotional weakness" (p. 200).

During periods of extraordinary functioning, however, a complete reversal takes place:

> Although theoretically one would predict a lack (or at least a denial) of depression and anxiety in patients with NAR, clinical experience suggests that they seek treatment in response to overwhelming discomfort brought about by failure of their typical modes of defense against precisely these feelings of depression and/or anxiety. In such cases, it is likely that elevations will then occur on these facets of Neuroticism, at least in the early stages of treatment. In other words, a poorly defended narcissist may produce elevations on Neuroticism (an accurate portrayal of his or her vulnerability), whereas a rigidly defended narcissist may produce extremely low scores (reflecting a defensive denial of vulnerability). (p. 200)

Corbitt's use of parenthetical statements in this quotation exemplifies the essential alternating and contradictory pattern of behavior that is characteristic of the person with a narcissistic personality organization (NAR). The rigid and controlling behavior is a defense against severe anxiety, a primitive defense, that breaks down when overloaded and leads directly to an outbreak of compulsive and, in the more extreme case, addictive behavior (Kernberg 1985A, pp. 22, 222; Albanese 1990, 1991). If the person is observed over time, through ordinary and extraordinary situations in which the defense works and when it does not, respectively, a chaotic pattern of alternating and contradictory behavior emerges. It does not make the scores, or configuration of scores, on the FFM straightforward, but it does contribute to an appropriate interpretation of the meaning of these scores. This complexity is characteristic of personality organizations in the primitive range of the Personality Continuum.

PERSONALITY AND ORGANIZATIONAL BEHAVIOR

Personality organizations at the lower levels of personality development—neurotic, primitive, and even psychotic—may have some advantages as leaders by virtue of their particular personality organization. The literature on personality and organizational behavior is germane here. Kernberg (1978, 1979) and Manfred F.R. Kets de Vries and Danny Miller (1984, 1988) have investigated how the personality of the leader influences the functioning of the organization.

Can a person with a narcissistic personality organization lead an organization? The answer is yes, but the question is how? In the ruthless and exploitative way that is characteristic of a person with a narcissistic personality organization: "In general, their relationships with other people are clearly exploitative and sometimes parasitic. It is as if they feel they have the right to control and possess others and to exploit them without guilt feelings—and behind the surface which very often is charming and engaging, one senses coldness and ruthlessness" (Kernberg 1985A, p. 17).

In addition, the political psychology literature is relevant here, for example, the charismatic personality (Zaleznik 1988). Entrepreneurship, innovation and bringing a business into existence to apply an invention in the pursuit of profit, is another type of leadership that can be explored. The creative destruction of the entrepreneur (Schumpeter 1934) is the engine of economic growth. How does the entrepreneur pursue profit? By what overall pattern of behavior? With the (ego) capacity of sympathy for others and the (superego) capacity to experience guilt for violating the moral system of society? Simply stated, "What kind of person is the entrepreneur?" At what level of personality development? What personality organization?

A person with a narcissistic personality organization is never satisfied. For an entrepreneur with a narcissistic personality organization, the pursuit of profit is relentless and ruthless, because he is never satisfied. This is greed. But success and failure oscillate, just like all the other contradictory aspects of his chaotic life. Stability is absent, and maintenance is not his strong suit. Winning does not just mean coming out ahead, it also means getting the other fellow down and destroying his opponent (Sullivan 1953, p. 232).

NOTES

1. In fact, the Hall and Lindzey reference in Kassarjian and Sheffet (1991) is erroneous; the second edition was published in 1970, not 1969. The third edition was published in 1978. In Kassarjian and Sheffet (1981), the reference is to a publication of the Advertising Research Foundation, "Are There Consumer Types?" (1964), which is a study of personality differences in the purchase of one- versus two-ply toilet paper using the Edwards Personal Preference Schedule. There are no references for consistency in Kassarjian and Sheffet (1975). In Kassarjian (1971), the reference is to the first edition of Hall and Lindzey in 1957, and there is an erroneous reference to the second edition in 1969. Kassarjian and Sheffet would have been better off if they had quoted the famous observation attributed to Hall and Lindzey (1957) that there are as many definitions of personality as there are theorists.

2. Wells made this comment as a discussant on a "Special Topics Session on Personality and Psychoanalytic Theory: Current Theoretical and Empirical Research" at the 1991 Association for Consumer Research Conference in Chicago, Illinois.

3. For a valiant effort to resuscitate this approach in marketing, see John C. Mowen, *The 3M Model of Motivation and Personality: Theory and Empirical Applications to Consumer Behavior* (2000).

Chapter 2

SHRINKING ECONOMIC MAN

Shrinking economic man down to his preferences was largely the result of the transformation from cardinal to ordinal utility theory, which left economic theory resting on the superficial conception of the consumer as merely a scale of preferences or preference ordering—virtually the last vestige of a human being left in economic analysis. Making the conception of economic man more realistic, shrinking economic man, as in psychoanalyzing, is a primary objective of this book. Once we recognize how little is left to work with, the consumer's scale of preferences, it must be apparent that we must go beyond the boundaries of economics to accomplish this overriding objective.

Although I am an economist by training and am essentially interested in economic behavior (i.e., consumer behavior), I am taking a decidedly psychological approach to the analysis, drawing heavily on psychoanalytic object relations theory. What intrigues me most is the interpretation of the meaning of individual patterns of behavior, and the psychological perspective stems from the equation of the personality with a particular pattern of behavior. Personality is reflected in a particular pattern of behavior, or, more baldly, the personality is a package containing a pattern of behavior. The interpretation of the meaning of a pattern of behavior in terms of the individual personality shifts the analysis to a predominantly psychological perspective.[1]

Economics is not being abandoned. Quite the contrary, the limits of applicability of economic theory are being expanded by going beyond the boundaries of the discipline to broaden the behavioral foundations of economic analysis. Broadening the behavioral foundations of economic analysis and expanding the limits of applicability of economic theory are two powerful motivations for relating psychology and economics. As an economist, going beyond the boundaries of economics to make contributions to the foundations of economics puts me into a bit of a double bind; however, as an unabashed behavioral economist, I am compelled to begin with the observation of human behavior.

NORMAL, COMPULSIVE, AND ADDICTIVE CONSUMPTION BEHAVIOR

Two general patterns of individual behavior will be analyzed throughout this book: A pattern of stable and consistent behavior and a chaotic pattern of alternating and contradictory behavior. A pattern of stable and consistent consumption behavior should be somewhat more familiar to economists, since consistency is the behavioral basis of the rationality postulate in economic theory. A rational consumer will make consistent choices and therefore will have a transitive preference ordering.

Transitivity is a mathematical property of a preference ordering that has been stretched to consistency, a behavioral postulate reflecting the actual choices of the consumer, and has become enshrined in the vaunted concept of rationality in economic analysis. Rationality is an attribute of a person, not a preference ordering, and should be equated with the personality of the individual. This must be recognized if we are to make any progress toward the goal of making the conception of economic man more realistic.

The description of a pattern of consumption behavior as stable will not be as familiar to economists and heretofore has not been considered a part of the rationality postulate. By stability, I mean that the consumer consistently makes consistent choices over time. Stability is a dynamic property of the consumer's preferences, as the term *dynamic* is used in economics, pertaining to choices over time. This is essential to any definition of a "rational" person. A pattern of stable and consistent consumption behavior is designated here as *normal* consumption behavior.

Object relations theory defines normal personality development and, therefore, the normal person. This may surprise some economists who seem more willing to talk vaguely about "rationality," yet bridle at the notion that normality can somehow be defined. Surely such talk about rationality is more often than not nothing more than a disguise for an absence of a deeper understanding of just what it really means. It may be equally grating, however, to critics of neoclassical orthodoxy to learn that, mutatis mutandis, the normal person and normal personality development strikingly support the theoretical conception of the consumer of ordinal utility theory.

This does not imply that the reality of the rationality postulate is that it represents an ideal level of personality development. The rational consumer is not a perfect person, although the theoretically perfect person would be a perfectly rational consumer. The implication that economic man does not represent the pinnacle of personality development should not be surprising, and the implications of going beyond economic man will prove to be surprisingly illuminating.

A chaotic pattern of alternating and contradictory consumption behavior is described by the following observation: Consumers behave as if they had two separate sets of contradictory preferences that are alternately expressed in their observable consumption behavior (Schelling 1980; Winston 1980). It will be argued that a chaotic pattern of alternating and contradictory behavior is the basis for compulsive consumption behavior and, in the more extreme case, addictive consumption behavior.

In such cases, individuals are in conflict over their consumption behavior—at one point in time, they want to consume the commodity, and at another point, they do not want to consume the very same commodity. Their consumption behavior oscillates between these two contradictory preference states, and this alternating and contradictory pattern of behavior results in an intransitive preference ordering. Ordinal utility theory should not be applied in this case, since inconsistent consumption behavior violates the transitivity property of the consumers' preference ordering.

The characterization of preferences as alternating and contradictory has been explored by Thomas C. Schelling in "The Intimate Contest for Self-Command" (1980). Schelling is an astute observer of human behavior with an acute interest in, and an institute on, smoking behavior. He has advanced an insightful hypothesis for this compulsive consumption behavior: "People behave sometimes as if they had two selves, one who wants clean lungs and long life and another who adores tobacco, or one who wants a lean body and another who wants dessert, or one who yearns to improve his mind by reading *The Public Interest* and another who would rather watch an old movie on television. The two are in continual contest for control" (pp. 95–96). Schelling's two-selves hypothesis proves to be a highly illuminating explanation for this commonly observed pattern of alternating and contradictory behavior and has spawned an interdisciplinary literature on compulsive and addictive behavior. An excellent example is *The Multiple Self* (1985), a volume of essays edited by Jon Elster.

In "Addiction and Backsliding: A Theory of Compulsive Consumption" (1980), Gordon C. Winston carried Schelling's observations of behavior into a mathematical optimization model that recognizes the significance of contradictory preferences: "Simultaneously two sets of preferences order an individual's choices and they don't agree," and furthermore, "the individual's preferences are not rigidly fixed over time; instead they flip-flop between two different preference states" (p. 303). Winston's model is an important step toward operationalizing the contributions of behavioral economics and will be elaborated subsequently along with the analysis of addiction.

This raises a difficult question for economists: If ordinal utility theory does not apply, does that imply that this alternating and contradictory behavior is irrational? This issue is extremely telling of the misuse of the description of behavior as "irrational" by economists. Compulsive and addictive consumption includes commonplace everyday behavior; to take Schelling's examples, smoking, eating, and watching television. While these constitute problems for the individual, they hardly warrant being labeled "irrational." This is pure nonsense from a psychological perspective; an irrational person is psychotic, lacking even the most rudimentary level of reality testing. Psychotic personalities, like schizophrenics and manic-depressives, often require institutionalization. The lack of economic uses of the psychotic personality is very telling of the flagrant misuse of the designation of any inconsistent behavior as "irrational" by economists.

Schelling (1980) asked the following critical question:

> Does it matter, for theory or policy, whether we know how to characterize such behavior, even just to describe it in the language of preferences and values, choices and decisions, utility, welfare, and rationality? We could be interested in casting suspicion on the entire individualistic-utilitarian foundation of neoclassical economics by adding a large fraction of the literate adult population to that already large population disqualified by infancy, senility, or incompetence from being represented in our theory of the consumer. Alternatively, we could just be interested, as I am, in getting a better idea of what is going on and how

much it matters when people behave in these apparently contradictory fashions. (p. 96)

Yes, it does matter, because we can and must circumscribe the limits of applicability of ordinal utility theory (and its extensions to the new household production function approach) as a way of making it more useful, not less. The crucial implication for economic analysis is that there is a vast area between the extremes of the perfectly rational and the truly irrational person, representing numerous patterns of behavior that must be investigated.

This is a critical contribution that psychology can make to economics—the recognition that there are ranges of behavior that exist along a Personality Continuum between the extremes of rationality and irrationality. These ranges represent behavior that does not conform to the conventional economic theory of the consumer, but is nonetheless patterned and persisting behavior that can be modeled in an optimization framework.[2]

A pattern of consistent behavior is a central theme in the exploration of normal consumer behavior. From the perspective of observable behavior, a rational consumer makes consistent choices. Should a person be expected to behave consistently from situation to situation? That depends on the person's level of personality development. The answer is "yes" for normal personality development, and "yes" under ordinary circumstances for the neurotic personality organizations, but "no" under extraordinary circumstances, that is, interpersonal situations fraught with severe anxiety. Under extraordinary functioning, a person with a neurotic personality organization is likely to behave inconsistently. Inconsistent behavior under extraordinary functioning is indicative of the neurotic consumer.

In comparison, even under ordinary circumstances the answer is "no" for primitive personality organizations. For personality organizations in the primitive range of the Personality Continuum, behavior is not merely inconsistent, but is actually contradictory. In general, a chaotic pattern of alternating and contradictory behavior characterizes personality organizations in the primitive range of the Personality Continuum. Fairbairn (1952, p. 10) observes that a person with a primitive personality organization would manifest evidence of contradictory behavior under the most ordinary conditions of life.

Under very favorable circumstances, a person with a primitive personality organization can function at a higher-than-ordinary level and behave neurotically according to Fairbairn's hypothesis. Neurotic behavior is still inconsistent under extraordinary functioning, but this is far from the chaotic pattern of alternating and contradictory behavior characteristic of primitive personality organizations.

Finally, for psychotic personality organizations, characterized by the absence of reality testing and by a changing and capricious pattern of behavior, resulting in truly irrational behavior, the answer is a resounding "no."[3] It is important to recognize that the changing and capricious pattern of behavior characteristic of psychotic personality organizations is qualitatively different from the chaotic, but rigidly alternating and contradictory pattern of behavior characteristic of the primitive personality organizations, the merely inconsistent pattern of behavior of the neurotic personality organization, and the stable and consistent pattern of behavior of a normal person.

Economics only distinguishes between the extremes of "rational" and "irrational" behavior at the normal and psychotic levels of personality development, respectively, without recognizing the useful patterns of variations of neurotic and primitive consumer behavior between these extremes. What are missing from the rational-irrational dichotomy of economics are the neurotic and primitive ranges of the Personality Continuum and all the variations in patterns of behavior that go with these qualitatively different levels of personality development. In this way, the Personality Continuum facilitates the comparison of variations in general patterns of behavior, related to the qualitatively different levels of personality development and the contrast between particular personality organizations arrayed into discrete ranges (Albanese 1990).

THE FOOLISH CONSISTENCY OF RALPH WALDO EMERSON: RIGIDLY PATTERNED BEHAVIOR

The primitive range of the Personality Continuum is occupied by personality organizations intermediate between neurosis and psychosis, representing the most rigid kind of structure, and not transitory states fluctuating between neurosis and psychosis (Kernberg 1984A, p. 20; Kernberg 1985A, p. 3). According to Kernberg (1984A), "There is no doubt that this state of affairs represents an ego weakness, but it also shows itself a most rigid kind of structure" (p. 20).

Personality organizations in the primitive range of the Personality Continuum represent a manifestation of one global, rigid characterological pattern (Kernberg 1984A, p. 19). "The rigidity of characterological patterns is sometimes mistakenly considered to be a sign of ego strength" (Kernberg 1985A, p. 22). In a further elaboration, according to

Kernberg (1985A), "Neither excessive rigidity of character pathology nor its 'overfluidity' in itself represent ego strength or weakness, but rather both are specific modes of organization of the character pathology" (p. 22).

Ralph Waldo Emerson captured the rigidly patterned behavior of personality organizations in the primitive range of the Personality Continuum in "Self-Reliance," perhaps his most enduring essay: "A foolish consistency is the hobgoblin of little minds" (Emerson 1968, p. 152). Foolish consistency is the rigidity characteristic of personality organizations at the primitive level of personality development. Just as consistency should not be confused with rigidity, preferences that change in response to the specific circumstances of the situation should not be confused with inconsistency.[4]

The theme of the rigidity of behavior is characteristic of personality organizations in the primitive range of the Personality Continuum. It is a critical aspect of the complexity of personality classification. This is an explicit example of the difficulty in differentiating, at one point in time, the stable and consistent behavior of the normal consumer from the rigidly patterned behavior typical of primitive personality organizations.

Personality organizations in the primitive range of the Personality Continuum present the best opportunity to explore observable consumption behavior that is rigidly patterned, such as the redosing regime of an addict. In dealing with a simpler structure, rigid and uncomplicated by higher-level psychic structures, such as the schizoid, antisocial, narcissistic, infantile, and borderline personality organizations in the primitive range of the Personality Continuum, we must remember Freud's crystal analogy, see what is revealed to us about internal, psychic reality, and not be too critical, or hypocritical, of the individual's pattern of behavior.

The Personality Continuum represents an enormous source of theories and observations of human behavior that become available to economists by forging a theoretical relationship between economics and psychology. The explanation provided for these observed patterns of normal, compulsive, and addictive consumption behavior is that they represent different ranges along the Personality Continuum, reflect different personality organizations within these ranges, and, in short, represent entirely different persons. As has been previously stated, the Personality Continuum is divided into four discrete ranges of personality development—normal, neurotic, primitive, and psychotic. The economic implications of each range of the Personality Continuum, and particular personality organizations within each range, will be explored in depth.

Emphasis will be placed on a comparison of the normal and primitive ranges as the basis for the analysis of stable and consistent consumption behavior and a pattern of compulsive and addictive consumption behavior, respectively.

A BRIEF BEHAVIORAL HISTORY OF ECONOMIC THOUGHT FOR BEGINNERS

Paul A. Samuelson began his chapter "The Pure Theory of Consumer's Behavior" in the first edition of *Foundations of Economic Analysis* (1947) by expressing the view that the introduction of the subjective theory of value into economic theory was the "single criterion by which to distinguish modern economic theory from its classical precursors" (p. 90). He followed this with an observation that still rings true today: "Moreover, it is this part of economic doctrine that has proved to be the center of so much controversy. Indeed, many critics of the orthodox tradition have identified the whole body of economic theory with the belief in that abstraction, *homo economicus*" (p. 90).

At the heart of this controversy over *homo economicus*—the vaunted concept of the rational economic man—is the changing conception of the consumer in the transformation from cardinal to ordinal utility theory. The essence of cardinal utility is stated succinctly by Joseph A. Schumpeter in his "Note on the Theory of Utility" from his epic *History of Economic Analysis* (1954): "In the beginning, utility, both total and marginal, was considered a psychic reality, a feeling that was evident from introspection, independent of any external observation—hence, to repeat this also, *not* to be inferred from those externally observable facts of behavior in the market which were to be explained by it—and a *directly measurable* quantity" (p. 1060).[5]

I am equally interested in the interplay between introspection and the observation of behavior, and the contrast between cardinal and ordinal utility. Utility was considered the cause of value, and cardinal utility theory was believed to be a general psychology of values (Schumpeter 1954, p. 1058). The concept of cardinal utility was abandoned, along with the theory of value, and was replaced by an ordinal conception of utility, a more realistic theory of choice. In the classic article, "A Reconsideration of the Theory of Value" (1934), John R. Hicks gave generous credit to Vilfredo Pareto for the transformation from cardinal to ordinal utility theory:

> Of all Pareto's contributions there is probably none that exceeds in importance his demonstration of the immeasurability of utility. To most earlier writers, to

Marshall, to Walras, to Edgeworth,[6] utility had been a quantity theoretically measurable; that is to say, a quantity which would be measurable if we had enough facts. Pareto definitely abandoned this, and replaced the concept of utility by the concept of a scale of preferences. It is not always observed that this change in concepts was not merely a change of view, a pure matter of methodology; it rested on the positive demonstration that the facts of observable conduct make a scale of preferences capable of theoretical construction. (p. 52)[7]

Samuelson (1947) considered the movement away from the concept of utility as an introspective magnitude to be a fundamental shift in view for some economists: "It is not merely that the modern economist replaces experienced sensation or satisfaction with anticipated sensation, according to the now familiar distinction between ex post and ex ante analysis. But much more than this, many writers have ceased to believe in the existence of any introspective magnitude or any quantity of a cardinal, numerical kind" (p. 91). The reaction against the measurability of utility was quite extreme, according to Samuelson: "Indeed, so far has the reaction gone that it is the belief of many that nothing remains but an empty convention. Others, who do not admit the hollowness of utility, have in some cases embraced a formulation of the analysis which is meaningless in any operational, empirical sense. The result is a curious jargon of dogmatic precepts" (p. 91). Ordinal utility theory came to rest on a superficial conception of the consumer as simply a scale of preferences. As Hicks (1943) demonstrated, knowing the consumer's preferences does "not enable us to proceed from the scale of preferences to a particular utility function" (p. 52).

The personality organization becomes the organizational framework that can be used to explain variations in patterns of consumption behavior. The personality organization, the central conception of psychoanalytic object relations theory, is comprised of the intrapsychic structure and the predominant defensive organization of the personality. Personality organizations in the same range along the Personality Continuum are characterized by a common, or general, pattern of behavior, and, therefore, each personality organization will be represented by the same general form of the utility function. The general form of the utility function will depend upon the level of intrapsychic structural formation that characterizes the personality organization. After an object relations theory of personality development has been presented, the fundament of the utility function for each level of personality development will be provided.

The main achievement of this approach, according to Hicks, is that "by transforming the subjective theory of value into a general logic of choice, they extend its applicability over wide fields of human conduct" (p. 54). I shall proceed by beginning with human behavior, and I believe that this is the direction that the discipline of economics is taking with respect to consumer theory, most notably, with the innovation of the allocation of time introduced by Gary S. Becker (1965).

A cardinal measure of utility is, after all, unnecessary, and will remain so forever; however, introspection, as a technique of analysis, should not have been abandoned so easily by economists as a tool for investigating the nature of the consumer's preferences. In the early development of the economic theory of the consumer, the theory was known as the subjective theory of value. The economic theory of the consumer is quite properly a logic of choice. Subjective states are the field of study of psychology, not economics.

The concept of subjective experience provides a bridge that brings together the economic and psychological analyses bearing on choice. A person can come to know his subjective inner experience through introspection. This harks back to Samuelson's admonition that we—economists—went too far in eliminating any trace of introspection in the transition from cardinal to ordinal utility theory (1947, p. 91). To know more of reality includes one's inner reality known through introspection.[8]

CIRCULARITY AND PREFERENCE CHANGE

Schumpeter (1954) argued for open boundaries between economics and psychology in all their aspects: "If we ask how consumers come to behave as they do in all those wider problems of human behavior for which particular psychological propositions become relevant, we must in fact appeal to all that modern professional psychology—of all varieties, from Freudianism to behavioralism—might have to give us" (p. 1059). If we ask how consumers come to behave as they do, as economists, we invariably beg the question rather than answer it. We cannot question the motivation for the choices made by the consumer without being circular: The consumer's market behavior is explained in terms of preferences, which are in turn defined only by behavior in the market; the result, more often than not, is a circular statement saying that we behave as we behave or prefer what we prefer (Sweezy 1934, p. 181; Samuelson 1947, p. 91).[9]

This is not a problem with the theory per se, but with the applications of the theory by economists; as long as we do not question the motivation of the consumer, the theory is not circular. This is such an apparent limitation that it is often overlooked in the welter of assumptions and equations used to explain consumer behavior. Economists need to heed Tennyson's admonition, "Ours is not to reason why."

This admonition must not be confused with the open hostility within the economics profession toward the investigation of the nature of preferences. In his critical contribution to the extremely limited literature on preference change, *Shifting Involvements: Private Interest and Public Action*, Albert O. Hirschman (1982) made the following observation: "Any number of quotations from economists and economics textbooks could be supplied to the effect that economics had no business delving into the reasons why preferences are what they are, and it is implicit in such denials that it is even less appropriate for economists to inquire how and why preferences might change" (p. 9).

Such hostility must be openly acknowledged because it disguises the real limitations of economic analysis. Hirschman characterized this view with scathing clarity: "Such assertions about the proper province of 'scientific, positive,' economics are often made in so annoyed a tone and so aggressive a manner that one may well suspect here some basic sensitivity and vulnerability" (p. 9). This is undoubtedly a subtle reference to the apocryphal notions expressed by George J. Stigler and Gary S. Becker in "De Gustibus Non Est Disputandum" (1977).

THE ELEVATION OF THE SUBJECT OF TASTES IN ECONOMIC THEORY

In an important survey of research on economic factors in American fertility, "Towards a Socioeconomic Theory of Fertility," Richard A. Easterlin (1969) laid down a very clear challenge for economists: "Perhaps the greatest obstacle so far to development of a unified socioeconomic theory of fertility, and, correspondingly, the most promising opportunity for advance, lies in the subject of tastes" (p. 133). Easterlin's challenge with regard to a socioeconomic theory of fertility reverberates throughout the economic theory of the consumer, which starts with the assumption of a consumer of given tastes or preferences. In Easterlin's view, the elevation of taste considerations bearing on choice to a position equal to that of other factors in economic theory requires "explicit attention to preference phenomena and the factors entering into their formation" (p. 135).

Easterlin emphasized this challenge by chiding economists for their lack of interest in taste phenomena: "Nor can economists dismiss taste phenomena as non-economic in nature, for it is clear that economic variables enter into the shaping of tastes and affect behavior through this channel as well as via resource and price constraints traditionally emphasized" (p. 135). The consideration of the subject of tastes or preferences is a controversial area in economics, with the clearest lines drawn between Easterlin and his colleagues, who have become known as the Pennsylvania school, and Gary S. Becker and his colleagues, known as the Chicago-Columbia school. This controversy can be elaborated by comparing the views of Easterlin and his colleagues, particularly in a recent contribution with Robert A. Pollak and Michael L. Wachter, "Toward a More General Economic Model of Fertility Determination: Endogenous Preferences and Natural Fertility" (1980), with the views of Gary S. Becker and Robert T. Michael, "On the New Theory of Consumer Behavior" (1973), and a later statement by George J. Stigler and Gary S. Becker, "De Gustibus Non Est Disputandum" (1977). Easterlin's earlier views on the importance of investigating the formation of tastes or preferences in "Towards a Socioeconomic Theory of Fertility" (1969) have not changed in his more recent contribution: "A framework that incorporates research on taste formation along with other social and economic variables will extend the range of empirical problems potentially amenable to treatment" (Easterlin et al. 1980, p. 117).

The views of the Chicago-Columbia school were established by Becker and Michael (1973). The essential modification of the traditional theory of consumer choice that was introduced at that time was the household production function approach, in which "commodities are produced by the consumer unit itself through the productive activity of combining purchased market goods and services with some of the household's own time" (p. 381). According to Becker and Michael, the advantage of this approach is that "it systematically and symmetrically incorporates numerous constraints on the household's behavior, strengthens the reliance on changes in income and prices as explanations of observed behavior, and correspondingly reduces the reliance on differences in tastes or preferences" (p. 394). This view was subsequently elaborated by Stigler and Becker 1977): "The great advantage, however, of relying only on changes in the arguments entering household production functions is that all changes in behavior are explained by changes in prices and incomes, precisely the variables that organize and give power to economic analysis" (p. 89).

It is essential to investigate preference phenomena and the factors entering into their formation, since the economic conception of the consumer is limited to the assumption of a consumer of given preferences. The interest in preference formation has created a controversy in economics. Becker and Michael (1973) have simply asserted that no theory exists: "For economists to rest a large part of their theory of choice on differences in tastes is disturbing since they admittedly have no useful theory of the formation of tastes, nor can they rely on a well-developed theory of tastes from any other discipline in the social sciences, since none exists" (p. 380). This assertion, however, only serves to underscore the fundamental importance of investigating the formation of preferences as a way out of the limitations imposed by the assumption of a consumer of given preferences (see Easterlin 1969; Kapteyn and Wansbeek 1982).

Becker and Michael (1973) concluded that, "From this point of view, the Latin expression *de gustibus non est disputandum* suggests not so much that it is impossible to resolve disputes arising from differences in tastes but rather that in fact no such disputes arise!" (Becker and Michael 1973, p. 392). Thus, in the views of the Chicago-Columbia school, neither changes nor differences in tastes or preferences play any significant role in explaining economic behavior. According to their approach, "One searches, often long and frustratingly, for the subtle forms that prices and incomes take in explaining differences among men and periods" (Stigler and Becker 1977, p. 76).

Easterlin and his colleagues, while accepting the household production function approach, make it quite clear that substituting technology for tastes has simply obscured the fundamental question of the formation of tastes or preferences: "The notion that economists have an acceptable theory of systematic differences in household technology, but do not have a definitive theory of taste formation, is hardly a justification for excluding or neglecting hypotheses related to tastes" (Easterlin et al. 1980, p. 116). They take this view one step further to provide a more thoughtful approach: "Taste differences, like differences in technology, can be and often are used as a deus ex machina when other explanations fail. But the fact that specifications involving taste differences (or technology differences) can be misused is not a justification for ignoring them" (p. 133).

The elevation of taste considerations bearing on choice to a position equal to that of income and prices involves going beyond economic theory and searching long, but profitably, for a methodology that will contribute to an understanding of the formation of preferences. Easterlin (1969) established the essential criterion for a methodology to investigate the formation of preferences: "It must be a commonly accepted analytical framework which embraces the variety of factors which are considered important in the formation of preferences" (p. 127).

The way out of this circularity is to go beyond the boundaries of economics to investigate the nature of preferences, which I would classify into the formation, variation, and change of preferences. Amitai Etzioni (1985) has called for "opening the preferences," and I would expand this to a call for opening the profession. Object relations theory, concentrating on the formation of the intrapsychic structure of the personality, provides a superb theoretical framework to investigate the nature of preferences (Albanese 1982, 1987, 1988C, 1988D, 1990).

On the subject of preference change, economics does not fare much better. The consumer's scale of preferences represents what a person likes or dislikes, more or less, and we must come to a fundamental understanding of the motivation for preference change. This is a seemingly insurmountable task when one looks at the available literature in economics. In *Shifting Involvements*, Hirschman (1982) states this quite clearly: "Since change in tastes or preferences is an undeniable fact of considerable importance, particularly in Western societies, one might expect a sizable literature to have accumulated on the topic. Actually, at least insofar as economics is concerned, this expectation is largely contradicted. The reason for this is that economic analysis proceeds on the basis of preferences that are considered to be given" (p. 9).

Given the superficial conception of the consumer as merely a scale of preferences, it is imperative to overcome this limitation. Otherwise, preferences may appear to be changing capriciously. Hirschman (1982) has made a fundamental contribution to an understanding of the process of preference change by exploring the role of disappointment. His hypothesis is simply stated: "Acts of consumption, . . . , which are undertaken because they are expected to yield satisfaction, also yield disappointment and dissatisfaction" (p. 10).

The importance of the role of dissatisfaction in consumption was earlier recognized by Tibor Scitovsky in his highly influential book on psychology and economics, *The Joyless Economy: An Inquiry Into Human Satisfaction and Consumer Dissatisfaction* (1976). It is worth noting that in the preface of the paperback edition, Scitovsky related that his book had grown out of his trying to find out why a whole generation of young Americans had become disaffected and disappointed with the way of life and high standard of living of their parents' generation during the 1960s. More than a decade later Hirschman (1982), in the introduction to *Shifting Involvements*, attributed his insight about the role of disappointment in preference change to the resurgence of interest in the demonstrations, student uprisings, and strikes that had occurred in the late 1960s.

An understanding of the systematic way in which preferences change has proven to be an intractable area of economic theory. The reason for this strikes at the very foundations of the economic theory of the consumer. There is no mechanism for preference change in economic theory because the concept of "utility" has been interpreted to mean only satisfaction or pleasure. The theory had its origin in Jeremy Bentham's hedonic calculus, which was based on the belief that pleasure and pain could be quantified. When economists borrowed this theoretical framework, only the pleasurable side of the equation was chosen, and the painful aspects of the theory were completely ignored. This omission has direct relevance for understanding the intractability of preference change: What possible motivation could there be for the consumer to change his preferences if he is always satisfied with his choices? In the static analysis of ordinal utility theory, a rational consumer will maximize utility by choosing the most preferred consumption bundle. Thus there is no mechanism for change.

The primary motivation for changing preferences is disappointment, whether we call it dissatisfaction, disillusionment, or disgust, and this recognition will inform the inquiry into preference change. Yet this simple idea cannot be readily incorporated into consumer theory in a systematic way in its present form. This is why Hirschman's treatment of the subject is somewhat unsatisfying, and why the work of Richard L. Solomon on the opponent-process theory of motivation and Lester D. Taylor's brilliant adaptation of it to economic theory have gained increasing credibility in economics (Solomon 1980, 1988; Solomon and Corbit 1974; Taylor 1988).

NOTES

1. For a similar perspective, see Holbrook (1992).
2. For a similar insight, see Winston 1980, p. 304.
3. The characterization of irrational behavior as "changing and capricious" is taken from George J. Stigler and Gary S. Becker, "De Gustibus Non Est Disputandum" (1977), p. 76.
4. The significance of the interpersonal situation was introduced with Sullivan's interpersonal theory of personality. For an early exploration of the situational variables in marketing, see Russell W. Belk (1975), "Situational Variables and Consumer Behavior." For a more mature approach, see Gordon R. Foxall, *Consumer Choice* (1983). For an intriguing exploration of the situational determinants of behavior, see the research on situational ethnicity by Deshpande, Hoyer, and Danthu (1986).
5. Schumpeter began his "Note on the Theory of Utility," the appendix to chapter 7 of *History of Economic Analysis*, with this quite accurate statement:

"In this Note we shall survey, in the briefest possible compass, the whole career of the utility theory of value" (1954, p. 1053).

6. In deference to F.Y. Edgeworth, the opening of *Mathematical Psychics: An Essay on the Applications of Mathematics to the Moral Sciences* (1881) is a clear statement of the basic principle of ordinal utility theory: "The science of quantity is not alien to the study of man, it will be generally admitted, in so far as actions and effective desires can be *numerically* measured by way of statistics—that is, very far, as Professor Jevons anticipates. But in so far as our *data* may consist of estimates other than *numerical*, observations that some conditions are accompanied with *greater* or *less* pleasure than others, it is necessary to realize that mathematical reasoning is not, as commonly supposed, limited to subjects where numerical data are attainable. Where there are data which, though not *numerical* are *quantitative*—for example, that a quantity is *greater* or *less* than another, *increases* or *decreases*, is *positive* or *negative*, a *maximum* or a *minimum*, there mathematical reasoning is possible and may be indispensable. To take a trivial instance: a is greater than b, and b is greater than c, therefore a is greater than c" (Edgeworth 1967, pp. 1–2).

It was Pareto's extension of Edgeworth's concept of the indifference curve that revolutionized utility theory. In *Value and Capital* (1946), Hicks characterized Pareto's contribution in the following way: "Pareto turned his attention to the problem of related—complementary and competitive—goods. Here he made an extension of the earlier analysis; or rather, something which started as an extension but ended as a revolution. For the purpose of studying related goods, Pareto took over from Edgeworth a geometrical device—the Indifference Curve" (pp. 12–13).

7. According to Schumpeter (1954), "Pareto as a 'pure' economist became a familiar figure in England and the United States when Allen and Hicks developed his theory of value (indifference-curve approach), giving generous credit to him" (p. 859). As a further clarification, he later added: "Pareto proceeded to develop the idea of ordinal utility and eventually worked out what must in fairness be considered the fundament of the modern theory of value. He was not quite consistent about it and slid back again and again into the habits of thought he had acquired in his formative years. Further advance was made, however, . . . although it was not until 1934 that the job was completely done by Allen and Hicks" (p. 1063).

8. See Holbrook (1995) for a thorough exploration of, and strong advocacy for, the role of subjective personal introspection in consumer research.

9. This reminds me of the caricature of circularity of theories of the so-called Chicago school. In the remarkably readable *Minds, Markets, and Money*, Shlomo Maital (1982) described the applications of revealed preference theory by Gary S. Becker and his colleagues as tail-chasing: "At times, the circularity of deductive mathematical logic in economics almost becomes self-parody. We learn about husbands who 'would read in bed at night only if the value of reading exceeded the value (to him) of the loss of sleep suffered by his wife';

about persons who marry 'when the utility expected from marriage exceeds the utility expected from remaining single'; about couples who separate when 'the utility expected from remaining married falls below the utility expected from divorcing and possibly remarrying' " (pp. 13–14).

My favorite Becker bashing is his quality-quantity theory of the historical decline in fertility, where he begins with the observation that "the analysis developed here is far more suited to explaining fertility changes in Western countries during the last few centuries and in developing countries during this century," goes through some stupendous mathematical machinations, and, at the end of the analysis, concludes that "revealed preference shows us that the new equilibrium must be to the left of e_0, as is e_1" (Becker 1981, pp. 95, 108). Indeed, it is, exactly where it was when he started. For a more elaborate critique, see my "The Changing Motivation for Having Children" (1988A). I prefer to describe such applications as pin-the-tail-on-the-donkey, rather than tail-chasing; at least the dog is still chasing his tail and does not rest content having miraculously discovered the proper place for it.

Chapter 3

Individual Pursuit of Self-Interest and the Social Basis of Individual Behavior

For behavioral economists, establishing a relationship between economics and psychology is not the end of the process, but the beginning, because it provides a bridge to a social analysis of economic behavior, that is, a socioeconomic analysis. Psychological economics is something of a transitional phase to socioeconomics, with the progression of ideas going from the interpretation of observable patterns of individual behavior to the psychological foundations of consumer behavior as the bridge to a truly socioeconomic analysis.

Overcoming the overwhelmingly individual orientation of economic theory is an overriding objective of relating ordinal utility theory and object relations theory. Amartya K. Sen was highly critical of this conception of the economic man and the individual orientation of economic theory in his brilliant and concise critique of the limits of economic theory, "Rational Fools: A Critique of the Behavioral Foundations of Economic Theory" (1977). Sen raised many fundamental questions related to the economic theory of the consumer. His most profound questioning is addressed to the individual pursuit of self-interest. Sen quoted F.Y. Edgeworth: "In his *Mathematical Psychics*, published in 1881, . . . Edgeworth asserted that 'the first principle of Economics is that every agent is actuated only by self-interest' " (p. 317).

The predominant view of economic man as an isolated individual selfishly pursuing his own self-interest, maximizing his utility subject only to a budget constraint, raises many questions concerning the significance of social influences on individual behavior. Sen (1977) concluded that "the *purely* economic man is indeed close to being a social moron" and argued that "between the claims of oneself and all lie the claims of a variety of groups—for example, families, friends, local communities, peer groups, economic and social classes" (pp. 318, 336). This seemingly simple list of social groups is surprisingly comprehensive and bears repeating, because each of these groups will be systematically drawn into the analysis as significant social influences on personality development: family, friends, peer groups, the local community, and economic and social classes.

Sen (1977) prefaced this powerful critique with the following statement: "The economic theory of utility, which relates to the theory of rational behavior, is sometimes criticized for having too much structure; human beings are alleged to be 'simpler' in reality. If the argument so far has been correct, precisely the opposite seems to be the case: traditional theory has too *little* structure" (p. 335). Indeed, in the view of reality of the Chicago-Columbia school, the human is an exceedingly simple being, responding only to prices and income. The attitude of the Pennsylvania school, and the approach that will be elaborated here, is that economic theory has too little structure.

Tibor Scitovsky made important contributions toward relating psychology and economics in his pioneering work *The Joyless Economy: An Inquiry into Human Satisfaction and Consumer Dissatisfaction* (1976). Scitovsky opens the original preface to this highly stimulating and worthwhile book by deriding the use of the concept of consumer sovereignty: "This book is written by an economist, but it is concerned with matters not hitherto considered part of economics. People's tastes, the way they spend their money and arrange their lives, are matters economists have always regarded as something they should not poke their noses into. They seem to feel that analyzing people's tastes and their motivation would be an invasion of privacy and an abrogation of consumer sovereignty, and that it might expose them to the charge of pretending to know better than the consumer himself what is good for him. Instead, economists assume that the consumer is rational; in other words, they assume that whatever he does must be the best thing for him to do, given his tastes, market opportunities, and circumstances, since otherwise he would not have done it" (p. xi).[1]

In *Shifting Involvements*, Hirschman (1982) likewise ridiculed the concept of consumer sovereignty, interpreted to mean that consumers have independently acquired tastes, as a subterfuge for the alleged givenness of tastes and preferences and leveled a general criticism against much of economic decision theory: "Its subjects, while efficient and often ingenious and devious, are *without a history*" (p. 79). If we combine Sen's (1977) reproach of the social moron with Hirschman's critique, we arrive at the rather unflattering conception of economic man as a sovereign moron.

The brilliant Hungarian object relations theorist Michael Balint warned against the fallacy of seeing the simplest form of organization as the most *primitive*. He took economists and psychoanalysts to task for equating the earliest experience with the narcissistic state:

> But does it follow that the logically simplest form must be in reality the most primitive one? This is a fallacy of which we psycho-analysts are not the only victims. In the same way the economists, for quite a long time, put the so-called Robinson Crusoe situation at the beginning of economic development; in the same way it was assumed that the history of civilization started with logically simple conditions *à la* Rousseau, and in biology the apparently simplest living being, the amoeba, was presented as *primum vivens*. The psychological content of all these assumptions is the narcissistic state totally cut off on all sides, obviously a wish-fulfillment in a sublimated form. (Balint 1949, p. 273)

The socially isolated narcissistic personality organization should not be the model for the individual pursuit of self-interest.

BEYOND ECONOMICS

It is precisely because of the individual orientation of economic theory that psychological theories and, in particular, psychoanalytic theories of the personality are useful—there is a fundamental compatibility between the individual basis of behavior in both disciplines. Indeed, economic analysis and psychoanalysis are highly compatible in two fundamental ways, the overwhelmingly individual orientation of the analysis and the penchant for tight and concise models. The orientation toward tight and concise models in economic theory can be credited to David Ricardo and his victory over Thomas R. Malthus in their famous debate, and in psychoanalytic theory, of course, to Sigmund Freud and his formulation of the structural model of the id, ego, and superego.

By establishing a relationship between the personality of the individual and a particular pattern of behavior, a psychological approach offers a promising opportunity to deepen our understanding of individual behavior and contribute to the interpretation of the meaning and ultimately the motivation for observable patterns of behavior. Here I am drawing on the ideas of Clifford Geertz in his highly influential "Thick Description: Toward an Interpretive Theory of Culture" from his book *The Interpretation of Cultures* (1973). In response to the question "What does the ethnographer do?" Geertz answered, "He writes," then again, "more exactly, 'inscribes,' " and to the heart of the matter, "the ethnographer 'inscribes' social discourse" (p. 19). Thus, according to Geertz, "In so doing he turns it from a passing event, which exists only in its own moment of occurrence, into an account, which exists in its inscriptions and can be consulted" (p. 19).

I want to continue the progression from patterns of behavior, which can be observed, inscribed, and thickly described, to the social basis of behavior. Geertz argued that behavior and culture are based in social interaction: "Behavior must be attended to, and with some exactness, because it is through the flow of behavior—or, more precisely, social action—that cultural forms find articulation" (p. 17). Although I do want to bask in the aura of Geertz's concept of thick description and consider myself an ethnographer, very much interested in integrating cultural factors into the analysis, here I want to continue to lay emphasis on the social basis of behavior. As stated cryptically by Geertz, "Society's forms are culture's substance" (p. 28).

Geertz offers something of an indictment of economics, which fits his description of a "size-up-and-solve social science": "It is not against a body of uninterpreted data, radically thinned descriptions, that we must measure the cogency of our explications, but against the power of the scientific imagination to bring us into touch with the lives of strangers" (p. 16). I am drawing heavily on Geertz because he captures central concerns in the social sciences with uncommon clarity and resolves them into social issues; for example, "meaning varies according to the pattern of life by which it is informed" (p. 14). Here we have arrived at the heart of this endeavor, the interpretation of the meaning in the patterns of the everyday lives of people. Again, in Geertz's view, "A good interpretation of anything—a poem, a person, a history, a ritual, an institution, a society—takes us into the heart of that of which it is the interpretation" (p. 18).[2]

INTIMACY IN INTERPERSONAL RELATIONSHIPS

To elaborate on the social basis of individual behavior, we must recognize that it is, more concretely, the significant interpersonal relationships that characterize a person's life that constitute the social system within which the individual's personality develops. I would like to dwell on the significance of interpersonal relations through the concept of intimacy. The theme of intimacy penetrates to the heart of an interpersonal relationship and permeates the approach that I am taking to the analysis of human behavior.

I want to approach the concept of intimacy by way of Geertz's observation on what anthropologists do in villages: "Anthropologists don't study villages (tribes, towns, neighborhoods . . .); they study *in* villages," and what anthropologists study in villages is relevant because the findings "present the sociological mind with bodied stuff on which to feed" (Geertz 1973, pp. 22, 23). Thus Geertz concluded, "The famous anthropological absorption with the (to us) exotic . . . is, thus, essentially a device for displacing the dulling sense of familiarity with which the mysteriousness of our own ability to relate perceptively to one another is concealed from us" (p. 14).

To relate perceptively to one another in depth is a measure of *intimacy* in an interpersonal relationship. I want to explore intimacy as an avenue of analysis. According to Geertz, "If anthropological interpretation is constructing a reading of what happens, then to divorce it from what happens—from what, in this time or that place, specific people say, what they do, what is done to them, from the whole vast business of the world—is to divorce it from its applications and render it vacant" (p. 18).

The interpretation of the meaning of behavior from a social perspective, literally, from the basis of interpersonal relationships, is, of course, not original with Geertz, and his views clearly evoke in my mind the truly unique interpersonal theory of personality of Harry Stack Sullivan. In "The Illusion of Personal Individuality," Sullivan argued that "it makes no sense to think of ourselves as 'individual,' 'separate,' capable of anything like definitive description in isolation" (Sullivan 1964, p. 220). The following theoretical statement presents his views with characteristic clarity: "No great progress in this field of study can be made until it is realized that the field of observation is what people do with each other, what they can communicate to each other about what they do with each other" (pp. 220–221). What people do with each other, what they can communicate to each other, that is, what they relate perceptively to one another, confirms, or consensually validates, our own interpretations of the meaning of life:

> So we look again at our experience, and we consider, from the standpoint of illusory critics,[3] and so on: How can the thing be made to communicate? How can I tell somebody about this? And we finally, if we are fairly clever, get the

> answer. Once we have got that, the unique individuality of the experience begins to shrink, it becomes part of the general structure of life, we forget how strikingly novel the experience was and how peculiarly it had fringes which apply only to us—we lose all that in the process of validation. (p. 214)

Sullivan (1953) saw intimacy as bound up with one's personal worth and the capacity to collaborate in an interpersonal relationship: "Intimacy is that type of situation involving two people which permits validation of all components of personal worth. Validation of personal worth requires a type of relationship which I call collaboration, by which I mean clearly formulated adjustments of one's behavior to the expressed needs of the other person in the pursuit of increasingly identical—that is, more and more nearly mutual—satisfactions, and in the maintenance of increasingly similar security operations" (p. 246).

Sullivan (1964) was adamant about keeping the analysis at the level of interpersonal relations, and, therefore, on the basis of externally observable behavior, as the following passage from "Illusion" attests:

> As I say, the conceptual system has grown up which finds its subject matter not in the study of personality, which is beyond reach, but in the study of that which can be observed; namely, interpersonal relations. And when this viewpoint is applied, then one of the greatest difficulties encountered in bringing about favorable change is this almost inescapable illusion that there is a perduring, unique, simple existent self, called variously "me" or "I," and in some strange fashion, the patient's, or subject person's, private property. (p. 220)[4]

Once a person is convinced of this illusion, according to Sullivan (1964), "progress begins, life unfolds, and interpersonal relations improve" (p. 220).

Kernberg (1974A, 1974B, 1977), in his three contributions to the psychology of love relations, collapsed the determinants of intimacy into two preconditions. The advantage of collapsing the determinants of intimacy into two preconditions is that personality organizations representing qualitatively different levels of personality development can be arrayed along the Personality Continuum based on the degree of achievement of intimacy in an interpersonal relationship—an external and therefore observable pattern of behavior. Thus the classification of an individual into the appropriate range of the Personality Continuum can be made through observation of that person's behavior. Further, the differential diagnosis of a person's particular personality organization facilitates more refined interpretation of the meaning of any particular pattern of behavior. This opens the way to a vast array of variations in patterns of behavior that can be contrasted and compared along the Personality Continuum, including interpersonal comparisons of behavior; ultimately, we can investigate individual differences of behavior.

Through the conception of intimacy, personality theory has transcended its origins in the problems of personality and provides a general theoretical framework that encompasses normal personality development. There are no labels on personality organizations in the normal range of the Personality Continuum. A label on personality organization implies pathology at some level, neurotic, primitive, or psychotic, in descending order. Perhaps, for the normal person, the illusion of personal individuality disappears.

Hicks (1934) alerted us that we cannot proceed from an individual's scale of preferences to a unique utility function. In relating the economic conception of the consumer from ordinal utility theory to the personality organization of psychoanalytic object relations theory, the outcome will not be a unique utility function nor a cardinal measure of utility. Because object relations theory differentiates between personality organizations at qualitatively different levels of development, the general form of the utility function can be established for each range of the Personality Continuum. In the quest for a more realistic conception of economic man, Sullivan's illusion of personal individuality has profound economic implications. It implies that the search for a unique personality is unrealistic, or perhaps only unnecessary, at the normal level of personality development. This will be explored in greater depth with the normal consumer.

FROM ECONOMICS TO PSYCHOLOGY

Having shrunk economic man down to his preferences means that this is where we must perforce begin our endeavor to make the conception of economic man more realistic. According to Schumpeter (1954), "Once we recognize the purely formal character of the theorist's utility concept, we are naturally led to question the relations between the utility theory of value and psychology" (p. 1057). Schumpeter was a sincere advocate of using psychology in economics: "We do not become dilettantes in physics when we use the physical facts that are implied in the classical law of decreasing returns in agriculture. No more do we become dilettantes in psychology—or borrow from professional psychology—when we speak of motives or, for that matter, of wants or satisfactions" (p. 1059). But Schumpeter warned against "pseudo-psychology" in economics and repeatedly launched into tirades against Keynes's marginal propensity to consume, which he described as a "flagrant abuse" of psychology:

> Before proceeding I wish to advert to a type of pseudo-psychology which is nothing but an abuse. Keynes's well-known psychological law about the propensity to consume is an outstanding example. It avers that both individuals and societies will, if they experience an increase in income, normally increase their expenditure or consumption but by less than the increase in income. Whether this is so or not, it is a statement of statistically observable fact which Keynes raised to the rank of an assumption. Nothing is gained but a spurious dignity, by calling it a psychological law. Our experience with such "laws of human nature," from the seventh century on, is certainly not encouraging. (pp. 1059–1060; see also p. 28)[5]

In *The Joyless Economy*, Tibor Scitovsky (1976) lamented the loss of the last tiny bit of psychology from economics:

> Modern economics and psychology originated with the rationalist philosophers of the eighteenth century. Both disciplines claim Jeremy Bentham as an ancestor, although soon after his day they went their very separate ways. One of Bentham's shrewd psychological observations was that the second cup of coffee or the second helping of a dish is less enjoyable than the first, and the economists enshrined it into their celebrated Law of Diminishing Marginal Utility. But in the twentieth century they expurgated even that tiny bit of psychology, and today the economist's theory of consumer behavior is limited to exploring the logical implications of the assumption of man's rationality. (p. 15)

So this is where we must begin, shrinking economic man, to make the conception of the consumer more realistic.

NOTES

1. In the original preface, Scitovsky (1976) also relates the hostility he experienced in researching and writing *The Joyless Economy*: "Economists are deeply divided into the Establishment and its radical-left critics, but they were like a harmonious and happy family in their unanimous hostility to my ideas. I was taken aback at first by such an unbroken string of negative reactions, but then took comfort in its fitting in so well with one of the main points I make here: that man wants novelty but cannot take, and gets disturbed by, too much of it. After all, some of the greatest achievements of the human spirit were also too new for their day and encountered violent hostility at first. Such reception,

of course, is no proof of excellence; nevertheless, I decided to be reassured by it" (p. xv).

2. For the consumer behavior tradition drawing on hermeneutics, refer to Elizabeth C. Hirschman (1989).

3. Sullivan's use of the concept of an "illusory critic" reminds me of Adam Smith's use of the "impartial spectator" in *The Theory of Moral Sentiments* (1759).

4. The illusion of a separate "I" or "me" is indicative of the influence of the social psychology of George Herbert Mead on Sullivan's interpersonal theory (Sullivan 1953, pp. 16–18). In Sullivan's masterpiece, "The Illusion of Personal Individuality" (1950), he argued against limiting personality to the skin over your bones (Sullivan 1964, p. 226). In drawing on Mead's views, Alan Watts (1961) has stated, "Society gives us the idea that the mind or ego is inside the skin and that it acts on its own apart from society" (p. 37). Watts goes on to clarify that "the ego is almost invariably considered as something *in* the organism like the chauffeur in a car, or a little man inside the head who thinks thoughts and sees sights. It is just this ego feeling that is the social construct" (p. 37). I would characterize a more paranoid view as a brain in a bag of shit. This also brings to mind Freud's (1933) view that the ego's relation to the id might be compared with that of a rider to his powerful horse (p. 77).

5. I must continue Schumpeter's flagrant abuse of Keynes by ridiculing the latters's use of "animal spirits" as the motivation for economic behavior in *The General Theory of Employment, Interest, and Money* (1936). This indignity also must be leveled at the use of "altruism" by Gary S. Becker (1981); it must be regarded as a flagrant abuse of psychology.

Chapter 4

The Historical Misinterpretation of Adam Smith's Exquisite View of Human Nature

For far too long now the discipline of economics has been based on the erroneous conception of economic man as a selfish individual who pursues his own self-interest without regard for anyone else. Along with this unrepentant view of human nature, the goal of economic man qua consumer is to maximize utility, where utility is defined only as satisfaction or pleasure, constrained by the time and income he has to allocate toward consumption activity. As long as he makes consistent choices in the process of maximizing his utility, economic man is rational. What more could anyone ask for than to be rational while enjoying maximum pleasure? It is no wonder that greed is often mistaken for a positive motivation for economic behavior. This conception of economic man is ridiculed by Sen (1977):

> A person is given *one* preference ordering, and as and when the need arises this is supposed to reflect his interests, represent his welfare, summarize his idea of what should be done and describe his actual choices and behavior. Can one preference ordering do all these things? A person thus described may be "rational" in the limited sense of revealing no inconsistencies in his choice behavior, but if he has no use for these distinctions between quite different concepts, he must be a bit of a fool. . . . Economic theory has been much preoccupied

with this rational fool decked in the glory of his *one* all-purpose preference ordering. (pp. 335–336)

The character of economic man as an isolated individual, selfishly, if not ruthlessly, pursuing his own self-interest, has dominated the thinking of economists since Adam Smith formulated the concept of the invisible hand in *The Wealth of Nations*, first published in 1776:

> As every individual, therefore, endeavors as much as he can both to employ his capital in the support of domestic industry, and so to direct that industry that its produce be of the greatest value; every individual necessarily labours to render the annual revenue of the society as great as he can. He generally, indeed, neither intends to promote the public interest, nor knows how much he is promoting it. By preferring the support of domestic to that of foreign industry, he intends only his own security; and by directing that industry in such a manner as its produce may be of the greatest value, he intends only his own gain, and he is in this, as in many other cases, led by an invisible hand to promote an end which was no part of his intention. Nor is it always the worse for the society that it was no part of it. By pursuing his own interest he frequently promotes that of the society more effectually than when he intends to promote it. (p. 423)

This oft-quoted statement is commonly used to justify the overwhelmingly individual orientation of economic analysis. The *selfish* character of economic man is most often derived from a statement Smith made early in *The Wealth of Nations*: "It is not from the benevolence of the butcher, the brewer, or the baker, that we expect our dinner, but from their regard to their own interest. We address ourselves, not to their humanity but to their self-love, and never talk to them of our own necessities but of their advantages" (p. 14).

These two statements taken together form the basis for our current conception, or, as I will argue, misconception, of the rational economic man and represent the historical misinterpretation of Adam Smith's exquisite view of human nature. I would also argue that the selective quotation of any authority is more often than not self-serving, intended only to confirm one's own view rather than to support the view of the authority. This, I would argue, is the case with the misinterpretation of Adam Smith's rather profound, but unfortunately not prophetic, view of human nature. It is in the perspective of this attempt at historical reparation that I wish to approach the analysis of economic man.

Sen (1977) called for a more elaborate structure to make room for different concepts related to economic man's behavior and raised intriguing questions with regard to the place of the human capacity for sympathy and commitment (p. 336). We will not have to stray very far from the wellsprings of economics to find greater insight into the capacity for sympathy because sympathy is the central conception of Adam Smith's *The Theory of Moral Sentiments* (1759).

The opening sentence of *The Theory of Moral Sentiments* leaves no doubt that Smith's view of human nature recognized the higher side of life: "How selfish soever man may be supposed, there are evidently some principles in his nature, which interest him in the fortune of others, and render their happiness necessary to him, though he derives nothing from it, except the pleasure of seeing it" (Smith 1759, p. 47). Throughout *The Theory of Moral Sentiments*, behavior motivated by the capacity for sympathy is compared with truly selfish behavior. Although Smith sometimes uses "self-love" interchangeably with selfishness in his writings, more often he uses "self-love" to refer to a person who is in love with himself or herself. This is the excessive self-reference that is characteristic of the narcissistic personality organization.

The invidious comparison of selfish with sympathetic behavior is apparent in the following passage:

> But whatever may be the cause of sympathy, or however it may be excited, nothing pleases us more than to observe in other men a fellow-feeling with all the emotions of our own breast; nor are we ever so much shocked as by the appearance of the contrary. Those who are fond of deducing all of our sentiments from certain refinements of self-love, think themselves at no loss to account, according to their own principles, both for this pleasure and this pain. (Smith 1759, p. 54)

This statement anticipates by more than two centuries the argument that all behavior based on sympathy is still selfish because, according to Sen (1977, p. 326), "one is oneself pleased at others' pleasure and pained at others' pain, and the pursuit of one's own utility may thus be helped by sympathetic action."

As much as Adam Smith was able to grasp psychologically of what is described as the higher side of human life, in the words of Freud (1933, p. 67), is captured in the following profound passage from *The Theory of Moral Sentiments*: "And hence it is, that to feel much for others, and little for ourselves, that to restrain our selfish, and to indulge our benevolent, affections, constitutes the perfection of human nature; and can alone produce among mankind that harmony of sentiments and passions in which consists their whole grace and propriety" (Smith 1759, p. 71). I would argue that these statements reflect what Smith intended by the concept of sympathy throughout *The Theory of Moral Sentiments*, that sympathy represents a human capacity, the capacity for concern for another person and oneself: "Sympathy, though its meaning was, perhaps, originally the same, may now, however, without much impropriety, be made use of to denote our fellow-feeling with any passion whatsoever" (p. 49).

The capacity to sympathize with the sentiments of another person is a fundamental interpersonal experience. Interpersonal relations and the significance of the interpersonal situation are clearly recognized by Smith (1759): "As we have no immediate experience of what other men feel, we can form no idea of the manner in which they are affected, but by conceiving what we ourselves should feel in the like situation" (p. 47). According to Smith, "Sympathy, therefore, does not arise so much from the view of passion, as from that of the situation which excites it" (p. 51). The situation is quintessentially interpersonal, or, simply, social, and Smith's sentiments are human emotions. In Smith's view of human nature in *The Theory of Moral Sentiments*, sympathy, not selfishness, ought to be the basis for an understanding of consumer behavior, although he did not naively believe that all human behavior was motivated by sympathy for benevolent affections alone, and he felt that society would be much more agreeable if this were the case (p. 166).

Smith intended that *The Theory of Moral Sentiments* and *The Wealth of Nations* be read together as companion volumes. This explains why there is virtually no overlapping of critical ideas between the volumes. It is easy to see why reading only *The Wealth of Nations* can result in the misinterpretation of Smith's view of human nature.

Smith's brilliance lies in choosing a human capacity—the capacity for sympathy—as the basis for his view of human nature. In object relations theory, this same capacity is referred to as the capacity for concern. Object relations theory provides the specific interpersonal achievement in personality development that determines whether an individual will have this capacity or not and, therefore, provides the psychological foundations for the capacity for concern. In this way, using the personality organization of object relations theory as an organizational framework, I intend to make the conception of economic man more realistic and to broaden the behavioral foundations of economic analysis. This is not the end of the analysis, however, because establishing a sound methodological relationship between economics and psychology and, pertinently, between ordinal utility theory and psychoanalytic object relations theory opens the way for psychologists and other social scientists to delve more deeply into economic analysis. Further, economic analysis can be expanded by systematically linking the psychological, social, and cultural systems, using the Personality Continuum as the integrative framework.

The enduring usefulness of *The Theory of Moral Sentiments* for understanding human behavior stems from Smith's recognition of the significance of the capacity for concern, and it remains one of the best books ever written on the study of consumer behavior. We shall return often to Smith's penetrating interpretations of the meaning of human behavior, especially his understanding of the economic motivation for upward social mobility, to better one's lot in life. Smith also understood the darker side of human nature. Because he could appreciate the higher side of life, he understood the true nature of selfishness as a motivation for economic behavior, and his use of the term *self-love* will be elaborated with the narcissistic personality organization. His ideas on remorse will be explored in depth with the punitive superego and the dark side of consumer behavior. Smith's exquisite view of human nature will guide us in the quest to make the conception of economic man more realistic. Thus we begin our journey toward a human understanding of consumer behavior.

PART II

OBJECT RELATIONS THEORY OF PERSONALITY

Chapter 5

The Superego and the Origins of Object Relations Theory

It was Freud's formulation of the superego that gave rise to British object relations theory and later to American or psychoanalytic object relations theory. Object relations theory grew out of Freud's illuminating conception of the superego because it represented the internalization of an aspect of the interpersonal relationship with one's parents, rather than instincts or drives. In Freud's (1933) mature conception of the superego, "The part which is later taken on by the super-ego is played to begin with by an external power, by parental authority," and "the external restraint is internalized and the super-ego takes the place of the parental agency and observes, directs and threatens the ego in exactly the same way as earlier the parents did with the child" (p. 62).

There is no great mystery here. The superego starts out as all those things your parents told you to do and not to do—brush your teeth, wash your hands and face, don't stay out too late at night, and so on. These parental prohibitions and demands become internalized and form the contents of the superego. Then a little voice inside your head says, brush your teeth, wash your hands and face, don't stay out too late at night, and so on. On the higher side of human life, according to Freud, "The super-ego is the representative for us of every moral restriction, the advocate of a striving towards perfection—it is, in short, as much as we have been able to grasp psychologically of what is described as the higher side of human life" (pp. 66–67).

FREUD'S SUPEREGO AND THE ORIGINS OF OBJECT RELATIONS THEORY

In a series of brilliant essays published in the early 1940s, W.R.D. Fairbairn, the founder of British object relations theory, argued persuasively for the movement of psychoanalytic theory away from Freud's early libido theory based on instincts and toward a theory of personality development based on the significance of interpersonal or object relations: "The historical importance of the libido theory and the extent to which it has contributed to the advance of psychoanalytical knowledge requires no elaboration; and the merit of the theory has been proved by its heuristic value alone. Nevertheless, it would appear as if the point had now been reached at which, in the interests of progress, the classic libido theory would have to be transformed into *a theory of development based essentially on object-relationships*" (Fairbairn 1952, p. 31).

According to Fairbairn (1952), "Previous to my reaching the above-mentioned standpoint, however, I had already become very much impressed by the limitations of 'impulse psychology' in general, and somewhat skeptical of the explanatory value of all theories of instinct in which the instincts are treated as existing per se" (p. 84). In some ways, the assumption that instincts and impulses motivate behavior is similar to the assumptions in economics about quantitative conceptions of utility. Fairbairn's approach was simple and straightforward: "What an individual shall do with his 'impulses' is clearly a problem of object relationships" (p. 84). This is stated succinctly by Fairbairn: "The ultimate goal of libido is the object" (p. 31). Finally, and more simply, "My general position is that, from a psychological standpoint, all aims must be regarded as personal" (Fairbairn 1955, p. 145).

The superego became the basis for this transformation because it represented the internalization of an aspect of the interpersonal or object relationship with one's parents. In his highly influential essay "Endopsychic Structure Considered in Terms of Object-Relationships," first published in 1944, Fairbairn argued that this transformation was inevitable: "It seems to me to constitute an inevitable implication of the illuminating conception of internalized objects, which has been fruitfully developed by Melanie Klein, but which traces its scientific origin to Freud's theory of the superego (an endopsychic structure which was, of course, conceived by him as originating in the internalization of objects)" (Fairbairn 1952, p. 82).

The Protective, Prohibitive, and Punitive Superego of Object Relations Theory in Freud

In Freud's (1933) conception, the superego has three levels of functioning: "We have allotted it the functions of self-observation, of conscience and of [maintaining] the ideal" (p. 66). Freud's three levels of superego functioning provided the foundation for the refinement of the intrapsychic structural formation of the superego of object relations theory into the punitive, prohibitive, and protective superego. The function of self-observation is the self-consciousness of the punitive superego, persecuting the person with severe anxiety. The function of conscience is the capacity for experiencing guilt for violating the more realistic parental prohibitions and demands internalized in the prohibitive superego. The function of maintaining the ideal is the capacity for commitment to a value system shared with another person and internalized in the protective superego.

Freud (1933) clearly conceptualized the lofty position of a value system as the cultural contents of the protective superego: "Thus a child's super-ego is in fact constructed on the model not of its parents but its parents' super-ego; the contents which fill it are the same and it becomes the vehicle of tradition and of all time-resisting judgments of value which have propagated themselves in this manner from generation to generation" (p. 67). The "time-resisting judgments of value" passed on from generation to generation represent a value system, and, in this respect, the superego function of maintaining the ideal means living up to an internalized value system. The protective superego represents the refinement of one of Freud's most fundamental insights into the human personality.

Freud's superego function of conscience is closely related to the prohibitive superego of object relations theory. The contents of the prohibitive superego constitute a moral system, not a higher-level value system. Freud's superego function of maintaining the ideal is close to, but does not quite correspond to, the protective superego of object relations theory. Maintaining the ideal, in one respect, represents the ego ideal, which is part of the prohibitive superego. The intrapsychic structural formation of the superego will be elaborated in great depth subsequently.

The Synthetic Function of the Ego

To complete Freud's structural model, the ego is distinguished by its synthetic function: "But what distinguishes the ego from the id quite especially is a tendency to synthesis in its contents, to a combination and unification in its mental processes which are totally lacking in the id" (Freud 1933, p. 76). The ego, according to Freud, "must observe the external world, must lay down an accurate picture of it in the memory-traces of its perceptions, and by its exercise of the function of 'reality principle' must put aside whatever in this picture of the external world is an addition derived from internal sources of excitation" (p. 75).

Freud's classic statement on the plight of the ego is the following: "Thus the ego, driven by the id, confined by the super-ego, repulsed by reality, struggles to master its economic task of bringing about harmony among the forces and influences working in and upon it; and we can understand how it is that so often we cannot suppress a cry: 'Life is not easy!' " (p. 78). Finally, "No wonder that the ego so often fails in its task. Its three tyrannical masters are the external world, the super-ego, and the id" (p. 77).

The Id and the Ego

Freud's conception of the id has largely been abandoned by object relations theory.[1] *It* was considered by Freud to be the "dark, inaccessible part of our personality" and "a cauldron full of seething excitations" (Freud 1933, p. 73). According to Freud: "The id of course knows no judgements of value: no good and evil, no morality. The economic or, if you prefer, the quantitative factor, which is intimately linked to the pleasure principle, dominates all its processes" (p. 74).

THE MOTHER-INFANT RELATIONSHIP

The first interpersonal or object relationship is typically and ideally with the mother, and the significance of the vicissitudes of the infant's dependence on the mother became the basis for the object relations theory of personality development: "Accordingly, the nature of the relationship so established exercises a profound influence upon the subsequent relationships of the individual, and upon his subsequent social attitude in general" (Fairbairn 1952, p. 11).

Otto F. Kernberg (1972) sees the mother-infant relationship as a basic element in both the personality system and the social system (p. 244).

From an internal, or intrapsychic, perspective, Geertz's insight on relating perceptively to one another also evokes Kernberg's ideas on depth and stability in an intimate interpersonal relationship: "In more general terms, the internal resources that an individual has in the face of conflict and failure are intimately related to the maturity and depth of his internal world of object relations" (Kernberg 1984A, p. 73).

Kernberg, no doubt following Freud's use of the crystal analogy, uses the term *crystallization* to refer to psychic precipitates, or structural derivatives of object relationships (the title of Kernberg's classic 1966 article, reprinted as chapter 1 of 1984A) (Kernberg 1984A, pp. 34, 41; see also 1985A, pp. 26, 276). In a reference to personality organizations in the primitive range of the Personality Continuum, Kernberg (1984A) reaffirms the direct link between internal and interpersonal relations: "Under these pathological circumstances, early nonintegrated object-images come to the surface; but even then, . . . we never do have 'free-floating' internal objects but always confront specific ego structures into which they have crystallized" (p. 34).

Freud (1933) continued the crystal analogy by explaining the fascination that problems of personality have had for people: "Mental patients are split and broken structures of this same kind. Even we cannot withhold from them something of the reverential awe which peoples of the past felt for the insane. They have turned away from external reality, but for that very reason they know more about internal, psychic reality and can reveal a number of things to us that would otherwise be inaccessible to us" (p. 59).

Fairbairn (1952) echoed this insight in arguing for the analysis of the schizoid personality precisely because of the preoccupation with inner reality that characterizes such individuals:

> Contrary to common belief, schizoid individuals who have not regressed too far are capable of greater psychological insight than any other class of person, normal or abnormal—a fact due, in part at least, to their being so introverted (i.e. preoccupied with inner reality) and so familiar with their own deeper psychological processes (which, although not absent in individuals who would ordinarily be classified as simply "psychoneurotic," are nevertheless excluded from consciousness of such individuals by the most obstinate defenses and stubborn resistances). (p. 3)

It was Fairbairn's study of the schizoid personality organization that made it possible for him to understand the significance of interpersonal relationships in the development of personality: "What has convinced me of the paramount importance of the object-relationship is the analysis of patients displaying schizoid characteristics; for it is in such individuals that difficulties over relationships with objects present themselves most clearly" (p. 39).

FROM THE SUPEREGO TO THE SOCIAL SYSTEM

In the early 1950s, the central importance of the superego as a common frame of reference was rediscovered and extended in some important ways by Talcott Parsons, most notably in "The Superego and the Theory of Social Systems." Parsons recognized the social significance of the origin of the superego in the internalization of interpersonal relationships and argued that Freud's concept of the superego represented the basis for bringing together the main theoretical trends of psychology and sociology. In Parsons's view, "The superego provides exactly such a bridge because it is not explicable on any other basis than that of acquisition from other human beings, and through social interaction" (1964, p. 31).

Parsons extended Freud's view by considering more broadly the social and cultural implications of the internalization of interpersonal relationships. On the social implications, according to Parsons, "Freud and his followers, by concentrating on the single personality, have failed to consider adequately the implications of the individual's interaction with other personalities *to form a system*" (p. 20). Thus significant interpersonal relationships form a social system within which the individual personality develops. Object relations theory, by concentrating on the internalization of interpersonal relations and the formation of the intrapsychic structure of the personality, once again, and this bears repeating, automatically transcends the individual to the wider social system.

THE ECONOMIC MOTIVATION FOR UPWARD SOCIAL MOBILITY

It is important to recognize that the social system in which the personality develops is a system of significant interpersonal relationships and does not constitute society as a whole. Society is stratified into relative economic and social classes, or a hierarchy of status groups, and the social system of the individual will be contained within a specific stratum of society. It is also important to recognize that individuals not only relate to one another as individuals, but as social groups or classes. This idea is worth exploring for many reasons, not the least of which is to overcome the overwhelmingly individual orientation of economic analysis.

James S. Duesenberry (1949) was the first economist to explicitly recognize the social significance of consumer behavior: "Ours is a society in which one of the principal social goals is a higher standard of living. Now the fact that the attainment of a higher standard of living as an end in itself is a major social goal has great significance for the theory of consumption" (p. 28). Indeed, Duesenberry's *Income, Saving, and the Theory of Consumer Behavior* (1949) was remarkably prescient, as the following passage indicates: "When the attainment of any end becomes a generally recognized social goal, the importance of attainment of this goal is instilled in every individual's mind by the socialization process. In psychoanalytic terms the goal is incorporated into the ego-ideal. When this occurs the achievement of a certain degree of success in reaching the goal becomes essential to the maintenance of self-esteem" (p. 28).

Michael Piore (1979) has argued that it is "basically the accumulation and maintenance of social status, and not income, that induces people to work. People work either to advance up the hierarchy of jobs (and, hence, of social status) or to maintain the position they have already achieved" (p. 33). He arrived at this conclusion through the recognition that "economic activity is embedded in a wider social system" (p. 34). This startling observation (for an economist, that is) gave rise to the dual-labor-market hypothesis.

The dual labor market of an industrial market economy is comprised of a primary and a secondary labor market. Jobs in the primary labor market are characterized by a steady, stable, and preferably rising source of income and, most importantly, the opportunity for upward social mobility, while jobs in the secondary labor market "tend to be unskilled, generally but not always low paying, and carry or connote inferior social status" (p. 17). The increasing stratification of the primary labor market in the course of economic development increases the opportunity for upward social mobility by moving social classes closer together and, thereby, facilitating social mobility. In the analogy of a social ladder, the ladder has more rungs.

In *Schooling in Capitalist America* (1976), Samuel Bowles and Herbert Gintis provide a clear conception of this idea from a radical economic perspective: "Classes are important because individuals in U.S. society do not relate to each other as individuals alone, but as groups. That is, class is a social concept, and classes are defined only through how they relate to other classes" (p. 67). As a consequence, "The common daily experiences give rise to a common—not identical—set of values and perceptions, or a common consciousness, within a class" (p. 68).

Adam Smith (1759) referred to the economic motivation for upward social mobility as "that great purpose of human life which we call bettering our condition" (p. 113). Smith often referred to the motivation to "pursue riches and avoid poverty" (p. 112), and he was acutely aware of the significance of the stratification of society, which he referred to as "the distinction of ranks and the order of society" (pp. 115, 408). Leibenstein (1975) differentiated a variety of manifestations of the economic motivation for upward social mobility: A strong desire to maintain the new higher social class and status that has been successfully achieved; the desire to emulate those in higher social classes and statuses for oneself or for one's children and family; a strong desire to differentiate oneself from lower social classes and statuses; and a strong desire to avoid a fall in social class or status (p. 6).[2]

Economic success is thus defined as the achievement of upward social mobility. In America, the ultimate goal of the individual pursuit of self-interest is the successful achievement of upward social mobility. In an industrial market economy, like that of the United States at the end of the nineteenth and throughout the twentieth century, economic success is most often manifested in the movement from the secondary to the primary labor market. The result is the achievement of a steady, stable, and preferably rising source of income for the individual (Piore 1979, p. 78).

The hierarchy of social statuses, the stratification of society into economic classes, or the class structure of society is critical to the motivation of the labor force. Even economic man, the social moron, knows that the motivation for upward social mobility—to better one's lot in life for the individual, and to improve the relative social position of oneself and one's family—is the most powerful economic motivation.

NOTES

1. Kernberg's rather tortured attempts to rehabilitate the concept of the id in object relations theory will be addressed in some depth subsequently.
2. See also Frank 1985.

Chapter 6

The Crossroads

In "Early Ego Integration and Object Relations" (1972), Kernberg described psychoanalytic object relations theory as a crossroad and as a bridge between various theories of personality: "Psychoanalytic object relations theory has come a long way, it seems to me, toward bridging the gap between the sociocultural theories of personality on the one hand, and the constitutionally focused, instinct-centered theories within psychoanalysis and other related personality theories on the other" (p. 243). "Psychoanalytic object relations theory," according to Kernberg (1984A), "represents, in my opinion, a major integrative framework which can link the psychosocial approach to, and the subjective, experiential nature of human life, on the one hand, with the intrapsychic structures comprehended in general metapsychology, on the other" (p. 58; see also pages 55, 59).[1]

Further, according to Kernberg (1984A), "Psychoanalytic object-relations theory, thus defined, has been referred to as a 'middle language' between the metapsychological and clinical ones" (p. 56). The middle language provided by psychoanalytic object relations theory of the personality facilitates the integration of the metapsychological and clinical approaches to personality. I am creating (not just writing) the middle language of psychoanalytic object relations theory to integrate metapsychological and clinical approaches to personality and economic approaches to consumer behavior.

By providing a general integrative analytic framework for psychology, psychoanalytic object relations theory creates a variety of promising opportunities for establishing a theoretical relationship between preferences and the personality. The personality organization of the individual is the central conception to be used in the interpretation of patterns of consumption behavior. The methodological task of relating economics and psychology must begin with the establishment of a theoretical relationship between the consumer's scale of preferences from ordinal utility theory and the personality organization of psychoanalytic object relations theory.

THE COMMON GROUND OF ANALYSIS: THE INTERNAL OBJECT RELATION

The internal object relation provides the common ground of analysis: "In more general terms, internalized object relations may be considered as the crossroad where instinct and the social system meet and contribute to the development of the personality of the individual" (Kernberg 1972, p. 244; see also Kernberg 1984A, p. 59).[2] According to Kernberg (1984A), object relations theory includes a common unit of internalization that relates the works of authors of different schools: "It also allows one to bring together findings and conceptualizations [very reminiscent of Geertz] which at times have been artificially separated because of the difficulties of communication between various psychoanalytic groups. As I see it, object-relations theory, already implied in Freud's writings, transcends any particular psychoanalytic school or group and represents a general psychoanalytic development to which authors of very different orientations have contributed significantly" (p. 58).

The methodological unit of internalization is the internal object relation. It will provide the common ground of analysis to accomplish the task of relating the consumer of economic theory to the conception of the personality organization from object relations theory. Upon this common ground of analysis, the Personality Continuum is established, an integrative framework that brings together the contributions of psychology, sociology, anthropology, and economics for the study of consumer behavior.

THE FORMATION OF THE INTRAPSYCHIC STRUCTURE OF THE PERSONALITY

Object relations theory concentrates on the internalization of interpersonal relationships and the formation of the intrapsychic structure of the personality. Internalization is at first a process based on the primary autonomous functions of perception and memory. These processes result in patterned and persisting "structures" that represent internalized organizations of interpersonal experience or internal object relations (Kernberg 1984A, p. 25). The formation of the intrapsychic structure of the personality develops in levels that are hierarchically organized and reflect the increasing maturation of the primary autonomous functions of perception and memory (Rapaport and Gill 1959, pp. 157–158). The intrapsychic structure of the personality is one of two definitional criteria that operationalize the personality organization, along with the predominant defense against severe anxiety in interpersonal relationships.

The basic methodological unit of the internal object relation consists of three components: (1) an image or representation of the object or other person; (2) an image or representation of the self relating to that person; and (3) the feeling, emotion, or affect experienced in the relationship with the other person, based on specific inborn physiological dispositions (Kernberg 1984A, p. 26). In simple terms, an interpersonal relationship, as it exists in the external world, is made up of you, the other person you are relating to, and how you feel in the interpersonal situation. When that interpersonal relationship becomes internalized, it consists of three components, the self, object, and affect, respectively. The internal object relation, the self relating to the object and the affect, is the common ground of analysis. From this common ground, we shall explore the psychological foundations of consumer behavior.[3]

The changes in the levels of internalization and the structural formation of the personality can be apprehended through the changing relationship between the self, object, and affective components of internal object relations. Following Kernberg's (1984A) use of terminology, the levels of internalization are designated as introjection, identification, and the formation of an ego identity.

Paul T. Young's Definition of Perception and Sullivan's Perception of Internalization

In Sullivan's view, reality is filtered through one's own perceptions, and this includes our perception of another person:

> Between a doubtless real "external object" and doubtless real "my mind" there is a group of processes—the act of perceiving, understanding, and what not—which is intercalated, which is highly subject to past experience and increasingly subject to foresight of the neighboring future. Therefore, it would in fact be one of the great miracles of all time if our perception of another person were, in any greatly significant number of respects, accurate or exact. (Sullivan 1953, p. 167, single quotes in the original)

Sullivan's view of perception is filtered through his own disdain for Freud's concept of internalization of another person. Sullivan (1953) was quite antagonistic toward the conception of the internalization of interpersonal relationships: "The idea that one can, in some way, take in another person to become part of one's personality is one of the evils that come from overlooking" these processes of perception (p. 167). Sullivan regarded such concepts as "reckless oversimplification, if not a great magic verbal gesture the meaning of which cannot be made explicit" (p. 166). He adopted the convention of using single quotation marks around 'in' to indicate its special social or interpersonal meaning (see, e.g., pp. 87–88 and especially p. 112). But surely Sullivan's skepticism here is not realistic for a normal person with the capacity for foresight of the future.

Perception, in the exceptional definition of Paul T. Young (1961), is essentially the meaning derived from the experience: To perceive is to see, hear, touch, taste, smell, or sense internally some thing, event, or relation, and to organize, interpret, and derive meaning from the experience (pp. 298–299). While perception includes mere sensations, impinging on the sense organs, and sensations that arise internally, the perception is the meaning derived from the experience.[4]

Introjection: The First Level of Internalization

Introjection is the earliest process of internalization, and the internal object relations that result, the introjects, represent the basic level of the intrapsychic structure of the personality. The introjects are characterized as self undifferentiated from object, intense and overwhelming, positive and negative affect (Kernberg 1984A, pp. 29, 35). That is the terminology of object relations theory. But what does it mean?

In the beginning, the original interpersonal relationship is with the mother, and that is where the analysis of the levels of internalization and the structural formation of the personality must begin. The early infant does not have the physiological capacity to see that the mother is a separate person. In Sullivan's view, the early infant experiences the world as a cosmic whole and has no awareness of itself as an entity separate from the rest of the world:

> All that the infant "knows" are momentary states of being, the distinction of before or after being a later acquirement. The infant vaguely feels or "prehends" earlier and later states without realizing any serial connection between them. He has no awareness of himself as an entity separate from the rest of the world. In other words, his felt experience is all of a piece, undifferentiated, without definite limits. It is as if his experiences were "cosmic." (Sullivan 1953, p. 28)

The momentary states of being experienced by the early infant are biologically determined, inborn affect dispositions (Kernberg 1985B, p. 108).

Perhaps the most cogent and influential conception of the earliest phase of personality development has been provided by Michael Balint, especially in his "Early Developmental States of the Ego. Primary Object Love," first published in German in 1937, and in English in 1949. Balint (1949) elaborated on the active object-seeking behavior of the infant: "In all these instances we are faced with active behavior on the part of the infant, even with an activity directed towards an object" (Balint 1949, p. 269). Balint's (1937) recognition of the object-seeking behavior of the infant, instead of Freud's early libido theory, precedes Fairbairn's basic stance in his 1941 essay: "The ultimate goal of libido is the object" (Fairbairn 1952, p. 31).

According to Balint (1979), on the very earliest experiences of life, "To start with biological facts, we know that the fetus's dependence on its environment is extreme, certainly more intense than an infant's or an adult's" (p. 66). Balint's view of the quality of dependence in interpersonal relationships is a fundamental consideration in object relations theory. Balint referred to this as the phase of "primary object love" and described it as a harmonious interpenetrating mix-up characterized by the absence of any structural formation: "This environment, however, is probably undifferentiated; on the one hand, there are as yet no objects in it; on the other hand, it has hardly any structure, in particular no sharp boundaries towards the individual; environment and individual penetrate into each other, they exist together in a 'harmonious mix-up' " (p. 66). A similar conception is built into Kernberg's developmental schema, which begins with a primary undifferentiated stage (Kernberg 1984A, p. 59).

What can be observed? The behavioral manifestations of introjection are less apparent because the capacity of the early infant for emotional experience is limited to only pleasurable and painful affective states (Kernberg 1984A, p. 31). Whatever these affective states are called, there are only two, and they represent biologically determined inborn affect dispositions: "The affect states activated in the context of object relations are either positive, rewarding, gratifying, or negative, aversive, frustrating: this will give to their respective object relations a basic quality of 'good' or 'bad' " (Kernberg 1985B, p. 108). To this list I would add libidinal and aggressive. Sullivan (1953), from a developmental perspective, "similarly refers to the period early in infancy, when situations approach the 'all-or-nothing' character" (p. 160).

Balint (1949) describes the pleasurable experience of the infant as a "tranquil quiet sense of well-being" that is observable only with difficulty, while the frustration of the infant's needs calls forth the most stormy reaction:

> If the satisfaction arrives at the right moment, and with the right intensity, it causes reactions that are observable only with difficulty because the experience of gratification happens so quietly. Properly this feeling of pleasure could be described as a *tranquil quiet sense of well-being*. If, however, these wishes must remain unsatisfied, their gratification will be demanded very vehemently and an eventual frustration will call forth the most stormy reactions. (Balint 1949, p. 269)

Freud, a gifted writer as well as a brilliant lecturer, described the pleasurable aspects of the early interpersonal situation of the mother and infant in a similar way: "When children fall asleep after being sated at the breast, they show an expression of blissful satisfaction" (Freud 1917C, p. 313).[5]

Affect, Internalization, and Motivation

For the early infant, the first interpersonal relationship is ideally with the mother, and this relationship has been used as the prototypical interpersonal relationship. The affective experience of the early infant represents the major motivation for organizing the intrapsychic structure of the personality. This begins the critical and legitimate exploration of the concept of motivation. The integrative function of affect in motivation is elaborated by Kernberg (1984A): "Affect dispositions constitute the primary motivational systems which integrate the perception of (1) central (pleasurable or unpleasurable) states, (2) physiological discharge phenomena, (3) inborn perceptive and behavior patterns, and (4) envi-

Figure 6.1
Intrapsychic Structure of the Personality Organization

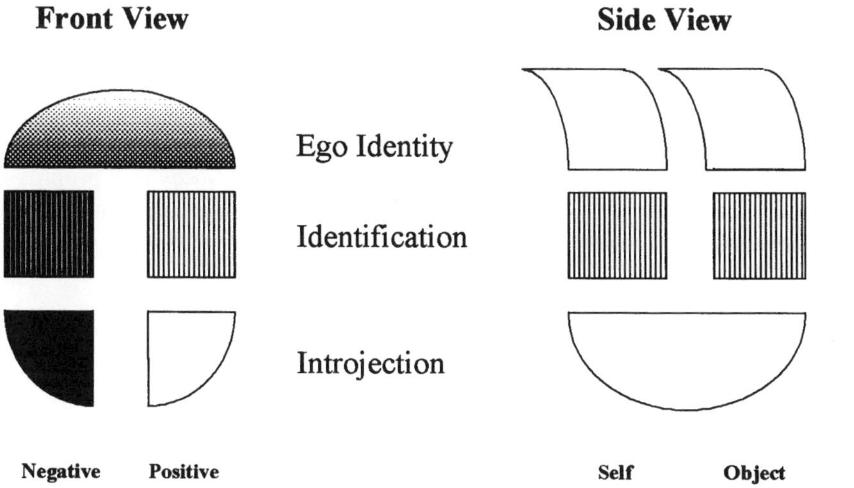

ronmental responses as they impinge on specialized extroceptive and introceptive perceptions" (p. 87).

The intensely positive and negative affective dispositions are the earliest motivation for internalizing the relationship with the mother as two separate, completely different mothers, representing the "all-good mother" and "all-bad mother" or, more precisely, the good and bad introjects (Kernberg 1984A, p. 30). They are not integrated into one image or representation of the mother simply because the infant does not have the physiological capacity to bring together the good and bad internal object relations (Kernberg 1984A, p. 35).

The first level of structural formation of the personality is made up of these two structures, the good and bad introjects. The all-good and all-bad introjects, without the differentiation of self from object, are somewhat loosely referred to as the good and bad internal objects and are also sometimes suggestively referred to as the good and bad mothers (Kernberg 1984A, p. 30). These are known as "part-object relationships," because each represents only a part of the whole relationship with the mother. Figure 6.1 provides a schematic representation of the intrapsychic structure of the personality organization. All the aspects of internalization of the early object relations through introjection are brought together in the following summary statement by Kernberg (1984A), using the rather horrendous, but necessary, terminology of object relations theory:

> To summarize, my general proposal is that affects represent inborn dispositions to a subjective experience in the dimension of pleasure and unpleasure; that they are activated simultaneously with inborn behavior patterns, which elicit reciprocal environmental (mothering) reactions, and with general arousal, which increases the perception of external and internal stimuli occurring during the interaction; and that all this leads to fixation of memory traces in a primitive, "affective memory" constellation or unit incorporating self components, object components, and the affect state itself. (Kernberg 1984A, p. 104)

The mother's role in the relationship with the infant is described by Donald W. Winnicott as being good enough: "The good enough 'mother' (not necessarily the infant's own mother) is one who makes active adaptation to the infant's needs, an active adaptation that gradually lessens, according to the infant's growing ability to account for failure of adaptation and to tolerate frustration" (Winnicott 1953, p. 94).

Sullivan constantly referred to "the mothering one," rather than to the mother, to describe the role played by anyone whose relatively enduring recurrent pattern of interpersonal situations characterizes the early interpersonal environment of the infant. According to Sullivan (1953): "Consideration of the composition of the family group may indicate that persons other than the mother have exerted great influence on the earliest phase of developmental history, long before these other persons enter into significant, direct, interpersonal relations with the infant. Moreover, in a good many instances some person other than the mother does have recurring, significant, direct, interpersonal relations with even the young infant" (p. 115).[6]

At birth, the early infant has no awareness of being separate from the mother and experiences life as momentary states of being, previously described as intense and overwhelming positive and negative affective states (Sullivan 1953, pp. 28–29). The infant's earliest interpersonal need is for reassuring physical contact with the mother:

> The only nonphysicochemically induced need that is probably somewhere near demonstrable during very early infancy and which certainly becomes very conspicuous not much later than this, is the *need for contact*, by which I mean just about what the word ordinarily means. The very young seem to have very genuine beginnings of purely human or interpersonal needs in the sense of re-

quiring manipulations by and peripheral contact with the living, such as lying-against, and so on. (p. 40)

This early need for reassuring physical contact with the mother is part of the infant's general need for tenderness: "The manifest activity by the mothering one toward the relief of the infant's needs will presently be experienced by the infant as the undergoing of tender behavior; and these needs, the relaxation of which require cooperation of another, thereon take on the character of a general *need for tenderness*" (p. 40).

Although the suckling situation represents an intense instance of the satisfaction of this need, it is not necessary for a human being to have been breast-fed at this stage of personality development, because the general need for tenderness can be satisfied by the mother, or the mothering one, in the process of bottle-feeding the early infant and, in general, caring for the infant's needs. It is the fundamental quality of dependence that matters most in the relationship of the early infant with the mother (Fairbairn 1952, p. 40). Because the infant has no awareness of being separate, according to Sullivan (1953), "Thus there is no differentiation of a tender real mother from a tender mother's helper in the situations in which the infant satisfies his needs" (p. 120).

Nevertheless, the infant nursing at the mother's breast will be used to explore early infancy as a heuristic stage of personality development. In the earliest interpersonal relationship, the relationship is essentially one of the infant's lips with the nipple of the mother's breast: "The nipple-in-lips, our first example of such an interpersonal situation, is integrated and maintained by the infant's need for water and food and the mother's need to give tenderness in this connection" (Sullivan 1953, p. 111). In Sullivan's interpersonal theory, the infant's behavior toward the mother's nipple, "come, nipple, into my mouth," as he colorfully puts it (p. 67), is comparable to Fairbairn's (1952) fundamental insight on the object-seeking behavior of the infant that transformed the foundations of psychoanalytic theory to an object relations theory of the personality.

In the view of Sullivan (1953), "The nursing situation still includes as its central detail the nipple-in-lips, its oldest core" (p. 123). The infant's mouth becomes central to their relationship because the earliest experiences of the infant with the mother are typically with her breast. In Fairbairn's (1952) view, "So far as the infant is concerned, the mouth is the chief organ of desire, the chief instrument of activity, the chief medium of satisfaction and frustration, the chief channel of love and hate, and, most important of all, the first means of intimate social contact" (p. 10).

Thus, according to Fairbairn (1952), this gives the earliest internalization through introjection an oral and incorporative component:

> This process of internalization is promoted, if not actually instigated, by the very nature of the oral attitude itself; for the inherent aim of the oral impulse is incorporation. The incorporation in question is, of course, originally physical incorporation; but we must believe that the emotional mood accompanying incorporative strivings has itself an incorporative colouring. Hence, when a fixation in the early oral phase occurs, an incorporative attitude inevitably becomes woven into the structure of the ego. (p. 18)

The view of Sullivan (1953) is similar: "In other words, the zone of interaction which is involved in a particular course of events gives a particular kind of mark, or color, to the experience which the living creature undergoes" (p. 65). Fairbairn (1952) draws far-reaching social implications from the relationship between the mother and the early infant: "The child's oral relationship with his mother in the situation of suckling represents his first experience of a love relationship, and is, therefore, the foundation upon which all his future relationships with love objects are based. It also represents his first experience of a social relationship; and it therefore forms the basis of his subsequent attitude to society" (pp. 24–25).

The earliest internalization process, introjection, results in the first level of intrapsychic structural formation of the personality, the all-good and all-bad internalized objects, the positive and negative introjects. The self is not differentiated from the object, and the positive and negative affect is characterized by its intense, overwhelming nature (Kernberg 1984A, pp. 34–35). This earliest level of intrapsychic structural formation typically develops over the first three to four months of life, and Kernberg has referred to this stage of personality development as early infancy (p. 37).

The methodological unit of the internal object relation is made up of self, object, and affect. The affective component of an introject is intense and overwhelming, positive and negative, and has an irradiating effect on all other perceptual elements of the introjection, in the precise terminology of the object relations theory (Kernberg 1984A, p. 35). In a similar way, the affective component of introjection was previously described by Fairbairn (1952) as *colouring* and Sullivan (1953) as *color*.

The positive introject starts with the infant nursing at the mother's breast. All that pure positive affect is bound up in the positive introject. The positive introject is the all-good mother, the infant sated at the mother's breast, in Freud's description, and the tranquil quiet sense of well-being, in Balint's observation.[7] That is why it is so precious and protected.

Economic Implications: Preference Change and Barely Observable Utility

While economic implications may seem remote at this point, nonetheless a fundamental contribution has been made to the inadequacy of utility theory for explaining preference change. Since ordinal utility theory incorporates only the pleasurable aspects of consumption behavior, there is no basis for dissatisfaction and, therefore, change. The foundation of the personality is the good and bad aspects of the relationship with the mother. In this way, psychoanalytic object relations theory provides a basis for understanding the process of preference change.

Balint's description of the behavioral manifestations of the early infant sheds light on the potency of Pareto's challenge to the cardinal utility theorists: "Show me a utility or satisfaction that is, say, three times as great as another." It would seem that utility, as pleasure or satisfaction, is not only immeasurable but barely observable.

Identification: The Next Higher Level of Internalization

The developmental phase of late infancy begins with the discovery by the infant that the mother is separate. Fairbairn (1952) marks the beginning of the transition from infantile to mature dependence in personality development by the discovery of separateness. This discovery is based on the increasing maturation of the primary autonomous functions of perception and memory, and the growth of cognitive abilities. The perceptions of touch and increasingly of sight and hearing are the most important senses involved in the growing infant's discovery of being separate. According to Balint in *Thrills and Regressions* (1959), "Both sight and touch, together with hearing, are projective senses; they feel, place, or construct the object outside the body, either at distance (sight and hearing) or at its surface (touch)" (pp. 62–63).

The infant is born into a state of intense relatedness with the mother, described by Balint as primary love "represented by the structureless friend, expanses" (Balint 1959, p. 91). With birth, according to Balint (1959), "This harmonious relation is but short-lived, the traumatic discovery that vitally important parts of it are both independent and inscrutable creates a structure, and from then the world will consist of firm and resistant objects and of spaces separating them" (p. 91).

Sullivan (1953) describes the infant's growing awareness of the mother as separate: "The infant's experience of the relevant oral behavior, and the mother's experience nursing the infant are just as significantly a part of any particular nursing situation as are the physiological structures which are involved. In the ever-expanding world of the infant, it comes to be the nipple, which is a discernible characteristic of the good mother, with which he is orally integrated. In the world of the mother, it is the lips of the more-or-less personified particular infant with which her nipple is invested" (p. 111).

Sullivan describes his conception of the personification of the good mother in the following way: "The infant's personification of the good mother is the prehended pattern of her participation in recurrent nursing situations and integrations of other needful sorts which have been resolved by satisfaction. She—the infant's personification of the good mother—symbolizes in turn the integration, maintenance, and resolution of situations that include her, through appropriate and adequate activity on the infant's part" (p. 111). Thus, according to Sullivan, "The good mother begins as a discrimination or differentiation of the good and satisfactory nipple" (p. 122). The recognition of the ever-expanding world of the infant reinforces the argument made earlier with regard to bottle-feeding that it is not necessary to have been breast-fed as an infant, because the growing infant's awareness expands rapidly with physiological maturation, beyond the mother's nipple to her breast, then to the mother as separate object and, ultimately, as a whole person, in the course of normal personality development.

The next higher process of internalization is identification. It begins with the physiological maturation of the growing infant's ability to recognize that the mother, and then itself, are separate (Jacobson 1964, p. 67). The internal object relations that result represent a self-component that is increasingly differentiated from the object component, the internalization of the role aspects of the relationship between the object and self, and the affective experience becomes less intense and more differentiated, demonstrating a broader range of modified affective states (Kernberg 1984A, pp. 30–31).

With the discovery of being separate, the nature of the internalization process changes to reflect the increasing differentiation of the self from the object. The internalization process of identification is formulated by Kernberg (1984A) in the following way: "The cluster of memory traces implicit in identification comprises then: (i) the image of an object adopting a role in an interaction with the self, (ii) the image of the self more clearly differentiated from the object than in the case of introjection (and possibly playing a complementary role), (iii) an affective coloring of the interaction of a more differentiated, less intense quality than in the case of introjection" (p. 31).

In late infancy, with the increasing differentiation of self and object, there are now multiple selves and objects, rather than just two internal objects. The various good and bad mothers are utterly different to the infant (Sullivan 1953, p. 72). The physiological capacity to integrate the different selves and objects is absent; therefore, identifications are "all-good" and "all-bad" and constitute part-object relations. The affective component of an identification is modified and more diversified than that characteristic of introjection, reflecting the more elaborate emotional experience of the growing infant. This is illustrated schematically in Figure 6.1.

The growing infant must increasingly be socialized by the mother, and this requires that the mother forbid behavior that is considered to be inappropriate in the culture in which she lives. With the recognition of being separate, indifference becomes a significant socializing influence. Whether the mother is satisfying, forbidding, or indifferent can increasingly be differentiated by the infant. According to Sullivan (1953), "As interpersonal relations grow, this element of socialization under the influence of indifference—which is a case neither of reward by tenderness nor of anxiety, but just a case where nothing happens—becomes pretty powerful" (p. 181).

An implication for economic theory is that, with the addition of subjective experience of indifference, the analysis of consumer behavior can no longer revolve solely around simple concepts of pleasure and pain. This was recognized by Vilfredo Pareto and constitutes the fundamental observation behind the transformation from cardinal to ordinal utility theory, that is, a quantitative concept of utility is unnecessary and was replaced by a scale of relative preferences.

The internalization of the role aspects of the relationship with the mother in late infancy embeds the developing personality in the social system within which it develops (Kernberg 1972, p. 244). Kernberg states the implications for personality development in the following passage: "As the self-concept develops, role integration and differentiation of the self occurs automatically with it; and as the child develops differentiated relationships with both parents and his siblings, these role differentiations acquire a highly sophisticated organization embedding the developing personality in the social system within which it develops" (p. 244).

The crucial economic implication of this development in personality that can be drawn at this point pertains to the social basis of consumption behavior. Through the internalization process of identification, the growing child learns behavior that is socially acceptable, and more important, roles that are socially sanctioned. The child comes to know his or her roles in the social system. According to Sullivan (1953), "No matter what kind of social organization there is, everyone who is born into it will, in certain ways, be adapted or adjusted to living in it" (p. 5).

It is through the internalization process of identification that the personality is embedded in the social system. This harks back to Sullivan's interpersonal definition of personality as the relatively enduring pattern of recurrent interpersonal situations that characterize a person's life (p. 11). This pattern of interpersonal relationships constitutes the social system of the person, and through the processes of internalization, the intrapsychic structure of the personality comes to reflect that social system. Thus the consumption pattern of the individual is socially determined and will reflect the social system within which the personality develops. This is stated incisively by Kernberg (1972): "In this way, the social system (represented by socially determined status-role bundles) becomes integrated into the personality from infancy on, and the mother-child interaction is considered, in effect, as a basic element of both the personality and the social system" (p. 244). Thus the socially determined status-role bundles reflect the individual's roles in his or her social system and his or her relative status in society.

The profound theoretical implication for the analysis of consumer behavior is that through this process of embedding the developing personality in the social system, the intrapsychic structure of the personality organization is reflected in the structure of preferences. The theoretical implication for economic theory is that by relating the structure of preferences to the intrapsychic structure of the personality organization, the individual orientation of the economic theory of the consumer is transcended. In this way, psychoanalytic object relations theory relates the intrapsychic structure of the personality organization to the preference structure of the consumer to provide a social foundation for the analysis of consumer behavior.

The behavioral manifestations of identifications have direct implications for the study of consumer behavior. The observable behavior is described as either wanting to be like another person, or not wanting to be like that person (Kernberg 1984A, pp. 78–79; Freud 1933, p. 63; Jacobson 1964, p. 66; Sullivan 1953, p. 209). By behaving like a parent in some selective way, the child will express a set of preferences that represent the specific aspects of the role of that parent in the interpersonal relationship. This must be considered a nascent expression of preference behavior and will be elaborated subsequently.

Ego Identity: The Highest Level of Internalization

Ego identity, the highest level of internalization, begins when the physiological integrative capacity of the child matures to the point where the child recognizes that all of the good mothers and all of the bad mothers are just one mother. The child can no longer regard the multiple good and bad mothers as different and is faced with the realization that there is only one mother who is both good and bad. This can be a startling discovery.

The child has now reached the stage of ambivalence in the relationship with the mother. The significance of ambivalence in the child's relationship with the mother has been elaborated by D.W. Winnicott (1955, 1963).[8] The child must be able to tolerate loving and hating the same person simultaneously before whole object relations can be integrated. If ambivalence can be tolerated by the child in the relationship with the mother, then the contradictory images can be integrated. This represents the integration of whole object relations, an intrapsychic structural formation, perhaps the most critical in personality development. It is the basis for identity formation, or an ego identity, and for the development of the prohibitive superego.

As previously noted, the mother's role in the relationship with the infant is described by Winnicott as being good enough. If the child's relationship with the mother has been good enough, that is, more positive than negative, with a preponderance of good introjections and identifications over the negative, this is not a difficult achievement in personality development.

The achievement of the integration of whole object relations is based on the quality of dependence upon the object (Fairbairn 1952, p. 40). In a moving and beautiful statement, Fairbairn draws profound implications for the quality of dependence in the early interpersonal relationship of the mother and child: "What emerges as clearly as anything else from the analysis of such a case is that the greatest need of a child is to obtain conclusive assurance (a) that he is genuinely loved as a person by his parents, and (b) that his parents genuinely accept his love" (p. 39).

The failure of such assurances from the mother is described by Fairbairn as "the greatest trauma that a child can experience": "It is only in so far as such assurance is forthcoming in a form sufficiently convincing to enable him to depend safely upon his real objects that he is able gradually to renounce infantile dependence without misgiving. In the absence of such assurance his relationship to his objects is fraught with too much *anxiety over separation* to enable him to renounce the attitude of infantile dependence; for such renunciation would be equivalent in his eyes to forfeiting all hope of ever obtaining the satisfaction of his unsatisfied emotional needs. Frustration of his desire to be loved as a person and to have his love accepted is the greatest trauma that a child can experience" (pp. 39–40).

According to Fairbairn (1952), "The outstanding feature of the child's personal relationship with the mother is . . . one of extreme *dependence*" (p. 145). Therefore, a transition must occur from infantile dependence to mature dependence: "The development of object-relationships is essentially *a process whereby infantile dependence upon the object gradually gives place to mature dependence upon the object*" (p. 34). Fairbairn preferred " 'mature dependence' rather than 'independence,' since a capacity for relationships necessarily implies dependence of some sort" (p. 145).

The integration of whole object relations is a precondition for mature dependence; however, the full achievement of mature dependence goes with the second precondition for intimacy, the full integration of satisfying genital sexual relations into an interpersonal relationship, but that is premature here. Indeed, independence can only be achieved economically, as an economic implication. Kernberg (1984A) described this achievement simply as "growing up and becoming independent" (p. 220).

Sullivan's Heuristic Stage of Childhood

Sullivan (1953) marks the beginning of the developmental epoch of childhood with the learning of language, which plays an important role in the development of personality by bringing about the integration, or fusion, of opposite internalized object relations (p. 188). Sullivan states his view on language in a powerful passage from *The Interpersonal Theory of Psychiatry* (1953):

> Thanks in no small part to the incredible power which verbal behavior seems to exercise in interpersonal situations, and to the great energy devoted by the more mature people around the very young child to equip him with this most

important of all human tools, language, it becomes quite impossible for the child to carry forward any striking surviving evidence of his earliest impression of two mothers—one who gives tenderness and cooperation in the satisfaction of needs, and one who carries anxiety and interferes with the satisfaction of needs. Although this dichotomy pertaining to one real person can go on at the lower strata, you might say, of personality, it can scarcely survive very long the high-pressure acculturation which makes one person "mama," and possibly another person "sister," or something like that. Thus no matter how thoroughly organized the two separate personifications of the good mother and the bad mother were, their individuality is lost or fused into the later personification, in the process of learning language. (p. 189)

The Coming into Existence of the Ego and Ego Identity

If the child can accept the fact that there is only one mother, who is both good and bad and therefore whole and more realistic, then the integration of whole object relations will be successfully achieved, and a new, higher level of structural formation begins with the internalization of an ego identity. The recognition in early childhood that the mother is one person represents the coming into existence of the ego. Sullivan called it the coming of the "I":

> In all this process of being socialized and particularly of developing the ability to communicate by verbal behavior, quite a time after little Willie has gotten to talking about "me wanting" bread and jam, little Willie begins to talk about "I"; and when little Willie gets to talking about "I," just as when you hear other people talking about "I," you will notice that something is going on that wasn't there when it was "me" that wanted bread; and it is really much more important than when he finally gets around to saying that he is Willie Brown, or something like that. The coming of "I," as a term, is great stuff. (1964, p. 214)

The Integration of Whole Object Relations

The intrapsychic structural formation is the integration of whole object relations in the terminology of American object relations theory. Kernberg (1985A) describes the integration of whole object relations the following way: "Thus, idealized 'all good' object images have to be integrated with 'all bad' object images, and the same holds true for good and bad self images. In this process of synthesis, partial images of the self and of the objects are integrated into total object and self representations, and thus self and object representations become further differentiated from each other, and also more realistic" (p. 27). Fairbairn (1952) describes the integrative function of the ego in the following way: "It must be remembered, however, that the ego also performs integrative functions, among the most important of which are (1) the integration of perceptions of reality, and (2) the integration of behaviour" (p. 9).

The outcome of the synthetic function of the ego is the formation of the stable ego identity. According to Kernberg (1985A), "One essential task in the development and integration of the ego is the synthesis of early and later introjections and identifications into a stable ego identity" (p. 25). "Ego identity," therefore, "refers to the overall organization of identifications and introjections under the guiding principle of the synthetic function of the ego" (Kernberg 1984A, p. 32). Thus, according to Kernberg (1984A), "Ego identity . . . is a structure characteristic of the ego, a fundamental outcome of the synthetic function of the ego" (p. 32).

The integration of whole object relations is a momentous achievement in personality development (Kernberg 1984A, pp. 39–40; 1985A, p. 35). What this means for the child is that the mother is both good and bad and, therefore, a whole and more realistic person. The internalization process changes to ego identity to reflect this new higher level of personality development. Ego identity represents the highest level in the organization of internalization processes; however, this internal world of object representations never reproduces the actual world of real people, with whom the individual has established relationships in the past and present (Kernberg 1984A, p. 33; Sullivan 1953, p. 167). This is represented schematically in Figure 6.1.

The mother and father are not perfect, but are good and bad and, therefore, whole and more realistic human beings. When parents remain godlike later in life, there is a problem in personality development. This issue will be explored in depth with the failure to achieve the integration of whole object relations and arrest of personality development in the primitive range of the Personality Continuum.

A Sense of Continuity of the Self

The integration of whole object relations also means that the child has accepted itself as both good and bad and, therefore, a whole and more realistic person. The child must integrate the contradictory self-images, as well as object images. The result of the achievement of whole object relations is an integrated self-concept and an integrated object concept.

The integration of whole object relations contributes to a sense of continuity of the self, where the self is the organization of the self-components of introjections and identifications (Kernberg 1984A, p. 32). According to Kernberg (p. 32), "The child's perception of its functioning in all areas of its life, and its progressive sense of mastering the basic adaptational tasks, contribute significantly" to the sense of continuity of the self.

Behavioral Manifestations of Ego Identity: Consistent Behavior

The behavioral manifestations of the integration of whole object relations are crucial to an understanding of the psychological foundations of consumer behavior. The integration of whole object relations is the psychological foundation for a pattern of consistent behavior. According to Kernberg (1984A):

> This organization implies: a consistent, overall conception of the "world of objects" derived from the organization of the object-image components of introjections and identifications and a sense of consistency in one's own interpersonal interactions, the behavioral aspects—that is, general consistency in the behavior patterns—being even more important aspects of ego identity than those of identifications; and a recognition of this consistency in interactions as characteristic of the individual by his interpersonal environment, and, in turn, the perception by the individual of this recognition by the environment ("confirmation"). (p. 32)

The fundamental behavioral manifestation of ego identity is the general pattern of consistent behavior, including the recognition of this consistency in the interpersonal relations of the person. The crucial implication for economic theory is that consistent consumption behavior is the sine qua non of ordinal utility theory, since consistency is the essential element of rationality. The postulate of rationality can be considered a positive limitation on economic analysis, because the validity of its behavioral implications can be verified or refuted by the observation of market behavior, and it imposes meaningful limitations on the shape of demand functions (Samuelson 1947, p. 92).

Thus, according to Sen (1977), "The requirement of consistency does have surprising cutting power" (p. 325). Consistency is a surprisingly powerful behavioral postulate. Psychoanalytic object relations theory has provided an analysis of the determinants of consistent behavior. The manifestation of a pattern of consistent behavior has been explained by a specific achievement in personality development, the integration of whole object relations. This is a critical contribution to the exploration of the psychological foundations of consumer behavior.

THE FAILURE TO ACHIEVE THE INTEGRATION OF WHOLE OBJECT RELATIONS

The object relations theory provided up to this point has dealt with the development of the normal personality. In fact, we have largely dealt with the "theoretically perfect person whose development has been optimum" (Fairbairn 1952, pp. 8–9). The failure to achieve the integration of whole object relations results when the child is unable to accept the mother as being both good and bad because of a preponderance of negative introjections and identifications over the positive. In this situation, integration threatens to contaminate, or even destroy, the good internalized interpersonal relations (Kernberg 1985A, p. 17). The child cannot tolerate the ambivalence of simultaneously loving and hating the mother. The situation becomes fraught with too much anxiety. If ambivalence cannot be tolerated, splitting will be maintained as an active and powerful defense against the intolerable anxiety of the mother behaving in an ambivalent way (Fairbairn 1952, p. 172).

Anxiety, in Sullivan's (1953) interpersonal conception, is an anticipated unfavorable appraisal of one's current activity by someone whose opinion is significant (p. 113). The origin of anxiety is exclusively interpersonal (Sullivan 1964, p. 238). Although the mother-infant relationship has been used as the prototypical relationship, anyone can induce anxiety, according to Sullivan (1953): "Incidentally, for all I know, anybody can induce anxiety in an infant, but there is no use cluttering up our thought by considering that, because frequency of events is of very considerable significance in all learning processes; and at this stage of life, when the infant is perhaps nine or ten months old, it is likely to be the mother who is frequently involved in interpersonal situations with the infant" (p. 162).

As a result of the maturation of primary autonomous functions of perception and memory, the ego comes into existence and is not present at birth (Kernberg 1984A).[9] According to Kernberg, "It is suggested that the ego as a differentiated psychic structure, in the sense of Freud's (1923) description comes about at the point when introjections are used for defensive purposes, specifically in an early defensive organization against overwhelming anxiety" (p. 35). This is further elaborated by Kernberg (1984A) in the following summary statement:

> The maturation and development of primary ego apparatuses give rise, at one point, to introjections, which in turn become an essential organizer of what is going to be the ego as an integrated structure. After some development of in-

trojections as psychic structures, a point is reached when introjections are actively kept apart or split for defensive purposes. Now the ego as a centralizing, synthetic function (in the sense of overall organizational purpose) and as a definite organizational structure comes into existence. (p. 37)

Splitting is a very powerful and primitive defense against intolerable anxiety. It represents the failure to integrate whole object relations. Personality development becomes arrested in the primitive range of the Personality Continuum. According to Sullivan (1953):

> Arrest of development does *not* imply that things have become static, and that from thenceforth the person will be just the same as he was at the time that development was arrested. The conspicuous evidence of arrest and deviation of personality development is, at first, delay in the showing of change which characterizes the statistically usual course, and later, the appearance of eccentricities of interpersonal relations, which are often anything but self-evident signs of the developmental experience which has been missed or sadly distorted. Thus there is nothing static about arrest of development; but the freedom and the velocity of the constructive change are very markedly reduced. (217–218)

The failure to achieve the integration of whole object relations arrests personality development in the primitive range of the Personality Continuum. The consequences of this failure for consumer behavior will be dealt with in depth subsequently under the rubric of compulsive and, in the more extreme case, addictive consumption behavior, the dark side of consumer behavior. At this point, I want to continue with the normal personality development.

This chapter has concentrated on the processes of internalization and the formation of the intrapsychic structure of the personality. It has provided the essential concepts and terminology of object relations theory. The terminology of object relations theory, however horrendous, is nonetheless necessary to describe the phenomena in question and to connect to the vast literature of object relations theory, especially the clinical case studies, and to the history of thought on psychoanalytic theory. Because it is useful, no effort has been made to abandon the terminology of object relations theory; however, I have endeavored to juxtapose translations of this terminology in the text whenever appropriate. I will follow this procedure throughout the book. With this framework in place, we can now turn to a fuller exposition of an object relations theory of normal personality development and to an elaboration of the normal range of the Personality Continuum.

NOTES

1. This links to the experiential aspects of consumption in marketing. See Hirschman and Holbrook 1982; and Holbrook and Hirschman 1982; and Holbrook 1995.

2. Kernberg's ideas on instincts and his effort to rehabilitate Freud's concept of instincts are unfathomable to me. See "Instincts, Affects, and Object Relations" (Kernberg 1984A, pp. 85–107). I am more in line with the underlying sentiment expressed by Sullivan (1953) in the following observation on the copulatory posture and movement: "They are one of the few things which faintly support the notion that the concept of instinct is not utterly irrelevant to human beings, for they come without calling, almost as if a little instinct still survived in our incredibly culture-ridden life" (p. 285).

3. Kassarjian and Sheffet (1991, p. 294) remark, "Unfortunately, no simple methodology for research of this sort has yet emerged." Why should it be simple? Should there be a simple explanation for President Clinton's disgraceful behavior while in the Oval Office? Is there a simple explanation for why O.J. Simpson, I believe, murdered Nicole Brown and Ronald Goldman? If you think so, you should stop reading here and give up trying to understand human behavior.

4. Sullivan was not concerned with reconciling his approach with Freud's, as I am: "Please do not bog down unnecessarily on the problem of whether my self-system ought to be called the superego or the ego. I surmise that there is some noticeable relationship, perhaps in the realm of cousins or closer, between what I describe as the personification of the self and what is often considered to be the psychoanalytic ego. But if you are wise, you will dismiss that as facetious, because I am not at all sure of it; it has been so many years since I found anything but headaches in trying to discover parallels between various theoretical systems that I have left that for the diligent and scholarly, neither of which includes me" (1953, p. 167, n. 3).

5. In this passage from Lecture XX, "The Sexual Life of Human Beings," Freud is actually equating the infant's expression of blissful satisfaction sated at the mother's breast with a similar expression "repeated later in life after the experience of sexual orgasm" (Freud 1917C, p. 313). The significance of the experience of sexual orgasm in an intimate interpersonal relationship will be elaborated subsequently with the subjective experience of transcendence. For a mature person, transcendence means the capacity to let go of all firm boundaries around self and objects and becoming one with another person.

Unfortunately, in this paragraph, and at this point in Lecture XX, Freud introduced the concept of the libido as sexual instinct. Since that time, the term *libido* has become too diffuse in meaning; it has acquired far more clarification in the refinement process by object relations theorists since Fairbairn. Sullivan's conception of *lust* stands in sharp contrast to Freud's earlier libido theory: "And let me make it clear that lust, in my sense, is not some great diffuse striving, 'libido' or what not. By lust I mean the felt aspect of the genital drive" (1953, p. 295). The term *libidinal* is laden with too many sexual and instinctual connotations, and ultimately harks back to Freud's belief in infantile sexuality, an idea thoroughly repudiated by object relations theory.

Psychoanalytic object relations theory represents the refinement of Freud's most fundamental insights, but infantile sexuality is not one of them. Freud (1933), in Lecture XXXI, is contrasting the prohibitive superego with infantile sexuality: "Even if conscience is something 'within us', yet it is not so from the start. In this it is a real contrast to sexual life, which is there from the beginning of life and not only a later addition" (pp. 61–62).

Freud is being ambiguous and somewhat enigmatic. What is added later is genital sexuality and the physiological maturation of puberty marking early adolescence as a heuristic stage of personality development.

In Goethals's brilliant article "The Evolution of Sexual and Genital Intimacy" (1976), he concluded, "It is fair to say that Sullivan sees what Freud would call infantile sexuality as existing in the mind of the parent rather than in the psychological repertoire of the child" (p. 536). Infantile sexuality is in the mind of the mother. In object relations theory, the term *genital* is typically used in conjunction with *sexuality* as a direct foil against Freud's concept of infantile sexuality. In much the same way, Sullivan used sexual and genital drives interchangeably (Sullivan 1953, p. 267).

6. Sullivan was acutely aware of the influence of culture on personality. In the fall of 1931, Sullivan began regularly attending Edward Sapir's seminar on culture and personality at Yale University (Perry 1982, p. 344). The manuscript for Sullivan's *Personal Psychopathology*, posthumously published in 1972, was supplemental reading for this seminar (p. 358). Harold Lasswell, founder of personality and political psychology, also participated in this seminar, and later Erik H. Erikson, starting in 1936, when he arrived at the Institute of Human Relations at Yale (p. 357). Sullivan's interpersonal theory of personality is uniquely suited to investigate the influence of culture on personality.

7. Although women have two breasts, and it is true that at any one time, the infant can nurse at only one, I interpret this to mean that there are good and bad introjects, and seeing the world as divided into two opposite extremes is a principal manifestation of splitting at the primitive level of personality of development.

8. Fairbairn's (1952) use of *ambivalent* and *pre-ambivalent* is different from Winnicott's *stage of ambivalence*. The capacity for ambivalence, in Winnicott's conception, is an achievement in personality development and is equated with the achievement of the integration of whole object relations. The capacity for concern, or depressive position, is based on the achievement of the integration of whole object relations (1955, p. 89). In the preambivalent, early oral phase, there is no separation between mother and infant, the infant has a cosmic view of the world, and there is no boundary between mother and infant (Sullivan 1953, p. 28). In the internalization process of introjection, the self is undiffer-

entiated from the object, and the affect is intense and overwhelming, and either positive or negative.

In my use of the heuristic stage, late infancy begins with the differentiation of self from object and the internalization of interpersonal relations through identification. The depressive position in Fairbairn (1952), however, is definitely abandoned. Fairbairn's (1952) early views on biting (and hating) are too simple now, too pat, too much of an attempt by Fairbairn to be too tidy as a theoretician. In Fairbairn (1952, p. 24), substitue "aggressive" tendencies for "biting" tendency and we are fully back to Kernberg and American object relations theory. We simply need to ask, "Why is the late infant biting the mother's nipple?" The answer is frustration, frustrated oral-dependent needs.

It is imperative to designate to what point in personality development and the human life cycle an observation or statement pertains. Here I am dismissing Fairbairn's ideas on biting as part of normal personality development; however, as soon as frustration becomes extreme and aggression intense, we are then looking at pathological personality development, a chronologically adult person arrested at a primitive level of personality development.

9. The view that the ego is not present at birth varies from that of Fairbairn that it does. See particularly "Synopsis of an Object-Relations Theory of the Personality," *International Journal of Psycho-Analysis* 44, no. 2 1963, pp. 224–225.

Chapter 7

Normal Personality Development

The intrapsychic structure of the personality—Freud's crystal, polished for nearly a century—has provided the psychological foundations for the study of consumer behavior. The common ground of analysis is provided by the methodological unit of the internal object relation made up of the self, the object, and the affect. The changing relationship between the self, the object, and the affect during physiological growth and maturation results in three levels of internalization—introjection, identification, and ego identity—and in the hierarchical formation of the intrapsychic structure of the personality.

The overview of the intrapsychic structural formation of the personality provided in the previous chapter is meant to serve as a bridge to a broader consideration of human behavior. The personality organization of object relations theory provides the organizational framework for the study of human behavior. The Personality Continuum provides the overall integrative framework that brings together contributions from many disciplines for the study of consumer behavior.

In this chapter and the following one, I will ascend the Personality Continuum to the normal level of personality development and to an exploration of normal consumer behavior. I will descend the Personality Continuum to the lower neurotic and primitive levels of personality de-

Figure 7.1
Intrapsychic Structure of the Normal Personality Organization

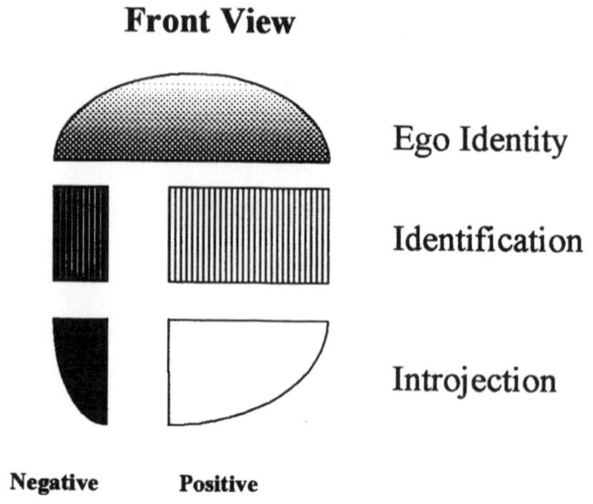

velopment, and to an exploration of the dark side of consumer behavior primarily in the primitive range, in the chapter "The Basic Fault." The psychotic range of the Personality Continuum will be dealt with comparatively and will not be explored in any great depth.

ASCENDING THE PERSONALITY CONTINUUM TO THE HIGHER NEUROTIC AND NORMAL LEVELS OF PERSONALITY DEVELOPMENT

As an achievement in personality development, the integration of whole object relations represents the maturation of a person's capacity to experience concern for another person and oneself—an ego capacity—and the capacity to experience guilt for violating the more realistic parental prohibitions and demands, a capacity of the prohibitive superego. The capacity for concern is closely related to Adam Smith's (1759) capacity for sympathy. The integration of whole object relations fosters a broader spectrum of affect dispositions of the ego (Kernberg 1984A, p. 40) and the use of the higher-level defense of repression (Kernberg 1985A, p. 25). Superego formation is integral to the higher neurotic and normal levels of personality development. The intrapsychic structural formation of the prohibitive superego and higher level protective superego will be elaborated here. Refer to Figure 7.1, for a schematic representation of the intrapsychic structure of the normal personality organization.

With the achievement of the integration of whole object relations, the primitive defense of *splitting* is overcome and gives way to the higher-level defense of *repression.* According to Kernberg (1985A). "This mechanism [splitting] is normally used only in an early stage of ego development during the first year of life, and rapidly is replaced by higher level defensive operations of the ego which center around repression and related mechanisms such as reaction formation, isolation, and undoing, all of which protect the ego from intrapsychic conflicts by means of the rejection of a drive derivative or its ideational representation, or both, from the conscious ego" (p. 25).

Modification of the Pure Affect of Introjections and a Broader Spectrum of Affect Dispositions

Drive derivatives are drives derived from the intense and overwhelmingly positive and negative affect incorporated into the positive and negative introjects and the modified and more diversified affect of the higher-level identifications. With introjection, according to Kernberg (1984A), "What is important is the intense, overwhelming nature of the early affect and its *irradiating* effect on all other perceptual elements of the introjection" (pp. 34–35).

The intense and overwhelming early affect states are described as pure by Kernberg (1984A): "The irradiating effect of earlier 'pure' affective states exerts a powerful regressive pull in the direction of primary process thinking" (p. 51). Primary process thinking refers to "primitive fantasies," and particularly to the use of "peculiar verbalizations" (Kernberg 1985A, p. 24), as opposed to higher-level secondary-process thinking, which involves "goal directed, ordered, and logical forms of thought" (Rapaport 1957, p. 179).[1] Primary process thinking represents "primitive cognitive processes intimately linked with primitive affect states" (Kernberg 1984A, p. 69). These pure affective states exercise a powerful regressive pull on the ego. Primary process thinking is particularly characteristic of the borderline personality organization; it will be dealt with again in the chapter on that personality organization.

The integration of whole object relations fosters a broader spectrum of affect dispositions of the ego: "The fusion of positive and negative introjections implies a fusion and concomitant modification of their affect components. The irradiating effect of purely positive and purely negative affective states diminishes, and the mutual compenetration of libidinal and aggressive drive derivatives fosters a broader spectrum of affect dispositions of the ego" (Kernberg 1984A, p. 40). Thus, as a result of the achievement of the integration of whole object relations, affect becomes modified and more diversified, and the ego has the capacity to experience a broader range of emotions (p. 40).

The integration of whole object relations results in the neutralization of aggression and gives rise to repression: "*The synthesis of identification systems neutralizes aggression and possibly provides the most important single energy source for the higher level of repressive mechanisms to come*, and implicitly, for the development of secondary autonomy in general" (Kernberg 1984A, pp. 45–46). This integration also results in the emancipation of thought processes from the related, underlying feelings, emotions, or affect: "The modification of affective dispositions available to the ego also indirectly fosters the emancipation of thought processes because the irradiating effect of earlier 'pure' affective states exerts a powerful regressive pull in the direction of primary process thinking which decreases when modification of affect occurs" (Kernberg 1984A, p. 51).[2]

Freud, Repression, and the Unconscious

In "The Unconscious," Freud (1915B) explored the defense of repression as an unconscious process. "Repression results not only in withholding things from consciousness, but also in preventing the development of affect and setting off muscular activity" (p. 179). According to Freud, "Affects and emotions correspond to processes of discharge, the final manifestations of which are perceived as feelings" (p. 178). Freud thus clarified the relationship between affect, emotion, and feelings: *affect* has a basic quality of good and bad and is characteristic of introjection; *emotion* has the modified and more diversified affect representative of identification; *feelings* are the perception of the behavioral manifestations. The terms *affect* and *cognition*, *feelings* and *thoughts*, and *emotion* and *ideation* are typically used interchangeably.

Repression is much more effective as a predominant defense against anxiety than splitting because discharge is blocked: "After repression has become predominant, . . . the ego protects itself against the anxiety connected with intolerable conflicts by eliminating these conflicts from consciousness. Repression is thus a much more effective defensive operation . . . unlike splitting, it is characterized by the blocking of discharge" (Kernberg 1984A, p. 45). This rejection from the conscious ego contributes to the delimination of ego boundaries at the neurotic and normal levels of personality development:

Repression, by contrast, is a central defensive mechanism of the ego at a later stage and consists in the rejection of an impulse or its ideational representation, or both, from the conscious ego. Just as splitting, at a more primitive level of development, is reinforced by projection, denial, and other primitive defenses, repression, on its higher level of ego development, is reinforced by mechanisms such as isolation, displacement, and other typical neurotic or normal defensive operations. Repression consolidates and protects the core of the ego and contributes crucially to the delimitation of ego boundaries. (p. 45)

Affect and cognition become more independent over the course of personality development. According to Freud (1915B), "In repression a severance takes place between the affect and the idea to which it belongs, and . . . each then undergoes its separate vicissitudes" (p. 179). Three such vicissitudes are possible, according to Freud (1915B): "Either the affect remains, wholly or in part, as it is; or it is transformed into a qualitatively different quota of affect, above all into anxiety; or it is suppressed, i.e. it is prevented from developing at all" (p. 178). Further, according to Freud, "We know, too, that to suppress the development of affect is the true aim of repression and that its work is incomplete if this aim is not achieved" (p. 178).[3]

When the affect is not prevented, it can be transformed into anxiety: "The affect always has the character of anxiety, for which all 'repressed' affects are exchanged" (p. 179). Thus the aim of repression is to prevent the affect from occurring, but the person is left feeling anxious as a warning signal.

Freud makes an important clarification of the use of "unconscious" in reference to affect: "In every instance where repression has succeeded in inhibiting the development of affects, we term those affects . . . 'unconscious' " (p. 178). Thus, according to Freud (1915B), "Strictly speaking, then, and although no fault can be found with the linguistic usage, there are no unconscious affects as there are unconscious ideas" (p. 178). Freud concluded, "Even within the limits of normal life we can recognize that a constant struggle for primacy over affectivity goes on between the two systems *Cs.* [conscious] and *Ucs.* [unconscious]" (p. 179).[4]

The Prohibitive Superego

The internalization of more realistic parental prohibitions and demands reflects the formation of the prohibitive superego as an integrated intrapsychic structure. The more realistic parental prohibitions and demands represent the contents of the prohibitive superego (Kernberg 1984A, pp. 42, 71). The prohibitive superego corresponds to the level of superego functioning that Freud (1933) loosely described as the conscience:

> There is scarcely anything else in us that we so regularly separate from our ego and so easily set over against it as precisely as our conscience. I feel an inclination to do something that I think will give me pleasure, but I abandon it on the ground that my conscience does not allow it. Or I have let myself be persuaded by too great an expectation of pleasure into doing something to which the voice of conscience has objected and after the deed my conscience punishes me with distressing reproaches and causes me to feel remorse for the deed. (pp. 59–60)

(As a clarification, it is guilt, and not something as dreadful as remorse, that a person with a conscience experiences, as we shall see.)

The integration of whole object relations triggers the development of images of the ideal self and ideal object. The image of the ideal self represents the striving for reparation of guilt and for the reestablishment of an ideal, positive relationship between self and object. The image of the ideal object represents the unharmed, all-loving, all-forgiving object (Kernberg 1984A, p. 40). The image of the ideal object and the prohibitive parental images constitute forerunners of the prohibitive superego (Kernberg 1984A, p. 41).

At the neurotic and normal levels of personality development, the ideal self and ideal object are integrated to form the ego ideal (Kernberg 1984A, p. 41). The formation of the ego ideal is part of the development of the prohibitive superego: "Normally, idealized images of the parental figures and idealized self images are first condensed into the ego ideal, which is further modified by the integration and incorporation of more realistically perceived parental demands, of the sadistic forerunners of the superego, and of the more advanced aspects of the prohibitive superego" (Kernberg 1985A, p. 240). Kernberg (1985A) provides these poignant portrayals of the real self, the ideal self, and the ideal object: "The real self (the 'specialness' of the child reinforced by early experience), the ideal self (the fantasies and self images of power, wealth, omniscience, and beauty which compensated the small child for the experience of severe oral frustration, rage and envy) and the ideal object (the fantasy of an ever-giving, all-loving and accepting parent in contrast to the child's experience in reality; a replacement of the devalued real parental object" (pp. 265–266).

Freud (1933) described the ego ideal in the following way:

> One more important function remains to be mentioned which we attribute to this super-ego. It is also the vehicle of the ego ideal by which the ego measures itself, which it emulates, and whose demand for even greater perfection it strives to fulfill. There is no doubt that this ego ideal is the precipitate of the old picture of the parents, the expression of admiration for the perfection which the child then attributed to them. (pp. 64–65)

Living up to the ideal parental images, internalized in the ego ideal, reinforces the person's self-esteem: "Such a 'toned down,' less grandiose, and more attainable ego ideal permits one the normal narcissistic gratification of living up to the internalized ideal parental images, and this gratification in turn reinforces self-esteem, one's confidence in one's own goodness and one's trust in gratifying object relationships" (Kernberg 1985A, 240). Normal and narcissism do not go together, and gratification, especially when crude, is characteristic of primitive behavior, far from the normal range of the Personality Continuum. But what I believe Kernberg means by normal narcissism is a sense of self-esteem, which he describes as confidence in one's own goodness and basic trust in one's interpersonal relationships.

Living up to Cultural Prescription and Prohibitions

An exploration of Sullivan's (1953) conception of the self-system will shed further light on the contents of the prohibitive superego:

> The origin of the self-system can be said to rest on the irrational character of culture or, more specifically, society. Were it not for the fact that a great many prescribed ways of doing things have to be lived up to, in order that one shall maintain workable, profitable, satisfactory relations with his fellows; or, were the prescriptions for the types of behavior in carrying on relations with one's fellows perfectly rational—then, for all I know, there would not be evolved, in the course of becoming a person, anything like the sort of self-system that we always encounter. If the cultural prescriptions which characterize any particular society were better adapted to human life, the notions that have grown up about incorporating or introjecting a punitive, critical person would not have arisen. (p. 168)

The cultural prohibitions and prescriptions that have to be lived up to are the more realistic parental prohibitions and demands, respectively, that represent the contents of the prohibitive superego. According to Sullivan (1956), "The things that become terrifying and generalized in these primitive processes are the cultural mandates—the prohibitions and prescriptions—that I have not been able to live up to, or to live with" (p. 184). Sullivan's (1956) characterization of the superego as primitive darkly echoes Freud's (1933) classic statement on the higher side of human life.

The Pursuit of Perfection and the Narcissistic Personality Organization

The normal process of striving toward perfection goes awry in a person with a narcissistic personality organization. This is presented by Kernberg (1985A) in the following case observation: "I also explored with him his fear that I would not accept him as a person in his own right if he did not live up to some kind of perfect standards, which reflected a projection onto me of his own, highly unrealistic, aspirations for perfection that we had explored in the past" (p. 292). In this way, according to Kernberg (1985A), the obsessive personality organization at the neurotic level of personality development is comparable to the narcissistic personality organization at a primitive level of personality development: "In obsessive personalities, living up to primitive ideals of perfection and cleanliness may be a most effective protection against anal-sadistic guilt and conflicts" (p. 241). Although the term *primitive* is not typically used to characterize the behavior of a person with a personality organization at the neurotic level of personality development, the obsessive personality organization represents an extreme variation, in particular, because the person is trying to live up to primitive ideals of perfection as a defense against guilt that has become sadistic.[5]

In a further comparison, Kernberg (1985A) returns to the fundamental quality of interpersonal relationships as the basis for differentiating between the obsessive and narcissistic personality organizations: "Thus, for example, the stubbornness or oppositionalism of obsessive personalities often have a strong narcissistic quality; however, there is much more stability and depth in the interpersonal relationships of obsessive personalities, in spite of the fact that both may appear superficially as quite 'cold.' Also, the value systems of narcissistic personalities [at the primitive level of personality development] are generally corruptible, in contrast to the rigid morality of obsessive personalities [i.e., a personality organization at the neurotic level of development with an integrated prohibitive superego and the capacity for experiencing guilt]" (p. 238).

It is important to clarify that a person with a narcissistic personality organization does not have a value system shared with another person. Higher-level moral and value systems are missing in personality organizations at the primitive level of personality development. Personality organizations in the primitive range of the Personality Continuum rigidly adhere to a system of ideals that they will pursue without concern for others or within a moral system. Personality organizations at the higher neurotic and normal levels of personality development have an internalized moral system that constitutes the contents of the prohibitive superego. At the normal level of personality development, a person has an internalized value system that constitutes the contents of the protective superego.

Depersonification and the Process of Individuation

Beyond the parental figures, other authority figures step into place, so to speak, and influence the formation of the superego: "In the course of development the super-ego also takes on the influences of those who have stepped into the place of parents—educators, teachers, people chosen as ideal models. Normally it departs more and more from the original parental figures; it becomes, so to say, more impersonal" (Freud 1933, p. 64).

To become more impersonal is the process of depersonification, which is closely related to the process of individuation:

> The normal outcome of identity formations is that primitive identifications are gradually replaced by selective, partial, sublimatory identifications in which only those aspects of object relations are internalized which are in harmony with the individual identity formation. Actually, the enrichment of one's personal life by the internal presence of such selective partial identifications representing people who are loved and admired in a realistic way without indiscriminate internalization constitutes a major source of emotional depth and well-being. The normal process of individualization is marked by the shift from identifications to partial, sublimated identifications under the influence of a well-integrated ego identity. One might say that *depersonification* of internalized object relations, *reshaping* of part of them so that they come to *resemble more the real objects*, and *individualization* are closely related processes. (Kernberg 1984A, pp. 33–34)

The process of identity formation is elaborated by Edith Jacobson (1964):

> While identifications thus display the child's touching dependency on his parents, they bring him closer step by step to the state of independence and to the time when the parents become dispensable. Moreover, the selectivity of identifications increasingly expresses the child's rebellious struggle for the development and maintenance of his own independent identity, since it means: "In this

respect I like you and want to be like you, but in other respects I don't like you and don't want to be like you; I want to be different, in fact myself." (p. 66)

We can choose. We are not amoebas.[6]

To Know More of Reality: The Realistic Aspects of Normal Personality Development

Kernberg (1984A) captures with rare eloquence the importance of being realistic to the integration of the ego and superego at the normal level of personality development:

> Gradually, the sharp opposition between superego and ego decreases. An integrated superego also fosters further integration and consolidation of ego identity. Here, ego identity continues to evolve by means of an on-going reshaping of the experiences with external objects in light of internal object-representations, and of these object-representations in the light of real experiences with others. The self-concept, in turn, undergoes continuous reshaping on the basis of real experiences with others and experiences with the internal world of objects. An integrated self, a stable world of integrated, internalized object-representations, and a realistic self-knowledge reinforce one another. The more integrated the self-representations, the more self-perception in any particular situation corresponds to the total reality of the person's interactions with others. The more integrated the object-representations, the greater the capacity for realistic appreciation for others and reshaping one's internal representations on the basis of such realistic appraisals. A harmonious world of internalized object-representations, including not only significant others from the family and immediate friends but also a social group and a cultural identity, constitutes an ever growing internal world providing love, reconfirmation, support, and guidance within the object relations system of the ego. Such an internal world, in turn, gives depth to the present interaction with others. In periods of crisis, such as loss, abandonment, separation, failure, and loneliness, the individual can temporarily fall back on his internal world; in this way, the intrapsychic and the interpersonal worlds relate to and reinforce each other. (pp. 72–73)

The significance of the total reality of the person's interactions with others, essential to being a normal person, represents an elaboration of Freud's reality principle. For Sullivan (1953), to know more of reality, to grasp realistically the world as known, internal and external, is integral to being a normal person (p. 156). To temporarily fall back on one's internal world of object relations represents the refinement of one of Freud's most fundamental insights on the regression to identification as a reaction to loss: "If one has lost an object or has been obliged to give it up, one often compensates oneself by identifying oneself with it and by setting it up once more in one's ego, so that here object-choice regresses, as it were, to identification" (Freud 1933, p. 63).

According to Kernberg (1985A), the development of the normal capacity for tolerating depression broadens and deepens a person's feelings: "Many authors have pointed out that the capacity for tolerating depression, linked to the capacity for mourning over a lost good object or a lost ideal image of oneself, is an important prerequisite for emotional development and especially for the broadening and deepening of feelings" (p. 237). This conception of regression to identification is further refined as regression in the service of the ego by Kernberg (1985A):

> The normal reaction to loss, abandonment and failure is the reactivation of internalized sources of love and self-esteem intimately linked with internalized object relations, and reflects the protective function of what has been called "good internal objects." Regression in the service of the ego often takes the form of regression to such reactivated internalized object relations of a protective kind, a regression which in turn activates, strengthens, and broadens the patient's capacity for meaningful relations with others and with humanity and with value systems at large. The capacity to work through mourning processes, to be in love, to feel empathy and deep gratification in identifying with loved people and values, a sense of transcendence with nature, of continuation within the historical process, and of oneness with a social or cultural group, are all intimately linked to the normal activation of internalized object relationships at the time of loss, failure, and loneliness. (p. 312)

Genuine Insight and the Urge to Change

In normal personality development, a person has the capacity for meaningful insight and the urge to change in an appropriate way: "Meaningful insight, in contrast to the simple availability of primary process material in conscious and preconscious mental life of borderline patients, refers to the combination of intellectual and emotional understanding of deeper sources of one's psychic experience, accompanied by concern for and an urge to change the pathological aspects of that experience" (Kernberg 1985A, p. 141). The urge to change is what makes the insight meaningful for a person: " 'Authentic' insight is a combination of the intellectual and emotional understanding of deeper sources of one's psychic experience accompanied by concern for and an urge to change the pathological aspects of that experience" (p. 93).

SULLIVAN'S HEURISTIC STAGES OF PERSONALITY DEVELOPMENT AND THE GROWTH OF THE INTERPERSONAL NEED FOR INTIMACY

Sullivan's heuristic stages of personality development are useful in understanding intimacy from an interpersonal perspective (1953, pp. 260–264, 290–291). The need to love and be loved grows from the beginning of life. In infancy, the need for love is expressed as a need for reassuring physical contact with the mother. In childhood, with the learning of language, the need for love is expressed as a need for the active participation of the mother and father in the child's play: "This activity takes the form of expressive play necessary to provide the child with equipment for showing what he feels, in manual play necessary for the coordination of the very delicate and intricate relationship of vision and prehensile hands, and so on, and in verbal play, which is the basis of all the enormously important acquisitions to personality which are reflected by verbal behavior and abstract thought" (p. 291).

The juvenile era begins with the entrance into school and requires the learning of social subordination and social accommodation. The development of the interpersonal need for intimacy in the juvenile era involves learning to live with one's peers and is expressed as a need for acceptance by one's peers. In the juvenile era, according to Sullivan, "there is added the need for compeers, as indispensable models for one's learning by trial and error; and this is then followed by a need for acceptance which is perhaps better known by its reverse, the fear of ostracism, fear of being excluded from the accepted and significant group" (p. 291).

In the preadolescent era of personality development, a brief period just before puberty, the interpersonal need for intimacy matures as the need for a relationship with someone very much like oneself that Sullivan referred to as the *chumship*: "A specific new type of interest in a particular member of the same sex who becomes a chum or a close friend" (Sullivan 1953, p. 245). In the chumship, the needs of the other person become as important as one's own, and this change represents the maturation of love into a need for intimacy: "The other fellow takes on a perfectly novel relationship with the person concerned: he becomes of practically equal importance in all fields of value. Nothing remotely like that has ever appeared before" (p. 245). In a 1939 lecture series that was later published as *Conceptions of Modern Psychiatry* (1940), Sullivan captured the essence of love in the preadolescent stage of personality development: "The capacity for love in its initial form makes appearance as the mark that one has ceased to be juvenile and has become preadolescent. What this means in the outline of situations which it brings about is this: at this point the satisfactions and security which are being experienced by someone else, some particular other person, begin to be as significant to the person as are his own satisfactions and security" (p. 42).

Sullivan saw loneliness as the motivating force behind the need for intimacy, "which reaches its full significance during the preadolescent expansion of personality, and goes on relatively unchanged from thenceforth throughout life" (Sullivan 1953, pp. 261–262). According to Sullivan, "Only as we reach the preadolescent stage of development does our profound need for dealings with others reach such proportions that fear and anxiety actually do not have the power to stop the stumbling out of restlessness into situations which constitute, in some measure, a relief from loneliness" (p. 262). Loneliness, in its full driving force, will bring one person together with another person despite really severe anxiety: "In other words, the fact that loneliness will lead to integrations in the face of severe anxiety . . . means that loneliness in itself is more terrible than anxiety" (p. 262).

Early adolescence begins with the physiological maturation of puberty and the eruption of true genital interest and culminates in late adolescence with the patterning of preferred genital sexual activity in an interpersonal relationship (Sullivan 1953, pp. 263, 297). The need for intimacy shifts to a person of the opposite sex in Sullivan's heuristic stage of early adolescent personality development, and cultural attitudes toward sexuality become increasingly significant as a complicating factor in interpersonal relationships. Adolescence begins with the eruption of the special sentience of the genitals at puberty, which Sullivan (1953) refers to as "lust" and defines in his crisp, operational way as the "felt aspect of the genital drive" (p. 295; Goethals 1976, p. 540). From the psychological standpoint, the abrupt change during adolescence culminates in the experience of sexual orgasm (Sullivan 1953, p. 263).

The developmental relationship of intimacy and lust is clearly formulated by Sullivan (1953) in the following passage: "The need for intimacy has been gradually developing along its own lines from very ancient roots, while lust has only recently and vividly appeared" (p. 274). Fairbairn (1952) takes a similar view of the relationship between intimacy and sexuality: "On the contrary, it is in virtue of the fact that satisfactory object-relationships have been established that true genital sexuality is attained" (p. 32). It is important to realize, according to Sullivan (1953), that "one cannot, except for the purpose of clarity of thinking, separate the manifestations of these two very powerful motivating systems of human life" (p. 290).

The full integration of satisfying genital sexual activity into an interpersonal relationship is the interpersonal achievement in personality development that defines the heuristic stage of late adolescence: "In other words, a person begins late adolescence when he discovers what he likes in the way of genital behavior and how to fit it into the rest of life" (Sullivan 1953, p. 297). Sullivan saw this as an interpersonal achievement in personality development: "The mark which, to my way of thinking, separates early adolescence from late adolescence is not a biological maturation but an achievement" (p. 297).

Late adolescence ends in the fully mature human being: "Late adolescence extends from the patterning of preferred genital activity through . . . the establishment of a fully human or mature repertory of interpersonal relations, as permitted by available opportunity, personal and cultural" (p. 297). This interpersonal achievement in personality development that marks late adolescence represents the second precondition for an intimate relationship with another person (p. 297).

Sullivan captured this interpersonal achievement in personality development rather graphically in the following passage: "In this culture the ultimate test of whether you can get on or not is whether you can do something satisfactory with your genitals or somebody else's genitals without undue anxiety and loss of self-esteem [to this I would add guilt]" (p. 294). In a similar way, Sullivan captured the confusion of intimacy and genital sexuality: "Now even at this late stage in my formulation of these ideas, I still find that some people imagine that intimacy is only a matter of approximating genitals one to another" (p. 246).

According to Alan Watts (1970), intimacy is "The feeling that one can express one's thoughts to the other just as they are, since there is not the slightest compulsion to assume a pretended character. This is perhaps the rarest and most difficult aspect of any human relationship, since in ordinary social converse the spontaneous arising of thought is more carefully hidden than anything else" (p. 200). Further, the relationship between intimacy and sexuality is explicated by Watts in the following clarification: "Yet this is quite the most important part of a deep sexual relationship, and it is in some way understood even when thoughts are left unsaid" (p. 200).

Sullivan (1953) goes further to make explicit that sexual difficulties are actually the result of earlier difficulty: "The failure to achieve late adolescence is, in fact, the last blow to a great many warped, inadequately developed personalities. Because this kind of experience is such an all-absorbing and all-frustrating preoccupation, it often constitutes the presenting difficulty which precedes the eruption of very grave personality disorder in a large number of people; it is of course by no means

Figure 7.2
Intrapsychic Structure of the Neurotic Personality Organization

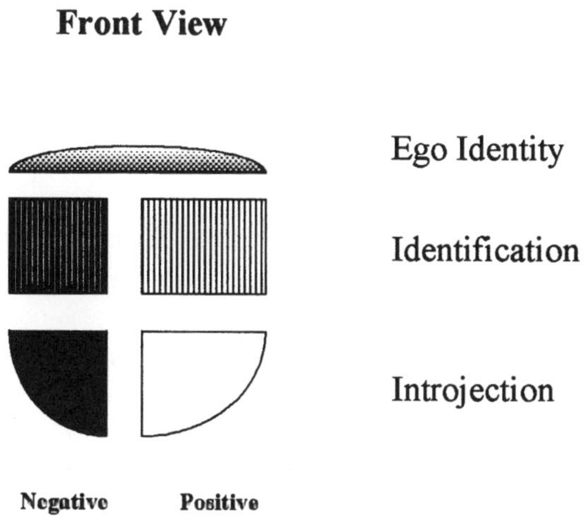

the actual difficulty" (p. 297). This "all-absorbing and all-frustrating preoccupation" with the failure to achieve late adolescence represents the arrest of personality development at the neurotic level.

This brings to fruition Freud's fundamental insight on the origin of neuroses: "People fall ill in one way or another of *frustration*, when reality prevents them from satisfying their sexual wishes" (1917B, p. 300), and again with a specific reference to neurosis, "It is possible . . . to fall ill of a neurosis as a result of a frustration of normal sexual satisfaction" (p. 300). Refer to Figure 7.2 a schematic representation of the intrapsychic structure of the neurotic personality organization.[7]

INTIMACY AND THE NORMAL RANGE OF THE PERSONALITY CONTINUUM

The integration of whole object relations contributes to the continuity of the self, the increasing consistency of behavior, and provides the basis for the capacity to experience concern and guilt. It also represents the first precondition for intimacy in an interpersonal relationship.

Intimacy represents a positive approach to the higher neurotic and normal levels of personality development. The concept of interpersonal intimacy has been brought to fruition by Otto F. Kernberg in three important articles on the psychology of love relations: "Barriers to Falling and Remaining in Love" (1974A), "Mature Love: Prerequisites and Characteristics" (1974B), and his most advanced work, "Boundaries and Structure in Love Relations" (1977).

We can build on the analysis of intimacy by examining the second precondition for intimacy, the *full integration of satisfying genital sexual relations into an interpersonal relationship* (Kernberg 1984A, pp. 185, 215; 1985B, pp. 277–278). Satisfying this precondition means that parental prohibitions against genital sexual relations, internalized in the prohibitive superego, have been overcome in an interpersonal relationship. The person now has the human capacity to remain in love and to form stable and deep intimate interpersonal relationships (Kernberg 1984A, p. 185).

This interpersonal achievement in personality development defines normal personality development in terms of the achievement of the human capacity for intimacy in an interpersonal relationship and demarcates the normal range of the Personality Continuum. Within the normal range of the Personality Continuum, there are differences in the degree of achievement of intimacy. From the interpersonal perspective, Sullivan (1953) describes the higher side of normal personality development: "If they are fortunate, their growth goes on and on; they observe, formulate, and validate, more and more; and at the same time, their foresight continuously expands so that they can foresee a career line, not as it inevitably will be, but in terms of expectation and probability, with perhaps provisions for disappointment" (p. 300).

The Subjective Experience of Transcendence and Sexual Orgasm

We are now in a position to investigate the highest position in the normal range of the Personality Continuum. Kernberg's work on intimacy focuses on the relationship of the married couple to elaborate on the consequences of satisfying the second precondition for intimacy. This perspective will also be taken here for the purposes of illustration. Sexual relations culminating in orgasm in an intimate interpersonal relationship can result in the subjective experience of *transcendence*. Transcendence involves abandoning the boundaries of the self, and this is required for the full experience of sexual orgasm:

> The central dynamic expression of sexual passion and the potential core of its culmination is the experience of orgasm in intercourse; in the experience of orgasm, gradually mounting sexual excitement culminates in an automatic, bi-

> ologically determined response with a primitive ecstatic affect, which requires for its full experience a temporary abandonment of the boundaries of the self, or rather, an expansion—or an invasion—of the boundaries of the self into an awareness of the subjectively diffuse biological roots of existence. (Kernberg 1985B, pp. 291–292)

Michael Balint has made important contributions to the understanding of sexual relations and personality development in "Eros and Aphrodite" (1936). Balint (1936) brings out the relationship of the experience of orgasm to the level of personality development:

> The concept of the "strength of the ego" is one which we have frequently employed, especially of late years. It has not yet been exactly defined, but it is clearly based on a quantitative idea. I would now suggest that the strength of the ego at a given moment may be measured by the maximum tension or excitation which it can tolerate without disturbance. Where conditions are fairly normal, the only excitation which approximates to this maximum in adults is the excitation before and during orgasm. Even supposing that it were not the only one, it is certainly the most frequent, for it is one of the conditions of adult life. (Balint 1986, p. 86)

In "On Genital Love" (1947), Balint brings out the problems encountered in sexual relations when the protective superego has not been integrated:

> The most important anxiety connected with this situation is that of losing the mature attitude, and once having lost it, of not being able to regain it. In these cases, maturity is mainly a defence against the wish of infantilism, which means conversely that these people had a very hard task to become mature, achieved maturity only with considerable difficulty, and therefore do not dare let themselves go. For such people every pregenital pleasure is childish, disgusting, even despicable, they cannot give up their "mature dignity," they do not dare lose their heads in or before an orgasm. (Balint 1986, p. 136)

Further, from "Primary Object Love" (1949), Balint contributed to an understanding of sexual intercourse culminating in orgasm and the subjective experience of transcendence: "Coitus, it is true, begins as an altruistic act, but the higher one's excitement grows the less regard is paid to the partner until finally immediately before and during orgasm the partner's interests are completely forgotten, and thus in the safe belief of being united with him (her) in perfect harmony one is able to enjoy together the highest pleasure" (Balint 1949, p. 270).

Goethals (1973) elaborates on the perils that transcendence poses: "In the act of regression during the climax of love-making one can not only experience sexual ecstasy and return to profound harmony but one can, in addition, in the intensity of this experience anticipate the agonies of what would happen if this were ever lost" (p. 94). Thus, according to Goethals, "It is a short step from this phenomenological statement to infer that it is possible also in this experience, or in the anticipation of this experience, to not only return to an experience of profound harmony but to rekindle, since regression may be non-selective, past experiences of profound object–loss" (p. 94).

"The experience of orgasm, however, does not by itself represent sexual passion," according to Kernberg (1985B, p. 292), who elaborates further: "Sexual passion implies the simultaneous crossing of the boundary of the self into awareness of biological functioning beyond the control of the self and a crossing of boundaries in a sophisticated identification with the loved object while yet maintaining the sense of a separate identity" (p. 292). The experience of transcendence creates a sense of oneness with the loved person: "Sexual passion is the facilitating core of a sense of oneness with a loved person as part of adolescent romanticism and, later, mature commitments to the beloved partner in the face of the realistic limitations of human life, the unavoidability of illness, decay, deterioration, and death" (p. 293). In a similar way, the capacity to experience transcendence can apply equally to art, nature, and religious experiences as well: "This reaction to inanimate objects, as well as to nature and art, is intimately connected with the transcending aspect of a full love relation in which the capacity for total object relation and the capacity for genital enjoyment are integrated" (Kernberg 1984A, pp. 227–228). For a brilliant application of object relations theory to art, see Ernst Kris, *Psychoanalytic Explorations in Art* (1952).

The Protective Superego and a Value System

The subjective experience of transcendence in an intimate interpersonal relationship results in an identification with the value system shared with the loved person: "This new type of idealization represents the idealized identification with the value system of the love object, an idealization, not of the body or even the person, but of the values for which this person stands" (Kernberg 1984A, p. 210). This process involves the basic creation of meaning in the person's life, according to Kernberg (1977, reprinted in 1985B): "In this process, there is a basic creation of meaning, of a subjective ordering of the world outside the self, which actualizes the potential structuring of human experience in terms of biological, interpersonal, and value systems" (1985B, p. 289).

In terms of the formation of the intrapsychic structure of the personality organization, transcendence represents the formation of a new boundary around the couple: "Shared secrets and mystery increase the couple's freedom from the surrounding social world; and each partner's secrets and mystery maintain and create new boundaries in the couple's relationship" (Kernberg 1985B, p. 304). The new boundary that forms around the couple protects them from the internal world and the surrounding interpersonal world. This is elaborated by Kernberg (1977) in the following statement:

> From the broader perspective, the couple's discovery vis-à-vis each other of the enjoyment of full genitality may cause it to change radically from submitting to cultural conventions and ritualized prohibitions and superstitions that erect barriers against mature genitality in both sexes. This degree of sexual freedom, together with the final overcoming of oedipal inhibitions, may constitute the ultimate potential for sexual enjoyment in love relations and reinforce passion by creating a new mystery of sexual secrets shared by the couple which frees it from the surrounding social group. In other words, crossing the sexual boundaries so strongly impelled by the mystery of oedipal longings from early childhood on may result in the couple's establishing a new common social boundary which protects the secret and the mystery of their sexual communion. (Kernberg 1985B, pp. 299–300)[8]

This new common social boundary represents the formation of the intrapsychic structure of the *protective superego*, the highest level of superego functioning. The protective superego protects the person from the guilt experienced for violating the internalized more realistic parental prohibitions and demands that represent the contents of the prohibitive superego, and from the parents and other authority figures who may continue to make demands and prohibitions.

The internalization of a system of values shared with the loved person represents the contents of the protective superego. The protective superego contributes to an understanding of the role of culture in human behavior, because a value system reflects the culture shared by the couple and represents the contents of the protective superego. Kernberg (1974A, reprinted in 1984A) elaborates on the cultural implications of the protective superego in the following way: "At the same time, in this establishment of identification with the love object involving value systems, a movement from the interrelation of the couple to a relationship with their culture and background is achieved, and past, present, and future are thereby linked in a new way" (1984A, p. 210).

The protective superego represents a refinement of Freud's fundamental insight into the values of the culture and the highest level of superego functioning (Freud 1933, p. 67). The human capacity to make a commitment is based on the internalization of a value system and structural formation of the protective superego. The implications of the capacity to make a commitment for the normal consumer will be elaborated subsequently.

Sublimatory Capacity, the Pursuit of Self-Interest, and the Normal Person

The integration of whole object relations is the psychological foundation for the development of the normal capacity for sublimation: "The capacity for developing a total object relationship, for integrating loving and hateful aspects of the relationships with others and with one's own self is a prerequisite for full development of sublimation" (Kernberg 1985A, p. 134). Sullivan (1953) has elaborated on sublimation, and his definition is relevant here: "Sublimation is the unwitting [Sullivan is loath to say *unconscious* because of his rejection of Freud's conception of introjection as an early internalization process] substitution, for a behavior pattern which encounters anxiety or collides with the self-system, of a socially more acceptable activity pattern which satisfies part of the motivational system that caused trouble" (p. 193). Kernberg (1985A) specifies the advantages of having a sublimatory capacity for a mature person: "Creative enjoyment and creative achievement are the main aspects of sublimatory capacity; they may be the best indicators of the extent to which a conflict-free ego sphere is available, and their absence, therefore, is an important indicator of ego weakness" (pp. 23–24).

Sublimatory capacity in a mature person is manifested in the capacity to transcend self-interest: "An individual's sublimatory potential involves an authentic dedication to something which transcends his self-interest" (Kernberg 1985A, p. 134). This becomes an important positive prognostic indicator: "The capacity to establish and maintain values transcending the self—abstract as it may sound, and difficult at times as it is to evaluate—is an eminently practical link between the vicissitudes of internalized object relationships on the one hand, and the capacity to benefit from a psychotherapeutic relationship, on the other" (p. 134).

Kernberg elaborates on the upper reaches of the higher side of life with this eloquent definition of sublimatory capacity in the mature person: "In more general terms, it involves concern for what is good and valuable in other people and in one's own self, the awareness of and appreciation for values or realities invested with love and from which love is received in turn in symbolic ways" (p. 134). It is remarkable how reminiscent Kernberg's observation of human nature is to the opening sentence of *The Theory of Moral Sentiments* "How selfish soever man may be supposed, there are evidently some principles in his nature, which interest him in the fortune of others, and render their happiness necessary to him, though he derives nothing from it, except the pleasure of seeing it" (Smith 1759, p. 47). Adam Smith's conception of the capacity for sympathy leaves no doubt that Smith's view of human nature recognized the higher side of life. With this eloquent definition of sublimatory capacity in the mature person, I believe that Kernberg has reached the heights of Fairbairn's (1952) profound understanding of the child's need to love and be loved: "The greatest need of a child is to obtain conclusive assurance (a) that he is genuinely loved as a person by his parents, and (b) that his parents genuinely accept his love" (p. 39).

Self-Respect and Human Maturity

Sullivan (1953) saw self-respect as an indication of a high level of human maturity: "Self-respect is necessary for adequate respect of others" (p. 309). A person at the normal level of personality development is high in self-respect, "and people who are very high in self-respect—that is, whose life experience has permitted them to uncover and demonstrate to their own satisfaction remarkable capacity for living with and among others—are people who find no particular expense to themselves connected with respecting any meritorious performance of anyone else" (pp. 308–309). A person high in self-respect does not feel impoverished when an invidious comparison is made with another person: "Insofar as self-respect has been permitted to grow without restrictions, because of comparatively unwarped personal development or because warp of personal development has been remedied, there is no excuse, no feeling of impoverishment, no hints of anxiety connected with discovering that somebody else is much better than you are in a particular field" (p. 309).

The Unstable Equilibrium at the End of the Road

Although we are at the pinnacle of normal personality development, we must not end unrealistically with some utopian notion. Kernberg

(1977, reprinted in 1985B), in a remarkably open opinion, describes the unstable equilibrium at the end of the developmental sequence:

> The observation of patients in the later stages of their psychoanalysis, the follow-up of patients who have successfully completed psychoanalytic treatment, and also the knowledge about colleagues and friends that one acquires in the course of a professional life, and self-analysis, all led me to a sense of the instability of the equilibrium reached at the end of the road of the developmental sequence, . . . and seemed to justify further study of what constitutes normality in love relations. (1985B, p. 281)

Even in an intimate interpersonal relationship, there are vicissitudes as a result of personal growth and development or changing circumstances of either or both of the persons in the relationship:

> One might, of course, say that in this case only one of the partners had been able to achieve change, thus threatening a previous equilibrium, and that under ideal circumstances change and growth in both participants may reinforce and renovate their relationship. This certainly happens in many cases; however, the assumption that change and growth will develop in the direction of reconfirming the couple can be wishful thinking: children grow up and leave home, education and professional developments of the couple take place which change the couple's life space and style, and external challenges and stress may bring about circumstances under which individual growth and the couple's growth do not necessarily coincide. (p. 280)

Object relations theory of normal personality development has described in detail what it means to be a normal person. A precise statement of the critical criteria for normality is provided by Kernberg (1984A): "Finally, this approach focuses upon such special criteria for mental health and normality as: (1) the depth and stability of internal relations with others; (2) the tolerance of ambivalence toward loved objects; (3) the capacity for tolerating guilt and separation and for the working through of depressive crises; (4) the extent to which the self-concept is integrated; and (5) the extent to which behavior patterns correspond to the self-concept" (p. 59).

NOTES

1. Primary-process thinking is related to Sullivan's prototaxic mode of experience, which he referred to as the earliest experience and as primitive, and is clearly related to introjection (Sullivan 1953, pp. 23, 67, 89, 108). In a similar

way, Sullivan's parataxic mode of experience is related to identification and cognitive elaboration in recall and foresight (p. 108), and the syntaxic mode of experience is related to the synthetic function of the ego and ego identity (p. 23).

2. I have always marveled at the dialogue in the movie *Philadelphia Story*, where Katharine Hepburn and Cary Grant were able to say the most anxiety-inducing things to one another, in the most articulate language, seemingly without emotion.

3. Suppression, a defense in the normal range of the Personality Continuum, involves a deliberate decision to postpone paying attention to a conscious impulse or conflict (Vaillant 1977, p. 386). The Predominant Defenses panel of the Personality Continuum expands the list of defenses at each level of personality development. I am drawing heavily on the work of George E. Vaillant, *Adaptation to Life* (1977), which represents the refinement of the earlier contributions of Anna Freud, *The Ego and the Mechanisms of Defense* (1966), first translated into English in 1937.

4. Two additional ideas in Freud's paper on "The Unconscious" (1915B) are worth noting: "It is a remarkable thing that the unconscious of one human being can react upon that of another, without passing through the conscious" (p. 194), and an idea that will become relevant to the subsequent analysis of subliminal stimuli used in advertising: "Normally all paths from perception to the unconscious remain open, and only those leading on from the unconscious are subject to blocking by repression" (p. 194).

5. Sullivan's *Clinical Studies in Psychiatry* (1956) is an invaluable source of case material on particular personality organizations. His portrait of the obsessional neurotic is an unparalleled exploration of the developmental history of the obsessive personality organization (pp. 229–282). Sullivan attributed the interpersonal origins of the obsessive personality organization to the atrocious disappointment of an utterly desolate childhood (pp. 269, 283).

6. According to Michael Balint (1937), this is slighting the amoebae: "Thus, biology, for instance, had to learn that the logically so-simple amoeba is in fact a secondary form; in its individual (not phylogenetic) youth it shows forms which swim freely about like flagellata, have a rather complicated structure, and above all are sexually dimorphous, which means that they develop proper object-relations to each other" (Balint 1986, p. 107). Sullivan (1953) used the amoebae to explain the effects of anxiety: "The appearance of just a little anxiety serves to deflect living away from the situation, just as the amoebae are deflected away from the hot water" (p. 301).

7. The intricacies of the neurotic range of the Personality Continuum are relatively underdeveloped in this book and need further elaboration. Indeed, there is an enormous potential for expanding the analysis of neurotic consumer behavior. George Ainslie's (1985, 1987) conception of precommitment devices—one's bargain with oneself to shore up self-control—essentially represents the striving for consistency of the neurotic personality organization.

8. Goethals (1980), commenting on Kernberg's views on intimacy, elaborates

on feelings of anger and aggression: “In a good passionate committed relationship you have the space—and safety—to work out the feelings of anger and aggression that you could never unleash on your parents because of your fear of them leaving you, or worse, punishing you” (p. 2). Stated in a somewhat less subtle way: “One way I read him is that in passionate sexual intercourse one does with the partner what one always wanted to do with one’s parents. . . . It is in a legitimate way fucking your mother/father and thus being part of the stream of human history” (p. 2).

Chapter 8

THE NORMAL CONSUMER: RATIONAL ECONOMIC MAN, MUTATIS MUTANDIS

Normal personality development represents the highest level of personality development on the Personality Continuum. A normal person has achieved the normal level of personality development and therefore would be a normal consumer. It is worth noting that there are no labels for personality organizations in the normal range of the Personality Continuum.

The maturation of the protective superego represents the pinnacle of personality development and the highest position in the normal range of the Personality Continuum. The contents of the protective superego represent the internalization of a value system shared with another person. An internalized value system is the basis for the human capacity for commitment. A person with the capacity to make a commitment will follow through under ordinary circumstances. Commitment is a dynamic concept because we make a commitment for the future. A person at the normal level of personality development has the capacity for foresight and the ability to plan for the future. The protective superego is the intrapsychic structure that provides a person with a future orientation (Kernberg 1985B, p. 291). A normal consumer's future behavior, therefore, is more predictable.

The achievement of the normal range of the Personality Continuum results in a general pattern of stable and consistent human behavior. This goes beyond consistent behavior at one point in time to the stability of behavior over time; therefore, the normal consumer will have a dynamic pattern of consumption behavior, as the term is used in economic analysis.

The stable and consistent pattern of behavior of a normal person, however, does not imply rigidity, because a person in the normal range of the Personality Continuum maintains the human capacity for concern and the capacity to experience guilt, to fall in and remain in love, and to establish stable intimate interpersonal relationships. In any given situation, the behavior of the normal person will be flexible and informed by a value system.

The achievement of the highest position in the normal range of the Personality Continuum thus has direct relevance for the determination of the individual's rate of time preference, that is, the relative valuation of the present and the future. The concept of commitment provides a firm foundation for altruism and gives substance to Becker's dynamic use of altruism to explain intergenerational wealth transfers (Becker 1981). The capacity for commitment, as a function of the protective superego, is quite properly a metapreference consideration in economic terms, that is, preferences about one's own preferences (Sen 1977, p. 337; Hirschman 1982, p. 71). The maturation of the protective superego, however, clearly refutes another definition of commitment proposed by Sen (1977): "One way of defining commitment is in terms of a person choosing an act that he believes will yield a lower level of personal welfare to him than an alternative that is also available to him" (p. 327).

It was with the earlier internalization process of identification that the exploration of the psychological foundations of consumer behavior became directly relevant for investigating nascent preference behavior. The essential behavioral implication of the process of identification, to want to be or to not want to be like another person in some selective way, will be revealed in the consumer's preference ordering or scale of preferences. Ultimately, for a person with a protective superego, the highest level of the superego functioning at the highest level of personality development, preferences are a reflection of the value system of the culture.

In this way, the analysis of the psychological foundations of consumer behavior makes a substantive contribution to overcoming Schumpeter's admonition that the economic theory of the consumer "does not state or imply anything about the nature of the wants and desires from which it starts" (1954, p. 1057). Thus one's preference ordering would reflect his or her concern, commitment to a value system, and actual choices in Sen's (1977) terms.

A CLARIFICATION OF THE THEORETICAL CONCEPTION OF THE RATIONAL ECONOMIC MAN

The theoretical conception of the normal personality organization, or simply the normal person, has provided the basis for a deeper understanding of the normal consumer. The analysis of personality development at the normal level presented thus far has, in fact, largely dealt with the "theoretically perfect person whose development had been optimum" (Fairbairn 1952, pp. 8–9). The optimally adjusted personality organization would occupy the very highest position in the normal range of the Personality Continuum and would represent the pinnacle of personality development.

The protective superego has provided many useful insights into the psychological foundations of normal consumer behavior and into the behavioral foundations of the economic theory of the consumer. It should be clear, however, that the abstraction of the rational economic man does not represent the pinnacle of personality development. The postulate of rationality only requires that the person's behavior be consistent, which begins with the integration of whole object relations. This structural formation in the personality also contributes to the increasing self-control over individual behavior (Kernberg 1984A, p. 32; Schelling 1980). The intrapsychic structural formation of the prohibitive superego—the internalization of the more realistic parental prohibitions and demands—constitutes an internal moral system that tells a person what is good and bad and helps distinguish between right and wrong. The prohibitive superego reinforces our self-control and enforces behavior that is consistent with our moral system through the experience of guilt.

The normal person would be rational from an economic point of view, because the normal consumer would reveal a transitive preference ordering and make consistent choices. The neoclassical economic theory of the consumer, ordinal utility theory, finds remarkable support in the normal range of the Personality Continuum. However, in economics, the rational consumer has a transitive preference ordering and makes consistent choices at one point in time, but that is not sufficient to qualify a person for the normal range of the Personality Continuum.

In general, a person at the normal level of personality development will behave in a stable and consistent pattern of behavior, and the normal consumer will have a dynamic pattern of consumption behavior. Therefore, the economic conception of the rational consumer must be modified to include a general pattern of consistent behavior that is stable over time, not just consistent at one point in time. Under this modification of the theoretical conception of rational economic man, mutatis mutandis, the new and improved conception of economic man, as we might say in marketing, would qualify as a normal consumer with a dynamic pattern of consumption behavior.

INTRAPSYCHIC STRUCTURE AND STRUCTURE OF PREFERENCES

The psychological foundations or, more precisely, the psychoanalytic object relations theory foundations of consumer behavior concentrates on the level of formation of the intrapsychic structure of the personality organization. This is not just a reference to the general level of personality development, but a specific reference to the intrapsychic structure of the personality organization and a direct application to economic analysis: The intrapsychic structure of the personality is reflected in the structure of the preferences. The crucial implication for the economic analysis of consumer behavior is that the nature of preferences is determined primarily by the level of intrapsychic structural formation that has been achieved in the development of the personality organization.

The internalization of interpersonal relationships and the structural formation of the personality has provided the structures that are missing from the economic theory of the consumer. Psychoanalytic object relations theory has provided a methodology for investigating the determinant of consistent preferences—the integration of whole object relations. Establishing a relationship between economics and psychoanalytic object relations theory has provided a methodology for investigating the formation of preferences (Albanese 1982).

THE OPEN ROAD

The integrative framework provided by the Personality Continuum opens the way to established economic theories of consumer behavior for the edification of noneconomists. Formidable mathematical models of consumer behavior are made even more useful by the careful circumscription of the limits of applicability through the exploration of the psychological foundations of consumer behavior. The objective is to establish the theoretical connections between the disciplines, and to open the way to economic theory for other disciplines, rather than to elaborate on the economic theories.

The theoretical connection has been established between object relations theory of the personality and ordinal utility theory of the consumer, and between object relations theory and the innovation of the theory of the allocation of time and the new household production function approach (although I have some objections to the confounding of technology and tastes) (Becker and Michael 1973). The term *commodity* is being used here as in the theory of the allocation of time and the new household production function approach to consumer behavior. The commodities in the consumption bundle of the normal consumer represent the internalized status-role bundles of the intrapsychic structure of the personality. Beyond the individual consumer the analysis can proceed to the concept of demand and the magic of the market.

ORDINAL UTILITY THEORY: THE FIRST- AND SECOND-ORDER CONDITIONS FOR THE EQUILIBRIUM OF THE INDIVIDUAL CONSUMER

Ordinal utility theory does remarkably well in modeling the normal pattern of stable and consistent consumer behavior. The rational economic consumer, mutatis mutandis, will maximize utility by equating the additional utility of the last dollar spent on every commodity, where *utility* is understood as the net of good and bad aspects of consumption activity and the outcome in satisfaction and dissatisfaction of any consumption activity. The utility function for an individual consumer is

$$U = f(q_1, q_2),$$

where q_1 and q_2 are commodities. The marginal utility of $q_1 MU_1$, is dU/dq_1. The marginal utility of q_2, MU_2, is dU/dq_2 The total differential of the utility function is

$$dU = f_1 dq_1 + f_2 dq_2,$$

where f_1 is the marginal utility for q_1, dU/dq_1, and f_2 is the marginal utility of q_2, dU/dq_2, along any indifference curve $\bar{U}$, and $dU = 0$.

Indifference curves cannot intersect, because this violates the transitivity property of the consumer's preference ordering. This reflects the consistent behavior of the consumer at one point in time. This clarification is provided to avoid confusion: Consistency has to do with the position of indifference curves in the commodity space q_1q_2, not the first-order condition for equilibrium of the consumer.

Marginal Rate of Substitution

The slope of the indifference curve, dq_2/dq_1, is the rate at which the consumer would be willing to substitute q_1 for q_2 or q_2 for q_1 in order to maintain a given level of utility. If the consumer substitutes one commodity for another, marginal utility decreases for the commodity he now has more of and increases for the commodity he now has less of. The marginal rate of substitution or the rate of commodity substitution is the negative of the slope of the indifference curve, $-dq_2/dq_1$, and is equal to the ratio of the partial derivatives of the utility function, the marginal utilities of q_1 and q_2, MU_1/MU_2:

$$\textit{marginal rate of substitution (MRS)} = -dq_2/dq_1 = MU_1/MU_2.$$

This clarification is provided to avoid confusion: The shape of the indifference curve—negatively sloped and convex—does not represent the first- and second-order conditions for equilibrium of the individual consumer.

The First-Order Condition for the Equilibrium of the Individual Consumer

Set up a constrained Lagrangian multiplier problem:

$$\text{Max } U = f(q_1, q_2) \text{ such that } y = p_1q_1 + p_2q_2.$$

The first-order condition for the equilibrium of the individual consumer is the equilibrium condition

$$MU_1/MU_2 = f_1/p_2,$$

that is,

$$\textit{marginal rate of substitution (MRS)} = MU_1/MU_2 = f_1/p_2.$$

Everything in Moderation: The Normal Consumer

The equilibrium condition can be stated as $MU_1/p_1 = MU_2/p_2$. The marginal utility divided by the price must be the same for all commodities; that is, the last dollar spent on every commodity must yield the same additional utility.

A behavioral interpretation of the generalized equilibrium condition for the individual consumer, $MU_1/p_1 = \ldots = MU_n/p_n$, the marginal utility of the last dollar spent on each commodity is equal, literally translates into everything in moderation (Albanese 1991, p. 31). In other words, all marginal utilities are positive, and no commodities are consumed to excess, where the marginal utility becomes negative, $MU < 0$. This is still the first-order condition for the static equilibrium of a normal consumer generalized to *n* commodities.

The Second-Order Condition for the Equilibrium of the Individual Consumer

The consumer's indifference curves must be strictly convex: At an equilibrium point, the rate of change of the slope of the indifference curve at the equilibrium point must be positive: $d^2q_2/dq^2{}_1 > 0$.

In economics, the second-order condition pertains to the stability of the static equilibrium of the individual consumer. While the stability of the equilibrium is a manifestation of the general pattern of stable and consistent behavior for the normal person, the equilibrium of the individual consumer is static. This is a limitation of ordinal utility theory and not the normal consumer: The behavior of the normal consumer, with the capacity for foresight, to plan for the future, and a future orientation, would be stable over time, a dynamic pattern of consumption behavior. This goes beyond the static-equilibrium analysis of ordinal utility theory. This clarification is provided to avoid confusion of the stability of a dynamic pattern of consumption behavior over time for the normal consumer with the mathematical property of the second-order condition for the static equilibrium of the individual consumer.

THE JOYLESS ECONOMY OF TIBOR SCITOVSKY AND THE EXPERIMENTAL PSYCHOLOGY OF PAUL T. YOUNG

With a conception of the normal consumer, we can begin to build bridges to integrate contributions from other disciplines. The analysis can be extended by a foray into neurophysiological and experimental psychological research. In *The Joyless Economy* (1976), Tibor Scitovsky has explored the neurophysiological concept of arousal. His approach can be profitably combined with the experimental psychology of Paul T. Young in *Motivation and Emotion: A Survey of the Determinants of Human and Animal Activity* (1961).

In Kernberg's (1984A) view, subjective states act as a bridge: "We have now come full circle: Neurophysiological and experimental psychological research have reinforced the central theory of affects and stressed the importance of exploring subjective states, which, of course, constitute the primary field of psychoanalytic research. At the same time, ethological, neurophysiological, and experimental psychological research all point in the direction of the intimate connection between instinct, as presently conceived, and affects" (pp. 103–104).

We can begin with the findings of a survey reported by Scitovsky (1976):

> In a questionnaire survey of man's happiness, people were asked a number of questions about the frequency with which they experienced annoyances such as pain, worry, and unpleasantness on the one hand and elation, praise, good news, and various other pleasant sensations on the other. The two groups were called negative and positive affect, respectively, and a quantitative index was established for each. As we would expect, both the absence of negative affect and the presence of positive affect were correlated with people's self-related happiness. But one totally unexpected result emerged from the study: there was a complete lack of correlation between positive and negative affect. In other words, the frequency with which a person had pleasant feelings was quite independent of the frequency with which he had unpleasant feelings. (p. 61)

Scitovsky related this to the discovery by neurophysiologists of the existence of separate pleasure and pain centers of the brain and drew the following conclusion: "In accepting that hypothesis, we must abandon the old-fashioned notion that pain and pleasure are the negative and positive segments of a one-dimensional scale, something like a hedonic gauge, calibrated from utter misery to supreme bliss, on which a person's hedonic state registers the higher the better off he is" (p. 61).

It was Scitovsky's contention that the independence of positive and negative affect contradicted the notion that a "hedonic gauge" could be constructed. Young (1961), however, has constructed just such a gauge, called the "hedonic continuum," which combines the motivational aspect of affect with arousal and provides striking support for the economic theory of choice. According to Young (1961): "The view that there are two dimensions of arousal—an activating and an hedonic dimension—is supported by physiological studies in electroencephalography and studies upon the physiology of 'reward' and 'punishment.' There are degrees or levels of activation and also degrees of positive and negative hedonic intensity" (pp. 203–204). Young's statement is virtually identical to a similar finding reported by Scitovsky (1976) on the two dimensions of stimulation:

> All stimulation is now believed to have two parallel effects on the central nervous system: it activates direct neural pathways to the associative areas of the brain, those parts which do the thinking and decision-making, thus transmitting specific information about each specific stimulus for possible action. At the same time it causes a diffuse, non-specific, general raising of the activation level of the arousal system, which increases alertness and so provides a more appropriate background for the efficient and prompt functioning of the brain's direct stimulus-response mechanism. (p. 19)

The hedonic dimension of stimulation is represented by the intensity of positive and negative affective arousal: "Positive affective arousals tend to facilitate and negative inhibit activities that were instrumental in producing them. Through a kind of primitive evaluation ('good' or 'bad') the organism is oriented towards or against certain kinds and intensities of stimulation. This organizing process is something very basic and widespread throughout nature" (Young 1961, p. 202).

Young's concept of the hedonic continuum, representing the intensity of affective arousal, can now be elaborated. According to Young (1961): "The affective processes can be represented as varying along a bipolar continuum extending from negative, through indifferent, to positive values" (p. 153). This harks back to Hicks's classic statement of Pareto's transformation of utility theory: "We can say, of any two sets, whether he will prefer one to the other, or whether they will be indifferent to him" (1934, p. 53).

Young's concept of the hedonic continuum was taken over from the earlier work of J.G. Beebe-Center in his *The Psychology of Pleasantness and Unpleasantness* (1932). The following statement confirms that the concept of indifference is being used by the psychologists in the same way that it is used by economists: "It would seem, then, that there is a definite concept called indifference which refers to contents of experiences different from those referred to by the concepts of pleasantness and unpleasantness" (Beebe-Center 1932, p. 6). The graphical analysis of Beebe-Center's experimental work leaves no doubt that the hedonic continuum represents a remarkable parallel development to the indifference curve analysis of economics. Even a brief perusal reveals numerous convex indifference curves (pp. 31, 172, 174, 175, 179).

The concept of affective arousal has very direct relevance to the economic theory of choice. The following statement by Young (1961) of the "hedonic principle" should leave no further doubt: "Neurobehavioral patterns are organized according to the hedonic principle of maximizing the positive and minimizing the negative affective arousal. This principle has a very wide range of application. It is seen most clearly in situations that involve choice" (p. 201).

The most important outcome of the experimental psychology of Paul T. Young is that he has developed practical techniques for the actual testing of preferences that correspond in a remarkable way with the theoretical constructs of the economic theory of the consumer. Thus the statement on testing made earlier by Hirschman (1982) is only relatively true—there have, in fact, been very few systematic attempts at actual testing by economists, but there have been systematic attempts at preference testing made by experimental psychologists. In fact, a systematic technique for preference testing has been developed, and Young's *Motivation and Emotion* should become required reading in any course on the economic theory of the consumer.

To see just how direct the relationship is between Young's experimental psychology and the economic theory of consumer choice, consult Young's development of "brief exposure preference testing": "In a brief-exposure test the animal is offered a series of choices between two test foods (A and B). The series of choices reveals whether a preference develops for one food (A) or the other (B)" (p. 152). Further, in perfect recognition of the law of diminishing marginal utility, Young states why the preference test should involve only a brief exposure: "A brief-exposure test is recommended because with prolonged exposures the level of acceptability of test foods declines as the terminal state of satiation is approached" (p. 152). Finally, the last statement confirms that Young is dealing with relative preferences: "A preference test does not reveal the absolute level of affective intensity but only the relative levels associated with two incentives." "A preference test, therefore, reveals only the relative affective intensities" (pp. 166, 168).

The analysis can be brought full circle at this point with Young's concept of the stable hierarchy of preferential values: "Such a value system is based upon affective processes. It has a stability and permanence (dependent upon the nervous system) that is independent of current affective arousals. The sign of an evaluative disposition is based upon the sign of the affective process aroused by the object" (p. 169).

A NOTE ON SUBJECTIVE EXPERIENCE

Subjective experience is a person's inner experience and has both a cognitive and affective component. The affective and cognitive components are integral to the person's subjective experience. The cognitive component is the idea or ideation, thoughts and the process of thinking. The affective component is the feeling or emotion experienced by a person. It is the relationship between the affective and cognitive component, not the primacy of one or the other, that is imperative to the analysis. The developmental approach provided by object relations theory explicates the relationship between affect and cognition. The three levels of internalization—introjection, identification, and ego identity—and the changing relationship between the self, the object, and the affect at each level of personality development provide the framework to analyze the hierarchical formation of the intrapsychic structure of the personality organization. This is a distinct strength of the approach provided by object relations theory.

The developmental perspective of object relations theory on affect is presented in a concise statement by Kernberg (1984A): "Affect states first determine the integration of both internalized object relations and the overall drive systems; later, affect states signal the activation of the drive and represent it in the context of the activation of specific internalized object relations" (p. 104). A developmental approach is the solution to the fallacious chicken-and-egg debate over primacy of affect versus primacy of cognition. In the same way, the developmental approach will enable us to explore the independence hypothesis (Zajonc 1980).[1] What has been missing from the debate on the primacy of affect or cognition is a developmental perspective. In a later article in this debate, one literally sees Lazarus (1991) groping toward the need for a developmental approach. The developmental relationship between affect and cognition will be explored at every opportunity throughout this book.

In America, the extreme separation of head and heart replicates the relationship between cognition and affect, respectively. According to Barker-Benfield (1976) in his exploration of male attitudes toward women and sexuality in nineteenth-century America: "Man's division of sex roles according to head and heart by definition corresponded to a division within himself. . . . 'Head' connoted self-control, will, intellect, undeviating persistence in the pursuit of success, hardness, educability, political, scientific, artistic, inventive, and mercantile activity; the capacity to master the sordid traffic beyond the home, and the progressive conquest of the West and the world in the interest of Christianity and civilization. 'Heart' connoted feelings and their expression, morality, sensibility, softness, gentleness, spontaneity, lack of staying power, intuition, eruptibility, nervousness; it was very easily influenced (as Ray pointed out in his account of 'sympathy')" (p. 199).

A NOTE ON THE MEASUREMENT OF ATTITUDES IN MARKETING

In marketing, the cognitive component of an attitude is made up of perceptions and knowledge and is measured by the construct of beliefs. The affective component of an attitude is made up of feelings and emotions and is measured by an overall evaluation, good or bad. Drive derivatives are feelings and emotions, the affective component of an internal object relation, or an attitude, as measured by a single-component attitude model in marketing. The ideational representations are thoughts and mental images, the cognitive component of an attitude, as measured in marketing by a modified single-component attitude model and the more elaborate multiattribute structural models of attitudes. Multiattribute structural models in marketing represent important approaches for measurement of attitudes (Bagozzi 1992; Fishbein 1963; Miniard and Cohen 1979, 1981, 1983).[2]

ALFRED MARSHALL AND NEOCLASSICAL ECONOMICS

Economists have shown a certain fascination for an observation made by Alfred Marshall with regard to the law of diminishing marginal utility, which can be fruitfully addressed at this point using Young's (1961) work: "There is, however, an implicit condition in this law which should be made clear. It is that we do not suppose time to be allowed for any alteration in the character or tastes of the man himself. It is, therefore, no exception to the law that the more good music a man hears, the stronger is his taste for it likely to become" (Marshall 1920, p. 79).

C.C. von Weizsäcker (1971) has analyzed Marshall's observation as an "example of endogenously changing tastes" (p. 146). Stigler and Becker (1977) analyzed Marshall's observation as an example of "beneficial addiction":

> We believe that the phenomenon Marshall is trying to explain, namely that exposure to good music increases the subsequent demand for good music (for some persons!), can be explained with some gain in insight by assuming constant tastes, whereas to assume a change in tastes has been an unilluminating "explanation." The essence of our explanation lies in the accumulation of what might be termed "consumption capital" by the consumer, and we distinguish "beneficial" addiction like Marshall's good music from "harmful" addiction like heroin. (Stigler and Becker 1977, p. 78)

What was "good music" to Marshall, in his hierarchy of preferential values, was part of his value system, and his appreciation of this music represented a pleasurable affective experience to him. In Young's (1961) view, "The relative hedonic intensities determine the rate of growth of preferential discrimination" (p. 168). Thus, the phenomenon Marshall is trying to explain, namely, that exposure to good music increases the demand for good music, is the growth, that is, the formation of a preference for music that is judged to be good in the person's value system.

While this comes closer to Weizsäcker's explanation, Marshall was not trying to explain a change in preferences, as Stigler and Becker charge, but simply the growth or formation of preferences over time. Thus, at a given point in time, a consumer's preferences can be assumed to be constant, but over time, "It is therefore no exception to the law that the more good music a man hears, the stronger is his taste for it likely to become." Stigler and Becker's (1977) explanation of this phenomenon as "the accumulation of what might be termed consumption capital" must be considered a deus ex machina, and, as will be shown subsequently, their application of neoclassical consumer theory to addiction, beneficial or otherwise, is an inappropriate use of the model.

Thus, with regard to the development of normal personality, one of the assertions made by Stigler and Becker is substantiated: Preferences are stable. However, a value system, which is ultimately reflected in a person's preferences, represents the culture in which the personality develops. In the United States, with a population based on successive waves of immigration, cultural variations in value orientations refute their assertion that preferences are uniform (p. 89).

NOTES

1. There is a vast literature in the field of marketing on affect, emotions, feelings, and moods. References have been made to the experiential aspects of consumption in marketing (Hirschman and Holbrook 1982; Holbrook and

Hirschman 1982; Holbrook 1995). This only scratches the surface. See any consumer behavior textbook, like Blackwell, Miniard, and Engel, 2001.

2. The treatment of cognition in marketing is considered too narrow by Holbrook (1995), such as in the role of unconscious thoughts. The virtual neglect of the unconscious was addressed in the introduction.

Chapter 9

The Basic Fault: Failure to Achieve the Integration of Whole Object Relations

The personality organization is defined by the level of intrapsychic structural formation and the predominant defense used against severe anxiety in interpersonal relations. Anxiety was introduced in the context of the failure to achieve the integration of whole object relations, resorting to the primitive defense of splitting against severe anxiety, and arrest of personality development in the primitive range of the Personality Continuum. Personality organizations arrested at the neurotic level of personality development have achieved the integration of whole object relations but have failed to achieve the full integration of satisfying genital sexual activity into an intimate interpersonal relationship. In terms of relative emphasis, the comparison of the normal and primitive personality developments will be central to the analysis of consumption behavior; less emphasis will be placed on the neurotic level of personality development, and the least amount of emphasis on the psychotic range of the Personality Continuum.

Problems of personality are primarily interpersonal for personality organizations arrested at the neurotic and primitive levels of personality development. For a child who would become a primitive personality organization as an adult, the transition from infantile dependence to mature dependence on another person confronts the developing ego with a great conflict, according to Fairbairn (1952):

> The great conflict of the transition stage may now be formulated as a conflict between a progressive urge to surrender the infantile attitude of identification with the [internalized] object and a regressive urge to maintain that attitude. During this period, accordingly, the behavior of the individual is characterized both by desperate endeavors on his part to separate himself from the object and desperate endeavors to achieve reunion with the object—desperate attempts "to escape from prison" and desperate attempts "to return home." (p. 43)

This is a classic statement of the alternating and contradictory behavior characteristic of the person with a primitive personality organization. In a metaphorical foray, Fairbairn further describes the chronologically adult person with a schizoid personality organization confronting this conflict as a timid mouse: "During the course of analysis, such an individual provides the most striking evidence of a conflict between an extreme reluctance to abandon infantile dependence and a desperate longing to renounce it; and it is at once fascinating and pathetic to watch the patient, like a timid mouse, alternately creeping out of the shelter of his hole to peep at the world of outer objects and then beating a hasty retreat" (p. 39).

It is this conflict that is at the center of the use of neurotic defenses by primitive personality organizations designated as Fairbairn's hypothesis: "It is also illuminating to observe how, in his indefatigable attempts to emerge from a state of infantile dependence, he resorts by turns to any or all four of the transitional techniques which have been described—the paranoid, obsessional, hysterical, and phobic" (p. 39). Further, "Each of the various techniques in question may now be interpreted as a specific method in attempting to deal with the characteristic conflict of the transition stage in so far as this conflict remained unresolved. The conflict is one between (a) a developmental urge to advance to an attitude of mature dependence upon the object, and (b) a regressive reluctance to abandon the attitude of infantile dependence upon the object" (p. 38). In his seminal contribution to founding British object relations theory, "Schizoid Factors in the Personality," published in 1940, Fairbairn, commenting on what he considered to be the insuperable difficulties of constructing a Personality Continuum, gives the earliest statement of Fairbairn's hypothesis and attributes it to Freud: "In actual practice, of course, the construction of a scale such as that just imagined would involve quite insuperable difficulties, of which only one is that arising out of the fact that quite a number of schizoid manifestations, as indeed Freud pointed out, are really defences against splitting of the ego" (Fairbairn 1952, p. 10).

In the terminology of object relations theory, American as opposed to British, the primitive defense of splitting characterizes all personality organizations in the primitive range of the Personality Continuum. Under ordinary circumstances, with the primitive defense of splitting intact, a person with a primitive personality organization can function at the higher neurotic level of personality development and therefore utilize a range of neurotic defenses.[1]

The analysis of the borderline personality organization is central to the analysis of all personality organizations in the primitive range of the Personality Continuum. The extreme frustration and intense aggression that characterize the personal history of a person with a borderline personality organization are characteristic of the personal history of all personality organizations arrested at a primitive level of personality development. The exploration of the borderline personality organization by Kernberg occupies the same position in American object relations theory that Fairbairn's earlier exploration of the schizoid personality organization occupies in British object relations theory.

FAIRBAIRN ON THE PERSONALITY CONTINUUM

It was a brilliant stroke that led Fairbairn to study the schizoid personality organization, a simple structure, rigid and uncomplicated by higher-level intrapsychic structures, a primitive personality organization, hanging just above the psychotic range. According to Fairbairn (1952), "What has convinced me of the paramount importance of the object-relationship is the analysis of patients displaying schizoid characteristics; for it is in such individuals that difficulties over relationships with objects present themselves most clearly" (p. 39).

From this vantage point, Fairbairn formed a clear conception of a personality continuum: "Accordingly, we must recognize the possibility of development resulting in all degrees of integration of the ego; and we may conceive a theoretic scale of integration such that one end of the scale represents complete integration and the other end represents complete failure of integration, with all intermediate degrees" (p. 9). The top of the Personality Continuum, according to Fairbairn, would represent only a theoretical possibility: "A place at the very top of the scale, which would represent perfect integration and absence of splitting, must be regarded as only a theoretical possibility" (p. 9).

The theoretically perfect person would have had an optimum personality development (optimum is a concept that economists can appreciate, much like the concept of marginal anxiety): "This would hold true, of course, in the case of a theoretically perfect person whose development had been optimum; but then there is nobody who enjoys such a happy lot. Indeed it is difficult to imagine any person with an ego so unified and stable at its highest levels that in no circumstances whatever would any evidence of splitting come to the surface in recognizable form" (p. 8). Even a "normal person" may at times show signs of splitting: "There are probably few 'normal' people who have never at any time in their lives experienced an unnatural state of calm and detachment in face of some serious crisis, or a transient sense of 'looking on at oneself' in some embarrassing or paralysing situation; and probably most people have had some experience of that strange confusion of past and present, or of phantasy and reality, known as 'déjà vu' " (p. 8; see also p. 51).

On the other hand, according to Fairbairn, some people manifest splitting under the most ordinary conditions of life:

> If we keep such a scale in mind, it should help us understand how it would be possible for any individual to display some schizoid feature under sufficiently extreme conditions, and how it comes about that some individuals manifest evidence of a split in the ego only in situations involving such readjustments as are involved in adolescence, marriage, or joining the army in wartime, whereas others again may manifest such evidence even under the most ordinary conditions of life. (pp. 9–10)

The important qualification, according to Fairbairn, is that everything depends upon the mental level that is being considered:

> The criticism for which I must now prepare myself is that, according to my way of thinking, everybody without exception must be regarded as schizoid. Actually I am quite prepared to accept this criticism, but only with a very important qualification—one in the absence of which my concept of "Schizoid" would be so comprehensive as to become almost meaningless. The qualification which confers meaning on the concept is that everything depends upon the mental level which is being considered. The fundamental schizoid phenomenon is the presence of splits in the ego. . . . The all-important factor here is the mental depth which requires to be plumbed before evidence of splitting of the ego declares itself. (pp. 7–8)

The mental level to be plumbed is the intrapsychic structure of the personality organization, and the qualification that everything depends on the mental level is fundamental to the understanding that everything depends upon the level of personality development along the Personality Continuum. This represents the remarkable progress that has been made in the movement from British object relations theory to American object relations theory.

A CAVEAT ABOUT THE CHRONOLOGICALLY ADULT PERSON'S PERSONALITY ORGANIZATION

An important caveat is in order here: It is the chronologically adult person's personality organization that is classified along the Personality Continuum. This caveat is important because, at this point, I am using the Personality Continuum for pedagogical purposes to present an object relations theory of personality development. It would be easy to misconstrue the analysis. Although an early infant and a chronologically adult person with a psychotic personality organization have in common an absence of boundaries between oneself and others, it would be wrong to conclude that the early infant starts out life psychotic. The early infant, utterly helpless and unconditionally dependent, is on the way to achieving higher levels of personality development. For the chronologically adult person, however, the psychotic personality organization represents an absence of reality testing and personality development arrested in the psychotic range of the Personality Continuum. For psychotic personality organizations, problems of the personality are primarily physiological and not interpersonal in origin.

In a similar vein, personality organizations in the primitive range of the Personality Continuum are often described as being childlike, particularly the borderline personality organization. A man with a narcissistic personality organization is often described as an eternal little boy or *puer aeternus* (Franz 1981; Kernberg 1977). Childlike behavior by a chronologically adult person is indicative of arrest of personality development at a primitive level.

It is critical to keep in mind whether an observation is being made from a developmental perspective (i.e., at a particular point of personality development in early or late infancy, childhood, and so on) or from the perspective of a chronologically adult person. I will endeavor to specify whether the perspective is developmental or that of the chronologically adult person.

The terminology of the heuristic stages of personality development—early infancy, late infancy, childhood, and so on—becomes less useful and more awkward when personality development diverges from the normal course. The integration of whole object relations could have been achieved by the age of two with fortunate interpersonal experience, that is, good-enough mothering.

SPLITTING AND THE PRIMITIVE LEVEL OF PERSONALITY DEVELOPMENT

At first, splitting is the result of the lack of physiological integrative capacity. It is only subsequently that splitting is used as a primitive defense against severe anxiety in interpersonal relationships. The early infant does not have the physiological capacity to integrate the good and bad aspects of the relationship with the mother, and these aspects of the relationship are internalized completely separately in the good and bad introjects and identifications (Kernberg 1984A, pp. 34–39). There are multiple good and bad mothers that are completely separate. With the physiological maturation of perception and memory, the later infant comes to recognize that there is only one mother, who is both good and bad.

If the later infant can accept the mother as both good and bad and, therefore, a whole and more realistic person, and then accept oneself as whole and more realistic, the integration of whole object relations has been achieved. This interpersonal achievement in personality development demarcates the neurotic range of the Personality Continuum for the chronologically adult person. The internalization process changes to ego identity.

Kernberg (1984A) describes the origin of the primitive defense of splitting in the language of object relations theory: "Introjections with positive valence and those with negative valence are thus kept completely apart. They are kept apart at first simply because they happen separately and because of the ego's incapacity to integrate introjections not activated by similar valences, but then gradually, in response to anxiety, because of the ego's active use of this separation for defensive purpose. This is actually the origin of splitting as a mechanism of defense" (p. 35). When the primitive defense of splitting is working, anxiety is prevented: "Under these pathological circumstances, contradictory ego states are alternately activated, and as long as these contradictory ego states can be kept separate from each other, anxiety is prevented" (Kernberg 1985A, p. 26). In contrast to the higher-level defense of repression, splitting largely occurs in consciousness: "The conflict is not 'unconscious' in the strict sense connected with repression, and as long as the rigid barrier between contradictory ego states is maintained, the patient [person with a primitive personality organization] is free from anxiety" (Kernberg 1984A, p. 46).

THE PREDOMINANCE OF NEGATIVE INTROJECTIONS, SPLITTING, AND PRIMITIVE IDEALIZATION

The failure to achieve the integration of whole object relations means that the later infant has not been able to accept that the mother is only one person who is both good and bad and, therefore, a whole and more realistic person. Splitting is an active and powerful defense against severe anxiety that involves separating contradictory images of the self and object as a way of denying that the mother is not all-good, thereby protecting the primitive fantasy of the ideal, all-good mother (Kernberg 1984A, pp. 40, 68).

In the borderline personality organization, the predominance of negative introjections leads to a dangerous primitive idealization (Kernberg 1984A, p. 49). According to Kernberg (1985A), primitive idealization "refers to the tendency to see external objects as totally good, in order to make sure that they can protect one against the 'bad' objects, that they cannot be contaminated, spoiled, or destroyed by one's own aggression or by that projected onto other objects" (p. 30). Further, according to Kernberg (1985A), "Primitive idealization creates unrealistic, all-good and powerful object images, and this also affects negatively the development of the ego ideal and the [prohibitive] superego" (p. 30).

Splitting is primarily a conscious defense in comparison to the unconscious defense of repression at the higher neurotic level of personality development. According to Kernberg (1984A), a chronologically adult person with a primitive personality organization "may be conscious of the severe contradiction in his behavior, but he can alternate between opposite strivings with a bland denial of this contradiction and with what is, seen from the outside, a striking lack of concern over it" (p. 46). A person with a primitive personality organization "is aware of the fact that at this time his perceptions, thoughts, and feelings about himself or other people are completely opposite to those he has had at other times; but this memory has no emotional relevance, it cannot influence the way he feels now" (Kernberg 1985A, p. 31).

The alternately activated contradictory ego states are manifested in a chaotic pattern of alternating contradictory behavior that characterizes all personality organizations arrested at the primitive level of personality development and arrayed in the primitive range of the Personality Continuum. This chaotic, alternating, and contradictory behavior is rigidly patterned. It is displayed in observable behavior, in what appears on the surface as a lack of impulse control, which is highly selective and specific: "The mechanism of splitting is reflected in what appears on the surface as simple lack of impulse control rather than in alternating expression of complementary sides of a conflict. Such 'lack of impulse control' is often of a highly selective, specific kind and represents the emerging into consciousness of a split identification system" (Kernberg 1984A, p. 47). The behavioral manifestations of splitting in a person with a borderline personality organization may at first appear chaotic, but "gradually, however, repetitive patterns emerge, reflecting primitive self-representations and related object-representations under the influence of the conflicts mentioned above" (Kernberg 1985A, p. 78).

An impulse is a sudden driving force acted on with conscious thought. This begins the analysis of the origin of compulsive and, in the more extreme case, addictive consumer behavior, the dark side of consumer behavior, that will be analyzed in greater depth subsequently. The breakdown of splitting is manifested in an outbreak of observable behavior, the often crude gratification of impulses by a person with a primitive personality organization. It is the chronic character of the episodic outbreaks of this behavior over time that forms the patterns of compulsive and addictive consumption behavior, and it is the chronic character of the compulsive and more extreme addictive behavior that is ultimately self-destructive.

SPLITTING, SUPEREGO PATHOLOGY, AND TOLERATING CONTRADICTORY BEHAVIOR

The essential structural formation that has not taken place in the personality organizations in the primitive range of the Personality Continuum is the integration of whole object relations—precisely the development that contributes to the consistency of behavior. The failure to integrate whole object relations means that neither the ego nor the superego are integrated as structures in the personality: "Thus, excessive splitting operations of the ego preventing the integration of the self-concept, and lack of integration within the superego reinforce each other" (Kernberg 1985A, p. 144). The failure to integrate the superego reinforces the splitting in the ego by tolerating contradictory behavior: "It is only a pathological superego that tolerates the contradictions between mutually dissociated or split-off ego states" (p. 144).

The consequences of the failure to integrate higher-level superego structures in Kernberg's clinical observations begin to sound more and more like Sen's (1977) general critique of neoclassical consumer theory as having too little structure: "What is especially missing in patients with severe superego pathology is concern for oneself, for one's relations to others, and for what one is doing to others in terms of moral values" (Kernberg 1985A, p. 141). The absence of concern, or sympathy, represents the lack of structural formation, most importantly, the integration of whole object relations. Without the integration of whole object relations, the higher-level structural formation related to commitment cannot take place: "The absence of internalized value systems, lack of awareness of such value systems in others, and lack of awareness of the interpersonal implications of such value systems are important indicators of absence of advanced superego structures and functions" (p. 141).

MARGINAL ANXIETY AND THE LACK OF ANXIETY TOLERANCE IN PRIMITIVE PERSONALITY ORGANIZATIONS

The critical aspect of the lack of anxiety tolerance in a person with a primitive personality organization is the inability to tolerate any additional anxiety, or marginal anxiety, translated into the terminology of neoclassical economic analysis. Additional anxiety overloads the primitive defense of splitting, and it breaks down, leaving the person subject to intense and overwhelmingly severe anxiety. The breakdown of splitting is manifested in variations in behavior: "*Lack of anxiety tolerance* is reflected in the degree to which any additional anxiety to that habitually experienced moves the patient [in this case, a person with a borderline personality organization] toward further symptom formation, alloplastic behavior, or ego regression. It has to be stressed that it is not the degree of anxiety which is important here, but how the ego reacts to any additional anxiety 'load' " (Kernberg 1985A, p. 22).

The breakdown of splitting represents a mental breakdown—a regression to a lower level of psychic functioning and a return to earlier patterns of behavior. This regression is the hallmark of all mental illness. The behavioral manifestation of the breakdown of splitting in "symptom formation, alloplastic behavior, or ego regression" includes compulsive and, in the extreme case, addictive behavior. For personality organizations in the primitive range of the Personality Continuum, the breakdown of splitting is the focal point for the exploration of the psychological foundations of compulsive and addictive patterns of consumer behavior.

The lack of anxiety tolerance in primitive personality organizations is a manifestation of ego weakness: *"Splitting, then, is a fundamental cause of ego weakness. Since . . . a weak ego falls back easily on splitting, . . . a vicious circle is created by which ego weakness and splitting reinforce each other"* (Kernberg 1984A, p. 46).[2] Ego weakness is the result of the basic fault in personality development—the failure to achieve the integration of whole object relations. This is characteristic of personality organizations arrested at the primitive level of personality development and in the primitive range of the Personality Continuum.

THE BASIC FAULT: THE FAILURE TO LOVE AND BE LOVED AS A PERSON

The central issue at this point is what caused the failure to integrate whole object relations. What brought about what Balint (1979) has called the basic fault? A history of extreme frustrations and intense aggression during the first few years of life is at the core of the etiology of all primitive personality organizations (Kernberg 1985A, p. 41). The mothering was not good enough.

In the particular case of the borderline personality organization, according to Kernberg (1984A), "The most important cause of failure in the borderline pathology [personality organization] is probably a quantitative predominance of negative introjections. Excessive negative introjections may stem both from a constitutionally determined intensity of aggressive drive derivatives and from severe early frustrations" (p. 48). The predominance of negative over positive interpersonal and internal object relations is designated by Kernberg (1984A) as the quantitative factor, and by Freud (1933) as the economic factor. Kernberg (1984A) identifies three factors that contribute to the predominance of negative interpersonal and internal object relations: "Quantitative factors involving the degree of aggressive drive derivatives, the degree of objective deprivation and frustration, and the degree of the early ego's anxiety tolerance may also be crucially involved" (p. 50). Refer to Figure 9.1, for a schematic representation of the intrapsychic structure of the primitive personality organization.

In Fairbairn's conception the cause of the basic fault is the failure of the mother, or mothering one, to use Sullivan's term, to convince her child by spontaneous and genuine expressions of affection that he or she is loved as a person, and that his or her love is accepted by her in return (p. 13). This is a good use of *child* as a heuristic stage of personality development because primitive personality organizations are characterized as childlike.

Figure 9.1
Intrapsychic Structure of the Primitive Personality Organization

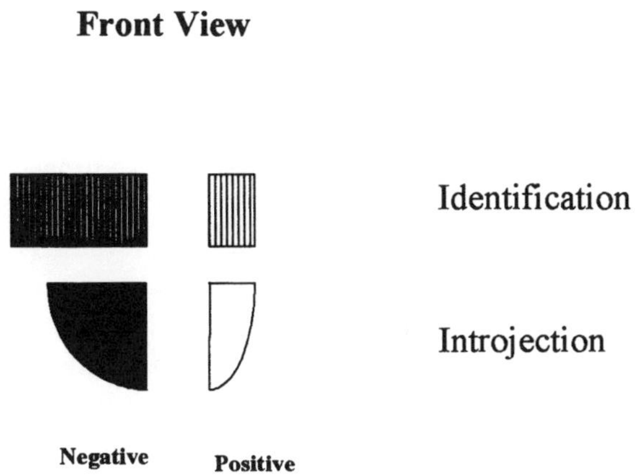

Personality development is arrested at the primitive level because of the excessive frustration in the early interpersonal relationship with the mother and the predominance of negative introjections and identifications, the all-bad internal object relations. The result is the failure to integrate whole object relations and to accept another person, and oneself, as both good and bad and, therefore, a whole and more realistic person, and thus to achieve the higher neurotic level of personality development.

FRUSTRATION OF ORAL-DEPENDENT NEEDS

In the terminology of object relations theory, excessive pregenital aggression, especially oral aggression, and the unusual intensity of pregenital aggression predominate for personality organizations in the primitive range of the Personality Continuum (Kernberg 1985A, pp. 7–8, 40). *Pregenital* means the premature development of the oedipal strivings. In the case of the little boy, this means perceiving the father as his rival for his mother. The result is a premature development of genital striving typical of the oedipal situation, premature because it is preadolescent, before puberty, prepubescent, too soon, and too early in life. With the premature development of genital striving, typical of the oedipal situation, we arrive at *pregenital*, a term densely packed with meaning in object relations theory.

The premature development of genital striving typical of the oedipal situation does not mean sexual arousal of the little boy's genitals—an erection, ejaculation, or masturbation—all directed toward the mother. After all, we are talking about two or three year olds, chronologically speaking, although age is not a good predictor of anything when it comes to personality development. In the case of the borderline personality organization, according to Kernberg (1985A), "I suggest that what is characteristic of the borderline personality organization, in contrast to less severe pathological conditions [personality organizations at a neurotic level of personality development], is a specific condensation between pregenital and genital conflicts, and a *premature* development of oedipal conflicts from the second or third year on" (p. 40).

Pregenital also does not mean the premature development of the oedipal situation, because the typical three-person oedipal situation of mother, child, and father cannot form without the integration of whole object relations (Kernberg 1984A, p. 216). In the absence of this interpersonal achievement in personality development—accept another person, and oneself, as both good and bad and, therefore, a whole and more realistic person—an attitude of mature dependence on the mother and father cannot develop. Instead, an attitude of immature dependence on primitively idealized part-object relations prevails, precluding the formation of the three-person oedipal situation.

The chronologically adult person who is arrested at the primitive level of personality development has failed to integrate whole object relations because of the intense frustrations in interpersonal relations during the early stages of personality development. The interpersonal achievement in personality development, to recognize oneself as separate from another person, that demarcates the primitive range of the Personality Continuum has been achieved. Splitting, however, compromises even this achievement in varying degrees, according to Fairbairn (1952): "Another important function of the ego is discrimination between inner and outer reality. Splitting of the ego has the effect of compromising the progressive development of all these functions, although, of course, in varying degrees and varying proportions" (p. 9).

The analysis of the interpersonal origins of the borderline personality organization presented thus far, focusing on aggressive drive derivatives stemming from the excessive frustration of oral-dependent needs in early interpersonal relations with the mother, applies to all personality organizations in the primitive range of the Personality Continuum. The extreme frustration and deprivation of the infant's oral-dependent needs has the effect of intensifying and imparting an aggressive quality to these needs, according to Fairbairn: "In circumstances of deprivation, emptiness comes to assume quite special significance for the child. Not only does he feel empty himself, but he also interprets the situation in the sense that he has emptied his mother—particularly since deprivation has the effect not only of intensifying his oral need, but also imparting an aggressive quality to it. Deprivation has the additional effect of enlarging the field of his incorporative need" (p. 11).

The oral incorporative aspects of early interpersonal relations color introjections. This is addressed by Fairbairn (1952) in a rare bit of overstatement:[3]

> This process of internalization is promoted, if not actually instigated, by the very nature of the oral attitude itself; for the inherent aim of the oral impulse is incorporation. The incorporation in question is, of course, originally physical incorporation; but we must believe that the emotional mood accompanying incorporative strivings has itself an incorporative colouring. Hence, when a fixation [arrest of personality development at the primitive level] in the early oral phase [of infancy] occurs, an incorporative attitude inevitably becomes woven into the structure of the ego. (p. 18)

THE DANGEROUS, FRUSTRATING MOTHER

In the terminology of American object relations theory, the "emotional mood" of an interpersonal relationship is the intense and overwhelming affect experienced in early infancy that is internalized in the positive and negative introjects. The mother is perceived as dangerous and frustrating, denying oral gratification (Kernberg 1985A, p. 42). The purpose of the premature development of oedipal striving is to deny oral dependent needs (p. 41). The extreme frustrations and intense aggression of the early interpersonal experiences, primarily with the mother, lead to the premature development of genital striving typical of the oedipal situation as a means of escape: "At the same time, in an effort to escape from oral rage and fears, premature development of genital strivings takes place" (p. 41). In a densely worded summary statement in the terminology of object relations theory, Kernberg captures the essential developmental aspects of the borderline personality organization: "In summary, in both sexes *excessive development of pregenital, especially oral aggression tends to induce a premature development of oedipal strivings, and as a consequence a particular condensation between pregenital and genital aims under the overriding influence of aggressive needs*" (p. 43).

In the case of the little boy who would become a borderline personality organization as a chronologically adult person, the frustrating mother is characterized as *dangerous* and *castrating*: "Premature development of genital strivings in order to deny oral-dependent needs tends to fail because oedipal fears and prohibitions against sexual impulses toward the mother are powerfully reinforced by pregenital fears of the mother, and a typical image of a dangerous, castrating mother develops" (p. 41). The father's role in the family reinforces the fears and anxiety of the little boy: "The projection of pregenital aggression reinforces oedipal fears of the father and castration anxiety in particular, further reinforcing, in turn, pregenital aggression and fear" (p. 41).

In the case of the little girl who would become a borderline personality organization as a chronologically adult person, "Genital strivings for the father are used as a substitute gratification of oral-dependent needs that have been frustrated by the dangerous mother" (p. 42). The father's role is, again, one of reinforcing the dangerous and frustrating mother: "This effort tends to be undermined by the contamination of the father image with pregenital aggression deflected from the mother and projected onto him, and also because oral rage and especially oral envy powerfully reinforce penis envy in women" (p. 42).

Under the overriding influence of aggressive drive derivatives, the integration of whole object relations fails, and the child does not develop a whole and more realistic conception of the mother or the father. The differentiation of the mother and father is compromised, and the projection takes on a sadistic character: "Excessive pregenital and particularly oral aggression tends to be projected and causes a paranoid distortion of the early parental images, especially the mother. Through the projection of predominantly oral-sadistic but also anal-sadistic impulses, the mother is seen as potentially dangerous, and hatred of the mother extends to both parents, who are later experienced as a 'united group' by the child" (p. 41).

In addition to the failure of the integration of whole object relations, the realistic differentiation between the mother and father is compromised: "A 'contamination' of the father image by aggression primarily projected onto the mother and lack of differentiation between mother and father under the influence of lack of realistic differentiation of different objects under the influence of excessive splitting operations tend to produce, in both sexes, a combined and dangerous father-mother image" (p. 41).

HAUNTED BY THE RETURN OF BAD OBJECTS

At this point, I want to continue the analysis of the significance of frustration in early interpersonal relations, and the predominance of negative introjects and identifications, for personality organizations in the primitive range of the Personality Continuum. Under ordinary functioning, a person with a primitive personality organization has good reality testing at the level of differentiating the self from the object, representing the interpersonal achievement in personality development to recognize oneself as separate from other. This achievement does not represent the formation of firm ego boundaries, because there is no integrated ego or ego identity with the failure to achieve the integration of whole object relations at the primitive level of personality development. Under ordinary functioning at the primitive level of personality development, there are multiple separate selves and objects.

Under ordinary functioning, a person with a primitive personality organization can barely tolerate the already high level of anxiety in his or her everyday life. Under extraordinary functioning, additional anxiety breaks down the primitive defense of splitting, and the negative introjects and identifications return, persecuting the person with severe anxiety (Fairbairn 1952, pp. 9–10). The breakdown of splitting represents a regression to a lower level of personality development and a return to earlier patterns of behavior.

Just what emerges into consciousness when splitting breaks down? The all-bad, negative internal part-object relations, internalized through introjection and identification. But it is the return of the negative introjects that is the most frightening and dangerous. The negative introjects are the all-bad past internalized part-object relations, the negative aspects of the relatively enduring pattern of recurrent significant interpersonal situations that characterized early infancy, internalized through the process of introjection—self undifferentiated from object and affect intense and overwhelming. The reactivation of the negative introjects persecutes the person with severe anxiety. Severe anxiety is inside the person's head, the brain running endlessly in thought about the unfavorable appraisal of one's current activity by someone whose opinion is significant. The persecution of the punitive superego with severe anxiety is represented by thoughts of being worthless. When the primitive defense of splitting breaks down, severe anxiety becomes intolerable.

Because the self is undifferentiated from object, there is no boundary between self and object in interpersonal relations internalized through introjection in early infancy before the physiological maturation of the cognitive capacity to recognize oneself as separate from another object, before a separate self existed. This is the one significant interpersonal achievement in personality development achieved by a person with a personality organization at the primitive level of development.

What is frightening about the return of the negative introjects is the loss of the boundary between self and object, the loss of a sense of a separate self, the loss of separate self. There is no longer a separate self to defend. All defenses have broken down. In Fairbairn's chilling statement on the return of bad objects, the person is "haunted by bad objects against the return of which all defenses have broken down, and from which there is no escape (except in death)" (1952, p. 166).[4]

ONE POSITIVE INTROJECT AND ONE NEGATIVE INTROJECT

There is only one negative introject and one positive introject. In early infancy, the mother and father are introjected—the mother and father are internalized through the process of introjection. But there is only one positive introject and one negative introject as intrapsychic structures, with the self undifferentiated from the object, and the affect is intense and overwhelming.

Kernberg (1984A) referred to this stage of personality development as the *primary undifferentiated phase.* Since there are no boundaries between self and object, there is no separate mother, father, or infant. The positive and negative introjects are the intrapsychic structures that result from the introjection of the positive and negative relations with the mother and the father, along with any other significant person with whom the early infant has a relatively enduring pattern of recurrent interpersonal situations.

The positive and negative introjects are internalized completely separately, and the primary motivation for organizing these experiences together is the intense and overwhelming positive and negative affect. With introjection there is a clear primacy of affect over cognition. The cognitive capacity to see the mother as separate does not even exist in early infancy. Thus, as intrapsychic structures, there is only one positive introject and one negative introject; the contents of the positive and negative introjects represent introjections of the mother, the father, and any other significant person.

The positive introject represents the internalization of the earliest positive interpersonal relations, starting with the mother's breast and the tranquil quiet sense of well-being of the infant sated at the mother's breast. The introjection of the early infant's relationship with the mother's breast represents only one of the possible contents of the positive introject. It is tempting to call the positive introject the Big Tit. Likewise, there is only one negative introject, representing the oral frustration, rage, and aggression, and it would be tempting to call the negative introject the Big Bad Mother. But in both cases it is not mothers, as in multiple bad mothers internalized through identification with the self differentiated from object, because there is no conception of the mother as a separate object at this point in personality development, and even that is lost with the regression to the lower level of personality development for a person with a primitive personality organization.

In a surprisingly ironic way, the negative introject is the Big Bad Mother, because there is no boundary between the self and the object, and the regression to the lower level of introjection involves the loss of boundary between self and object, a psychotic regression. Fairbairn's interpretation of the Little Red Riding Hood myth is germane here: "In the story, it will be remembered, the little girl finds to her horror that the grandmother whom she loves has disappeared, and that she is left alone with her own incorporative need in the form of the devouring wolf. The tragedy of Little Red Riding Hood is the tragedy of the child in the early oral phase" (1952, p. 24). But the interpretation here is quite different in a significant respect: The little girl's dread terror of being devoured by the Big Bad Wolf is the fear of loss of self, the ultimate psychopathological disaster, a psychotic regression (p. 52). Substitute the Big Bad Object for wolf, and we have the negative introject.

THE FAILURE TO ACHIEVE THE INDEPENDENCE OF AFFECT AND COGNITION: THE INDEPENDENCE HYPOTHESIS

The independence of affect and cognition varies with the level of personality development. The borderline personality organization in the primitive range of the Personality Continuum represents a failure to achieve this independence: "The emancipation of cognitive functions is, of course, always a relative one, but rather severe failure of such an independent development occurs in the borderline personality organization" (Kernberg 1984A, p. 51).

When the normal neutralization and the modification of affect do not occur, affect remains intense and overwhelming, and these pure affective states influence thought processes: "Under these circumstances, thought processes remain strongly linked to 'nonmetabolized' identification systems, abstraction and generalization are interfered with, and the regressive pull of 'pure' affective states influences thought processes" (p. 51). The regressive pull of pure affective states will be explored again with the lure of addiction.

These "nonmetabolized" internal object relations are the positive and negative introjects, nonintegrated internalized early object images close to the surface, ready to erupt into consciousness at any time. In the language of object relations theory: "*The persistence of 'nonmetabolized' early introjections is the outcome of a pathological fixation of severely disturbed, early object relations*, a fixation which is intimately related to the pathological development of splitting. Splitting, in turn, interferes with the integration of self- and object-images and the depersonification of internalized object relations in general. Under these pathological circumstances, early nonintegrated object-images come to the surface" (p. 34). As a result, intense and overwhelming drive derivatives exist dangerously close to the *surface* of consciousness, "directly influencing all aspects of psychic life" (p. 50).

In a brief foray into addiction, Fairbairn (1952) referred to these early nonintegrated object images coming to the surface as the return of bad objects, specifically an intrapsychic structure he labeled the internal saboteur, which punishes the person with severe and intolerable anxiety. It is the return of bad objects that drives the person with a primitive personality organization to compulsive and, in the more extreme case, addictive behavior. The further symptom formation, alloplastic behavior, and ego regression manifested in the crude gratification of impulses, substitutive satisfaction in Fairbairn's (1952) sense, in compulsive and addictive consumption behavior is an escape from this persecution.

For a person with a primitive personality organization, the motivation for the compulsive or addictive consumption behavior is to restore the defense of splitting. This is done by regressively reactivating the positive introjects and the pure affective states that go with the earliest internalized object relations to escape from the return of the all-bad negative introject, which persecutes the person with severe anxiety.

SADISTIC SUPEREGO FORERUNNERS AND THE PUNITIVE SUPEREGO

The punitive superego persecutes the person who does not have a prohibitive superego and the capacity for experiencing guilt with severe anxiety. Splitting interferes with the integration of the higher levels of the superego, because it interferes "with the normal internalization of more realistic parental prohibitions and demands," or cultural prohibitions and prescriptions in Sullivan's terminology, which represent the contents of the prohibitive superego (Kernberg 1984A, p. 50). Instead, the person with a primitive personality organization has to resort to "primitive idealization [that] creates unrealistic, all-good and powerful object images, and this also affects negatively the development of the ego ideal and [prohibitive] superego" (Kernberg 1985A, p. 30). Further, splitting interferes with the integration of the ego: "One other consequence of all these developments is that both excessive splitting and the lack of superego integration interfere with further synthesis of the ego core" (Kernberg 1984A, p. 50).

The failure to integrate the prohibitive superego gives the punitive superego a sadistic character: "Failure of superego integration may occur at various levels. First, failure to integrate preoedipal superego forerunners interferes with the internalization of more realistic oedipal parental images and perpetuates the primitive, sadistic, and unintegrated quality of the superego" (Kernberg 1984A, p. 71). Quantitative factors determine the degree of this sadistic character of the unintegrated superego forerunners: "The stronger the pregenital frustration and aggression, the more predominant are these sadistic superego forerunners" (p. 71).

As a consequence, according to Kernberg (1985A), "These patients respond with an 'all or nothing' superego reaction instead of the normal, flexible one" (p. 143). A clinical judgment by Kernberg (1985A), based on his case material, bears out this oversensitivity to criticism by a person with a borderline personality organization: "It is remarkable to observe how some borderline patients with a harsh superego [i.e., punitive superego] who are quite paranoid and unrealistically oversensitive to reactions of others often show a complete lack of sensitivity and of self-appropriate criticism where uncertainty about their functioning would be appropriate; for example, when a failure in work is pointed out to them in a friendly way" (p. 143). Individuals with a borderline personality organization "react only if stronger criticism of them is expressed, but then with the experience of being cruelly attacked or persecuted" (p. 143). In other words, the borderline personality organization reacts to additional anxiety only if it overloads the defense of splitting.

For a chronologically adult person, arrested at the primitive level of personality development, higher-level intrapsychic structures are missing: "The normal integration of the ego ideal with other superego structures is missing, the forerunners of later value systems are missing, so is the precondition for the internalization of later superego components, mainly the more realistic parental images derived from the oedipal conflicts which normally constitute a major cement of superego integration" (Kernberg 1985A, p. 283; also see p. 36 on the borderline personality organization; Jacobson 1964). Thus, the prohibitive and the protective superego are missing.

Kernberg's Attempt at a Reformulation of Freud's "Id"

In his endeavor to incorporate all useful contributions to understanding human personality into American object relations theory, I do not agree with some aspects of Kernberg's (1984A) attempt to reformulate Freud's conception of the "id" (Kernberg 1984A, pp. 69–70). Freud (1933) considered the id to be the "dark, inaccessible part of our personality" and "a cauldron full of seething excitations" (p. 73). I do agree that the contents of the id are "the most frightening and disturbing units involving self- and object-images under the influence of primitive affect," but I do not agree that they "are repressed, and this interferes with their ultimate differentiation and integration within the total personality" (Kernberg 1984A, p. 70).

Kernberg's (1984A) reformulated id comes into existence after the integration of whole object relations, and it is repressed, a defense that comes into existence only after the integration of whole object relations. If the integration of whole object relations has been achieved in personality development, the synthetic function of the ego brings the partial, all-good and all-bad self- and object images together to form whole and more realistic images of another person and oneself. Good and bad mean more realistic, but not perfect. Only then does repression become the predominant defense over splitting, and only then can the intense and overwhelmingly negative interpersonal relations internalized in the all-bad part-object relations be repressed.

Kernberg's reformulated id, therefore, pertains to neurotic personality organizations in the neurotic range of the Personality Continuum and not to primitive personality organizations in the primitive range of the Personality Continuum. Kernberg (1984A) describes the reformulated id and its contents "as an overall intrapsychic structure containing the sum of those internalized object relations which are unacceptable because of the dangerous, anxiety- and guilt-producing experiences" (p. 70). It only applies to personality organizations at a neurotic and normal level of personality development, with an integrated prohibitive superego with the capacity for experiencing guilt, and an integrated ego with the capacity for experiencing concern. Prior to the integration of whole object relations, repression is not an available defense.

Confusion results, however, whenever levels of personality development are transcended without explicit acknowledgment, in this case, descending to the qualitatively different primitive level of personality development. At that level, the primitive defense of splitting predominates, and the integration of whole object relations has not been achieved because of the preponderance of negative over positive interpersonal relations and internal object relations. Positive and negative introjections and identifications have not been integrated; "the overall organization of identifications and introjections under the guiding principle of the synthetic function of the ego" has not taken place (Kernberg 1984A, p. 32).

Where is the id now? When Kernberg (1984A) writes that the "primitive, unrealistic self- and object-representations remain relatively unchanged in the id, and so do the correspondingly primitive, overwhelming affect dispositions," he is clearly describing the contents of the punitive superego, "the most frightening and disturbing units involving self- and object-images under the influence of primitive affect" (p. 70). In this interpretation, at the primitive level of personality development, the id is the punitive superego. The confusion results from blurring the levels of personality development, because everything depends on the level of personality development. The id is the punitive superego for both neurotic and primitive personality organizations. The neurotic range of the Personality Continuum represents a higher level of personality development than the primitive range. For a person with a neurotic personality organization, the punitive superego is at a lower level of intrapsychic structural formation and the prohibitive superego is at a higher level, along with the higher-level human capacity for guilt and concern. The point here is that the punitive superego is repressed in neurotic personality organizations, but for the primitive personality, the punitive superego exists dangerously close to consciousness, persecuting the person with severe anxiety.

Fairbairn's Internal Saboteur

Fairbairn's (1952) internal saboteur is also the punitive superego, and he abandoned the id. According to Fairbairn:

> The "internal saboteur" is unlike the "super-ego" in that it is conceived as, in itself, devoid of all moral significance. Thus I do not attribute the affect of guilt to its activity, although this activity is unquestionably a prolific source of anxiety. Such anxiety may, of course, merge with guilt; but the two affects are theoretically distinct. Here it should be noted that, whilst introducing the conception of the internal saboteur, I am not prepared to abandon the conception of the super-ego as I now come to abandon the id. On the contrary, it seems to me impossible to offer any satisfactory psychological explanation of guilt in the absence of the super-ego; but the super-ego must be regarded as originating at a higher level of mental organization than that at which the internal saboteur operates. (p. 107)

The punitive superego is the internal saboteur, devoid of guilt, with no affect of guilt, and guilt is not anxiety. There is no prohibitive superego and, therefore, no capacity for experiencing guilt. The punitive superego is devoid of all moral significance—a moral system represents the contents of the prohibitive superego. It is the return of the all-bad objects, the Vague "they," that persecute the person with severe anxiety.

The end of this exegesis is that the id in Kernberg's reformulation is the punitive superego, and Fairbairn's internal saboteur is also the punitive superego. The contents of the punitive superego are the (nonmetabolized) internal part-object relations that are all negative, both introjections and identifications. According to Kernberg (1984A), "The repressed portion of the id would possess an internal organization, as well as specific structures composed of self-image, object-image and unacceptable impulse components" (p. 43).

The aspect Freud (1933) described as "a cauldron full of seething excitations" reflects the intense and overwhelming nature of early affective experience (p. 73). When one considers Freud's most cogent characterization of the id, the parallels are clear: "The id of course knows no judgements of value: no good and evil, no morality. The economic or, if you prefer, the quantitative factor, which is intimately linked to the pleasure principle, dominates all its processes" (p. 74).

The contents remain the same. What changes is the level of personality development. Everything depends on the level of personality development, defined by the level of intrapsychic structural formation and the predominant defense against severe anxiety. For the neurotic personality organization, the punitive superego represents a lower level and an earlier stage of personality development; it has been repressed. According to Kernberg (1984A): "Let us now contrast splitting and repression as defensive operations. Freud (1915A) stated that 'the essence of repression lies simply in turning something away, and keeping it at a distance, from the conscious' " (p. 43).

Although this salvages some aspects of the id in Freud's 1933 conception, as the "dark, inaccessible part of our personality" (p. 73), it is only inaccessible to the person with a neurotic personality organization. For the person with a primitive personality organization, the punitive superego is on the surface when the defense of splitting breaks down.

Sullivan's Not-Me

To this effort to relate the punitive superego, Freud's id and Kernberg's attempt at reformulating it, and Fairbairn's internal saboteur, we can now add Sullivan's not-me. According to Sullivan (1953), the not-me is always relatively primitive, made up of poorly grasped aspects of living that will presently be regarded as dreadful: "This rudimentary personification of not-me evolves very gradually, since it comes from experience of intense anxiety" (p. 163), although the not-me is internalization through identification, because the self is differentiated from the object, and not earlier introjection (p. 164).

The integration key concepts from different theoretical perspectives at the crossroad, just as Kernberg said, and the language and terminology of object relations theory facilitates this integration. The Personality Continuum is a monument to the integration facilitated by the "middle language" of psychoanalytic object relations theory of the personality (see Kernberg 1984A, pp. 56–59).

SEVERE ANXIETY: A SUDDEN BLOW ON THE HEAD

How could anyone endure such severe anxiety? According to Sullivan (1953), "When anxiety is severe, it has almost the effect of a blow on the head; one isn't really clear on the exact situation in which the anxiety occurred" (p. 300). The circumstances of the situation immediately surrounding the occurrence of severe anxiety are obliterated: "And this severe anxiety, as I have said before, has a little bit the effect of a blow on the head, in that later one is not clear at all as to just what was going on at the time anxiety became intense" (p. 160).

Severe anxiety is sudden and intense because the primitive defense of splitting breaks down and leaves the person defenseless. When the primitive defense of splitting is working, severe anxiety is not experienced by the person. The experience of severe anxiety is sudden because of the breakdown of splitting, and it is intense because the affect of introjection is intense and overwhelming

Have you ever had the experience of having someone whose opinion is significant to you say something to your face that is truthful and at the same time very painful, yet you cannot remember immediately afterward exactly what was said? You know it was true, but you just cannot consciously recall exactly what was said. But you will remember later; maybe days, maybe years, or even decades later, what was said will come back to you, either during a vulnerable time when your defenses are down or when you have grown to the point where you can accept the criticism.

According to Sullivan (1953), "The sudden occurrence of severe anxiety practically prohibits any clear prehension, or understanding, of the immediate situation. It does not, however, preclude recall, and as recall develops sufficiently so that one recalls what was about to occur when severe anxiety intervened—in other words, when one has a sense of what one's action was addressed to at the time when everything was disorganized by severe anxiety" (pp. 160–161). There is little information to be elaborated into foresight for the future as a result of this practically obliterative sudden severe anxiety (p. 161):

> It is a peculiarity of the difference between anxiety and fear that, under fortunate circumstances, the factors in the situation in which one was hurt can be observed, analyzed, identified, and incorporated in foresight for the future, while in the case of anxiety that is only relatively true, at best; and if the anxiety is very severe, it has, as I have said before, almost the effect of a blow on the head. Thus one has very little data on which to work in the future—we might almost say there is nothing in particular to be elaborated into information and foresight. (p. 205)

Foresight, however, is not a human capacity characteristic of individuals with a primitive personality organization, who do not learn from their mistakes, because they do not foresee the consequences of their behavior and stumble blindly into situations fraught with sudden severe anxiety, like a blow on the head.

NOTES

1. It should not be surprising that the earliest statement of Fairbairn's hypothesis is attributed to Freud. In his brilliant lectures on the psychology of the human life cycle, George W. Goethals would often say that "Freud said everything," and that "there was nothing new under the sun."

2. This evokes Aristotle's notion of "akrasia"—the weakness of will, which has been drawn upon by Sen (1977, p. 340) and Winston (1980, p. 295) as a possible explanation for compulsive and addictive consumption behavior.

3. Fairbairn writes with such precision in his essays collected in *Psychoanalytic Studies of the Personality* (1952) that it is easy to forget just how complex personality organizations arrested at the lower levels of development are in reality. In a similar vein, Sullivan's lectures, transcribed in *The Interpersonal Theory of Psychiatry* (1953), are so crisply operational (or observational) that they seem to be a perfect picture of reality. Kernberg, standing on the shoulders of these great theorists, combines precision with all the complexity of human personality. George Goethals, my mentor in psychology, once compared reading Kernberg's writing to reading fudge. It is this rich detail that makes the reading so rewarding. I would prefer *thick*, as in thick description.

4. Despair, the loss of hope in this situation, the belief that nothing will ever

change, can lead to suicide. Kurt Cobain, denied the escape from severe anxiety granted by heroin, was driven to end his life by blowing his head off with a shotgun to terminate the thoughts and stop the persecution. I have a Kurt Cobain poster, a portrait with the caption "I hate myself, and I want to die." That is despair—the loss of all hope. Sullivan (1956) characterized despair in this way: "Thus in despair there is a feeling of total, utter isolation and utter incapacity to do anything that would change an exceedingly undesirable situation favorably" (p. 352).

PART III

COMPARATIVE ANALYSIS OF PERSONALITY ORGANIZATIONS

Chapter 10

W.R.D. Fairbairn, the Schizoid Personality Organization, and British Object Relations Theory

Fairbairn's conception of the schizoid personality organization has illuminated the origins of British object relations theory: "What has convinced me of the paramount importance of the object-relationship is the analysis of patients displaying schizoid characteristics; for it is in such individuals that difficulties over relationships with objects present themselves most clearly" (p. 39). In Fairbairn's theoretical conception of the schizoid personality organization, the basic character constellation is comprised of three common characteristics: a preoccupation with inner reality, an attitude of isolation and detachment, and an attitude of omnipotence and superiority (p. 6). To this characterization, Fairbairn added this caveat concerning the complexity of the schizoid personality organization:

> It is important, however, to bear in mind that these characteristics are by no means necessarily overt. Thus the attitude of omnipotence may be conscious or unconscious in any degree. It may also be localized within certain spheres of operation. It may be over-compensated and concealed under a superficial attitude of inferiority or humility; and it may be consciously cherished as a precious secret. Similarly the attitude of isolation and detachment may be masked by a façade of sociability or by the adoption of specific roles; and it may be accompanied by considerable emotionality in certain contexts. (pp. 6–7)

FAIRBAIRN'S PORTRAIT OF THE CHRONOLOGICALLY ADULT PERSON WITH A SCHIZOID PERSONALITY ORGANIZATION

For a chronologically adult person with a schizoid personality organization, Fairbairn (1952) regarded the preoccupation with inner reality as "undoubtedly the most important of all schizoid characteristics" (p. 7). In his seminal contribution to British object relations theory, "Schizoid Factors in the Personality" (1940), Fairbairn described the fascination with intellectual pursuits for a person with a schizoid personality organization:

> It is further to be noted that intellectual pursuits as such, whether literary, artistic, scientific, or otherwise, appear to exercise a special attraction for individuals possessing schizoid characteristics to one degree or another. Where scientific pursuits are concerned, the attraction would appear to depend upon the schizoid individual's attitude of detachment no less than upon his over-valuation of the thought processes; for these are both characteristics which readily lend themselves to capitalization within the field of science. (Fairbairn 1952, p. 6)

The caricature of the absent-minded professor, preoccupied with his own internal thought processes, is a typical schizoid personality organization. In individuals with a schizoid personality organization, meaning tends to be derived from the internal world:

> In the case of an individual with a schizoid component in their personality, accordingly, there is a great tendency for the outer world to derive its meaning too exclusively from the inner world. In actual schizophrenics [a psychotic, as opposed to a primitive, personality organization] this tendency may become so strong that the distinction between inner and outer reality is largely obscured. Such extreme cases apart, however, there is a general tendency on the part of individuals with a schizoid component to heap up their values on the inner world. (p. 18)

Schizoid individuals experience great difficulty with giving emotionally in interpersonal relationships because it makes them feel impoverished: "In the case of individuals whose object-relationships are predominantly in the inner world, giving has the effect of depreciating values, and of lowering self-respect. When such individuals give, they tend to feel impoverished, because, when they give, they give at the expense of their inner world" (p. 18). "Such individuals," according to Fairbairn, "are commonly described as 'shut in personalities'; and, in view of the extent to which they keep their emotional contents shut in, the description is singularly apt" (p. 15).

For a person with a schizoid personality organization, giving genuine human emotion means "parting with something too *precious* to be lost" (p. 15). This makes contact in social situations exhausting: "This overvaluation of mental contents shows itself, for example, in the difficulty experienced by the individual with a schizoid tendency over expressing emotions in a social context. For such an individual, that element of giving which is involved in expressing emotion towards others has the significance of losing contents; and it is for this reason that he so often finds social contacts exhausting" (p. 15).

Fairbairn (1952) describes the defense of substitution of showing for giving often utilized by schizoid artists and authors:

> An artist may defend himself against a sense of loss of contents by continuing to regard his pictures as his own possessions, in an unrealistic sense, even after they have been acquired by others. In this connection, reference may be made again to that form of defence, which consists in a substitution of showing for giving. The artist "shows" or exhibits his pictures, of course; and, in so doing, he reveals himself indirectly. Similarly, the author reveals himself to the world from a distance through the medium of his books. The various arts thus provide very favorable channels of expression for individuals with a schizoid tendency. For by means of artistic activity they are able both to substitute showing for giving and, at the same time, to produce something which they can still regard as part of themselves even after it has passed from the inner into the outer world. (pp. 19–20)

To defend against this loss, Fairbairn's case of a schizoid artist treated what he had created as worthless:

> To mitigate a sense of impoverishment following giving and creating, the individual with a schizoid component often employs an interesting defence. He adopts an attitude that what he has given or created is worthless. Thus, the artist whose case has just been quoted lost all interest in his pictures once they had been painted; and the completed pictures were characteristically either dumped in the corner of the studio or treated simply as commodities for sale. (p. 19)

In character with the chaotic pattern of alternating and contradictory behavior of all primitive personality organizations, "On the other hand, a totally opposite form of defence against loss of contents may be adopted by individuals with schizoid attributes; for they may attempt to safeguard themselves against a sense of loss by treating what they have produced as if it were still part of their own contents" (Fairbairn 1952, p. 19). An analogous phenomenon within a more mental sphere, according to Fairbairn (1952), "may be illustrated in the case of an artist who, after completing a picture, used to feel, not that he had created or gained something as a result, but that virtue has gone out of him. Such a phenomenon goes a long way to explain the periods of sterility and discontent which follows periods of creative activity in the case of certain artists, and which did so in the case of the artist to whom I have referred" (p. 19).

The Attitude of Detachment: The Divorce of Thought and Feeling

The attitude of detachment—the divorce of thought and feeling—often leaves the individual with a schizoid personality organization utterly devoid of affect: "In the case of those with whom the schizoid tendency is marked, defence against emotional loss gives rise to *repression of affect* and an attitude of detachment which leads others to regard them as remote—and, in more extreme cases, even as inhuman" (Fairbairn 1952, p. 15).

The use of the concept of repression for a personality organization at a primitive level of personality development, however, is not apt for American object relations theory. Primitive personality organizations cannot resort to the higher-level neurotic defense of repression. Fairbairn tentatively makes this distinction in "A Revised Psychopathology of the Psychoses and Psychoneuroses" (1941): "Whether such a mass-withdrawal of libido can properly be ascribed to repression is a debatable question, although where the process is restricted to a withdrawal from object relationships it gives that impression" (Fairbairn 1952, p. 51).

Fairbairn is using "libido" diffusely to mean simply good, positive, satisfying, loving relations that have been frustrated by the mother (who becomes dangerous and frightening). By libido Fairbairn does not mean sexual or genital aims, as yet. According to Guntrip (1973), Fairbairn "later gave up the use of the term 'libido' for the same reason and spoke always of the libidinal ego" (p. 34).

What is the "libidinal ego" in the terminology of American object relations theory? Fairbairn's concept of the *libidinal object* is related to the *positive introject*, since it represents the mother's breasts, and the *antilibidinal object* is related to the *punitive superego*. According to Kernberg (1984A), "These early, sadistically determined superego forerunners probably correspond to Melanie Klein's primitive, sadistic superego and to Fairbairn's antilibidinal object" (p. 71).

Rather than argue that the unconscious repression of affect follows in the train of the preoccupation with the inner world of the schizoid personality organization, it would have been more precise to describe the process as the withdrawal of affect, a conscious choice made by the person with a schizoid personality organization. Thus by replacing repression with withdrawal, Fairbairn's conception of a schizoid personality organization can be restated in the following way: "Owing to the preoccupation with the inner world and the withdrawal of affect which follows in its train, he has difficulty expressing his feelings naturally and spontaneously in his relations with them. This leads him to make an effort to work out his emotional problems intellectually in the inner world" (Fairbairn 1952, p. 20).

Fairbairn provided the following clinical observations of manifestations of the splitting processes in individuals with a schizoid personality organization: "Amongst other schizoid phenomena which may be mentioned here are a sense of being wasted, a sense of unreality, intense self-consciousness and a sense of looking at oneself. Taken together, these various phenomena clearly indicate that an actual splitting of the ego has occurred" (p. 51). Further, according to Fairbairn:

> On the basis of an analytical study of cases belonging to the various categories which have now been mentioned, it becomes possible to recognize as essentially schizoid not only such phenomena as full-fledged depersonalization and derealization, but also relatively minor or transient disturbances of the reality-sense, e.g. feelings of "artificiality" (whether referred to the self or the environment), experiences as "plate-glass feeling," feelings of unfamiliarity with familiar persons or environmental settings, and feelings of familiarity with the unfamiliar. Allied to the sense of familiarity with the unfamiliar is the experience of "déjà vu"—an interesting phenomenon which must likewise be regarded as involving a schizoid process. (p. 5)

Depersonalization represents a regression in an interpersonal relationship: "This type of regressive process may perhaps best be described as *Depersonalization of the Object*; and it is characteristically accompanied by a regression in the quality of the relationship desired. Here again the regressive movement is in the interests of a simplification of relationships; and it takes the form of a substitution of bodily for emotional contacts. It may perhaps be described as *De-emotionalization of the Object-relationship*" (p. 14).

The attitude of detachment in a person with a schizoid personality organization represents an extreme manifestation of the divorce between thought and feeling characteristic in varying degrees of all personality organizations in the primitive range of the Personality Continuum. In Fairbairn's view, the divorce between thought and feeling is based fundamentally upon a split within the ego (p. 21). In the terminology of American object relations theory, the primitive defense of splitting against severe anxiety is characteristic of all personality organizations in the primitive range of the Personality Continuum.

Affect and Cognition: Divorce of Thought from Feeling and the Independence Hypothesis

The attitude of detachment raises the debate on the primacy of affect or cognition. In the field of marketing, this goes with the independence hypothesis—the independence of affect and cognition. Affect and cognition vary qualitatively with the level of personality development.

At the primitive level of personality development, the attitude of detachment is manifested as a conscious divorce of thought and feeling. The ideation and impulse are both consciously experienced, but not together. It is imperative to keep in mind that this is a chapter on Fairbairn's theoretical conception of the schizoid personality, a primitive, not a neurotic, personality organization. The schizoid personality organization represents the extreme in the degree of isolation and detachment within the primitive range of the Personality Continuum.

At the neurotic level of personality development, the repression of affect and ideation results in no conscious thought or actual affective experience, but a residual anxiety as a warning signal of danger in the situation. The analysis of the unconscious processing of information previously presented, and the analysis of subliminal stimuli to be presented subsequently, clearly pertain to personality organizations at the neurotic level of personality development. The unconscious processing of subliminal stimuli embedded in an advertisement leaves the person hyperalert to the supraliminal elements of the advertisement, that is, the explicit elements pertaining to the image of the brand.

We look away from images that offend us in general, not just in advertising. We do not want to look into the model's crotch along with the camera. Our attention is selective because our defenses are effective in protecting us from the unwanted stimuli in the environment we do not want to know about, or be consciously aware of, or even be exposed to; however, these things do exist in the unconscious. We can hold contradictory ideas simultaneously in the unconscious (Freud 1915B).

In a similar way, Adam Smith, in *The Theory of Moral Sentiments* (1759), described how we do not want to look at the poor: "They turn their eyes away, or if the extremity of his distress forces them to look at him, it is only to spurn so disagreeable an object from among them. The fortunate and the proud wonder at the insolence of human wretchedness, that it should dare to present itself before them, and with the loathsome aspect of its misery presume to disturb the serenity of their happiness" (pp. 113–114). "The poor man," according to Smith, "is ashamed of his poverty" (p. 113).

Positive Intention behind the Schizoid Person's Attempt to Solve Emotional Problems

Fairbairn (1952) saw a positive interpersonal intention behind the schizoid person's adaptive behavior in trying to solve his emotional problems in the internal world:

> It would appear that, so far as conscious intention is concerned, his attempts to solve his emotional problems intellectually are meant in the first instance to pave the way for adaptive behavior in relation to external objects; but since emotional conflicts springing from deep sources in the unconscious defy solution in this way, he tends increasingly to substitute intellectual solutions of his emotional problems for attempts to achieve a practical solution of them within the emotional sphere in his relationships with others in the outer world. (p. 20)

This is not the stumbling out of restlessness into interpersonal situations that offer some relief from loneliness that Sullivan (1953) equated with preadolescence, because for loneliness to motivate a person's behavior, at least a neurotic level of personality development must have been achieved. Nonetheless, the positive intention behind the schizoid person's adaptive behavior is that it may provide an opportunity for fortunate interpersonal experience and perhaps a relatively enduring interpersonal relationship.

This intellectualization intensifies the extent of the splitting processes: "It would seem, however, that withdrawal of libido from external objects has the result of intensifying not only the effects of the splitting process, but the actual extent of the splitting process itself" (Fairbairn 1952, p. 51). The withdrawal of affect reduces the person with a schizoid personality organization to a state of utter impotence:

> Failure to direct libido towards the object is, of course, equivalent to loss of the object; but, since, from the point of view of the schizoid individual, libido itself seems destructive, the object is equally lost when libido *is* directed towards it. It can thus readily be understood that, if the dilemma becomes sufficiently, pronounced, the result is a complete *impasse*, which reduces the ego to a state of utter impotence. (p. 51)

Futility is the characteristic affect of an individual with a schizoid personality organization. Fairbairn (p. 113) describes the futility of a schizoid person as exploding ineffectively into an emotional vacuum and provides the following clinical observation from a case study of a person with a schizoid personality organization:

> The ego becomes quite incapable of expressing itself; and, in so far as this is so, its very existence becomes compromised. This is well exemplified by the following remarks of a patient of mine during an analytical session: "I can't say anything. I have nothing to say. I am empty. There's nothing of me. . . . I feel quite useless; I haven't done anything. . . . I've gone quite cold and hard; I don't feel anything. . . . I can't express myself; I feel futile." (p. 51)

"The last quoted remark of this patient," according to Fairbairn, "is perhaps particularly significant as drawing attention to the characteristic state; for *the characteristic affect of the schizoid state is undoubtedly a sense of futility*" (p. 51).

An individual with a schizoid personality organization is constantly struggling with the loss of the ego, according to Fairbairn:

> *Loss of ego* is the ultimate psychological disaster which the schizoid individual is constantly struggling, with more or with less success, to avert by exploiting all available techniques (including transitional techniques) for the control of his libido. In essence, therefore, the schizoid state is not a defence, although evidence of the presence of defences may be detected in it. It represents the major disaster which may befall the individual who has failed to outgrow the early oral phase of dependence. (pp. 52–53)

The loss of one's ego is poignantly rendered by Brian Wilson of the Beach Boys in the song titled "Hang on to Your Ego." On his masterpiece, *Pet Sounds* (1966), the lyrics to this song were changed to "I Know There's an Answer." When the compact disc was reissued, "Hang on to Your Ego" was released as a bonus track. Here are the original opening lyrics:

I know so many people who think they can do it alone.
They isolate their heads and stay in their safety zone.
But what can you tell them?
What can you say that won't make them defensive.
Hang on to your ego,
Hang on, but I know that you're going to lose the fight.

This is an expression of the extreme attitude of detachment and isolation and the loss of the ego, the ultimate psychopathological disaster. The alternative lyrics are, "I know there's an answer. I know now but I had to find it by myself." Poignantly for Brian Wilson, the answer was "I know that you're going to lose the fight." *Good Vibrations*, the Beach Boys boxed set, contains recordings of alternate takes of various tracks for the sessions that went into making "Hang on to Your Ego." Before one take, Wilson first refers to it as "Let Go of Your Ego" and before the next take jokingly refers to it as "Let Go of Your Libido," mispronouncing "libido."

In the awkward early 1960s, Brian Wilson sized up the zeitgeist of his times and captured it in a music so compelling it could not be ignored. In the process, he created the California Myth based on surfin', so to speak. With an almost innocent sexuality, it was short-lived and was eclipsed by the more sexually explicit rock revolution of the 1964 British invasion and the Beatles.

DEVELOPMENTAL HISTORY: DYNAMIC ANALYSIS OF THE SCHIZOID PERSONALITY ORGANIZATION

The orientation toward partial objects is a characteristic feature of the schizoid personality organization. In the following statement, Fairbairn (1952) delves deeply into the developmental history of the person who would become a schizoid personality organization as an adult:

Here it may be remarked that the orientation towards partial objects found in individuals displaying schizoid features is largely a regressive phenomenon determined by unsatisfactory emotional relationships with their parents, and particularly their mothers, at a stage in childhood subsequent to the early oral phase in which this orientation originates. The type of mother who is specially prone to provoke such a regression is the mother who fails to convince her child by spontaneous and genuine expressions of affection that she herself loves him as a person. Both possessive mothers and indifferent mothers fall into this category. Worst of all perhaps is the mother who conveys the impression of both possessiveness and indifference—e.g. the devoted mother who is determined at all costs not to spoil her only son. Failure on the part of the mother to convince the child that she really loves him as a person renders it difficult for him to sustain an emotional relationship with her on a personal basis; and the result is that, in order to simplify the situation, he tends regressively to restore the relationship to its earlier and simpler form and revive his relationship to his mother's breast as a partial object. (p. 13)

Possessive mothers, according to Fairbairn (1952), are unable to see their children as separate persons: "Thus, so far from being indifferent to her child once he is born, a mother may continue to regard him in light of her own contents and to overvalue him accordingly. Such mothers are unduly possessive of their children and are unable to accord them the status of separate persons—with grievous consequences for the unfortunate children" (p. 19).

Regressive Reactivation of the Early Infant's Relationship with the Mother's Breast

The relationship of the early infant with the mother's breast can be regressively reactivated later in interpersonal situations fraught with frustration: "Regressive reinstatement of the early oral attitude would appear to be most readily brought about by a situation of emotional frustration in which the child comes to feel (*a*) that he is not really loved for himself as a person by his mother, and (*b*) that his own love for his mother is not really valued and accepted by her" (Fairbairn 1952, p. 17). "The net result," according to Fairbairn, "is that the child tends to transfer his relationships with his objects to the realm of inner reality" (p. 18). The secret possession of such internalized objects leads to feelings of being different for the person with a schizoid personality organization:

The secret possession of such internalized objects has the effect of leading the individual to feel that he is "different" from other people—even if not, as often happens, actually exceptional or unique. When this sense of difference from others is investigated, however, it is found to be closely associated with a sense of being the "odd man out"; and, with individuals in whom it is present, dreams embodying the theme of being left out are a common occurrence. Such an individual is only too frequently found to have been the boy who, although apparently his mother's boy at home, was anything but a boys' boy at school, and who devoted to personal achievement in study the energy which more ordinary boys devoted to participation in school games. Sometimes, it is true, personal achievement may have been sought within the realm of sport. Even so, however, there is usually evidence to show that there has been difficulty over

> emotional relationships within the group; in any case, it remains true that it is towards attainment within the intellectual sphere that attempts to circumvent such difficulties are more commonly directed. Here we can already detect evidence of the operation of the intellectual defence; and it is remarkable how often the previous history of an actual schizophrenic [a psychotic, not a primitive personality organization] reveals that he (or she) was regarded as a promising scholar during some part at least of his (or her) school career. (pp. 22–23)

Kernberg (1985A) has made a similar observation with regard to the narcissistic personality organization, also a primitive personality organization: "Quite frequently these are the 'promising' geniuses who then surprise other people by the banality of their development" (p. 230).

In Sullivan's interpersonal conception of the schizoid personality organization, such unfortunate early interpersonal experience leads to a strikingly isolated way of life:

> Isolated juveniles, people whom one would expect to go on indefinitely in a rather "schizoid" way of life, sometimes, by very fortunate preadolescent experience, come out remarkably well able to handle themselves, to develop the social accommodation which did not really reach them in the juvenile period; and this is because of the peculiarly intimate consensual exchange which goes on in preadolescence. On the other hand, social isolation may make it very difficult to establish the type of intimacy which preadolescence calls for; and it may often delay preadolescence so that there is only a brief time, before the puberty change, in which to consolidate the benefits of the preadolescent period. (p. 254)

In the absence of such fortunate interpersonal experience in the preadolescent stage of personality development, Sullivan (1964) argued that even puberty can be delayed, especially in the case of the person with a schizoid personality organization: "Even internists recognize the condition of delayed puberty; it happens to coincide statistically very closely with what I as a psychiatrist describe as a schizoid type of interpersonal relations. Both the latter and the former, I believe, are explicable as a result of what are ordinarily called strongly repressive influences applied much earlier in life to operations and thought pertaining to the genital regions and genital acts" (p. 225).

By *repressive*, Sullivan (1964) is referring to interpersonal influences: "Thus puberty, the appearance of lust in the human, the furthest very dramatic maturation from birth, is much more susceptible of disturbance in its timing than other maturation of things that come earlier" (p. 225). Sullivan concluded that "what would certainly be described as purely interpersonal influences, interpersonal manifestations of cultural views, and so on, have a marked effect on the maturation rate" (p. 225). This reinforces the basic view in object relations theory, first espoused by Fairbairn, that problems of personality in the primitive range are primarily interpersonal and not physiological in origin.[1]

The Attitude of Superiority

The attitude of superiority, characteristically found in the chronologically adult person with a schizoid personality organization, is based on an orientation toward internalized objects and represents ego weakness:

> We invariably find an attitude of superiority which may manifest itself in consciousness to varying degrees as an actual sense of superiority. It should be noticed, however, that this attitude of superiority is based upon an orientation towards internalized objects, and in relation to objects in the world of outer reality the basic attitude of the schizoid individual is essentially one of inferiority. It is true that the externally oriented inferiority may be masked by a façade of superiority based upon an identification of external with internalized objects. Nevertheless, it is always present; and it is evidence of ego weakness. (Fairbairn 1952, pp. 50–51)

The secret sources of the sense of superiority for a person with a schizoid personality organization are summarized in a succinct statement by Fairbairn: "When its sources are uncovered, however, this sense of superiority is found to be based upon: (1) a general *secret* over-valuation of personal contents, mental as well as physical; and (2) a narcissistic inflation of the ego arising out of *secret* possession of, and considerable identification with, internalized libidinal objects (e.g., the maternal breast and the paternal penis)" (p. 22).

The identification with internal objects is the basis for the secretive and mysterious air of markedly schizoid individuals: "Here it would be difficult to exaggerate the importance of the element of *secrecy*. It is this that accounts for the secretive and mysterious air so commonly displayed by markedly schizoid individuals; but, even in the case of those in whom the schizoid component plays a relatively minor part, it still remains an important factor in the unconscious situation" (p. 22). In referring to "those in whom the schizoid component plays a relatively minor part," Fairbairn is distinguishing between the schizoid personality organization and a personality organization with a schizoid feature as a component and, therefore, exhibiting schizoid tendencies in behavior.

INTRAPSYCHIC STRUCTURE OF THE SCHIZOID PERSONALITY ORGANIZATION

In Fairbairn's conception of the schizoid personality organization, the inner necessity for secrecy is "in no small measure determined by fear of the loss of internalized objects which appear infinitely precious (even as precious as life itself), and the internalization of which is a measure of the importance and the extent of dependence upon them" (p. 22). There is a strong tendency to identify with internal objects: "Not only do their objects tend to belong to the inner rather than the outer world, but they tend to identify themselves very strongly with their internal objects. This fact contributes materially to the difficulty which they experience in giving emotionally" (p. 18). The strong identification with internal objects too precious to be lost is the key feature of Fairbairn's conception of the intrapsychic structure of the schizoid personality organization.

The dependence on internal objects represents the early attitude of infantile dependence. In the transition from infantile to mature dependence, the self becomes differentiated from the object, and I would add the further clarification that the integration of whole object relations has been achieved. This clarification is not as apparent in Fairbairn (1952) because he devoted his considerable intellect to investigating the schizoid personality organization, a simpler structure at the very bottom of the primitive range of the Personality Continuum.

This clarification is useful in understanding the following statement by Fairbairn on the failure to achieve mature dependence:

> It emerges clearly from the study of individuals with schizoid tendencies that the most characteristic feature of the state of infantile dependence is *primary identification with the object*. Indeed, it would not be going too far to say that, psychologically speaking, identification with the object and infantile dependence are but two aspects of the same phenomenon. On the other hand, mature dependence involves a relationship between two independent individuals, who are completely *differentiated* from one another as mutual objects. (pp. 41–42)

Fairbairn followed this statement with a conclusion on mature dependence that sounds somewhat cynical: "The relationship involved in mature dependence is, of course, only theoretically possible" (p. 42). While this is certainly the case for the schizoid personality organization, it is not true for the normal person who has achieved the integration of whole object relations and has the capacity to accept another person, and oneself, as both good and bad and, therefore, a whole and more realistic person. "Nevertheless," according to Fairbairn, "it remains true that *the more mature a relationship is, the less it is characterized by primary identification*; for what such identification essentially represents is failure to differentiate the object" (p. 42).

"I employ the term '*primary identification*' here," states Fairbairn, "to signify the cathexis of an object which has not yet been differentiated from the cathecting subject" (p. 34). Translated into the terminology of American object relations theory, this means an identification with the positive introject internalized through introjection. The positive introject represents the internalized all-good, all-loving, and all-forgiving mother and is essentially an internalization of the relationship with the mother's breast as a partial object—the self has not been differentiated from the object, and the affect is intense and overwhelming—the Big Tit.

The early oral situation of the infant is a relationship with the mother's breast as a partial object. The early infant lacks the physiological capacity to see the mother as a separate object, let alone as a whole object or a real person:

> Although the emotional relationship involved is essentially one between the child and his mother as a person, and although it must be recognized that his libidinal object is really his mother as a whole, nevertheless his libidinal interest is essentially focused upon her breast; and the result is that, in proportion as disturbances in the relationship occur, the breast itself tends to assume the form of a bodily organ or *partial object* (in contrast to that of a person or whole object). (p. 11)

In early infancy, according to Fairbairn, "the libidinal situation is one that confers tremendous significance upon states of *fullness and emptiness*" (p. 11). The theme of the subjective experience of emptiness will be dealt with in greater depth subsequently in the discussion of the narcissistic personality organization and the analysis of addictive consumer behavior.

The identification with internal objects is a regressive phenomenon representing a return to what Fairbairn (p. 23) described as an attitude of the early oral phase. Since the infant's relationship is largely with the mother's breast in the early oral phase, this means "regressively to restore the relationship to its earlier and simpler form and revive his relationship to his mother's breast as a partial object" (p. 13).[2]

A CLARIFICATION OF FAIRBAIRN'S EARLY AND LATE ORAL PHASES

There would not be an early oral phase to regress to unless at least some aspects of the infant's early interpersonal relations with the mother were good enough, to some extent at least, during early infancy as a heuristic stage of personality development (Winnicott 1953). Therefore, the excessive frustration must have been more characteristic of the later oral phase in Fairbairn's (1952) conception, or late infancy in the terminology of Sullivan's heuristic stages of personality development.

The phrase *early interpersonal relations with the mother* is too vague, sometimes far too vague. Clearly, the distinction between the early and late oral phase is the recognition of oneself as separate from another person. I sensed it in something Fairbairn (1952) wrote about the later oral phase, which I would equate with late infancy as a heuristic stage of personality development, and the interpersonal achievement in personality development—to recognize oneself as separate from another person and internal object relations with self differentiated from object. Fairbairn's distinction between early and late oral phases has been clarified by American object relations theory. The terminology is important, because Freud's heuristic stages, sugarcoated in Erikson (1950), are based on zones or parts of the body, not interpersonal relationships.

The excessive frustration of the oral-dependent needs of the late infant leads to strong aggressive tendencies. The premature (i.e., pregenital) development of oedipal strivings toward the mother, brought about by the excessive frustration of oral-dependent needs, prematurely sexualizes the relationship with the mother. No wonder she—the mother—rejects him, the later infant. The frustrations begin when the infant, sucking for pleasure, sexually arouses the mother and makes her uncomfortable. (The "libido" at this early stage of the relationship of the mother and infant could be considered the taste or sensation of the warm milk in the infant's mouth.) Can this really be the case? The answer must be yes, because the oral-dependent needs of the early infant have been frustrated, and that frustration has been extreme. Much of what has been written previously has been about the excessive frustration of oral-dependent needs, oral aggressiveness, and oral rage among personality organizations in the primitive range of the Personality Continuum.

Fairbairn (1955) related his late oral phase to his conception of his depressive position. What is Fairbairn's depressive position? Winnicott (1955) defined the depressive position as the *capacity for concern* determined by the achievement of the integration of whole object relations.

What I believe Fairbairn (1952) has captured in his conception of the depressive position, and the late oral phase, is that it involves more anger. This will be borne out subsequently with an exploration of the aggressiveness of the borderline personality organization, the rage of the narcissistic personality organization, and the overt violence of the antisocial personality organization, in descending order in the primitive range of the Personality Continuum.

Fairbairn (1952) does refer to the early oral phase as pre-ambivalent and the late oral phase as ambivalent. Indeed, this is the basis for Fairbairn's depressive position: "In the latter case the child, being essentially ambivalent, interprets the situation in the sense that it is his hate, and not his love, that has destroyed his mother's affection. It is then in his hate that his badness seems to him to reside; and his love is thus able to remain good in his eyes" (p. 25). The individual with a schizoid personality organization comes to regard love as dangerous, according to Fairbairn: "We are now in a position to appreciate that the individual with a schizoid tendency has another motive for keeping his love inside himself besides that arising from the feeling that it is too precious to part with. He also keeps his love shut in because he feels it is too dangerous to release upon his objects. Thus he also keeps his love in a cage" (pp. 25–26).

References to a *cage* or a *prison* occur frequently in Fairbairn's descriptions of the schizoid personality organization. A line from an Oscar Wilde poem captured the dilemma of the schizoid personality organization for Fairbairn: "It is small wonder then that individuals with any considerable schizoid tendency experience such difficulty in showing [this should be *giving*] love; for they always entertain the deep anxiety expressed by Oscar Wilde in *The Ballad of Reading Gaol* when he wrote, 'Each man kills the thing he loves' " (p. 25).

As a child, the person who would become a schizoid personality organization, according to Fairbairn, "seeks to circumvent the dangers of expressing both libidinal and aggressive affect towards his object by *using a maximum of his aggression to subdue a maximum of his libidinal need.* In this way, he reduces the volume of affect, both libidinal and aggressive, demanding outward expression" (pp. 114–115). The result is the mass withdrawal of affect characteristic of individuals with a schizoid personality organization.

It would be hard to overestimate Fairbairn's contributions to the foundations of object relations theory of the personality. It is Fairbairn's understanding that is at the broken heart of the basic fault: The failure to love and be loved as a person. According to Fairbairn: "Valuable as it is to understand the nature of these 'relationships by default,' such understanding is much less important than a knowledge of the factors which compromise spontaneous relationships. By far the most important of these factors is a situation in childhood which leads the individual to feel that his objects neither love him as a person nor accept his love" (p. 40).

NOTE

1. In *Clinical Studies in Psychiatry* (1956), Sullivan argued that problems of personality are primarily interpersonal, and he advanced the intriguing hypothesis that although problems of personality do not start out as primarily physiological, they may become manifested in that way.

2. It is interesting to note that this section on the intrapsychic structure in Fairbairn's theoretical conception of the schizoid personality organization is relatively terse and drew on American object relations theory for clarification.

Chapter 11

Otto F. Kernberg, the Borderline Personality Organization, and American Object Relations Theory

W.R.D. Fairbairn was a superb theorist and the founder of British object relations theory. His penetrating psychoanalytic studies of the schizoid personality organization established the foundations of the primitive level of personality development. He understood the difficulties in differentiating neurotic from high-functioning primitive personality organizations, and he recognized that problems of personality are primarily interpersonal in the primitive range of the Personality Continuum.

The schizoid personality organization is at the very bottom of the primitive range of the Personality Continuum, just above the psychotic range, but nonetheless, a qualitatively different personality organization at a higher level of personality development. Within the primitive range of the Personality Continuum, in descending order, the borderline, infantile, narcissistic, and antisocial personality organizations are all better off, relatively speaking, than the schizoid personality organization.

The borderline personality organization has been extensively investigated, both directly and indirectly, because it forms the fundament for Otto F. Kernberg's contributions to American object relations theory. The exploration of the borderline personality organization by Kernberg occupies much the same position in American object relations theory that the earlier explorations of the schizoid personality organization by

Fairbairn occupy in British object relations theory. In analyzing primitive personality organizations other than the schizoid personality organization, Kernberg and American object relations theory represent a refinement of the fundamental insights of Fairbairn and British object relations theory. It is critical to know when Fairbairn is clearly analyzing a schizoid personality organization, a strength, or generalizing to all primitive personality organizations, in which case Kernberg is clearly the superior authority, especially on the borderline and narcissistic personality organizations.

REPRISE OF THE PRIMITIVE RANGE OF THE PERSONALITY CONTINUUM

Personality organizations in the primitive range of the Personality Continuum are characterized by the failure to achieve the integration of whole object relations. Splitting is the predominant defense against severe anxiety in interpersonal relationships. Splitting is a fundamental cause of ego weakness, a weak ego falls back easily on splitting, and a vicious circle is created; ego weakness and splitting reinforce each other (Kernberg 1984A, p. 46).

A person with a primitive personality organization cannot tolerate additional or marginal anxiety because he or she is already tolerating a high level of severe anxiety. Any additional or marginal anxiety overloads the primitive defense of splitting, causing it to break down, and the person is subjected to severe anxiety that is intolerable. When splitting breaks down, the punitive superego persecutes the person with a primitive personality organization with severe anxiety. That drives the person to outbursts of compulsive and, in the more extreme case, addictive consumption behavior. The compulsive or addictive consumption behavior is a desperate effort to restore the primitive defense of splitting against severe anxiety. The repetitiveness of the behavior, as in Freud's repetition compulsion, represents the repeated breakdown of the primitive defense of splitting as the person is constantly confronted with reality that contradicts his or her primitively idealized conception of oneself and others. This is the interpersonal origin of the additional or marginal anxiety that breaks down the primitive defense of splitting.

KERNBERG'S PORTRAIT OF THE CHRONOLOGICALLY ADULT PERSON WITH A BORDERLINE PERSONALITY ORGANIZATION

The purpose of the comparative analysis of personality organizations is to add depth and detail to the portrait of the borderline personality organization. In doing so, the order of presentation is the character constellation, some aspects of the descriptive behavior of the chronologically adult person, the dynamic analysis of the developmental history,[1] and the structural analysis of the intrapsychic structure of the borderline personality organization.

The Basic Character Constellation of the Borderline Personality Organization

In Kernberg's theoretical conception of the borderline personality organization, the basic character constellation is comprised of three "nonspecific" manifestations of ego weakness: Lack of anxiety tolerance, lack of impulse control, and lack of developed sublimatory channels. The basic defense constellation characteristic of the borderline personality organization is comprised of splitting, primitive idealization, early forms of projection (especially projective identification), denial, and omnipotence.

The lack of anxiety tolerance—the inability to tolerate any additional or marginal anxiety and the breakdown of splitting—has been addressed already. The lack of impulse control likewise has also been addressed at the general level—the breakdown of splitting is manifested in an outbreak (although outburst may be more descriptive) of compulsive or more extreme addictive behavior. The chronologically adult person with a borderline personality organization, in particular, is subject to a panoply of compulsive behaviors and may engage in a variety of compulsive activities, as opposed to the more extreme case of an addict who has narrowed his dependency down to just one thing. Dependency in the borderline personality organization is often characterized as clinging and childlike, and in general, personality organizations in the primitive range of the Personality Continuum are characterized as childlike (Kernberg 1985A, pp. 75, 97, 153, 275).

The Capacity for Sublimation

Personality organizations in the primitive range of the Personality Continuum are characterized by the lack of developed sublimatory channels. In general, the absence of sublimatory capacity is yet another indicator of ego weakness for personality organizations in the primitive range of the Personality Continuum.

In the case of a person with a borderline personality organization, a facade of sociability may conceal a lack of enjoyment or creativity: "In a highly stimulating, culture-oriented social environment the lack of enjoyment and creativity of the borderline patient may be obscured by his surface adaptation to the optimal environment" (Kernberg 1985A, p. 22). The "surface adaptation to the optimal environment" can be traced back to the basic fault for the individual with a borderline personality organization—the failure to love and be loved as a person. The failure to achieve the integration of whole object relations results in the absence of the capacity to see another person as whole and more realistic, and the absence of the capacity for concern. In the case of the borderline personality organization, according to Kernberg (1985A), "These patients have little capacity for a realistic evaluation of others and for realistic empathy with others; they experience people as distant objects, to whom they adapt 'realistically' only as long as there is no emotional involvement with them" (pp. 36–37).

For a person with a borderline personality organization, the capacity to transcend the self is an important positive prognostic indicator:

> When borderline patients in some area of their life basically trust something good and valuable in their relationships with others (or with work, leisure, art, science, or religion) this is of important, positive prognostic value. The capacity to establish and maintain values transcending the self—abstract as it may sound, and difficult at times as it is to evaluate—is an eminently practical link between the vicissitudes of internalized object relationships on the one hand, and the capacity to benefit from a psychotherapeutic relationship, on the other. (p. 134)

Although the capacity to transcend the self is typically absent in a person with a borderline personality organization, the borderline personality organization, at the top of the primitive range, is relatively better off than the schizoid personality organization, at the bottom of the primitive range of the Personality Continuum. An extreme attitude of detachment and isolation is characteristic of the schizoid personality organization. At the lower end of the spectrum of variation of the narcissistic personality organization, withdrawal in splendid isolation is a characteristic feature (p. 282). But the narcissistic personality organization is still relatively better off than the schizoid personality organization.

Sexual Activity and the Borderline Personality Organization

A fortunate interpersonal relationship can afford a person with a borderline personality organization an opportunity for a favorable change in the personality organization and the achievement of a higher level of personality development. The opportunity presented by sexual activity in an interpersonal relationship is frequently neglected in the clinical situation: "With patients presenting borderline personality organization the opposite danger of seeing only their pregenital, destructive aims, to the neglect of acknowledging their efforts to overcome their inhibited sexual orientation, appears a frequent clinical problem" (Kernberg 1985A, p. 103).

Kernberg, however, has warned that for a person with a primitive personality organization, the premature development of genital strivings typical of the oedipal situation has to do primarily with pregenital aims: "There was a time when a typical misunderstanding of the implications of psychoanalytic theory and practice was the assumption that sexual activity in itself was a therapeutic factor. We have advanced a long way from such misunderstandings, and have learned that often what appears on the surface to be genital activity is actually in the service of aggressive, pregenital aims" (p. 103). Kernberg illustrates this with a case study of a promiscuous young woman with a borderline personality organization: "A promiscuous, divorced, young woman, hospitalized after a psychotic regression which followed years of disorganized behavior, was restricted in the hospital from male patients. On several occasions a few minutes of unobserved time had been enough for her to have intercourse in an impulsive way with other patients, practically strangers" (p. 103).

In the case of this promiscuous young woman, Kernberg sees her pattern of acting out her fantasy of being a prostitute as "submission to a primitive sadistic superego" (p. 104). For her, this was the only thing that provided escape from the unrelenting persecution of the punitive superego, punishing her with severe anxiety, becoming her worst fears in a sense, all bad, no good, worthless; namely, a prostitute. But remember, the gratification really sought is oral, not sexual and genital. What object relations theory explicitly refers to as genital sexual activity serves as substitute gratification for oral-dependent needs frustrated by the dangerous mother (p. 42). What reveals the premature development of genital strivings is the excessive aggressiveness with which the gratification is sought. Out of this crude gratification of sexual impulses, this woman was able to establish a fortunate relationship with a man:

> She was finally able to establish a good relationship with one patient, with whom she fell in love, went steady for a two-year period, and whom she eventually planned to marry. During the latter part of these years they had sexual intercourse, characterized by her being able for the first time in her life to have tender as well as sexual feelings toward just one man, and by her taking pre-

cautions not to get pregnant, which was in contrast to her previous behavior. (p. 104)

In contrast to the transitory infatuations and sexually promiscuous behavior of a person with a narcissistic personality organization, the impulsive sexual promiscuity of Kernberg's patient with a borderline personality organization may appear worse off: "Paradoxically, the type of falling in love described in this [borderline] patient has a better prognosis than the ephemeral infatuations of narcissistic personalities, not withstanding that narcissistic personalities appear to be much more 'reality oriented' than typical borderline patients without narcissistic personality structure" (Kernberg 1984A, p. 199). A person with a borderline personality organization is better off than the narcissistic personality organization because of the greater potential for fortunate interpersonal relationships:

> Paradoxically, disturbed, inappropriate, and immature as the ordinary borderline patients' falling in love, primitive idealization, and sexual promiscuity may appear, these patients do have a much better prognosis for further development than the descriptive pathology of their love relations would initially suggest. In contrast to the narcissistic patients, they have a better capacity for investment in others, or less active deterioration of their object relations. (Kernberg 1985B, p. 278)

DEVELOPMENTAL HISTORY: DYNAMIC ANALYSIS OF THE BORDERLINE PERSONALITY ORGANIZATION

The history of extreme frustrations and intense aggression in early interpersonal relations during the first few years of life is at the core of the etiology of the borderline personality organization (Kernberg 1985A, p. 41). Excessive pregenital aggression, especially oral aggression, and the unusual intensity of pregenital aggression are particularly characteristic of the borderline personality organization: "Pregenital aggression, especially oral aggression, plays a crucial role as part of the psychopathological constellation" (p. 40).

For a person with a borderline personality organization, in particular, there is a pathological condensation of pregenital and genital aims. In the language of object relations theory, "A predominant characteristic of the instinctual development of patients with borderline personality organization is the excessive development of pregenital drives, especially oral aggression, and of a particular pathological condensation of pregenital and genital aims under the overriding influence of aggressive needs" (p. 103). From the clinical point of view, according to Kernberg (1985A), the regressive reactivation of early internalized object relations under the overriding influence of aggressive drive derivatives, and the projection of aggressive drive derivatives, result in the paranoid distortion of the early parental images:

> The conflicts that typically emerge in connection with the reactivation of these early internalized object relations may be characterized as a particular pathological condensation of pregenital and genital aims under the overriding influence of pregenital aggression. Excessive pregenital aggression, and especially oral, aggression tends to be projected and determines the paranoid distortion of the early parental images, particularly those of the mother. From a clinical point of view, whether this is a consequence of severe frustration or actual aggression on the mother's part, whether it reflects excessive constitutional aggressive drive derivatives, whether it reflects a lack of capacity to neutralize aggression or lack of constitutionally determined anxiety tolerance, is not so important as the final result—the paranoid distortion of the early parental images. (p. 78)

THE RELATIONSHIP OF THE MOTHER AND FATHER IN THE CASE OF THE LITTLE BOY WHO WOULD BECOME A BORDERLINE PERSONALITY ORGANIZATION

From the case of a chronologically adult person with a borderline personality organization, Kernberg (1984A) describes the relatively enduring pattern of recurrent interpersonal situations that characterized his early life:

> In the case of this patient, I came gradually to understand that the depreciative, harsh, and haughty image of me that he had in times of intense anger corresponded to one image of his mother, while the image of the all-forgiving, all-loving and understanding therapist that he had during the times of positive feelings toward me reflected that of a fused ideal mother and weak but protective father image. In the intimate relationship with these two images were self-images of, respectively, the rejected, depreciated, attacked little boy (this is how he felt in his relationship with his harsh and rejecting mother) and the longing, guilt-ridden child (which represented his feeling about both parents together, seen as kind, weak, forgiving keepers of the home that he had lost). (p. 24)

Although a person with a primitive personality organization does not have an integrated prohibitive superego and, therefore, does not have the capacity for experiencing guilt, I do not disagree with Kernberg's use of *guilt* in his characterization of the "longing, guilt-ridden child" as a partial self-image related to the all-loving, all-forgiving, and understanding image of the ideal mother and weak but protective father. The borderline personality organization is at the top of the primitive range of the Personality Continuum, relatively speaking, and can function at the higher neurotic level of personality development under high functioning with fortunate interpersonal experience and favorable circumstances in the situation. The partial self-image of the longing, guilt-ridden child is an intrapsychic structure internalized though identification, with the self differentiated from the object, and the affect modified and more diversified. It is partial because this self-image is still all-good in the absence of the integration of whole object relations. In a sense, this intrapsychic structure is the repository for the child's positive feelings of longing and guilt.

STRUCTURAL ANALYSIS OF THE BORDERLINE PERSONALITY ORGANIZATION AND PRIMITIVE IDEALIZATION

The early history of extreme frustration and aggression leads to a primitive idealization that creates all-good and powerful object images to protect good internal and external objects from being contaminated, spoiled, or destroyed by all-bad internal and external objects (Kernberg 1984A, p. 49). The primitively idealized image of the all-good internal objects, the positive introjects and identifications, provides protection against a surrounding world of dangerous objects:

> Primitive idealization implies neither the conscious or unconscious acknowledgement of aggression toward the object, nor guilt over this aggression and concern for the object. Thus, it is not reaction formation [a higher-level neurotic defense], but rather is the direct manifestation of a primitive, protective fantasy structure in which there is no real regard for the ideal object, but a simple need for it as a protection against a surrounding world of dangerous objects. (Kernberg 1985A, p. 30)

Primitive idealization interferes with the integration of the prohibitive superego and the development of the ego ideal (Kernberg 1985A, p. 30). According to Kernberg (1984A), the sadistic superego forerunners (or nuclei) "interfere with the normal internalization of more realistic parental prohibitions and demands and with the integration of the [prohibitive] superego itself" (p. 50). The more realistic parental prohibitions and demands represent the contents of the prohibitive superego. There is a direct relationship between the predominance of aggressive drive derivatives in the borderline personality organization and the predominance of sadistic superego forerunners: "The stronger the pregenital frustration and aggression, the more predominant are the sadistic superego forerunners" (Kernberg 1984A, p. 71).

For a person with a borderline personality organization, reality testing is maintained at the level of recognizing oneself as separate from another object, as opposed to another person, since the integration of whole object relations has not been achieved: "Sufficient delimitation between self and objects (stability of ego boundaries) is maintained to permit practical immediate adaptation to the demands of reality, but deeper internalization of the demands of reality, especially social reality, is made impossible by the interference of these nonintegrated self and object images with superego integration" (Kernberg 1985A, p. 36). Further, according to Kernberg (1984A): "One other consequence of all these developments is that both excessive splitting and the lack of superego integration interfere with further synthesis of the ego core. Mutual reinforcements of ego weakness and splitting end up in a pathologically fixated personality organization in which early drive derivatives, as part of split-up ego states, persist dangerously close to consciousness and to directly influencing all aspects of psychic life" (p. 50).

PRIMITIVE PROJECTIVE IDENTIFICATION

The defense of projection is characteristic of the borderline personality organization: "The main purpose of projection here is to externalize the all-bad, aggressive self and object images" (Kernberg 1985A, p. 30), in other words, the negative introjects and identifications. "The high degree of projection of aggressive self- and object-images of negative introjections perpetuates a dangerous world of persecuting objects" (Kernberg 1984A, p. 49). Primitive idealization and projection work together to defend against persecution: "Constant projection of 'all bad' self and object images perpetuates a world of dangerous, threatening objects, against which the 'all good' self images are used defensively, and the megalomanic ideal self images are built up" (Kernberg 1985A, p. 36). The projection of aggression threatens the separation of self from object that has been achieved in the borderline personality organization: "While these patients do have sufficient development of ego boundaries to be able to differentiate self and objects in most areas of their lives, the very intensity of the projective needs, plus the general ego weakness characterizing these patients, weakens the ego boundaries in the particular area of the projection of aggression" (p. 31).

The primitive defense of projective identification is characteristic of the borderline personality organization, in particular. Projective identification blurs the boundary between self and object and represents a paranoid technique used to control the object:

> This leads such patients to feel that they can still identify themselves with the object onto whom aggression has been projected, and their ongoing "empathy" with the now threatening object maintains and increases the fear of their own projected aggression. Therefore, they have to control the object in order to prevent it from attacking them under the influence of the (projected) aggressive impulses; they have to attack and control the object before (as they fear) they themselves are attacked and destroyed. (p. 31)

It is the fear of an impulse—a sudden driving force acted on with conscious thought—that is driving the person with a borderline personality organization to control the external object.

"In summary, projective identification is characterized by the lack of differentiation between self and object in that particular area, by continuing to experience the impulse as well as the fear of that impulse while the projection is active, and by the need to control the external object" (p. 31). Fear of an impulse (e.g., a boy afraid of getting an erection in the shower of the boys' locker room or a little boy's fear of castration) is defended against by control of the external object, or person, upon whom the aggressive drive derivatives have been projected through the primitive defense of projective identification.

The rapid oscillation between the projection of, and identification with, primitive self- and object images contributes to the chaotic pattern of the alternating and contradictory behavior characteristic of the borderline personality organization:

> Primitive self- and primitive-object representations are actually linked together as basic units of primitive object relationships, and what appears characteristic of borderline patients is that there is a rapid oscillation between moments of projection of a self-representation while the patient remains identified with the corresponding object representation, and other moments in which it is the object-representation that is projected while the patient identifies with the corresponding self-representation. For example, a primitive, sadistic mother image may be projected onto the therapist while the patient experiences himself as the frightened, attacked, panic-stricken little child; moments later, the patient may experience himself as the stern, prohibitive, moralistic (and extremely sadistic)

primitive mother image, while the therapist is seen as the guilty, defensive, frightened but rebellious little child. (p. 81)

The combined image of a dangerous mother-father complicates later sexual relationships because pregenital aggression contaminates the genital striving:

Through projection of predominantly oral-sadistic and also anal-sadistic impulses, the mother is seen as potentially dangerous, and hatred of the mother extends to a hatred of both parents when later they are experienced as a "united group" by the child. A "contamination" of the father image by aggression primarily projected onto the mother and lack of differentiation between mother and father tend to produce a combined, dangerous father-mother image and a later conceptualization of all sexual relationships as dangerous and infiltrated by aggression. Concurrently, in an effort to escape from oral rage and fears, a "flight" into genital strivings occurs; this flight often miscarries because of the intensity of the pregenital aggression which contaminates the genital striving. (p. 78)

PRIMARY-PROCESS THINKING IN THE BORDERLINE PERSONALITY ORGANIZATION

In Kernberg's theoretical conception of the borderline personality organization, regression to primary-process thinking is the most important single structural indicator: "Whatever its origin, the regression toward primary-process thinking is still the most important single structural indicator of borderline personality organization. Its detection through the use of projective tests makes sophisticated psychological testing an indispensable instrument for the diagnosis of borderline personality organization" (Kernberg 1985A, p. 25). The psychological testing Kernberg is referring to is that of Rapaport, Gill, and Schafer (1968) and the use of projective testing to evaluate the degree to which secondary-process or primary-process thinking predominates: "On projective testing, and especially in response to unstructured stimuli, primary-process thinking tends to appear in the form of primitive fantasies, in a decrease in the capacity to adapt to the formal givens of the test material, and particularly in the use of peculiar verbalizations" (Kernberg 1985A, p. 24).[2]

REGRESSIVE LURE OF PURE AFFECT STATES

As a result of the failure to achieve the integration of whole object relations, affect remains intense and overwhelming and exerts a powerful regressive pull: "The modification of affective dispositions available to the ego also indirectly fosters the emancipation of thought processes because the irradiating effect of earlier 'pure' affective states exerts a powerful regressive pull in the direction of primary process thinking, which decreases when modification of affect occurs" (Kernberg 1984A, p. 51). The regressive pull of pure affect states will be elaborated subsequently with compulsive and addictive behavior and the regressive lure of addiction and the nature of the "high."

QUESTIONABLE INSIGHT IN THE BORDERLINE PERSONALITY ORGANIZATION

Meaningful insight and the urge to change in an appropriate way were addressed at the normal level of personality development. Here an invidious comparison is made between insight, at the normal level of personality development, and the mere availability of primary-process thinking for the borderline personality organization at the primitive level of personality development.

Severe superego pathology prevents the kind of genuine insight that brings about an understanding of one's own behavior that leads to an urge to change in a positive way:

> Superego pathology of the kind described above also implies a reduction in the more subtle aspects of reality testing in the realm of interpersonal relationships, and a reduction in the capacity for meaningful insight. Meaningful insight, in contrast to the simple availability of primary process material in conscious and preconscious mental life of borderline patients, refers to the combination of intellectual and emotional understanding of deeper sources of one's psychic experience, accompanied by concern for and an urge to change the pathological aspects of that experience. (Kernberg 1985A, p. 141)

Instead, in the borderline personality organization, primary-process thinking is mistaken for meaningful insight:

> The question of "insight" in borderline patients deserves discussion. Unfortunately, one frequently finds that what at first looks like insight into "deep" layers of the mind and into unconscious dynamics on the part of some borderline patients is actually an expression of the ready availability of primary process functioning as part of the general regression of ego structures. Insight which may come without any effort, is not accompanied by any change in the patient's intrapsychic equilibrium, and above all, is not accompanied by any concern on

the patient's part for the pathological aspects of his behavior or experience, is questionable "insight." (Kernberg 1985A, pp. 92–93)

RIFF ON DENIAL

The lack of impulse control is episodic, and is manifested in outbreaks of compulsive or more extreme addictive consumption behavior that characterizes the breakdown of splitting. In general, the result is a chaotic pattern of alternating and contradictory behavior. The person with a primitive personality organization defends the contradictions between his usual feelings and behavior and his behavior during the specific episodes with bland denial. In the language of object relations theory, according to Kernberg (1984A), "The episodic character of this lack of impulse control, the typical ego syntonicity of the impulses expressed during the time of emotional contact between that part of the patient's personality and the rest of his self-experience, and finally, the bland denial secondarily defending the contradictions between his usual feelings and behavior and his behavior during the specific episodes all reflect the presence of strong splitting operations" (p. 47).[3]

Denial as a defense for a person with a primitive personality organization represents the denial of contradictory behavior. This includes the self-destructive consequences of compulsive and addictive behavior patterns over time: "It is relatively easy to diagnose the operation of denial because of the glaring loss of reality-testing that it brings about. The patient acts as if he were completely unaware of a quite urgent, pressing aspect of his reality" (Kernberg 1985A, p. 100).

Denial varies qualitatively with the level of personality development. Vaillant (1977) places denial of external reality in the psychotic range and dissociation or neurotic denial in the neurotic range of the Personality Continuum. Dissociation or neurotic denial includes a number of different defensive mechanisms, including "a *short-term* refusal to perceive responsibility for one's acts or feelings" (p. 385).

Primitive fantasy, withdrawal, and denial through fantasy serve "to gratify unmet needs for personal relationships, and to obliterate the overt expression of aggressive or sexual impulses towards others" (p. 384). In the primitive range, fantasy is used in combination with acting out—the crude gratification of impulses to avoid becoming conscious of the affect that goes with an unconscious wish or desire. The crude gratification of impulses, manifested in compulsive or addictive patterns of consumption behavior, prevents the person at the primitive level of personality development from becoming conscious of the unconscious wish or desire that is the unconscious motivation for the behavior.[4]

Vaillant uses the term *dissociation* to designate denial at the neurotic level of personality development: "*Dissociation* is more comprehensible to others than distortion, more considerate of others, and less prolonged than *acting out*" (p. 385). In a comparison of dissociation at the neurotic level with fantasy at the primitive level of personality development, "Unlike *dissociation*, fantasy remakes the outer not the inner world" (p. 384). "In contrast to the psychotic *denial*," a person using primitive denial through fantasy, "does not fully believe in or insist upon acting out his fantasies" (p. 384).

In Vaillant's (p. 384) definition of acting out, I disagree with his characterization of a "direct expression of an unconscious wish or impulse," because the behavior is anything but direct. An impulse is the sudden driving force acted on with conscious thought. The person is not conscious of the wish or desire (the ideation) or the affect (feelings or emotions), only of the impulse. The impulse is crudely gratified in order to avoid becoming conscious of the ideation or the affect that goes with the wish or desire.[5] For example, Jim Morrison shouting, "Father, I want to kill you. Mother, I want to fuck you," in a live performance of the song "The End," is giving direct expression to his oedipal desires.[6]

The characterization of the denial of contradictory behavior as bland for a person with a primitive personality organization indicates that it is a conscious defense. Severe anxiety—the persecution of the punitive superego, the return of bad objects, especially the regressive reactivation of the negative introjects, the all-bad objects, the all-bad mother—erupts into consciousness. This episodic character of the behavior reflects the breakdown of splitting and the person's desperate behavior to restore it.[7] Thus, for a person with a primitive level of personality development, the impulse to eat, to masturbate, to smoke pot, and so on is a way to avoid the conscious recognition of the unconscious wish or desire that is the driving force behind the impulse.[8]

Fitting Vaillant (1977) into the Personality Continuum works well at the general level of personality development, but does not work as well for particular personality organizations. There is too much variation among particular personality organizations at the same level of development, and for each personality organization, there is a spectrum of variation. For these variations of the defense of denial for particular personality organizations, we must return to object relations theory.

For the borderline personality organization in the primitive range of the Personality Continuum, according to Kernberg (1985A), "Denial here is typically exemplified by 'mutual denial' of two emotionally independent areas of consciousness (in this case, we might say, denial simply reinforces splitting)" (p. 31). For the person with a borderline personality organization, "*emotions* are denied which he has experienced (and remembers having experienced) and awareness of the emotional relevance of a certain situation in reality is denied, of which the patient has been consciously aware or can again be made consciously aware" (p. 32). Thus, according to Kernberg:

> Denial in the patients [borderline personality organization] I am considering may also manifest itself only as simple disregard for a sector of their subjective experience or for a sector of the external world. When pressed, the patient acknowledges his intellectual awareness of the sector which has been denied, but again he cannot integrate it with the rest of his emotional experience. It has to be stressed that which is denied now is something that in other areas of his consciousness the patient is aware of. (p. 32)

On the spectrum of variation of the borderline personality organization at the primitive level of personality development, Kernberg characterizes the denial of emotions being experienced currently as an "intermediate" manifestation, relatively speaking: "An intermediate level of denial, which is also quite prevalent in patients with borderline personality organization, is the denial of emotions contrary to those which are strongly experienced at that point, especially the manic denial of depression" (p. 32). "In this form of denial," according to Kernberg, "an extreme, opposite affect is used to reinforce the ego's stand against a threatening part of the self experience" (p. 32).

The variations in the defense of denial within the primitive range of the Personality Continuum are hierarchical; that is, the nature of denial higher up in the primitive range compares favorably to the neurotic level of personality development, where repression is the predominant defense. The comparison is unfavorable for denial based on the predominant defense of splitting in the primitive range of the Personality Continuum: "Denial, then, is a broad group of defensive operations, and probably related at its higher [neurotic] level to the mechanisms of isolation and other higher level defenses against affects (detachment, denial in fantasy, denial 'in word and act') and at its lower level, to splitting" (pp. 32–33).

In comparison, *negation* as a defense at the neurotic level of personality development is related to denial and repression, as opposed to the splitting that characterizes primitive personality organizations:

> All of this [denial in the primitive range of the Personality Continuum] is different from the higher level form of denial such as is implicit in the mechanism of negation. In negation, a mental content is present "with a negative sign"; the patient says that he knows what he himself, his therapist, or others *might* think about something, but that particular possibility is rejected as a purely intellectual speculation. In this case, the emotional relevance of what is denied has never been present in consciousness, and remains repressed. Negation in this regard is a higher form of denial linked with repression, and is also quite close to isolation. (p. 32)

OMNIPOTENCE AND DEVALUATION

An attitude of superiority is particularly characteristic of individuals with a schizoid personality organization. An attitude of omnipotence is more characteristic of primitive personality organizations prone to more overt expressions of aggression, in particular, the antisocial personality organization, followed closely by the narcissistic personality organization, and, to a lesser degree, the borderline personality organization.

The defensive operations of omnipotence and devaluation are related to primitive idealization and to the primitive fantasies characteristic of primary-process thinking, and, ultimately, to the primitive defense of splitting. This contributes to the complexity of the characteristic defensive constellation of the borderline personality organization: "The fractionating of the defensive operations which are characteristic of borderline patients into completely separate forms may clarify their functioning but it does necessarily oversimplify the issue. There are complex intertwinings of these defensive operations, and they present themselves in various combinations" (Kernberg 1985A, p. 102). Furthermore,

> These two, intimately linked defensive operations of omnipotence and devaluation refer to the patient's identification with an over-idealized self- and object-representation, with the primitive form of ego-ideal, as a protection against threatening needs and involvement with others. Such "self-idealization" usually implies magical fantasies of omnipotence, the conviction that he, the patient, will eventually receive all the gratification that he is entitled to, and that he cannot be touched by frustrations, illness, death, or the passage of time. A corollary of this fantasy is the devaluation of other people, the patient's conviction of his superiority over them, including the therapist. The projection of that magical omnipotence onto the therapist, and the patient's feeling magically united with or submissive to that omnipotent therapist, are other forms which this defensive operation can take. (pp. 101–102)

NOTES

1. Kernberg (1985A, pp. 40–44), uses the term genetic-dynamic analysis of the Borderline Personality Organization. Kernberg's use of the term *genetic* in the psychotic range is appropriate because physiological problems appear to predominate—genetic in the case of manic depression or bipolar disorder, and genetic or congenital in the case of schizophrenia; however, problems of personality in the primitive range of the Personality Continuum are primarily interpersonal.

2. The capacity to adapt to the formal givens of the test material during marijuana intoxication has been explored by Lester Grinspoon, *Marihuana Reconsidered* (1971); see especially page 153.

3. Ego syntonic means in emotional equilibrium and responsive to environment. If it feels good, do it, so to speak.

4. According to Vaillant (1977), the crude gratification of impulses is a way to avoid becoming conscious of the affect that goes with the unconscious wish or impulse. If I substitute "desire" for "impulse," I believe that the statement is clearer.

5. This insight sheds some additional light on the comparative analysis of how subliminal stimuli in advertising would work for personality organizations at the neurotic and primitive levels of personality development. At the neurotic level of personality development, repression prevents the rejected idea or affect from becoming conscious, and it prevents the development of the affect, leaving only a residual anxiety as a warning signal. A person at the primitive level of personality development does not have resort to the higher-level defense of repression, and the anxiety, as a signal warning of danger, is severe and intolerable.

6. The recorded version appeared on *The Doors* self-titled album, sans the "fuck you." Instead, Morrison let out a primal scream, poignantly communicating the intense affect attendant on the conscious recognition of the wish.

7. I have not said what "it" is yet.

8. In the lyrics of the Grateful Dead, "Drivin' that train, high on cocaine." The lyric is from "Casey Jones" on *Workingman's Dead* (1970).

Chapter 12

PORTRAIT OF THE NARCISSISTIC PERSONALITY ORGANIZATION

In an endeavor to provide a fuller portrait of the narcissistic personality organization, I have culled clinical observations from Kernberg's case material. The intense observation of individual behavior in the clinical setting forms the basis for the theoretical conceptions of particular personality organizations and represents the foundation of an object relations theory of the personality. This reinforces the earlier arguments made for the use of an object relations theory of personality in economics—economics with an unparalleled theoretical conception of the rational consumer and object relations theory with an unparalleled theoretical conception of the personality organization. Economics, lacking the apparatus to observe actual consumer behavior—and economists lacking the inclination—can benefit from broadening the behavioral foundations of economic analysis and expanding the limits of applicability of economic theory. The qualitatively different patterns of consumer behavior can be modeled mathematically. The fundament of the mathematical form of the utility function for each range of the Personality Continuum will be presented subsequently in an expanded analysis of consumer behavior.

If economists had observed the actual consumer behavior of a person with a narcissistic personality organization, they would have been remarkably satisfied with the selfish behavior that is particularly characteristic of such individuals. The common misconception of rational economic man—the individual consumer maximizing his utility subject to a budget constraint and, increasingly, a time constraint—is a dead ringer for the selfish, self-absorbed, uncaring, coldly calculating, exploitative, and materialistic narcissistic personality organization. After all, it is a conception of the rational economic man, and rightly so; however, this characterization of a narcissistic economic man is little more than a caricature of normal consumer behavior.[1]

The narcissistic personality organization is particularly prominent among American men. Unfortunately, it is not unfair to say that the archetypal American male is essentially a narcissistic personality organization. Many of our cherished heroes in film and fiction are narcissistic personality organizations: In American literature, the character of Natty Bumppo in *The Leather Stocking Tales* of James Fenimore Cooper (Barker-Benfield 1976, pp. 8–9); in film, the sexually promiscuous behavior of the British James Bond, or perhaps Han Solo in the *Star Wars* trilogy, and, in some ways, even Henry Fonda in the John Ford western *My Darling Clementine*.

To mistake the behavior of a narcissistic personality organization for a rational economic consumer represents a misconception of Adam Smith's exquisite view of human nature. Adam Smith's *Theory of Moral Sentiments* (1759) represents a watershed in the human understanding of consumer behavior. Smith's conception of the capacity for sympathy and his conception of the prudent economic man have been addressed; his views on remorse will be elaborated subsequently in the chapter on the pursuit of self-interest in America.

The analysis of variations on the theme of the subjective experience of emptiness across particular personality organizations will facilitate the further exploration of addictive behavior. A person with a narcissistic personality organization is particularly prone to addiction. In this way, the personality organization serves as a useful organizational framework, and the Personality Continuum provides an integrative framework that facilitates the comparative analysis of personality organizations.

THE BASIC CHARACTER CONSTELLATION OF THE NARCISSISTIC PERSONALITY ORGANIZATION

In Kernberg's theoretical conception of the narcissistic personality organization, the basic character constellation is comprised of emptiness, restlessness, and boredom: "In these cases, emptiness, restlessness, and boredom constitute a constellation of what might be considered a baseline of pathological narcissistic experience" (Kernberg 1985A, p. 220). The basic mechanisms of defense characteristic of the narcissistic personality organization are comprised of defenses against intense envy, such as devaluation, omnipotent control, and withdrawal: "I stress the presence of chronic, intense envy, and defenses against such envy, particularly devaluation, omnipotent control, and narcissistic withdrawal, as major characteristics of their emotional life" (p. 264).

An attitude of indifference is characteristic of a person with a narcissistic personality organization. James Dean's "I don't care" is the basic attitude of indifference. The abrupt shift from primitive idealization into a basic attitude of indifference—to turn around and walk away from another person—is characteristic of the interpersonal relationships of an individual with a narcissistic personality organization (p. 291).[2] The basic character constellation of the narcissistic personality organization, therefore, is comprised of emptiness, restlessness, and boredom, the primitive defenses against chronic intense envy of devaluation, omnipotence, and withdrawal, and a basic attitude of indifference in interpersonal relationships.

A FULLER PORTRAIT OF THE NARCISSISTIC PERSONALITY ORGANIZATION

The diagnostic criteria for the narcissistic personality disorder from the *Diagnostic and Statistical Manual of Mental Disorders* (1994) can be integrated into the analysis. The *Diagnostic and Statistical Manual of Mental Disorders* (DSM-IV) is a standard clinical diagnostic tool published by the American Psychiatric Association. The clinical diagnostic criteria begin to fill out the portrait of the narcissistic personality organization. It is worth noting that the prevalence of the narcissistic personality organization is reported to be 2% to 16% in the clinical population and less than 1% in the general population (DSM-IV, p. 660).

Diagnostic Criteria for 301.81 Narcissistic Personality Disorder

DSM-IV defines the diagnostic criteria for narcissistic personality disorder as a pervasive pattern of grandiosity (in fantasy or behavior), need for admiration, and lack of empathy, beginning in early adulthood and present in a variety of contexts, as indicated by five (or more) of the following:

1. has grandiose sense of self-importance (e.g., exaggerated achievements and talents, expects to be recognized as superior without commensurate achievements)
2. is preoccupied with fantasies of unlimited success, power, brilliance, beauty, or ideal love
3. believes that he or she is "special' and unique and can only be understood by, or should associate with, other special on high-status people (or institutions)
4. requires excessive admiration
5. has a sense of entitlement, i.e., unreasonable expectations of especially favorable treatment or automatic compliance with his or her expectations
6. is interpersonally exploitative, i.e., takes advantage of others to achieve his or her own ends
7. lacks empathy: is unwilling to recognize or identify with the feelings and needs of others
8. is often envious of others or believes that others are envious of him or her
9. shows arrogant, haughty behaviors or attitudes (DSM-IV, p. 661)

Kernberg's Clinical Observations on the Narcissistic Personality Organization

In an effort to elaborate on the spectrum of variation of the narcissistic personality organization, clinical observations will be presented for the typical narcissistic personality organization, followed by an exploration of the intrapsychic structure and the developmental history. The extremes of the highest and lowest points on the spectrum of variation of the narcissistic personality organization will then be elaborated. Clinical descriptions will be presented to provide a fuller, albeit unflattering, portrait of a chronologically adult person with a narcissistic personality organization.

"In practice," according to Kernberg (1985A), "one can differentiate three levels of functioning of narcissistic personalities" (p. 332). The middle of the spectrum of variation is the typical narcissistic personality organization, representing the majority of narcissistic individuals who come for clinical treatment, according to Kernberg (p. 333). The highest point on the spectrum of variation of the narcissistic personality organization is characterized as a person who appears almost normal: "It seems worthwhile to invest much effort in the treatment of what so often on the surface, looks deceivingly as if we were dealing with an almost 'normal' person" (p. 313). The lowest point on the spectrum of variation of the narcissistic personality organization is represented by "narcissistic patients with overt borderline functioning, particularly those who present intense rage reactions or 'narcissistic rage' " (p. 334).

I offer these clinical observations culled from Kernberg's case material with little elaboration at first, as a way of filling out the unflattering portrait of the narcissistic personality organization. Increasing elaboration will be provided as this chapter progresses, and in a subsequent chapter on the dark side of consumer behavior.

On Excessive Self-Reference

Excessive self-reference is the central characteristic of the narcissistic personality organization:

> These patients present an unusual degree of self-reference in their interactions with other people, a great need to be loved and admired by others, and a curious apparent contradiction between a very inflated concept of themselves and an inordinate need for tribute from others. Their emotional life is shallow. They experience little empathy for the feelings of others, they obtain very little enjoyment from life other than from the tributes they receive from others or from their own grandiose fantasies, and they feel restless and bored when external glitter wears off and no new sources feed their self-regard. (Kernberg 1985A, p. 17)

Superficially Appropriate Social Adjustment and Effective Social Adaptation

The contradictory character of the narcissistic personality organization is elucidated by Kernberg (1985A):

> I describe patients with narcissistic personalities as presenting excessive self-absorption usually coinciding with superficially smooth and effective social adaptation, but with serious distortions in their internal relationships with other people. They present various combinations of intense ambitiousness, grandiose fantasies, feelings of inferiority, and overdependence on external admiration and acclaim. Along with feelings of boredom and emptiness, and continuous search for gratification of striving for brilliance, wealth, power and beauty, there are serious deficiencics in their capacity to love and be concerned for others. This lack of capacity for empathic understanding of others often comes as a surprise considering their superficially appropriate social adjustment. Chronic uncertainty and dissatisfaction about themselves, conscious or unconscious exploitiveness and ruthlessness toward others are also characteristics of these patients. (Kernberg 1985A, p. 264)

Superficially Smooth and Socially Charming

While the narcissistic personality organization is superficially smooth and socially charming on the surface, deeper exploration reveals a cold and ruthless person, with shallow interpersonal relationships that are exploitative and parasitic: "In general, their relationships with other people are clearly exploitative and sometimes parasitic. It is as if they feel they have the right to control and possess others and to exploit them without guilt feelings—and behind the surface which very often is charming and engaging, one senses coldness and ruthlessness" (Kernberg 1985A, p. 17). Indeed, a person with a narcissistic personality organization exploits without guilt because he or she does not have a prohibitive superego and therefore does not have the capacity for experiencing guilt.

While individuals with a narcissistic personality organization tend to conform to moral standards, they think of themselves as capable of antisocial behavior:

> Narcissistic patients characteristically adapt themselves to the moral demands of their environment because they are afraid of the attacks to which they would be subjected if they do not conform, and because this submission seems to be the price they have to pay for glory and admiration; however, one frequently finds that patients of this kind, who have never shown evidence of antisocial activity, think of themselves as "crooks" and as capable of antisocial behavior "if they could get away with it." Needless to say, they also experience other people as basically dishonest and unreliable, or only reliable because of external pressures. (p. 232)[3]

In comparison to a child who had a relatively normal upbringing, the child who would develop a narcissistic personality organization is characterized by a lack of warmth and engagement with others:

> The coldness and aloofness of patients with pathological narcissism at times when their capacity for social charm is not in operation, their tendency to disregard others except when temporally idealizing them as potential sources of narcissistic supply, and the contempt and devaluation prevalent in most of their relationships are in striking contrast to the warm quality of the [normal] small child's self-centeredness. Pursuing this observation into the historical analysis of narcissistic patients, one finds from the age of two or three years a lack of normal warmth and engagement with others, and easily activated, abnormal destructiveness and ruthlessness. (p. 273)

Lack of Depth and Productivity over Time

Kernberg (1985A) presents a devastating portrayal of the lack of depth and productivity over a long period of time that is characteristic of the typical narcissistic personality organization:

> Highly intelligent patients with this personality structure may appear as quite creative in their fields: narcissistic personalities can often be found as leaders in industrial organizations or academic institutions; they may also be outstanding performers in some artistic domain. Careful observation, however, of their productivity over a long period of time will give evidence of superficiality and flightiness in their work, of a lack of depth which eventually reveals the emptiness behind the glitter. (pp. 229–230)

Social Opportunity and Narcissistic Supplies

A person with a narcissistic personality organization does not have the capacity for concern. Interpersonal relationships present opportunities for the immediate gratification of impulses that may provide a temporary sense of meaningfulness:

> Patients with narcissistic personality, in contrast, do not have the capacity for empathizing with human experience in depth. Their social life, which gives them opportunities to obtain confirmation in reality or fantasy of their needs to be admired, and offers them direct instinctual gratifications [where *instinctual* refers to impulse gratification], may provide them with an immediate sense of meaningfulness, but this is temporary. When such gratifications are not forthcoming, their sense of emptiness, restlessness, and boredom take over. Now their world becomes a prison from which only new excitement, admiration, or experiences implying control, triumph or incorporation of supplies are an escape. Emotional reactions in depth to art, the investment in value systems or in creativity beyond gratification of their narcissistic aims is often unavailable and indeed strange to them. (Kernberg 1985A, p. 218)

Success and admiration often come easily to a person with a narcissistic personality organization who has a special gift. A more effective surface adaptation provides them with unusual availability of narcissistic supplies: "There are narcissistic personalities whose surface adaptation is more effective, and who present talents, skills, and/or high intelligence which grant them outstanding success in their social life and provide them with unusual availability of gratification from external sources in the form of success and admiration" (pp. 332–333). Further, according to Kernberg, "One might say that their gains from their illness often compensate for the disturbance in object relations" (p. 333). When such unusual availability of gratification from external sources is *not* forthcoming, a sense of emptiness, restlessness, and boredom pervades the person with a narcissistic personality organization and drives the person to consume narcissistic supplies as one source of escape.

These satisfactions compensate the individual for failures in interpersonal relationships and ultimately for the failure to achieve the higher neurotic and normal levels of personality development. The theme of compensatory satisfactions has been dealt with before as the additional symptom formation that goes with the breakdown of splitting, that is, the outbreak of compulsive or more extreme addictive consumption behavior to restore the primitive defense of splitting against severe anxiety. The panoply of compulsive behaviors characteristic of the borderline personality organization and the chronic pattern of addictive behavior characteristic of the narcissistic personality organization represent relative degrees of variation within the primitive range of the Personality Continuum.

THE GRANDIOSE SELF AND THE INTRAPSYCHIC STRUCTURE OF THE NARCISSISTIC PERSONALITY ORGANIZATION

The grandiose self is the central component of the intrapsychic structure of the narcissistic personality organization. In Kernberg's (1985A) conception, the grandiose self represents the condensation of components of the real self, the ideal self, and ideal objects:

> In my thinking, this grandiose self is a pathological condensation of rudiments of the real self, the ideal self, and the ideal objects of infancy and early childhood, and thus incorporates some components that would otherwise become integrated into the superego. As a result, superego integration is defective, ego and superego boundaries are blurred in certain areas, and the entire intrapsychic world of object relations deteriorates; it is replaced by the grandiose self and by devalued, shadowy representations of self and others and potentially persecutory images representing the nonintegrated sadistic superego-forerunners. (p. 332)

The pathological condensation of the real self, the ideal self, and the ideal object is the result of the excessive frustration and severe oral aggression, rage, and envy experienced in early interpersonal relations.

Kernberg (1985A) has provided these poignant portrayals of the internal objects of the real self, the ideal self, and the ideal object that are condensed into the grandiose self of the narcissistic personality organization: The real self is the specialness of the child reinforced by early experience; the ideal self is the fantasies and self-images of power, wealth, omniscience, and beauty that compensated the small child for the early experiences of severe oral frustration, rage, and envy; and the ideal object is the fantasy of an ever-giving, ever-loving, and accepting parent (pp. 265–266).

As a result of the failure to achieve the higher neurotic level of personality development, the intrapsychic structure of the narcissistic personality organization is missing higher-level intrapsychic structures: "As the normal integration of the ego ideal with other superego structures is missing, the forerunners of later value systems are also missing, and so is the precondition for the internalization of the later superego components, mainly the more realistic parental images derived from oedipal conflicts which normally constitute the major cement of superego integration" (p. 283). The more realistic parental images, derived from the successful resolution of the oedipal conflict, the prohibitive superego and the ego ideal, and the forerunners of later value systems and the protective superego are all missing in the intrapsychic structure of the narcissistic personality organization.

It is not just a case of missing higher-level intrapsychic structures, however, because the intrapsychic structure of the narcissistic personality organization has actively deteriorated: "There is not merely a 'lack' of internalization of certain normal idealized superego forerunners, but an active distortion of them simultaneously with pathological devaluation of the external objects. In more general terms, there is not simply an 'absence' of certain structures, but a pathological development of earlier structures so that the later normal ones cannot develop" (p. 284).

Kernberg, using the terminology of integration, condensation, and fusion somewhat interchangeably, concisely characterizes the intrapsychic structure of the narcissistic personality organization: "The pathological fusion between ideal self, ideal object, and actual self images prevents such integration of the superego, because the process of idealization is highly unrealistic, preventing the condensation of such idealized images with actual parental demands and with aggressively determined superego forerunners" (p. 232).[4] The superego forerunners have been internalized, but have not been integrated, and retain a distorted, primitive, and aggressive character: "Although some superego components are internalized, such as prohibitive parental demands, they preserve a distorted, primitive, aggressive quality because they are not integrated with the loving aspects of the superego which are normally drawn from the ideal self and object images and are missing in these patients" (p. 232).

Sadistic Superego Forerunners and the Punitive Superego

The forerunners of the superego that predominate in a person with a primitive personality organization have a sadistic character: "Insofar as superego elements and ego elements are condensed into the grandiose self, certain superego elements will not be available for superego integration, particularly the normal components of the ego ideal. Under these circumstances, the sadistic superego forerunners of the superego predominate, and superego integration would represent a terrible danger for the ego of pressure from a sadistic, primitive superego" (Kernberg 1985A, pp. 282–283). The sadistic, primitive superego is the punitive superego, persecuting the person with a narcissistic personality organization with severe anxiety.

The level of superego functioning is an important indicator of the level of personality development. In general, for the primitive range of the Personality Continuum, according to Kernberg, "The better the integration of the superego, the higher the level of character pathology" (p. 20). The better integrated the superego, therefore, the higher the relative ranking of the personality organization within the primitive range of the Personality Continuum.

In comparison to the higher neurotic and normal ranges of the Personality Continuum, the integration of the prohibitive superego and the ego ideal are prevented in the narcissistic personality organization at the primitive level of personality development: "In my view, idealized object images which normally would be integrated into the ego ideal and as such, into the [prohibitive] superego, are condensed instead with the self-concept" (p. 282). The condensation of actual self-images with the ideal self and the ideal object images in the grandiose self blurs the boundaries between the ego and superego: "Actual self images, a part of the ego structure, are now pathologically condensed with forerunners of the superego, and therefore, they interfere with the normal differentiation of the superego and ego" (p. 232).

A person with a narcissistic personality organization is ignorant of the higher and more mature aspects of another person because the intrapsychic structures that provide the psychological foundations for these human capacities are missing: "The lack of superego development, and therefore the further lack of ego integration and maturation of feelings, aims, and interests, also keeps them in ignorance of the higher, more mature and differentiated aspects of other people's personalities" (p. 37).

Excessive Oral Aggression and the Narcissistic Personality Organization

The purpose of the pathological condensation of ideal self, ideal object, and actual self is to protect the self, and this is reinforced by the primitive defense of devaluation: "In narcissistic personalities, such a primitive fusion of the self with the ego ideal [i.e., the images of ideal object and ideal self that would have been integrated into the ego ideal], and the concomitant processes of devaluation of external objects and [internal] object images, do take place in order to protect the self against primitive oral conflicts and frustration" (Kernberg 1985A, p. 241).

Excessive oral aggression is at the core of the etiology of the narcissistic personality organization: "What brings about the crucial pathological fusion of ideal self, ideal object, and actual self images? These patients present a pathologically augmented development of oral aggression" (p. 234). Kernberg attributed the excessive oral aggression to three contributing factors: "It is hard to evaluate to what extent this development represents a constitutionally determined strong aggressive drive, constitutionally determined lack of anxiety tolerance in regard to aggressive impulses, or severe frustration in their first years of life" (p. 234).

INCAPACITY TO DEPEND ON ANOTHER PERSON

The incapacity to depend on another person is a crucial characteristic of a person with a narcissistic personality organization at the primitive level of personality development:

> These patients often admire some hero or outstanding individual and establish with such a person what on the surface looks like a dependent relationship, yet they really experience themselves as part of the outstanding person; it regularly emerges in treatment that the admired individual is merely an extension of themselves. If that person rejects them, they experience immediate hatred and fear, and react by devaluating the former idol. If the person disappears or is "dethroned," they immediately drop him. In short, there is no real involvement with the admired person and a simple narcissistic use is made of him. (Kernberg 1985A, p. 236)

For individuals with a narcissistic personality organization, these extensions of the self are projections of their own grandiose self-concepts: "Idealized people, on whom these patients seem to 'depend,' regularly turn out to be projections of their own aggrandized self concepts. Idealized representatives of the self, the 'shadows' of others, and—as we shall see—dreaded enemies, are all that seem to exist in the inner world of these patients" (p. 233).[5]

A person with a narcissistic personality organization tends to divide the world into two parts, diametrically opposite:

> This devaluated concept of the self can be seen especially in narcissistic patients who divide the world into famous, rich, and great people on the one hand, and the despicable, worthless, "mediocrity" on the other. Such patients are afraid of not belonging to the company of the great, rich, and powerful, and of belonging instead to the "mediocre," by which they mean worthless and despicable rather than "average" in the ordinary sense of the term. One patient, after years of analytic treatment, began to yearn to become "average," meaning he wanted to be able to enjoy being an ordinary person, without an overriding necessity to feel great and important in order to cancel feelings of worthlessness and devaluation. (p. 234)

Although the person with a narcissistic personality organization may appear to be dependent on others, appearances are deceiving, contributing to the contradictory character of the behavior: "There exists the danger of looking upon these patients as very dependent because of the satisfaction they obtain from such closeness" (p. 236). In reality, "Very often such patients are considered to be 'dependent' because they need so much tribute and adoration from others, but on a deeper level they are completely unable to really depend on anybody because of their deep distrust and depreciation of others" (p. 17).

Dependency on another person is dangerous, fraught with frustration and rage, hate and envy, that must be eliminated or denied: "Once, however, the kind of mechanism mentioned—defensive fusion of ideal self, ideal object and [actual] self images—comes into operation, it is extremely effective in perpetuating a vicious circle of self-admiration, depreciation of others, and elimination of all actual dependency. The greatest fear of these patients is to be dependent on anybody else, because to depend means to hate, envy, and expose themselves to the danger of being exploited, mistreated, and frustrated" (p. 235). "The grandiose self permits the denial of dependency on others, protects the individual against narcissistic rage and envy, creates the precondition for ongoing depreciation and devaluation of others, and contributes to distort both the future narcissistic and object investments of the patient" (p. 283).

Balint on the Thin Line between Love and Hate

The ideas of Michael Balint in "On Love and Hate" (1951) are illuminating here. Balint saw hate as the denial of dependence: "Love is the more general notion, more people and things can be loved than hated, because hate has the additional condition of a denial of dependence" (Balint 1986, p. 149). Thus hate is bound up with dependency, and according to Balint, "Only people and things on which we depend can be hated" (p. 149).

The conception of hate as the denial of dependency brings the analysis to a more fundamental level, the vicissitudes of dependency in an interpersonal relationship. According to Balint (1951), "Hate is a measure of inequality between the object and subject; the smaller the inequality, the more mature the subject, the less is his need for hate" (Balint 1986, p. 149). The unfortunate outcome, according to Fairbairn (1952), is "a persistence of the hatred which the child comes to feel towards himself for the dependence dictated by his need" (p. 115). This self-hatred is a significant contributing factor to the self-destructiveness of compulsive and addictive behavior.

Dependency varies with the level of personality development. The more mature a person is—the higher the level of personality development—the lower is the need for hate in interpersonal relationships. The more immature a person is—the lower the level of personality development—the greater is the need for hate. For personality organizations in the primitive range of the Personality Continuum, there is a thin line between love and hate. An additional elaboration by Balint (1951) brings the analysis around to the intrapsychic structural formation of the personality: "The change of love into hate is a subjective, intrapsychic process. The object need not take any part in it, may remain completely unaware of the process" (Balint 1986, p. 149).

The Grandiose Self and the Relatively Good Surface Functioning and Social Adaptation of the Narcissistic Personality Organization

The grandiose self explains the relatively good surface functioning and social adaptation of the narcissistic personality organization arrested at the primitive level of development: "The pathological grandiose self explains the narcissistic patients' paradox of relatively good surface functioning and social adaptation in the presence of a predominance of splitting mechanisms and severe ego pathology" (Kernberg 1985A, p. 332). In contrast to the borderline personality organization, occupying a relatively higher position in the primitive range of the Personality Continuum, the grandiose self gives a person with a narcissistic personality organization a better overall social adaptation on the surface, but this comes at a price, the loss of the capacity to depend on another person:

> Thus created, the pathological grandiose self permits a certain integration of the ego providing a better overall social adaptation than achieved by borderline patients in general. The splitting of the self characteristic of borderline patients is thus compensated for, but at a price of a further deterioration of object relationships, the loss of the capacity to depend and an ominous capacity for self-protection from emotional conflicts with others by withdrawing into splendid, grandiose isolation which gives the specific seal to the narcissistic [personality] organization. (p. 282)

There is a limit to the destruction of internal objects, however, because the person with a narcissistic personality organization needs to be admired and loved by others:

> One result of the defensive fusion [condensation] of ideal self, ideal object, and actual self images is the devaluation and destruction not only of external objects but also of internalized object images. Actually this process never goes so far that there are no internal representations of external objects: it would probably be impossible to live under such conditions. To want to be admired and loved by others requires that others should appear at least somewhat "alive," internally as well as externally. The remnants of the internalized object representations acquire the characteristics of real, but rather lifeless, shadowy people. This experience of other people, especially those who are not idealized, as lifeless shadows or marionettes is quite prevalent in the patients I am considering. (p. 233)

The remarkable absence of object relationships characteristic of the socially isolated narcissistic personality organization represents, on a deeper level, the incapacity to depend on internalized good objects: "On the surface these patients appear to present a remarkable absence of object relationships; on a deeper level, their interactions reflect very intense, primitive, internalized object relationships of a frightening kind and an incapacity to depend on the internalized good objects" (pp. 17–18). The intense, primitive, internalized object relationships of a frightening kind, the sadistic superego forerunners, represent the punitive superego. As a result of the deterioration of internal and external object relations, the subjective experience of emptiness is most intense and almost constant in the narcissistic personality organization: "In narcissistic personality organizations, where the normal relations between an integrated self and integrated internal objects are replaced by a pathological grandiose self and the deterioration of internal objects, the experience of emptiness is most intense and almost constant" (p. 220).

These primitive oral conflicts are internalized through introjection, forming the sadistic superego forerunners that later become the punitive superego. The punitive superego persecutes the person with a primitive personality organization with severe anxiety and drives the person to episodes of compulsive or more extreme addictive behavior. The motivation, unconscious, of course, that drives a person with a primitive personality organization to behave in compulsive or addictive behavior is to protect or defend the person from these internalized primitive oral conflicts and frustrations. The grandiose self, the devalued, shadowy representations of self and others, the persecutory images representing the nonintegrated sadistic superego forerunners, defective superego integration, and blurred ego and superego boundaries constitute the deteriorated intrapsychic structure of the narcissistic personality organization.

DEVELOPMENTAL HISTORY OF THE NARCISSISTIC PERSONALITY ORGANIZATION

An investigation of the interpersonal origins of the narcissistic personality organization is an examination of the person's developmental history, the relatively enduring pattern of recurrent interpersonal situations that characterized the person's life. These are the dynamic considerations, in the sense that Kernberg (1985A) uses this term when he refers to genetic-dynamic analysis. The analysis shifts from the chronologically adult person to the examination of the interpersonal origins of the narcissistic personality organization. What went wrong in those early interpersonal relationships with the mother and the father and in the person's wider social system (in the terminology of Piore 1979), or the entire social system (in the terminology of Parsons 1964), or Sullivan's interpersonal conception of the personality as the relatively enduring pattern of recurrent interpersonal situations that characterize a human life (1953, p. 111).

What makes a person with a narcissistic personality organization feel so grandiose? The term *grandiose* is often used disparagingly of a grandeur that is affected or assumed, an exaggerated self-importance. According to Kernberg (1985A), it is typical in the developmental history of a person with a narcissistic personality organization to have occupied a unique position in the family: "These patients often occupy a pivotal point in their family structure, such as being the only child, or the only 'brilliant' child, or the one who is to fulfill the family aspirations; a good number of them have a history of having played the role of 'genius' in their family during childhood" (p. 235).

The child who would develop a narcissistic personality organization typically does have a special gift: "Their histories reveal that each patient possessed some inherent quality which could have objectively aroused the envy or admiration of others. For example, unusual physical attractiveness or some special talent became a refuge against the basic feelings of being unloved and being the objects of revengeful hatred" (p. 235). This harks back to the basic fault in Fairbairn's (1952) conception: The failure of the mother to convince her child by spontaneous and genuine expressions of affection that he or she is loved as a person and that his or her love is accepted by her in return (p. 13).

Brutal Portrayal of the Parents of a Narcissistic Personality Organization

In the early relationship with the parental figures (I am tempted to say, in the vein of Sullivan), most importantly with the mother, the relatively enduring pattern of recurrent interpersonal situations of the person who will become a narcissistic personality organization was characterized as follows by Kernberg (1985A):

> Chronically cold parental figures with covert but intense aggression are a very frequent feature of the background of these patients. A composite picture of a number of cases that I have been able to examine or to treat shows consistently a parental figure, usually the mother or a mother surrogate [Sullivan's mothering one], who functions well on the surface in a superficially well-organized home, but with a degree of callousness, indifference, and nonverbalized, spiteful aggression. When intense oral frustration, resentment, and aggression have developed in the child within such an environment, the first condition is laid for his need to defend against extreme envy and hatred. (pp. 234–235)

In a particular case study of a male patient with a narcissistic personality organization, Kernberg relates that his treatment by a self-centered mother as a child had left him with intolerable feelings of unworthiness and abandonment: "There was abundant evidence in this case that his mother was, indeed, very self-centered, and had a chronic tendency to manipulate him through guilt feelings; but his feelings of abandonment and unworthiness were intolerable to him, because they were compounded by guilt over his anger toward his mother, and by the projection onto her of his own angry, revengeful feelings" (p. 294). It is severe anxiety, not guilt, that is appropriate here, because the person with a narcissistic personality organization does not have the capacity for experiencing guilt. The child experiences severe anxiety over his anger toward his mother and over the projection of that anger onto her.

Failure to Identify with the Penetrating Power of the Paternal Penis

Kernberg (1977, reprinted in 1985B), interpreting the view of a group of French writers, including the important contributions of Chasseguet-Smirgel (1975, 1974), observed that men with narcissistic personality organization often display or exhibit a playful sexual seductiveness toward women:

> Under these circumstances, narcissistic fixation may later result in a kind of infantile, playful sexual seductiveness toward women without the full identification with the "penetrating power" of the paternal penis. The fixation will interfere with full genital identity, with the internalization of the father into the ego ideal, and will foster the repression of excessive castration anxiety. The unresolved competition with the father and the defensive denial of castration anxiety are expressed in narcissistic enjoyment of infantile dependent relations with women who represent mother images. This constellation, for these authors as well as for Chasseguet-Smirgel (1975, 1974), is an important source of narcissistic fixation (I would say, fixation at a level of normal infantile narcissism)[6] and for failure to resolve the oedipal complex in boys, and is fostered by those aspects of mother's behavior through which she rebels against the "dominance" of the paternal penis and the "paternal law" in general. Hence, an unconscious collusion exists between eternally little boys—Don Juans—and seductive maternal women who utilize the rebelliousness of the Don Juan against father's "law and order" to express their own competitiveness with and rebelliousness against the father. (Kernberg 1985B, pp. 283–284)

Excessive castration anxiety and the defensive denial of castration anxiety are characteristic of personality organizations at the primitive level of personality development, in particular, the narcissistic personality organization. Denial is a primitive defense.

The failure to achieve a full identification with the father, including a complementary genital sexual identification, results in the enjoyment of infantile dependent relations with women representing mother images by men with narcissistic personality organization. This is one reason why such a man is often described as an eternal little boy—*puer aeternus*—without the full identification with the "penetrating power" of the paternal penis. The higher-level interpersonal achievements in personality development—the normal resolution of the oedipal complex in boys and the internalization of the father into the ego ideal—have not been reached by the person with a narcissistic personality organization, arrested at the primitive level of personality development.

A clarification is in order here. The failure of normal resolution of the oedipal complex—the full genital identification with the father and the internalization of the father into the ego ideal—is at the core of the etiology of the neurotic personality organization, not the primitive personality organization. The failure to resolve the oedipal conflict represents the failure to achieve the full integration of satisfying genital sexual relations into an interpersonal relationship, the interpersonal achievement in personality development that demarcates the normal range of the Personality Continuum. The result is the arrest of personality development of the chronologically adult person at the neurotic level.

Personality organizations in the primitive range of the Personality Continuum are characterized by the failure to achieve the integration of whole object relations. The three-person oedipal situation cannot develop until after the integration of whole object relations has occurred.

A Brutal Clarification of the Fear of Castration and Castration Anxiety

In the primitive range of the Personality Continuum, before the integration of whole object relations, and without resort to the more effective, higher-level defense of repression, the child who would develop a primitive personality organization utilizes the more primitive defense of splitting. In comparison, for personality organizations at the higher neurotic and normal levels of development, the fear of castration results in repression and the residual experience of castration anxiety as a warning signal of danger (Freud 1915B). The fear of being castrated is experienced consciously as a feeling and a thought, the emotion and the ideation or thought of the fear of being castrated—your cock on the chopping block, having your cock completely cut off, a cold shot in the crotch, Lorena Bobbitt carelessly tossing John Wayne Bobbitt's castrated penis out of the car window on the side of the road, the castration scene in the movie *Pelle the Conqueror* (1987), or even to some extent, the zipper scene in the movie *There's Something about Mary*.

The unconscious psychological defense of repression takes over to repress the ideation—the concept or thought of being castrated visualized in a mental image—so that the person does not become aware of the affect—the fear of the physical pain of actual castration. Thus when the defense of repression is working effectively, the unwanted emotion of fear does not occur, and the person is not aware of the fear of castration, but the person is left feeling anxious as a warning signal of danger in the interpersonal situation.[7]

Although it is called "castration" anxiety, for the neurotic and normal person, there is no conscious thought of being castrated when the defense of repression is working effectively, but the person does experience residual anxiety of varying degrees under the circumstances in the interpersonal situation. When repression works effectively, neither the idea nor the emotion are experienced consciously. Anxiety is the residual experience of effective repression of the fear of castration, the casting out of consciousness of the feeling and thought of being castrated. The term *castration anxiety*, therefore, must be used knowingly; it is anxiety that is being experienced, not the feeling or thought of being castrated. We (speaking for all mankind, at least, and not speaking loosely, of course) are spared the experience of castration, the idea or the emotion, but we are left feeling anxious, as a danger signal. We do not know why we are feeling anxious, because the unconscious defense of repression has worked effectively.

Fear, the Amygdala, and William James's Bear

Fear is the emotion that has been studied the most, largely from studies of classical conditioning. William James (1884) posed the key question about fear: "In an 1884 article in the philosophy journal *Mind*, he asked an unusually prescient question about the nature of emotion, using as an example a person's fear upon encountering a bear. Does he run because he feels he is afraid, or does he feel afraid *after* he has already started running? Put another way, does a person have time to think something is frightening, or does the reaction to fear precede the thought?" (Hall 1999, p. 45). James concluded that the fear precedes the thought.

Brain-functioning studies utilizing functional magnetic resonance imaging (fMRI) and positron-emission tomography (PET) have supported James's conclusion. The amygdala is, literally, the primitive part of the brain that reacts to fear first. The amygdala is known to project directly to the substantia innominata, where the cholinegric nucleus basalis of

Meynert neurons are located (Whalen et al. 1998, p. 416). Whalen et al. (1998) refer to "the well established role of the nucleus basalis of Meynert in the modulation of cortical neuronal excitability" (p. 416). After the initial fear stimulus, the result is an increase in the overall state of arousal: "The fact [is] that the activity of these neurons is more closely associated with an animal's overall state of arousal rather than with its response to specific stimulus presentations" (p. 416). The crucial implication for the area of information processing in the field of marketing is that in this hyperalert cognitive state, information is consciously processed more efficiently.

A Note on the Use of Subliminal Stimuli in Advertising

Anxiety represents an elevated level of arousal, a state of hyperalertness. The conscious processing of information becomes more efficient. This is germane to the discussion on the use of subliminal stimuli in advertising and the unconscious (Freud 1915B). An advertiser uses a subliminal stimulus in an advertisement precisely because the conscious processing of sensory information becomes more efficient. The objective of the advertiser is to increase recall of the brand image. Like stimuli designed to evoke castration anxiety, the subliminal stimulus embedded in the advertisement is negative.[8]

A Hole in Awareness: Sullivan's Primary Genital Phobia

At the primitive level of personality development, *pregenital* does not refer to the premature development of "genital" strivings, but to the premature development of oedipal strivings, because the genitals are split off and become part of what Sullivan (1958) designated the not-me: "In cases in which this is successful, that area of the body becomes distinctly related to that area of personality to which I long since referred as the not-me" (p. 267).

The fear of castration and castration anxiety are excessive for personality organizations at the primitive level of personality development, because the premature development of oedipal strivings is a means of escape from the oral rage and fears. This creates a hole in awareness, a hole where the genitals should be, "a hole punched in the totality of 'my body' " (p. 174). The result of the mother's forbidding gestures is "to segregate out these zones of 'ownness' " and relegate them to the not-me (p. 145).

Primary genital phobia represents an extreme variation of the forbidding mother as dangerous, frightening, and castrating: "I have commented on the incredible efforts made by certain parents to keep the young child from handling the genitals, from exploring and getting sensations from them" (p. 267). Infantile sexuality is in the mind of the mother (Goethals 1976, p. 536). The outcome is primary genital phobia: "By primary genital phobia I refer to an enduring warp of personality which is often inculcated in late infancy and early childhood and practically converts that area of the body into something not quite of the body" (Sullivan 1953, p. 267). Sullivan (p. 376) also referred to it as primitive genital phobia.

SEXUAL ACTIVITY IN THE SPECTRUM OF VARIATION OF THE NARCISSISTIC PERSONALITY ORGANIZATION

The spectrum of variation of the narcissistic personality organization can be illustrated by the patterns of sexual activity manifested in interpersonal relations. This is especially the case for men with a narcissistic personality organization. Kernberg (1984A) has delimited three patterns of sexual activity for men with a narcissistic personality organization: "Complete absence in sexual interest in women in the most severely ill patients; the frantic search for sexual excitement and sexual promiscuity linked with an incapacity for establishing a more permanent relationship, in less severe ones; and a limited capacity for transitory infatuation in still milder cases, represent the spectrum of narcissistic pathology of love life" (p. 195). A person with a narcissistic personality organization who has a limited capacity for transitory infatuations, and the sexually promiscuous person with a narcissistic personality organization, are both relatively better off than the person with a complete absence of sexual interest in another human being, because an infatuation or episode of sexual promiscuity provides an opportunity for fortunate interpersonal experience that holds the potential for favorable change in the personality organization and the achievement of a higher level of personality development.

Limited Capacity for Transitory Infatuations

A man with a narcissistic personality organization who has a limited capacity for transitory infatuations represents the highest point on the spectrum of variation of the narcissistic personality organization. At his point on the spectrum, problems in interpersonal relationships are often manifested in sexual difficulties that may appear neurotic on the surface:

"They frequently present complicating neurotic symptoms and sexual difficulties, and are disturbed by the serious defects in their capacity for establishing lasting emotional and sexual relationships and by their chronic feelings of emptiness" (Kernberg 1985A, p. 333).

For a narcissistic personality organization, neurotic difficulties in interpersonal relationships, especially sexual problems, represent high functioning, that is, a person with a primitive personality functioning at the higher neurotic level of personality development. This represents high functioning because the person with a narcissistic personality organization is not socially isolated: "These patients would not come for treatment unless they presented some serious neurotic symptoms, sexual disturbances, or chronic difficulties in intimate relations with others—in their marriage, for instance" (p. 333).

Sexually Promiscuous Behavior

Sexually promiscuous behavior—the frantic search for sexual excitement—represents a lower point, relatively speaking, on the spectrum of variation of the narcissistic personality organization. In the more extreme case in men, this pattern is manifested in predatory sexual behavior—the bachelor who goes from conquest to conquest, unable and unwilling to make a commitment to a relatively enduring relationship with a woman, the Don Juan, Casanova, playboy, the eternal little boy or *puer aeternus* (Franz 1981).

Complete Absence of Sexual Interest

The complete absence of overt sexual activity in an interpersonal relationship represents the lowest point on the spectrum of variation of the narcissistic personality organization. Intense paranoid fears of sexual involvement with women for men with narcissistic personality organization can result in social and sexual isolation: "Another frequent problem, particularly of narcissistic men in their relations with women, is the presence of intense, paranoid fears of sexual involvement, derived from their unconscious projection of their own hostility (toward primitive mother images) onto the women with whom they get involved. These fears may determine chronic social and sexual isolation, and contribute to the development of stalemates in the transference" (Kernberg 1985A, p. 336).

For a man with a narcissistic personality organization, the intense fear of a sexual involvement with a woman is derived from projection of his own hostility toward primitive images of the mother, the negative introject and the negative identifications. Sexual relations with women can be improved by reducing these paranoid fears in men with a narcissistic personality organization: "It is frequently possible to reduce these paranoid reactions and improve the nature of these patient's sexual relationships without full exploration or resolution of the underlying conflicts; the excessive demandingness, the arrogant, parasitic, and exploitive relationships these patients develop with women as well as in other interpersonal interactions, may be tactfully explored and modified by supportive, reeducative means" (p. 336).

A reduction in the excessive demandingness and parasitic and exploitative behavior may improve the opportunity for fortunate interpersonal experience and the potential for favorable change in the personality organization of a person with a narcissistic personality organization. The seeds of hope exist even with the destructive and self-destructive behavior of the individual with a narcissistic personality organization: "In the midst of the destructive and self-destructive instinctual [I would simply say *physiological*] manifestations are hidden potentials for growth and development, and especially that what appears on the surface to be destructive and self-destructive sexual behavior may contain the roots of further libidinal development and deepening interpersonal relationships" (p. 103).

These are very positive terms, the potential for growth and development, with a fortunate interpersonal relationship at any point in one's life (p. 103). Sullivan (1953) has made a similar observation: "But lust *combined with* the need for intimacy frequently does drive the victim toward correcting certain warps in personality and toward developing certain facilities, certain abilities, in interpersonal relations" (p. 270).

In the case of a man with a narcissistic personality organization, the episodes of promiscuous sexual behavior represent pseudogenital relationships with women:

> One other attempted solution may be the gratification of oral-aggressive needs in a heterosexual relationship, which on a deeper level represents the effort to "rob" mother sexually of what she denied orally. This constellation is frequently found in narcissistic, promiscuous men who unconsciously seek revenge against the oral, frustrating mother through pseudogenital relationships with women. Other solutions to the danger created by a premature condensation of the pregenital and genital aims can be found in the development of any of the polymorphous perverse infantile trends, especially those which permit the expression of aggression. (Kernberg 1985A, p. 42)

For a man with a narcissistic personality organization, this is a manifestation of the projection of his own angry, revengeful feelings toward his mother (p. 294). This is what is meant in mythology when a boy steals the key from under the mother's pillow at night while she sleeps with the father (Bly 1990).

As a consequence of this outcome, according to Sullivan (1953), the woman becomes idealized:

> Under these circumstances . . . a situation in which there are covert processes not accessible to awareness—in other words unconscious processes, to use the old-fashioned term—which are attended by pseudo-heterosexual practices. . . . This sort of thing is often a precursor of a lifelong course of searching for the "ideal" woman—or "ideal" man, if the person concerned is a woman—with the recurrent discovery of serious imperfections in each candidate for the ideal role. And this type of situation is the classical field for the appearance of the extremely unpleasant tension of jealousy. (p. 278)

Such pseudogenital heterosexual activity amounts to little more than mutual masturbation, according to Sullivan (p. 294). Although referring to premature ejaculation as an unfortunate outcome of early adolescent sexual experience, Sullivan captures the meaninglessness of the interpersonal situation that may result in the pseudogenital relationships of sexually promiscuous men with narcissistic personality organization:

> If there has been a lively lustful fantasy and little or no overt behavior with respect to the genitals—which incidentally will tend very strongly to characterize everyone who has this primary genital phobia I have spoken of—then it is almost certain that on the verge of an actual genital contact, precocious orgasm will occur in a man; this precocious orgasm suddenly wipes out the integration and just leaves two people in a practically meaningless situation although they had previously made immense sense to each other. Such an occurrence reflects very severely on the self-esteem of the man concerned. (p. 272)

The Fool Who Falls in Love Too Easily

A person with a narcissistic personality organization who has been wounded in love fits the profile of the fool who falls in love too easily.[9] A fool is someone who acts prematurely, without good sense or wisdom, and to behave foolishly means that something is done, happens, arrives or exists too early, before the proper or usual time. I believe that this is what William Blake meant, at least in part, when he wrote in the "Proverbs of Hell" from *The Marriage of Heaven and Hell* (1790): "If the fool would persist in his folly he would become wise" (Blake 1996, p. 76). The rub is if the fool would persist, since the failure to integrate whole object relations results in a chaotic pattern of alternating and contradictory behavior, lacking consistency and a sense of continuity of the self (Kernberg 1984A, p. 32).

The transitory infatuations and episodes of sexually promiscuous behavior for a person with a narcissistic personality organization represent a desperate search for love:

> And yet, hidden behind the transitory infatuations and sexual excitements of narcissistic personalities is not only greed and exploitativeness and the desperate need to escape involvement. It is true that there are some narcissistic people who live out lives completely devoid of meaningful object relations or even transitory infatuations, spending many years of their adult lives alone and lonely; they replace all sexual involvements with masturbation fantasies (usually of a primitive, polymorphous perverse kind) of such relations. But other narcissistic patients, those who do show the driven promiscuity of a narcissistic type, also reveal in analysis a desperate search for love, as if it were magically bound with body surfaces—breasts or penises or buttocks or vaginas. (Kernberg 1984A, pp. 187–188)

For a sexually promiscuous man with a narcissistic personality organization, the primitive idealization of woman represents a part-object relation, treating a woman as a bundle of body parts—breasts and buttocks and vaginas. This is the origin of the objectification of women by men.

Masturbation as a Substitutive Satisfaction for Genital Sexual Activity in an Interpersonal Relationship

Individuals with a narcissistic personality organization who live out their lives completely devoid of meaningful interpersonal relationships and replace all sexual involvements with masturbation fantasies, usually of a primitive, polymorphous perverse kind, of such relations, represent the lowest point on the spectrum of variation (Kernberg 1984A, pp. 187–188). In this case, masturbation is used as a way to avoid lust, according to Sullivan (1956): "You can avoid being disturbed by lust—which could be very troublesome in that it might draw you toward another person—by more or less continuously pulling your penis, or doing something of the sort" (p. 355). The unfortunate outcome of masturbation in this case is to avoid interpersonal relationships:

There is no way that I know of by which one can, all by oneself, satisfy the need for intimacy, cut off from the full driving power of loneliness, although loneliness can be manipulated or reduced to a certain extent. But through autosexual performance one can prevent lust from reaching tension sufficient to break down one's barriers. For that reason, the entirely exclusive use of autoerotic procedures can contribute to the prolongation of warp, which in turn contributes to the continued handicap for life of the person concerned. It is from this viewpoint alone that I would consider that masturbation, as the *only* solution for sundry collisions that lust enters into, is worse than almost anything else that is not definitely malevolent. (Sullivan 1953, pp. 270–271)

Loss of the Capacity for Crossing the Boundaries of the Self

The capacity for crossing the boundaries of the self is lost in a person with a narcissistic personality organization: "Sexual excitement and orgasm also lose their function of boundary-crossing into biology when mechanical, repetitive sexual excitement and orgasm are built into the self experience dissociated from the deepening of internalized object relations" (Kernberg 1985B, p. 294). The capacity for transcendence implies certain preconditions absent in a person with a narcissistic personality organization, most importantly, the integration of whole object relations and the capacity for concern:

As mentioned before, there has to be an awareness of and a capacity for empathy with the existence of a psychological field outside the self, hence, the erotically tinged states of manic excitement and grandiosity of psychotic patients cannot be called sexual passion; and the unconscious destruction of object representations and external objects that are so prominent in narcissistic personalities destroys their capacity for transcending into intimate union with another human being, therefore eroding and eventually destroying the capacity for sexual passion in such patients. (p. 294)

Thus it is the capacity for intimacy, love, as it were, that makes sexual activity satisfying in an interpersonal relationship:

I am suggesting that it is not the endless, compulsively repetitive gratification of instinctual urges that brings about a deterioration of the excitement, pleasure, and satisfaction derived from them, but the loss of the crucial function of crossing self-object boundaries, which is guaranteed by the normal investment in the world of object relations. In other words, it is the world of internalized and external object relations that keeps sexuality alive and provides the potential for "eternal" sexual gratification. (p. 294)

Masturbation, as a compulsive, repetitive activity, loses its transcendent function as well in the narcissistic personality organization:

> Here is where sexual excitement becomes differentiated from sexual passion; basically, masturbatory activity may (and usually does) express an object relation, typically the various aspects of the oedipal relations from early childhood on. But masturbation as a compulsive, repetitive activity, functioning defensely against forbidden sexual impulses and other unconscious conflicts in the context of a regressive dissociation from conflicted object relations, loses its transcendent function. (p. 294)

HARRY STACK SULLIVAN ON ENVY AND DISPARAGEMENT

In the basic character and defensive constellation of the narcissistic personality organization, devaluation is a primitive defense against intense envy, along with omnipotence and narcissistic withdrawal. Sullivan (1953) referred to the primitive defense of devaluation as *disparagement.* His interpersonal analysis of disparagement will set the stage for the subsequent object relations analysis of devaluation, the grandiose self, and the active deterioration of internal and external object relations characteristic of the narcissistic personality organization.

Envy is a feeling of acute discontent or discomfort because another person has something, some material thing or personal attribute, that one desires, and engenders ill will, resentful dislike, or hateful spite toward that person. In *Clinical Studies in Psychiatry* (1956), Sullivan defined envy in this way: "Envy is an acute discomfort caused by discovering that somebody has something one feels one ought to have" (p. 129).

According to Sullivan, "Envy is very unpleasant for the person who suffers it," and "there are perhaps two reasons for this" (p. 132). First, Sullivan (sounding somewhat cynical in his Irish Catholicism) refers to the ninth and tenth commandments against envy: "Thou shall not covet thy neighbor's house," and "Thou shall not covet thy neighbor's wife, servants, or anything that is your neighbor's," in the King James version of the Bible: "In the first place, in the Christian world, lip service at least is given to an ethical norm that one shall not envy—covet—the possessions of one's neighbor, and so envy carries heavy social disapproval" (p. 132). Such experiences of envy would evoke guilt in a person with a personality organization at the higher neurotic level of personality development; however, for a person with a personality organization at the primitive level of personality development, in particular, the narcissistic personality organization, without the capacity for experiencing guilt, envy provokes insecurity and the experience of severe anxiety. "In the second place," according to Sullivan, "envy is not pleasant because any formulation of it—any implicit process connected with it—necessarily starts with the point that you need something, some material thing that, unhappily, someone else has. This leads to the question, Why don't you have it? And this is itself enough in some cases to provoke insecurity" (pp. 132–133).

Thus envy leads to feelings of insecurity. Sullivan's implicit processes are, indeed, unconscious processes. Sullivan is loath to use Freudian psychoanalytic terminology. Insecurity provoked by envy—the heavy social disapproval of envy—is the experience of severe anxiety in interpersonal relationships for a person with a personality organization at the primitive level of personality development. The interpersonal origin of the severe anxiety is the invidious comparisons with others that evoked the intense envy: "In order to reduce anxiety from invidious comparisons with others," or "to avoid anxiety, he requires the security that comes from these other things" (Sullivan 1953, p. 309, and 1956, p. 128, respectively). Duesenberry (1949), an economist, drew a similar conclusion in arguing that strong barriers against association among individuals of different status are not maintained in American society: "This means that the frequency with which an individual can make invidious comparisons between the quality of his living standard and that of others is greatly increased" (p. 30).

The Defect in the Self: The Absence of Personal Worth in a Person with a Primitive Personality Organization

The absence of personal worth reflects a *defect in the self* in a person with a primitive personality organization: "This is where the defect in the self, which is somewhat parallel to the defect in the case of envy, steps in; and the most general way of describing this defect is to say that the person has grown into his present position in life with a deep, however unwelcome, conviction of relative unworthiness" (Sullivan 1956, p. 141). In Sullivan's conception, a person with such a defect in the self is at the mercy of intense envy:

> Returning to the self-system and looking into the history of its evolution, we find that the people who are much at the mercy of envy have learned to appraise themselves as unsatisfactory—that is, as inadequate human beings. Sometimes envious people have been taught this sense of their own inadequacy in a simple,

direct, and comprehensive way. That is, in the home environment and in the succeeding school society, they have been taught that they do not rate, that they are not the people that others wish they were. They have been children who have disappointed their parents' expectations and hopes for them. (pp. 129–130)

In early developmental history, children who would develop a narcissistic personality organization are "being taught of their inadequacy thus directly by being unsatisfactory to their parents and failing to live up to their parents' ideals," however unrealistic and rigidly held (p. 130). The failure to live up to parental ideals harks back to Fairbairn's piercing clear lament of the basic fault: "Failure on the part of the mother to convince the child that she really loves him as a person renders it difficult for him to sustain an emotional relationship with her on a personal basis" (Fairbairn 1952, p. 13).

Parents Who Disparage: Devaluation and the Learning of Disparagement

Disparaging another person represents the primitive defense of devaluation. To some extent, disparagement is learned from the parents: "It may occur because the parental figure has always disparaged all people who made her or him uncomfortable" (Sullivan 1953, p. 242). Uncomfortable, as in envy, but the focus here is on the origin of disparagement and the absence of personal worth:

This disparagement has its beginning for the most part in influence exerted by the parental group, who teach the juvenile to notice the shortcomings of others. And this necessity of maintaining self-esteem by pulling down the standing of others, if uncorrected in subsequent developmental eras, has unfortunate later outcomes. In the juvenile era this kind of security operation literally and importantly interferes with adequate appraisal of personal worth. Since one has to protect his feeling of self esteem by noting how unworthy everybody else is, this fails to provide any convincing data on one's having personal worth; one begins to think, "I am not as bad as the other swine." (pp. 345–346; see also p. 242)

"In other words," according to Sullivan, "one is encouraged to feel incapable of knowing what is good" (p. 243).

I prefer *protect* to *defend* because it refers to the use of primitive idealization to protect what little good early interpersonal experience a person with a primitive personality organization has had. Disparagement is used as a primitive defense: "And the usual solution in chronological maturity is to cover over one's chronic defect in self-esteem by disparaging others—a solution which is used by all of us in varying degrees" (p. 344). This is a somewhat dubious use of "self-esteem" in reference to the primitive range of the Personality Continuum, in general, and the narcissistic personality organization, in particular. Personality organizations in the primitive range of the Personality Continuum are characterized by chronically low self-esteem and the absence of personal worth. The use of disparagement is driven by severe anxiety and reflects this chronically low self-esteem of a person with a primitive personality organization:

> Disparaging and derogatory thought and action that make one feel "better" than the other person concerned, that expand one's self-esteem, as it were, at a cost, are always to be suspected of arising from anxiety. These processes are far removed from a judicious inquiry into one's relative personal skill in living. They do not reflect a good use of observation and analysis but rather indicate a low self-esteem in the person who uses them. The quicker one comes to a low opinion of another, other things being equal, the poorer is one's secret view of one's own worth in the field of the disparagement. (pp. 379–380)

In Sullivan's heuristic stages of personality development, the juvenile era is marked by the entry into the school system and the wider social system outside of the home: "I think that this is probably the most vicious of the inadequate, inappropriate, and ineffectual performances of parents with juveniles—this interference with sound development of appreciation of personal worth, by universal derogatory and disparaging attitudes toward anybody who seems to stand out at all" (p. 243).

Insults Reveal One's Own Faults

In general, at the primitive level of personality development, Sullivan (1953) equated disparagement with the lack of self-respect: "It is safe to say that people who respect no one except people they don't know do not respect themselves" (p. 308). For a person at the primitive level of personality development, disparagement reveals what one despises most about oneself: "In a good many ways one can read the whole state of a person's self-respect from his disparagement of others. The disparagement is built of two ingredients, that which one 'despises' about oneself, and a great many *not* operations" (p. 309).

According to Sullivan (1953), disparagement reveals a person's faults: "I think it has been known from the beginning of recorded thought that a person who is very bitter toward others, very hard on his fellow man for certain faults, is usually very sensitive to these particular faults because they are secret vices of his own" (p. 309). Thus the enhancement of one's self-esteem at the expense of others reveals one's own faults: "Enhancing one's prestige by the somewhat treacherous route of seeing one's faults in others" (Sullivan 1956, p. 134). When you reach down for an insult, you say the worst thing about yourself (Sullivan 1953, p. 309).

The *not* technique involves seeing others as if "they are different and opposite from you in one of your better aspects" (Sullivan 1953, pp. 302–303). This technique is essential to stereotyping: "Stereotypes reflect inadequate and inappropriate elements in one's own self-system; thus all the special stereotypes are either poor imitations of ingredients in the personified self, or—even more inadequate in terms of providing a guide in life—they are *not* elements from the personification of the self" (p. 303).[10]

THE HIGHEST POINT ON THE SPECTRUM OF VARIATION OF THE NARCISSISTIC PERSONALITY ORGANIZATION: THE DEVELOPMENT OF SUBLIMATORY CHANNELS AND THE CAPACITY TO TRANSCEND SELF-INTEREST

Kernberg (1985A) encourages the treatment of the described narcissistic personality organization at the highest point on the spectrum of variation: "It seems worthwhile to invest much effort in the treatment of what so often on the surface, looks deceivingly as if we were dealing with an almost 'normal' person" (p. 313). The development of sublimatory potential and investment in value systems transcending self-interest are good (prognostic) indicators of the highest point on the spectrum of variation of the narcissistic personality organization: "In simple terms, honesty in their daily life is a favorable prognostic indicator for the analysis of narcissistic personalities. In so much as a good development of sublimatory channels is intimately linked to the capacity for investment in value systems transcending narcissistic needs, the sublimatory potential of the patient is important too" (p. 307).

Transcending narcissistic self-interest in some activity or profession is a manifestation of sublimatory potential: "In general, the extent to which a patient is able to invest himself in a certain activity or profession beyond strictly narcissistic needs, the degree of gratification from such activity or profession, and the extent to which the patient is concerned about the intrinsic values of that activity or profession represent his sublimatory potential" (p. 133). Perhaps more important as a positive prognostic indicator for a person with a narcissistic personality organization is the ability to experience authentic human warmth and depth: "The extent to which there is authentic human warmth and depth may be more difficult to evaluate but is even more important than the extent to which there is commitment to ethical, intellectual, cultural or aesthetic values, the other major prognostic indicator in the special cases under examination" (p. 309).

The human capacity for concern for others and for oneself is the basis for authentic human warmth and depth. The absence of the capacity for concern pertains to the self:

> Narcissistic patients not only seem to love themselves excessively, but do so in a rather poor, often self-demeaning way, so that one concludes that these patients do not treat themselves better than the other people with whom they have relationships. Their conviction of being "phony," their deep lack of confidence in anything basically good and worthwhile that could emerge from honest self-exploration, and their occasionally surprising neglect and disregard for their "public image" in terms of honesty, decency and convictions about values, are poor ways of loving oneself. (p. 272)

Honesty in daily life, authentic human warmth and depth, and sublimatory potential represent the human capacity for concern and indicate that the person at the highest point on the spectrum of variation of the narcissistic personality organization is functioning at a high level. With fortunate interpersonal experience, a person with a narcissistic personality organization can achieve the integration of whole object relations and reach the neurotic level of personality development.

A Note on the Nature of Preferences and the Individual Pursuit of Self-Interest in the Primitive Range of the Personality Continuum

In general, the personality organizations in the primitive range of the Personality Continuum, in particular, the narcissistic personality organization, represent individuals who pursue their own self-interest selfishly. Their preferences are contradictory, rather than consistent, and do not reflect the capacity for concern, guilt, or commitment to a value system. In the normal range of the Personality Continuum, preferences are stable and consistent, and the pursuit of individual self-interest includes the capacity for concern, guilt, and commitment to a system of values. This analysis demonstrates that preferences are a reflection of the intrapsychic structure of the personality, even when preferences are contradictory, rather than consistent, and that preferences can be alternating and contradictory rather than stable.

Prognosis of Narcissism, Treated and Untreated: The Case of Prospective Psychoanalytic Candidates

Kernberg often uses potential candidates for psychoanalytic training to elaborate on the highest point on the spectrum of variation of the narcissistic personality organization: "A particularly difficult prognostic estimate is involved in the case of potential candidates for psychoanalytic training with narcissistic personality structure. Obviously, the problem only comes up in those relatively well-adjusted narcissistic personalities whose social and professional functioning is satisfactory, who present high intelligence and particular talents, and at times appear promising" (Kernberg 1985A, p. 307). This is reminiscent of Kernberg's use of case material on prominent professors at local universities to elaborate on the highest level of functioning on the spectrum of variation of the narcissistic personality organization.

The recognition of the quality of dependence upon the object is the heart of Fairbairn's contributions to British object relations theory (Fairbairn 1952, p. 40). Kernberg (1985A) builds on this foundation with the significance of the integrity and depth of the value system and superego functioning:

> In reviewing a number of cases in which, retrospectively, it appeared that mistakes had been made both in accepting and rejecting some candidates, the two major prognostic factors that stand out as prognostically significant are the quality of object relationships and the integrity and depth of the value systems and superego functioning. It needs to be stressed again that I use the concept "quality of object relations" to refer more to the quality of internalized object relations, i.e., the depth in the patient's internal relationships with others, rather than to the extent to which he is involved in social interactions. (pp. 307–308)

The therapist with a narcissistic personality organization may focus on small and complex issues and lose sight of the feelings, emotions, and affects: "Intelligent and gifted therapists with this character constellation may have a great sensitivity for 'small and complex issues' in the treatment, but lose sight of the emotional constellation expressing what is going on between them and the patient" (p. 291).

The integrity and depth of the value system represent the highest level of superego development, the intrapsychic structure of the protective superego. The contents of the protective superego represent an internalized value system shared with, at least, another person. The protective superego is the foundation for the highest level of superego functioning—the capacity for commitment. Here we see how clearly the study of simpler personality structures can shed light on normal personality development. Freud's mental patients were split and broken structures who "have turned away from external reality" in varying degrees, "but for that very reason they know more about internal, psychical reality and can reveal a number of things to us that would otherwise be inaccessible to us" (Freud 1933, p. 59). According to Kernberg (1985A), "Applying all this to the particular case of prospective psychoanalytic candidates, systematic attempts to evaluate the realness and aliveness of other people as they come through in the descriptions of the candidate, and the depth of the candidate as he describes himself, are important indicators of the quality of object relations, in addition to the more observable aspects of stability, depth, and richness of the relationships with others and himself" (pp. 308–309).

THE LOWEST POINT ON THE SPECTRUM OF VARIATION OF THE NARCISSISTIC PERSONALITY ORGANIZATION: NARCISSISTIC PERSONALITY ORGANIZATIONS WHO FUNCTION ON AN OVERT BORDERLINE LEVEL

Narcissistic personality organizations who function on an overt borderline level constitute Kernberg's third group, representing the lowest level of functioning, on the spectrum of variation of the narcissistic personality organization: "However, there are some narcissistic personalities who function on what I have called an overt borderline level, that is, they present the nonspecific manifestations of ego weakness characteristic of borderline personality organization, including severe lack of anxiety tolerance, generalized lack of impulse control, striking absence of sublimatory channeling, and primary-process thinking—evident in psychological testing" (Kernberg 1985A, p. 332).

The subjective experience of emptiness in a person with a narcissistic personality organization is what is typically meant by being burned out: "The persistent feelings of emptiness, the 'burned out' quality of interests and ambitions that one observes in narcissistic personalities functioning on a borderline level leaves them more willing to settle for rather conventional, often overconventional ways and styles, replacing their old ambitiousness and flamboyance with gratification of having their life and immediate needs stable and under control" (p. 290). This is what is meant by "beat" in reference to the Beat Generation.

Failure to resolve the narcissistic structure of the personality organization in therapy results in dissatisfaction with themselves and with life: "In contrast, the highly gifted, brilliant narcissistic personalities who have undergone psychoanalytic treatment which did not resolve their narcissistic personality structure, tend to experience more dissatisfaction with themselves and with life. They feel that while they can no longer hold on to their old grandiosity, they cannot accept the essentially 'mediocre' nature of ordinary life" (pp. 290–291). One can almost hear the Rolling Stones raging, "I Can't Get No Satisfaction," inside the head of the person with a narcissistic personality organization.

In contrast to these exceptional cases, a poorly functioning narcissistic personality organization may show more improvement with supportive psychotherapy: "Paradoxically, narcissistic personalities functioning rather poorly on an overt borderline level, who have undergone supportive psychotherapy, may present a higher level of improvement than patients who originally functioned more effectively and were more intelligent, creative and ambitious" (p. 290).

Narcissistic Rage: Projection of Oral Rage and Paranoid Traits

Rage is particularly characteristic of the lowest point on the spectrum of variation of the narcissistic personality organization. According to Kernberg (1985A), this group contains "some narcissistic patients with overt borderline functioning, particularly those who present intense rage reactions or 'narcissistic rage' " (p. 334). In these cases, Kernberg recommended an expressive psychotherapeutic approach.

Narcissistic rage, in particular, oral rage, is central to the etiology of the narcissistic personality organizations at the lowest point on the spectrum of variation: "Analytic exploration very often demonstrates that their haughty, grandiose, and controlling behavior is a defense against paranoid traits related to projection of oral rage, which is central to their psychopathology" (p. 17). Chronic rage in a person with a narcissistic personality organization functioning on an overt borderline level is a negative prognostic indicator: "In general, the prognosis for this subgroup of narcissistic patients with chronic rage who function on the borderline level is guarded" (p. 334).

The severe acting out of narcissistic rage must be controlled in a person with a narcissistic personality organization functioning on an overt borderline level: "Returning once more to the treatment of narcissistic personalities who function on an overt borderline level, one final technical problem is that of severe acting out, particularly of narcissistic rage. Acting out needs to be controlled, first by means of interpretive efforts, and then, if these are not effective, by a sufficient degree of structuring of the patient's life outside the treatment hours" (pp. 337–338).

Intense rage expressed in the clinical setting, however, may actually be a positive prognostic indicator: "A particular type of intense, devaluating rage evidenced by some narcissistic patients functioning on a borderline level, may have ominous immediate implications but, if worked through over a period of time, may actually indicate a beginning of the capacity for an intense emotional relationship with the therapist" (p. 208). This harks back to Balint's (1932) conception of the new beginning.

Narcissistic Personality Organization Functioning on an Overt Borderline Level with Antisocial Features

The analysis of the narcissistic personality organization with antisocial features is at least a step in the direction of differentiating the antisocial and narcissistic personality organizations. Kernberg (1985A) refers to the antisocial personality organization as a "subgroup" of the narcissistic personality organization. I would interpret this to mean that the relative ranking of the antisocial personality within the primitive range of the Personality Continuum is below the narcissistic personality organization: "The antisocial personality may be considered a subgroup of the narcissistic personality. Antisocial personality structures present the same general constellation of traits [of the narcissistic personality organization] that I have just mentioned, in combination with additional severe superego pathology" (p. 18).

The open expression of rage is a negative prognostic indicator for a person with a narcissistic personality organization functioning on an overt borderline level with antisocial features: "Early and open expression of rage represents a serious risk for the treatment. This is particularly true in narcissistic personalities functioning on a borderline level who present antisocial features or a sexual deviation with strong sadistic components, such as open physical violence toward the objects of their sexual exploits. Also, adolescents with narcissistic personality structure and antisocial behavior frequently show such rage reactions" (p. 268).

In a case study of rage in a patient with a narcissistic personality organization functioning on an overt borderline level with antisocial features, Kernberg (1984A) relates how the patient used rage to thwart any interpretation by the analyst that would provoke anxiety: "Open challenge brought about attacks of rage against me, the intensity of which I at first found almost frightening. I gradually realized that the main intent of his rage was to shut off any view of himself or of reality that contradicted his own, and that if I remained silent, his rage diminished. I had rarely experienced a more effective control over my psychotherapeutic efforts in the treatment of a nonpsychotic patient" (p. 175). Sullivan (1956) also observed this phenomenon of handling of severe anxiety by rage: "To such people, any little skid in their own performance is so oppressive that one can assume that they suffer terribly from anxiety, and their anger is an example of the handling of anxiety by rage" (p. 137).

Strong antisocial features in a narcissistic personality organization functioning on an overt borderline level are a negative prognostic indicator: "Finally, patients with narcissistic personality and overt borderline functioning who also present strong antisocial features have a very poor prognosis" (Kernberg 1985A, p. 334; see also p. 209).

ADJUSTMENT TO LATER STAGES OF LIFE FOR THE NARCISSISTIC PERSONALITY ORGANIZATION

According to Kernberg (1985A), "Because of the devastating effects of pathological narcissism on the adjustment to later stages of life, these patients, in spite of their good surface functioning, should be treated" (p. 333). Psychoanalysis is the therapeutic treatment of choice (p. 333). Although narcissistic personality organizations are particularly prone to frustrations in real life and may not be able to tolerate the additional or marginal anxiety that psychoanalysis may subject them to, Kernberg is notably optimistic:

> However, insofar as the treatment of choice in these cases is psychoanalysis, and psychoanalytic treatment requires a certain initial motivation to help withstand the serious increase in anxiety and awareness of conflicts unavoidable during analytic treatment, the decision of whether to treat or not sometimes becomes quite difficult. At times it may be preferable to provide the patient with immediate, short-term psychotherapeutic support in an acute crisis and wait for further increase in self-awareness or frustrations in real life—to which these patients are particularly prone—and start psychoanalytic treatment later. I have

recently become more optimistic about the treatment of some of these patients who start their analysis in their late thirties and forties, even though lengthy psychoanalytic treatment may be involved. (p. 333)

THE RELATIONSHIP OF THE NARCISSISTIC PERSONALITY ORGANIZATION WITH HIMSELF AND HIS FAMILY

Improvement in the relationship of a person with a narcissistic personality organization with his family and himself is a positive prognostic indicator: "In the course of this process, the patient's experience of me as an idealized person who could accept him as he was in his own right provided an important source of support to him, helped him tone down his own narcissistic aspirations and achieve further improvement in his relationship with himself as well as with his family" (Kernberg 1985A, p. 292). In general, a person's relationship with the self varies qualitatively with the level of personality development: "The clinical study of narcissistic personalities illustrates that the relationships of the individual with himself and with his surrounding human and inanimate world depends upon the development of normal or pathological internalized object relations" (p. 313).

INCOMPLETENESS OF THE PORTRAIT OF THE NARCISSISTIC PERSONALITY ORGANIZATION

This has been a long and difficult chapter, yet we are far from being through with the narcissistic personality organization. It will be elaborated in greater depth with the analysis of addiction. But before we turn to the dark side of consumer behavior, the comparative analysis of personality organizations will be expanded in the next chapter.

NOTES

1. It does matter what we teach our students in the classroom about the nature of economic man. Studies have shown that students of economics are more selfish than students of psychology (Marwell and Ames 1981; Frank, Gilovich, and Regan 1993).

2. Helen Swick Perry (1982), Harry Stack Sullivan's biographer, related the story of a young Harry at the train station in the little town of Smyrna in rural New York State where he grew up. He did not want to go back to Cornell for

the second semester of his freshman year. His mother Ella turned around and walked away, leaving him standing alone and abandoned at the train station.

3. For an elaboration of the gangster ideal, see Jacobson (1964, pp. 210–212).

4. In a clarification of terminology, *integration* pertains in a positive way to the formation of the intrapsychic structure of the personality and to the successful achievement of higher levels of personality development. *Condensation* appears primarily to refer to a pathological process that results in the deterioration of the intrapsychic structure of the personality of a narcissistic personality organization. *Fusion* as used here is synonymous with condensation; however, fusion will also be used to indicate the regressive loss of the boundary between self and object.

5. For an extension into marketing, see Belk (1988) on "Possessions and the Extended Self."

6. I would add to Kernberg's parenthetical comment that when an adult, chronologically speaking, is behaving in an infantile way, it is not normal, but primitive.

7. It is only with great difficulty that I was able to write this. To be brutally honest, while I was coming to this realization—that fear is the emotion of being castrated—unconsciously, I had been holding my crotch, as the recognition erupted into my consciousness. This is like men folding their arms when they deny experiencing any castration anxiety in response to advertising using subliminal stimuli designed to arouse castration anxiety. This is unambiguously clear body language.

8. I am somewhat reluctant to provide this analysis of the effective use of subliminal stimuli in advertising for fear that it will promote the already prevalent, if not rampant, use, of subliminal stimuli that I observe. I consider the use of subliminal stimuli in advertising unethical. I rationalize this ethical dilemma by noting, somewhat facetiously, that it is sufficiently well hidden that it will not be found by most advertisers. On a more serious note, education is the best way to deal with the use of subliminal stimuli in advertising. I intend to pursue this area of research in the future as an application of object relations theory in the field of marketing.

9. Another good song title, and very fitting music for a man with a narcissistic personality organization wounded in love, is "I Fall in Love Too Easily." Chet Baker did a devastating version on his *My Funny Valentine* album (a Pacific Jazz recording on February 15, 1954), and Frank Sinatra, I believe, has the acknowledged standard, recorded by Columbia on December 1, 1944.

10. Sullivan (1953) warned against the harm that careless wisecracks can make: "The Irish, who happen to be my ancestral people, are a little better known to me than are, for example, the Chinese; and so I feel—after the best modern pattern—perfectly free to make a wisecrack about the underlying religious attitude of my people. But, thank God, I know that it may or may not make

any sense; I wouldn't think of staking anything on it. It is all right for parlor conversation with good friends, preferably Irish. But if I say it often to other people, I may very unhappily present them with an opportunity to clinch an uninformed prejudice, which is usually done by nailing it onto a previous one" (pp. 303–304).

Chapter 13

Expanded Comparative Analysis of Personality Organizations

An examination of Kernberg's case material yields a wealth of clinical observations for the comparative analysis of personality organizations. The emphasis thus far has been on the schizoid, borderline, and narcissistic personality organizations in the primitive range of the Personality Continuum. The primary purpose here is to expand the comparative analysis to include the hysterical personality organization and, to some extent, the depressive personality organization in the neurotic range and the infantile personality organization in the primitive range of the Personality Continuum. Comparisons will be made to the normal range of the Personality Continuum, and within the primitive range, contrasts will be made to the borderline and narcissistic personality organizations, above and below the infantile personality organization, respectively. The relative ordering within each range can be seen on the Personality Organizations panel of the Personality Continuum. The comparative analysis of personality organizations will reach its zenith, or perhaps nadir, with the deeper exploration of the psychological foundations of compulsive and addictive behavior in the next chapter.

Kernberg's (1985A) continuum of classification of personality organizations can be related directly to the Personality Continuum:

> I shall briefly review a differential diagnosis of hysterical personalities, infantile personalities, and narcissistic personalities, which from my point of view do represent a continuum in that the hysterical personality is a typical "high level" character neurosis; the infantile personality a "middle range" one, actually reaching into the typical borderline field; and the narcissistic personality a typical "low level" character disorder, although it reaches up into the middle of the continuum. (p. 13)

I would translate this into the language of the Personality Continuum in the following way: The hysterical personality organization is classified into the neurotic range of the Personality Continuum, and the borderline, infantile, and narcissistic personality organizations are classified into the primitive range of the Personality Continuum. Within the primitive range of the Personality Continuum, the infantile personality organization occupies a relatively higher position than the narcissistic personality organization. When Kernberg argues that the narcissistic personality "reaches up into the middle of the continuum," I would interpret this to mean that, at best, the spectrum of variation of the narcissistic personality organizations reaches up into the middle of the primitive range of the Personality Continuum, below the infantile personality organization (but above the antisocial and lower schizoid personality organizations). The spectrum of variation of the borderline personality organization occupies a relatively higher position than the infantile and narcissistic personality organizations in the primitive range of the Personality Continuum. The spectrum of variation of the infantile personality organization occupies a "middle range" between the borderline personality organization and the narcissistic personality organization.[1]

A COMPARISON OF CONTINUOUS STRIVING IN THE NEUROTIC RANGE AND CONSTANT STRUGGLE IN THE PRIMITIVE RANGE OF THE PERSONALITY CONTINUUM

The neurotic person continuously strives to be consistent, whereas the primitive person constantly struggles with self-control. The normal person has a stable and consistent pattern of behavior. These are qualitatively different patterns of behavior representing qualitatively different levels of personality development.

The constant struggle characteristic of primitive personality organizations lacking in object constancy is a result of the failure to achieve the integration of whole object relations. Fairbairn (1952) observed that a person with a schizoid personality organization in the primitive range of the Personality Continuum struggles under the most ordinary conditions of life (p. 13). In a similar way, Freud (1915B) observed that even within the limits of normal life there is a constant struggle for primacy over affectivity (p. 179).

The continuous striving of the neurotic personality organization is the result of the integration of whole object relations that contributes to the continuity of the self (Kernberg 1984A, p. 32). A neurotic person will strive to behave consistently under ordinary functioning. A neurotic consumer under ordinary functioning, therefore, would fit the economic conception of the rational economic consumer. A person with a neurotic personality organization under extraordinary functioning does not fit the conception of rational economic man, mutatis mutandis, because a neurotic person has a tendency to behave inconsistently. This represents a regression to the lower primitive level of personality development and a return to earlier patterns of behavior. Stability of behavior—a pattern of consistent behavior over time—is lacking in a person with a neurotic personality organization.

In comparison, the mere inconsistency of a neurotic person's behavior under extraordinary functioning is qualitatively different from the chaotic and rigidly patterned, alternating and contradictory behavior under ordinary functioning characteristic of personality organizations at the primitive level of personality development. Chaos and constant struggle for self-control are characteristic of personality organizations at the primitive level of personality development.[2] An alternating and contradictory preference ordering clearly violates the transitivity property and therefore does not fit the economic conception of the rational economic man, mutatis mutandis or not.

The constant struggle for perfection can take on a sadistic character for personality organizations in the primitive range of the Personality Continuum. The sadistic character of the struggle for perfection is revealed in telltale self-destructive behavior. In the case of a person with an obsessive personality organization in the neurotic range of the Personality Continuum, the striving for perfection can result in primitive demands for perfection (Kernberg 1985A, p. 292). The sadistic demands for perfection by a person with an obsessive personality organization, therefore, represent an extreme variation in the neurotic range of the Personality Continuum.

VARIATIONS OF PATTERNS OF DEPENDENCY WITH THE LEVEL OF PERSONALITY DEVELOPMENT

Patterns of dependency vary qualitatively with the level of personality development along the Personality Continuum. Scitovsky's (1976) observation that addiction and falling in love are somehow related can be illuminated by the consideration of patterns of dependency in interpersonal relationships (p. 128). The stable and consistent pattern of behavior of a normal person represents what Fairbairn (1952) has described as "mature dependence" in an intimate interpersonal relationship (p. 34).

In comparison to the hysterical personality organization at the neurotic level of personality development, the childlike dependency of a person with infantile personality organization at the primitive level of personality development is deceptive: "Infantile personalities show a childlike 'dependency' of a more oral-demanding, aggressive kind than seen in the hysterical personality. On a deeper level [I would prefer *at a lower level*], patients with infantile personality structure really present an incapacity to depend on others, related to severe distortions in their internalized object relationships" (Kernberg 1985A, p. 16).

The childlike dependency of the infantile personality organization has a desperate oral-demanding character: "In the infantile personality, in contrast, childlike overidentification is of a more desperate, inappropriate nature; there is a gross misreading of the motives, of the inner life of others, even if on the surface there is a good adaptation to them. Long-term involvements show a regressed, childlike, oral-aggressive demandingness in the infantile personality which is not typical of hysterical patients" (p. 14). In a comparison of demandingness in the narcissistic personality organization with normal personality development, "the child's demandingness [is] related to real needs, while the demandingness of pathological narcissism is excessive, cannot ever be fulfilled, and regularly reveals itself to be secondary to a process of internal destruction of supplies received" (p. 273). The borderline personality organization in the primitive range of the Personality Continuum is characterized by clinging dependency, which, as in the case of the childlike dependency of the infantile and narcissistic personality organizations, conceals an incapacity to depend on another person (p. 91).

OEDIPAL VERSUS ORAL AND GENITAL VERSUS PREGENITAL: A COMPARISON OF THE HYSTERICAL AND INFANTILE PERSONALITY ORGANIZATIONS

The oedipal aspects of sexuality predominate in the hysterical personality organization at the neurotic level of personality development: "The hysterical personality reveals strong oedipal aspects of sexual involvements (such as chronic involvement with older or unavailable men), and there exists the capacity for a stable relationship with the sexual partner as long as certain neurotic preconditions for the relationship are fulfilled" (Kernberg 1985A, p. 15). Stable here refers to a high-functioning neurotic personality organization, that is, a neurotic personality organization functioning at a normal level of personality development. Stability mainly has to do with intimate interpersonal relationships, relationships that are deep and relatively enduring, involving a commitment to a shared value system and a future orientation, but nonetheless, with an unstable equilibrium at the end of the road (Kernberg 1985B, p. 281).

Genital sexual relations manifest problems of personality at all levels of personality development. For a person with a hysterical personality organization, according to Kernberg (1985A), "The need to be loved, to be the center of attention and of attraction, has more of a sexual implication in the hysterical personality, in which oral-dependent needs are linked with direct genital exhibitionistic trends" (p. 14).[3] In comparison, the infantile personality organization is more orally determined and inappropriately demanding: "In the infantile character the need to be the center of interest and attraction is less sexualized and it has a more helpless, mainly orally determined, inappropriately demanding nature, and the exhibitionism has a 'cold' quality, reflecting more primitive narcissistic trends" (pp. 14–15).

In comparison to the hysterical personality organization, the sexual provocativeness of the infantile personality organization is more orally determined: "In the infantile personality, sexual provocativeness tends to be more direct, more crude, more inappropriate socially, and reflects when it is present a more orally determined exhibitionism and demandingness than a really sexualized approach to the opposite sex" (p. 15). Sexual promiscuity is more characteristic of women with an infantile personality organization: "Sexual promiscuity in hysterical women is much less frequent than that in infantile women" (p. 15).

In comparison, oedipal conflicts predominate in the hysterical personality organization, and sexuality is more genital, while the infantile personality organization is more oral, and sexuality is more pregenital:

> The hysterical personality, in summary, gives evidence of a better integrated ego and superego, of a much broader range of conflict-free ego functions and structures, and of a predominance of oedipal conflicts over oral ones, although oral conflicts are also present. The sexual conflicts of the hysterical personality represent much more genital than pregenital conflicts. In the infantile personality, in contrast, pregenital and especially oral problems predominate. There is a reduced capacity for stable object relations in comparison to the hysterical personality, and there is a breakdown of repression [I believe that Kernberg means the breakdown of splitting here] with the emergence of primitive, polymorphous sexual fantasies. (p. 16)

Primitive sexual fantasies that are conscious in the infantile personality organization are repressed in the neurotic personality organizations: "In the infantile personality, in contrast, promiscuity is of a more 'drifting' quality, with very little stability of object relationships. Also, in contrast to general predominance of diffuse repression of sexual fantasies in the hysterical personality, there may be conscious sexual fantasies of a primitive, polymorphous perverse quality in the infantile personality" (p. 15).

The borderline personality organization is relatively better off than the infantile and the narcissistic personality organizations, in descending order within the primitive range of the Personality Continuum. Therefore, the sexual promiscuity of a person with an infantile personality organization functioning on an overt borderline level represents a real potential for emotional growth, because a person with a borderline personality organization is able to establish a relatively enduring relation with another human being:

> The impulsive, chaotic, infantile personality functioning on a borderline level has a better prognosis than the narcissistic patient, although superficially his love life may seem disturbed, inappropriate, and immature. Sexual promiscuity on this structural level may reflect the rapid breakdown of the primitive idealization typifying his sexual involvements and the desperate search for another object [not person] with whom a primitively idealized relation can be reestablished. The very fact that such borderline patients are able to establish a relatively stable relation with another human being—in the context of which tender and genital feelings can be expressed—represents a real potential for emotional growth. (Kernberg 1984A, pp. 215–216)

The use of *enduring* is preferable to *stable*, because stable should be equated with normal personality development. Sullivan's (1953) use of *enduring* is integral to his interpersonal conception of personality as the relatively enduring pattern of recurrent interpersonal situations that characterize a human life (p. 111). The extent to which a person with a borderline personality organization can establish a relatively enduring relation with another human being through fortunate interpersonal experience provides a favorable opportunity for the achievement of a higher level of personality development.

In contrast to the spectrum of variation of the narcissistic personality organization, the borderline personality organization has the capacity for clinging dependency on another person: "The absence of the capacity to depend upon others on the part of narcissistic personalities, in contrast to the clinging dependency and persistent capacity for a broad spectrum of object relations in borderline patients, contributes fundamentally to the differential diagnosis of narcissistic personalities functioning on an overt borderline level from usual borderline patients" (Kernberg 1985A, p. 275).

THE SPECIFICITY OF THE LACK OF IMPULSE CONTROL: NONSPECIFIC, SELECTIVE, AND SPECIFIC BEHAVIORAL MANIFESTATIONS

The nature of the lack of impulse control varies qualitatively with the level of personality development. In the primitive range of the Personality Continuum, the infantile personality organization is characterized by the nonspecific lack of impulse control; in contrast, the borderline personality organization is characterized by the selectivity of the lack of impulse control. In comparison, the hysterical personality organization, in the higher neurotic range of the Personality Continuum, is defined by the specificity of the lack of impulse control.

Kernberg's descriptions of the observable behavior of a chronologically adult person with an infantile personality organization as chaotic and impulse ridden resemble an infant in a high chair (Kernberg 1984A, p. 215). The lack of impulse control in the infantile personality organization is characterized as nonspecific, and the emotional lability of the infantile personality organization is generalized and diffuse (Kernberg 1985A, p. 14). In comparison, hysterical personality organizations manifest a lack of impulse control in specific areas and only at the height of some conflict:

> But these patients may appear to be quite stable emotionally and appropriate in their emotional reactions in nonconflictual areas [i.e., conflict-free ego spheres].

A hysterical patient who gets from one emotional crisis into the next in the relationship with her husband or in the transference may be remarkably stable and appropriate at her job. In contrast, the emotional lability in the infantile personality is generalized and diffuse. There are few, if any, conflict-free areas in their life, and this reflects a higher degree of social inappropriateness as compared to the hysterical personality. Hysterical personalities manifest a lack of impulse control in specific areas and only at the height of some conflict; infantile personalities manifest a lack of impulse control in a much more general way. (p. 14)

MANIFESTATIONS OF MARGINAL ANXIETY IN THE INFANTILE PERSONALITY ORGANIZATION

The erratic and impulsive behavior of the infantile personality organization is a simple reflection of an increase of anxiety—marginal anxiety—or of any particular drive derivative (Kernberg 1985A, p. 23). This represents the breakdown of splitting, the return of bad objects, and "the emergence into consciousness of a dissociated identification system" (p. 23). "In contrast" to the borderline personality organization, "nonspecific lack of impulse control can be seen typically in the infantile personality structure. Here it appears as unpredictable, erratic impulsivity, a simple reflection of an increase of anxiety [marginal anxiety] or of any particular drive derivative. It is an effort at the dispersion of intrapsychic tensions rather than the reenactment of a specific dissociated [but not repressed] identification system" (p. 23). The chaotic, unpredictable, and unstable character of the infantile personality organization manifests evidence of splitting behavior under the most ordinary conditions of life.

For the borderline personality organization, according to Kernberg (1985A), "I have noted elsewhere that what appears on the surface to be simply a lack of impulse control connected with ego weakness, may reflect highly specific defensive operations" (p. 23). The "specificity" of the lack of impulse control in the borderline personality organization is highly selective and rigidly patterned:

In this case, the specificity of this "lack of impulse control" is manifested typically by the ego syntonicity of the impulses being expressed during the time of the impulsive behavior, by the repetitive nature of the kind of lack of impulse control involved, by the lack of emotional contact between that part of the patient's personality and the rest of the self experience, and finally by the bland denial which secondarily defends this dissociated "breakthrough." (Kernberg 1985A, p. 23)

PRIMITIVE SELF-DESTRUCTIVENESS AND MASOCHISTIC TRAITS

Each range of the Personality Continuum represents a qualitatively different level of personality development. Dimensionality occurs within each range, where personalities at the same level of development vary continuously and quantitatively along the various trait dimensions (i.e., measurable dimensions, as in individual-difference or trait measures). Masochistic traits can be used for the purposes of exposition.

In the hysterical personality organization, at the neurotic level of personality development, masochistic traits represent an acting out of unconscious guilt over genital sexual relations: "I refer here to the masochistic traits that are frequently seen in hysterical personalities, and represent dynamically an acting out of unconscious guilt over genitality (for example, a hysterical patient with a severe superego representing mainly the internalized, prohibitive oedipal mother)" (Kernberg 1985A, p. 19).

The prohibitive superego—the internalized, prohibitive oedipal mother—and the capacity for experiencing guilt, present in the hysterical personality organization, are missing in the infantile personality organization: "In brief, what I call 'high level' masochism, as reflected in character traits dynamically related to a strict, punitive superego, is frequently a part of the hysterical personality structure. In contrast, 'middle range' or 'low level' masochistic character traits, with much less guilt and with direct interpenetration of sadistic and masochistic traits, are prevalent in the infantile personality" (p. 16).

Primitive self-destructiveness is particularly characteristic of the borderline personality organization in the primitive range of the Personality Continuum. In the extreme variation on the spectrum of the borderline personality organization, relief from anxiety is obtained by cutting or some form of self-mutilation. Masochistic tendencies represent the lowest point on the spectrum of variation of the borderline personality organization:

> There exists a "low level" group of masochistic characters, in which rather primitive sexualization of masochistic needs occurs, masochistic perverse trends may be present, and aggression is discharged indiscriminately toward the outside or toward one's own body. Patients with severe self-destructiveness (but without a well-integrated [prohibitive] superego and with a remarkable absence of the capacity to experience guilt) are members of this group. Typical examples are provided by patients who obtain nonspecific relief of anxiety by cutting them-

selves or by some form of self-mutilation, or by impulsive suicidal gestures carried out with great rage and practically no depression. From a dynamic point of view, preoedipal conflicts predominate in these patients, and rather primitive fusion and defusion of aggressive and sexual impulses occur. Most, if not all, of these patients present an underlying borderline personality organization. (pp. 19–20)

In varying degrees, primitive self-destructiveness is characteristic of all personality organizations in the primitive range of the Personality Continuum; the borderline personality organization represents an extreme degree in this regard. The further exploration of variations in patterns of self-destructiveness in the primitive range of the Personality Continuum will be addressed in the next chapter on the dark side of consumer behavior. All chronic patterns of compulsive and more extreme addictive consumption behavior are self-destructive.

A COMPARISON OF WOMEN WITH HYSTERICAL PERSONALITY ORGANIZATION AND THOSE WITH NARCISSISTIC TRAITS AND NARCISSISTIC PERSONALITY ORGANIZATION

In the hysterical personality organization at the neurotic level of personality development, the expression of narcissistic traits is limited by the capacity for concern. In comparison, a woman with a narcissistic personality organization at a primitive level of personality development may appear hysterical on the surface, but her seductiveness is cold and shrewdly calculating. According to Kernberg (1985A):

An exaggeration of narcissistic traits, especially those linked with exhibitionistic trends, is quite prevalent in hysterical personalities [at the neurotic level of development]; however, the need to be admired, to be the center of attention of the hysterical personality—usually a narcissistic reaction formation [a neurotic defense] against penis envy—goes together with a capacity for deep and lasting relationships with others. Women with narcissistic personalities [at a primitive level of personality development] may appear as quite "hysterical" on the surface, with their extreme coquettishness and exhibitionism, but the cold, shrewdly calculating quality of their seductiveness is in marked contrast to the much warmer, emotionally involved quality of hysterical pseudo-hypersexuality [a personality organization at the neurotic level of personality development]. (p. 238)

In a case of narcissistic character defenses in a female patient with hysterical personality organization, Kernberg (1985A) made the following clinical observation: "At no point did she completely devaluate the transference object, or oscillate between primitive, orally determined paranoid transference distortions on the one hand, and narcissistic withdrawal into a more primitive self-idealization on the other" (p. 242).

A COMPARISON OF PATTERNS OF COMPETITIVENESS IN WOMEN WITH HYSTERICAL AND INFANTILE PERSONALITY ORGANIZATIONS

Hysterical personality organizations at the neurotic level of personality development tend to differentiate their patterns of competitiveness with men and women: "In hysterical personalities there is usually a much clearer differentiation in the pattern of competitiveness with the same sex in contrast to that with the opposite sex. Hysterical women who tend to compete with men (in order to deny their sexual inferiority) tend to develop stable characterological patterns in this regard; in their competitiveness with women, oedipal rivalry tends to predominate over other origins of the competitiveness" (Kernberg 1985A, p. 15). I like the use of *stable* here, referring to a high-functioning neurotic personality organization, functioning at the higher normal level of personality development and displaying the stability of behavior representative of the normal level of personality development.

In comparison to the hysterical personality organization, the rapid shifting between intense positive and negative feelings of the infantile personality organization is an extreme manifestation of the chaotic pattern of alternating and contradictory behavior characteristic of primitive personality organizations: "In the infantile personality there is less differentiation in the typical behavior toward men and women; there is less chronic competitiveness in general, and there is rapid shifting between intense positive and negative feelings, between submission and childlike imitation of others, on the one hand, and stubborn, pouting oppositionalism of short duration, on the other" (p. 15).

REACTION TO LOSS OF A GOOD OBJECT RELATION

The reaction to loss of a good object relation, or good interpersonal relationship, varies with the level of personality development along the Personality Continuum. The reaction to loss of a good object relation for a normal person is sadness, loneliness, longing, and hope for the future.

The reaction to loss for a person with a neurotic personality organization is to suffer from an unconscious sense of guilt and the emptying of subjective experience by the harsh internal attack of the prohibitive superego on the self (Kernberg 1985A, pp. 214–215). The reaction to loss for a person with a primitive personality organization is the intensification of the splitting processes. The reaction to intolerable loss for a person with a psychotic personality organization is a regressive refusion of all-good self- and object images.

The emptying of subjective experience at the neurotic level is qualitatively different from the pervasive sense of emptiness characteristic of personality organizations at the primitive level of personality development under ordinary functioning. The subjective experience of emptiness serves as a point of comparison for the reaction to loss at the normal, primitive, and psychotic levels of personality development: "Emptiness stands midway between the longing, sadness, and loneliness that represents the hope for the re-establishment of significant object relations, on the one hand, and the regressive psychotic fusion of 'all good' self and object images (when the loss of the good relationship with an object cannot be tolerated), on the other" (pp. 220–221). For a person with a psychotic personality organization, therefore, the psychotic regression is precipitated by the loss of a good relationship with another person that cannot be tolerated.

In comparison to the regressive refusion of all-good self- and object images for a person with a psychotic personality organization, the reaction to intolerable loss for a person with a borderline personality organization, at the primitive level of personality development, is an intensification of splitting processes: because of the preponderance of aggressively determined self and object images "*In the psychoses their main effect is regressive refusion of self and object images; in the case of the borderline personality organization*, what predominates is not refusion between self and object images, but an *intensification and pathological fixation of splitting processes*" (p. 27).

Freud's Comparison of Normal Loss and Mourning and Melancholia

A comparison is made of normal loss and mourning at the normal and neurotic level of personality development with melancholia at the primitive level of personality development. In "Mourning and Melancholia" (1917A), Freud compares the normal emotion of grief and its expression in mourning and melancholia: "Mourning is regularly the reaction to the loss of a loved person, or to the loss of some abstraction which has taken the place of one, such as one's country, liberty, an ideal, and so on" (p. 243). In comparison, according to Freud, "The distinguishing mental features of melancholia are a profoundly painful dejection, cessation of interest in the outside world, loss of the capacity to love, inhibition of all activity, and a lowering of the self-regarding feelings to a degree that finds utterance in self-reproaches and self-revilings, and culminates in a delusional expectation of punishment" (p. 244).

In comparison, for the melancholic person at the primitive level of personality development, loss of a good object relation results in a fall in self-esteem and an impoverishment of the ego:

> The melancholic displays something else besides which is lacking in mourning—an extraordinary diminution in his self-regard, an impoverishment of his ego on a grand scale. In mourning it is the world which has become poor and empty; in melancholia it is the ego itself. The patient represents his ego to us as worthless, incapable of any achievement and morally despicable; he reproaches himself, vilifies himself and expects to be cast out and punished. (pp. 245–246)

The end result of the loss for the melancholic person is an identification of the ego with the abandoned object: "Thus the shadow of the object fell upon the ego, and the latter could henceforth be judged by a special agency, as though it were an object, like the forsaken object. In this way an object-loss way transformed into an ego-loss" (p. 240). Here we have arrived at Freud's seminal idea on the loss of the object—object choice regresses to identification: "If one has lost an object or has been obliged to give it up, one can compensate oneself by identifying oneself with it and by setting it up once more in one's ego, so that here, object-choice regresses, as it were, to identification" (Freud 1933, p. 63).

Reaction to Separation in the Primitive Range of the Personality Continuum: A Contrast of the Narcissistic, Borderline, and Infantile Personality Organizations

The reaction to separation varies qualitatively with the level of personality development along the Personality Continuum. Kernberg (1985A) has explored the theme of reaction to separation in the clinical situation: "The patient's reactions to separation from the therapist have important diagnostic, prognostic and therapeutic implications" (p. 208). Thus, according to Kernberg, "One might place the different type of separation reactions into a continuum, from the most severe distortions of internalized object relationships to the least" (p. 208). In a series of clinical observations, Kernberg has provided a contrast of the reaction to separation in the borderline, infantile, and narcissistic personality organizations in descending order within the primitive range of the Personality Continuum.

Intense mourning as a reaction to separation is particularly "characteristic of borderline patients with better integration of internalized object relations, and generally better prognosis" (p. 209). In addition, separation anxiety is an "intense, at times, disorganizing . . . experience with prolonged separations from the therapist" for the borderline and lower infantile personality organization" (p. 208). Rage as a reaction to frustration over separation is also characteristic of the borderline and infantile personality organizations: "In this case, fear of separation from the therapist usually reflects not only pathological dependency needs but fear of the destruction of the internalized image of the therapist because of the rage brought about by the frustration of separation from him" (p. 209).

A person with a borderline personality organization functioning at the higher neurotic level of personality development, with the integration of whole object relations, will have the capacity to tolerate mourning: "Finally, tolerance of normal mourning reactions to separations from the therapist is characteristic of advanced stages of treatment of borderline patients, and patients with less severe types of character pathology in general [i.e., at the higher neurotic level of personality development]" (p. 209).

The absence of any reaction to separation is particularly characteristic of the narcissistic personality organization, below the borderline and infantile personality organizations: "Next on the continuum would be open acknowledgement of not having any reaction to separation from the therapist, characteristic of most patients with narcissistic personality structure" (p. 208). Narcissistic personality organizations with antisocial features are relatively worse off: "The most ominous reaction is that of patients who are really unable to experience any emotional reaction at all to separations from the therapist, but who have learned to imitate such reactions from other patients, using them as rationalization for various acting out. These are usually narcissistic patients with strong antisocial features" (p. 208).

RIFF ON DEPRESSION

Depression varies with the level of personality development and with regard to particular personality organizations along the Personality Continuum. Symptomatic depression serves as a useful theme to delineate the qualitatively different ranges of the Personality Continuum and to differentiate between particular personality organizations. A combination of these three considerations will be used to elaborate the theme of symptomatic depression: Quality of depression, quantitative factors, and level of depressive-masochistic character organization.

The achievement of the integration of whole object relations determines the depressive position and the capacity for concern, guilt, and mourning at the neurotic and the higher normal levels of personality development. In the following passage, Winnicott (1955) provides a beautiful conception of the integration of whole object relations with normal personality development: "To reach the depressive position a baby must have become established as a whole person, and to be related to whole persons as a whole person. Here I am counting the breast as a whole person, because, as the baby becomes a whole person, then the breast, then the mother's body, whatever there is of her, any part, this becomes perceived by the baby as a whole thing" (p. 90). The "depressive position" is "a thoroughly bad name for a normal process." "My own suggestion was that it should be called '*the Stage of Concern*' " (p. 91).

A Comparison of Symptomatic Depression at the Neurotic Level of Personality Development and Depressive-Masochistic Character Traits at the Primitive Level of Personality Development

Depression as a symptom has to be differentiated from the depressive-masochistic character traits (Kernberg 1985A, p. 20). In the terminology of the Personality Continuum, the neurotic range has to be differentiated from the primitive range: Symptomatic depression pertains to the depressive personality organization in the neurotic range of the Personality Continuum; depressive-masochistic character traits are characteristic of personality organizations in the primitive range of the Personality Continuum.

At the neurotic level of personality development, "the quality of symptomatic depression is important, in that the more depression is combined with authentic guilt feelings, remorse, and concern about oneself, the more it is a reflection of superego integration" (p. 20). This is indicative of personality organizations at the neurotic level of personality development, with the ego capacity for concern and the superego capacity for guilt. Rather than *remorse*, I would prefer *regret*; remorse should be relegated to personality organizations in the primitive range of the Personality Continuum, and to the persecution of the punitive superego.

A person with a depressive personality organization at the neurotic level of personality development under ordinary functioning, and even more so under high functioning, will have an integrated ego identity, an integrated self, and an integrated world of internal objects, which sustains him during periods of extraordinary functioning, "when severe superego pressures threaten them with abandonment by their internal objects because of their internal sense of not deserving to be loved. However, under these circumstances, the capacity for normal object-relations always remains and may be actualized in the transference and in other interpersonal experiences" (p. 220).

This is essentially a description of the development of the normal personality organization: A normally constituted ego identity and a stable integrated self and stable integrated world of internal objects have been achieved (p. 220). Stability reflects the achievement of the normal level of personality development. In comparison, at the neurotic level of personality development, stability is lacking, because of the failure to achieve the full integration of satisfying genital sexual activity into an interpersonal relationship by successfully resolving the oedipal situation.[4]

At the neurotic level of personality development, there is evidence of the capacity for concern and guilt in the depression:

> In relation with a patient presenting a depressive personality structure or chronic neurotic depression, the therapist [the clinician observing and participating in the interpersonal relationship with the patient] may have a sense of intense human contact, a subjective experience of empathy, and at the same time, be aware that the patient cannot accept emotionally the very availability of the therapist as a real person. The unconscious sense of guilt that prevents the depressed patient's accepting love or concern as it is offered, is reflected in the transference and in the therapist's emotional reaction to it. (p. 215)

In comparison, at the normal level of personality development, loss and depression imply the experience of loneliness and a sense of longing for the now unavailable person, while at the neurotic level, depression is experienced as feelings of emptiness based on an unconscious sense of guilt and a harsh internal attack by the prohibitive superego:

> These depressed patients' feelings of emptiness come close to the feeling of loneliness, except that loneliness implies elements of longing and the sense that there are others who are needed, and whose love is needed, who seem unavailable now. Psychoanalytic exploration regularly reveals that these patients suffer from an unconscious sense of guilt and that the "emptying" of their subjective experience reflects their [prohibitive] superego's attack, as it were, on the self. The harsh internal punishment inflicted by the [prohibitive] superego consists in the implicit dictum that they do not deserve to be loved and appreciated, and that they are condemned to be alone. (pp. 214–215)

The normal capacity for tolerating depression and mourning over loss broadens and deepens the person's capacity for experiencing emotions: "Many authors have pointed out that the capacity for tolerating depression, linked to the capacity for mourning over a lost good object or a lost ideal image of oneself, is an important prerequisite for emotional development and especially for the broadening and deepening of feelings" (p. 237). In comparison, at the primitive level of personality development, depressive-masochistic character traits represent a qualitatively different experience: "Depression which has more of the quality of impotent rage, or of helplessness-hopelessness in connection with the breakdown of an idealized self concept, has much less value as an indicator of superego integration [i.e., indicates poor superego integration, a negative prognostic indicator]" (p. 20).

The better the integration of the superego, the higher the level of character pathology, and the person is relatively better off. Superego integration is a positive prognostic indicator of an integrated prohibitive superego and the capacity for experiencing guilt. In comparison, for personality organizations relatively lower in the primitive range of the Personality Continuum, "excessive depression and its absence may both indicate 'low level' character organization" (p. 20).

The highest point on the spectrum of variation of the borderline personality organization "borders on the neuroses" and is represented by a childlike clinging depression (p. 153). At the lowest point on the spectrum of variation of the borderline personality organization,

> severe depression approaching the psychotic degree of depressive reaction, which tends to produce ego disorganization in the form of "depressive depersonalization" and severe withdrawal from emotional relationships with reality, may be tentatively considered as one further presumptive indicator of borderline personality organization. In such instances, in spite of the fact (or rather because of the fact) of "intact" superego functioning, the ego is not able to withstand an excessively severe and sadistic superego. (p. 20)

The integrated prohibitive superego is missing in the intrapsychic structure of the primitive personality organization. Thus the "intact" superego functioning is the punitive superego, sadistically persecuting the person with severe anxiety and making him or her helpless and hopeless, exploding in impotent rage. Symptomatic depression is not characteristic of the borderline personality organization: "The combination of these three considerations (quality of depression, quantitative factors, and level of depressive-masochistic character organization) in regard to the presence of depression makes it evident that depression as a symptom should not be used directly as an indicator of borderline personality organization" (p. 20).

Loss of Meaning in Depression and the Narcissistic and Schizoid Personality Organizations

At the primitive level of personality development, depression is characterized by a loss of meaning:

> The loss of the world of loving and loved internal objects brings about the loss of meaning of the self and of the world. Psychotic depression represents, in many ways, the terrifying stage of awareness of the loss of love and meaning against which narcissistic personalities need to defend themselves, and schizoid emotional dispersal or a paranoid—not necessarily psychotic—reorganization of the world represents an alternative protection for these patients against depression, but at the cost of bringing about further dehumanization and emptiness. (Kernberg 1985A, p. 313)

Thus the loss of love brings about an intensification of the subjective experience of emptiness in the narcissistic personality organization, in contrast to the defensive emotional dispersal that brings about further dehumanization in the schizoid personality organization.

Prolegomena for a New Panel of the Personality Continuum

Range	**Depression**
Normal	Normal loss and mourning Normal emotion of grief and its expression in mourning Loneliness and longing

Neurotic	Mourning, loss, and symptomatic depression Concern and guilt feelings Stage of concern
Primitive	Impotent rage Helplessness and hopelessness Withdrawal from emotional relationships
Psychotic	Loss of meaning Depersonalization

NOTES

1. I am still not clear into which range of the Personality Continuum to put the obsessive-compulsive personality organization, or how it is related to the obsessive-compulsive personality disorder. My assumption is that the obsessive-compulsive personality organization is in the primitive range, owing to the self-destructive character of the obsessive-compulsive behavior. The complexity in classification and diagnosis is in distinguishing between a high-functioning primitive personality organization, utilizing an obsessional neurotic defense against severe anxiety in interpersonal relationships, and the obsessive personality organization, at the neurotic level of personality development and in the neurotic range of the Personality Continuum, that is, Fairbairn's hypothesis.

Kernberg (1985A), however, clearly classified the obsessive-compulsive personality organization as neurotic: "From a clinical point of view, most typical hysterical personalities are not borderline structures; the same holds true for most obsessive-compulsive personalities and 'depressive' personality structures or better integrated masochistic personalities" (p. 13). As a note of clarification, in this comparison, Kernberg is using the term *borderline structure* to refer generally to personality organizations at the primitive level of personality development and in the primitive range of the Personality Continuum.

2. In the lead editorial in the *New York Times* on Sunday, April 29, 2001, on the first 100 days in office of President George W. Bush, former president Bill Clinton's first 100 days were characterized in this way: "Bill Clinton struggled to enact his economic policies and health care reforms amid the chaos created by his swirling personal style and distracting issues like gays in the military."

3. I presume that this means a preference for the performance of fellatio by a hysterical woman and cunnilingus by a hysterical man. As previously stated, neurotic and primitive personality organizations have particular advantages.

4. In comparison to the stable ego identity of a person at the normal level of personality development, a person at the neurotic level experiences an identity crisis, and at the primitive level, identity diffusion, in particular, the borderline personality organization (Kernberg 1985B, p. 220).

PART IV

TOWARD A HUMAN UNDERSTANDING OF CONSUMER BEHAVIOR

Chapter 14

THE DARK SIDE OF CONSUMER BEHAVIOR

The analysis of the dark side of consumer behavior will focus primarily on the primitive range of the Personality Continuum. The borderline personality organization, subject to a panoply of compulsive behaviors, provides the organizational framework for the further analysis of a pattern of compulsive consumer behavior. The narcissistic personality organization, prone to addiction, provides the organizational framework for a deeper analysis of the more extreme pattern of addictive consumer behavior.

A person with a primitive personality organization, utilizing the primitive defense of splitting against severe anxiety, cannot tolerate additional or marginal anxiety because he or she is already tolerating a high level of anxiety. Any additional or marginal anxiety overloads the primitive defense of splitting, causing it to break down, and the person is subjected to severe anxiety that is experienced as intolerable. When splitting breaks down, the punitive superego persecutes the person with severe anxiety, and that is what drives the person with a primitive personality organization to outbursts of compulsive and, in the more extreme case, addictive consumption behavior. The outbreak of compulsive or more extreme addictive consumption behavior is an effort to restore the primitive defense of splitting against severe anxiety.

THE SUBJECTIVE EXPERIENCE OF EMPTINESS IN THE PRIMITIVE RANGE OF THE PERSONALITY CONTINUUM

A person with a primitive personality organization, utilizing the primitive defense of splitting against severe anxiety, experiences particularly strong feelings of emptiness: "This experience becomes particularly strong when active mechanisms of primitive dissociation or splitting constitute a predominant defense against intrapsychic conflict" (Kernberg 1985A, p. 220). Personality organizations in the primitive range of the Personality Continuum are characterized by a range of variations on the subjective experience of emptiness: "Among these experiences predominate a sense of emptiness and futility of life, chronic restlessness and boredom, and loss of the normal capacity for experiencing and overcoming loneliness" (p. 213).

Contrasts in variations of the subjective experience of emptiness will be made between personality organizations in the primitive range, and comparisons will be made to personality organizations in the neurotic and normal ranges of the Personality Continuum. In contrasting the subjective experiences of emptiness for personality organizations at the primitive level of personality development, a pervasive sense of futility is more characteristic of the schizoid personality organization, and a pervasive sense of emptiness is more characteristic of the narcissistic personality organization. In the narcissistic personality organization, emptiness is part of a constellation that includes restlessness and boredom (p. 220).

Exploring the theme of the subjective experience of emptiness reveals that there are variations among personality organizations at the same level of development, and between the personality organizations at different levels of personality development. The thematic analysis of the subjective experience of emptiness, therefore, is a superb way to differentiate personality organizations within the primitive range and to delineate the qualitatively different ranges of the Personality Continuum.

The subjective experience of emptiness will shed more light on the meaning of compulsive and addictive consumer behavior for the individual, although the use of "meaning" is ironic when emptiness is often characterized by a sense of meaninglessness for a person with a primitive personality organization. A person with a primitive personality organization is trying to escape from the subjective experience of emptiness by engaging in a panoply of compulsive and, in the more extreme case, addictive behaviors:

There are patients who describe a painful and disturbing subjective experience which they frequently refer to as a feeling of emptiness. In typical cases, it is as if this emptiness were their basic modality of subjective experience from which they attempt to escape by engagement in many activities or in frantic social interactions, by the ingestion of drugs and alcohol, or by attempts to obtain instinctual gratifications through sex, aggression, food, or compulsive activities that reduce their focusing on their inner experience. (Kernberg 1985A, pp. 213–214)

The conscious aspect of the motivation, for a pattern of compulsive or addictive behavior, a motivation that is largely unconscious for a person with a primitive personality organization, is to reduce focusing on one's own inner experience as an escape from the subjective experience of emptiness (p. 214). A person with a primitive personality organization is empty inside, and to escape from the emptiness, such a person engages in a range of compulsive and addictive behaviors.

Kernberg (1985A, p. 214) provides a long list of compulsive and addictive behaviors: Frantic social interactions, sex, aggression, ingestion of drugs, alcohol, and food, and many other *compulsive activities*. While the list does include the ingestion of substances like drugs and alcohol, and food, for that matter, it also includes many *activities*, like frantic social activities, sex, and aggressive behavior, and a panoply of compulsive activities, including work, as in a workaholic, compulsive buying behavior,[1] exercise, and polymorphous perverse sexual behavior, such as masturbating, predatory sexual behavior—fucking as opposed to the intimacy of making love. These are activities that do not involve ingesting any chemical substance, or any substance whatsoever, such as food and various chemical substances—alcohol, tobacco, heroin, cocaine, cannabis, and so on through a virtually endless list of illicit drugs. Sullivan (1953) referred to these as substitute activities: "Substitute activity, in contrast to indirect exploitative attitudes, is not addressed to an audience; instead it is addressed primarily to avoiding certain conscious clarity about one's own situation, one's own motivation, and so on" (p. 354).

It is the primitive level of personality development, not the substance or the activity, that determines the person's predisposition toward compulsive and, in the extreme case, addictive behavior. This is crucial to a deeper understanding of compulsive and addictive behavior. Personality organizations at the primitive level of personality development are prone to compulsive and addictive behavior. Further, since the defense of splitting has broken down, it is the underlying level of intrapsychic structural formation of the personality organization that primarily determines the nature of the compulsive or addictive consumer behavior. The critical implication for the economic analysis of consumer behavior is that the nature of preferences is determined primarily by the level of intrapsychic structural formation that has been achieved; that is, the intrapsychic structure of the personality is reflected in the structure of preferences.

THE SUBJECTIVE EXPERIENCE OF EMPTINESS: A COMPARISON OF THE NEUROTIC AND PRIMITIVE LEVELS OF PERSONALITY DEVELOPMENT

In comparison to the pervasive experience of emptiness and the more extreme experience of futility for personality organizations in the primitive range of the Personality Continuum, the subjective experience of emptiness is qualitatively different and occurs only intermittently for personality organizations in the neurotic range, in particular, the depressive personality organization:

> Some patients with chronic neurotic depressions or depressive personality structures present this subjective experience [of emptiness] only intermittently, and describe it as in sharp contrast to other types of subjective experience. For them, periods in which they feel empty are characterized by a sense of loss of contact with other people, who now appear distant, unavailable, or mechanical, while they themselves feel similarly. Life no longer seems to make sense, there is no hope for any future gratification or happiness, there is nothing to search for, long for, or aspire to. These patients may feel that they can no longer love anybody nor is there any reason why anybody should love them; the human world has become emptied of meaningful, loving relationships involving these patients. Their world of inanimate objects seems sharply delimited, as if such objects were protruding from their usual surrounding background and assuming a quality of impenetrability, lack of meaning, or unavailability. The usually appreciated and loved inanimate objects of their daily surroundings become strange and painfully meaningless. (Kernberg 1985A, p. 214)

In "Mature Love: Prerequisites and Characteristics" (1974B, reprinted in 1984A), one of Kernberg's three important articles on intimacy, he presents case material on a depressive-masochistic eighteen-year-old girl, a personality organization at the neurotic level of personality development. The patient was referred because of depression and consequent academic failure in her first year of college: "She had fallen in love with a boy she met at college, but after six months, he had left her, and this triggered off her depression" (Kernberg 1984A, p. 227).

This case is illuminating here because of the focus on the loss of meaning in the surrounding world of inanimate objects as a reaction to loss for a person with a neurotic personality organization: "The aspect I wish to focus upon is how she felt about the little town where her love affair and its end had taken place, her experience of the motel where they met, the streets, the park, and the buildings they had visited together. She had been afraid of going back to all those places and having to face again, in each of them, the painful loss of her boyfriend" (p. 227). (This represents what Freud described as a *withdrawal of cathexis*.) For a person with a neurotic personality organization, according to Kernberg (1974B),

> This is, of course, a quite typical experience when working through a mourning process, but I would like to stress the "coming alive" of inanimate objects—the background figures of human experience—illuminated by a love relation. This reaction to inanimate objects, as well as to nature and art, is intimately connected with the transcending aspect of a full love relation in which the capacity for total object relation and the capacity for genital enjoyment are integrated. (Kernberg 1984A, pp. 227–228)[2]

The capacity for genital enjoyment represents the full integration of satisfying genital sexual activity into an interpersonal relationship, the interpersonal achievement in personality development that qualifies a person for the normal level of personality development and demarcates the normal range of the Personality Continuum, a level of personality development higher than the neurotic level of the depressive personality organization. This interpersonal achievement of personality development constitutes the second precondition for intimacy. The first precondition for intimacy is the integration of whole object relations, or the capacity for total object relation.

Revisiting these places for the depressive-masochistic 18-year-old girl resulted in the intensification of her mourning reaction: "In the course of her exploratory interviews, she decided to visit those places again and discovered that, painful as the consequent intensification of her mourning reaction was, there was also something reassuring in the permanence of the buildings, of the room they had shared, the benches they had sat on, the whole world of inanimate objects that contained the memories of moments spent together" (p. 227).

In this case, according to Kernberg (1974B), her depressive-masochistic tendencies were relatively mild, and she had an overall well-organized personality structure (at the neurotic level of personality development) and the relative absence of serious character pathology (at the primitive level of personality development). She improved rapidly in the course of a few sessions geared mainly to psychological exploration of her presenting difficulties: "She returned to college, and follow-up information five years later revealed that she had continued functioning well, had married, and appeared to be leading a well-adjusted and satisfactory life" (Kernberg 1984A, p. 227).[3]

The Distinction between Loneliness and Emptiness

Loneliness is not emptiness. At the neurotic and higher normal levels of personality development, loneliness means a full awareness of the possibility of significant relations with others and a sense of longing for and of missing lost love relationships, thereby distinguishing the loneliness of the neurotic and normal personality organization from the emptiness of the primitive personality organization. Kernberg (1985A) makes this point in comparing personality organizations at the neurotic level of personality development to a schizoid personality organization at the primitive level of personality development: "The schizoid experience of emptiness is not close to a sense of loneliness; loneliness implies an intense, full awareness of the possibility of significant relations with others, which these patients do not have available to them for a long time in their treatment" (p. 217). The absence of the capacity to experience loneliness is particularly pronounced in narcissistic personality organizations, in contrast to the schizoid personality organization at the primitive level of personality development: "Narcissistic patients often do not have available the sense of longing for or of awareness of the possibility of a significant relation with others and of missing such a relation" (p. 219).

The Subjective Experience of Emptiness in the Narcissistic Personality Organization

For a person with a narcissistic personality organization, the subjective experience of emptiness is pervasive, intense, and almost constant (Kernberg 1985A, pp. 219–220). The narcissistic personality organization is particularly prone to addiction (p. 222). A deeper investigation of the theme of the subjective experience of emptiness in the narcissistic personality organization, therefore, offers an opportunity for further exploration of the psychological foundations of addictive consumer behavior. I want to examine the subjective experience of emptiness from the perspective of a chronologically adult person with a narcissistic personality organization, and specifically, the intrapsychic structure of the narcissistic personality organization—what is inside the person's head, so to speak.

In comparison to the normal and neurotic levels of personality development, a chronologically adult person with a narcissistic personality organization does not have the capacity to experience loneliness. A person with a narcissistic personality organization lacks higher-level intrapsychic structures: "In contrast, when there exists a lack of an integrated self and normal relations of the self with integrated internal objects, a more deep-seated, chronic sense of emptiness and meaninglessness of the ordinary life experience ensues" (p. 220). Thus, under ordinary life experience, under the ordinary conditions of life, under ordinary functioning, a sense of emptiness and meaninglessness is chronic for a person with a narcissistic personality organization.

The intrapsychic structure of the narcissistic personality organization is missing higher-level intrapsychic structures that would have reinforced the individual's self-control. The effectiveness of twelve-step programs for treating addiction, modeled on Alcoholics Anonymous, is based on putting another person in place of the missing higher-level intrapsychic structures. The group support shores up the addict's self-control. Hirschman (1992) provides a penetrating analysis of the surrogate family and community that twelve-step programs provide for the addict. She concludes that the bonding that takes place among group members is at an interpersonal level (p. 547).

In comparison to the depressive personality organization at the neurotic level of personality development, and in contrast to the schizoid personality organization at the primitive level of personality development, the subjective experience of emptiness for a person with a narcissistic personality organization is part of a constellation that is also characterized by strong feelings of boredom and restlessness (Kernberg 1985A, p. 217). In a short, brutal portrayal, Kernberg (1985A) characterizes the level of intrapsychic structural formation achieved in the narcissistic personality organization: "These patients' feelings of emptiness and boredom are intimately related to their stunted ego development" (p. 237).

Envy, Devaluation, and the Subjective Experience of Emptiness in the Narcissistic Personality Organization

The subjective experience of emptiness in a person with a narcissistic personality organization is a consequence of the devaluation of other persons and internal objects as a defense against envy:

The devaluation of objects and object images on the part of patients with pathological narcissism creates a constant emptiness in their social life and reinforces their internal experience of emptiness. They need to devaluate whatever they receive in order to prevent themselves from experiencing envy. This is the tragedy of these patients: that they need so much from others while being unable to acknowledge what they are receiving because it would stir up envy; in consequence, they always wind up empty. (Kernberg 1985A, p. 237)[4]

Sullivan (1956) equated envy with the thwarting of satisfactions: "Thus the personality of the markedly envious person is apt to show many evidences of the thwarting of satisfactions; but the thwarting is a result of the ubiquitous envy operations" (p. 131). A person with a narcissistic personality organization is characterized by low frustration tolerance and narcissistic vulnerability. The thwarting of satisfactions leads to excessive frustration and reactions of intense rage or protective withdrawal:

Another major technical problem in the treatment of these patients [with a narcissistic personality organization] is their low frustration tolerance; they combine nonspecific aspects of ego weakness and specific narcissistic vulnerability, and feel easily hurt or rejected because of minor frustrations from or shortcomings of the therapist. The therapist's awareness of their vulnerabilities to narcissistic frustrations and their reactive rage and/or protective withdrawal in their extratherapeutic interactions may help him to point out not only how and why they avoid getting involved in work, in social relationships, in marriage, but also how the need to escape from feared frustrations and rage about them operates in the transference, in the patient's hypersensitivity to the therapist and his narcissistic withdrawal from or rage with the therapist. (Kernberg 1985A, pp. 335–336)

Hungry, Enraged, Empty Self

Ultimately, the need to escape from feared frustrations and rage for a person with a narcissistic personality organization is the need to escape from the perfectionistic, never-satisfied mother (Kernberg 1985A, p. 292). The persecution of the punitive superego leaves such a person alone in a world now devoid of love: "On a deeper level, and in severe cases, internal fantasies determined by superego pressures are that because of their badness they have destroyed their inner objects and are therefore left alone in a world now devoid of love" (p. 215).[5] The emptying takes on a sadistic character because the persecution by the punitive superego with severe anxiety is sadistic.

Thus we are left with this devastating portrayal of a person with a narcissistic personality organization: "It is the image of a hungry, enraged, empty self, full of impotent anger at being frustrated, and fearful of the world which seems as hateful and revengeful as the patient himself" (p. 233). This characterization evokes Thomas Hobbes's in *Leviathan*, published in 1651: "And the life of man, solitary, poore, nasty, brutish, and short" (Hobbes 1950, p. 104). On the spectrum of variation of the narcissistic personality organization, this devastating portrayal represents the lowest point: "This, the deepest level of the self concept of narcissistic patients, can be perceived only late in the course of their psychoanalytic treatment, except in the case of narcissistic patients with overt borderline features who show it quite early" (Kernberg 1985A, pp. 233–234). Kernberg elaborates on the higher points on the spectrum of variation of the narcissistic personality organization:

> In less disorganized patients, that is, narcissistic personalities with relatively stronger egos, one eventually encounters in the transference [i.e., the reactivation of past internal object relations in the clinical setting] paranoid developments, with feelings of emptiness, rage, and fear of being attacked. On an even less regressed level, the available remnants of such self images reveal a picture of a worthless, poverty-stricken, empty person who feels always left "outside," devoured by envy of those who have food, happiness, and fame. Often the surface remnant of this line of primitive self images is undistinguishable from the shadowy remnants of devaluated object images. (p. 234)

The Subjective Experience of Emptiness in the Schizoid Personality Organization

Emptiness is experienced as a sense of being different in a person with a schizoid personality organization: "Other patients, that is, many patients with schizoid personality structure, may experience emptiness as an innate quality that makes them different from other people; in contrast to others, they cannot feel anything, and they may feel guilty because they do not have available feelings of love, hatred, tenderness, longing, mourning, which they observe and understand in other people but feel unavailable to experience themselves" (Kernberg 1985A, p. 215).

Kernberg's use of *guilt*, as in to feel guilty, is inappropriate for a personality organization at the primitive level of personality development. Personality organizations at a primitive level of personality development do not have the prohibitive superego capacity for experiencing guilt or the ego capacity for experiencing concern. A person with a schizoid personality organization cannot feel anything. Individuals with schizoid personality organization, in particular, like to intellectualize about feelings, but in actuality do not experience genuine feelings when appropriate, and, under extraordinary functioning, may regress to full-scale depersonalization (Fairbairn 1952, p. 6). At an intellectual level, perhaps, a person with a schizoid personality organization may understand love and hate, tenderness, longing, and mourning, but does not have the capacity to experience these feelings (Kernberg 1985A, p. 215).

The subjective experience of emptiness is strong in a person with a schizoid personality organization because of the characteristic defensive dispersal and fragmentation: "Schizoid personalities, in whom splitting processes are particularly strong and may lead to a defensive dispersal and fragmentation of affects as well as of internal and external relationships involving the self and significant objects, present strong feelings of emptiness" (p. 220). In comparison to a depressive personality organization at the neurotic level of personality development, the subjective experience of emptiness is qualitatively different and may be more tolerable for the schizoid personality organization at a primitive level of personality development:

> For such schizoid patients, the experience of emptiness may be less painful than for depressed patients because there is less of a contrast between periods in which they feel empty and other times in which they would have emotional relationships with others. An internal sense of drifting, of subjective unreality, and of a soothing quality derived from this very unreality, makes the experience of emptiness more tolerable to schizoid patients and permits them to adopt passive dependent reactions toward others and thus fill time with an awareness of external reality in contrast to their subjective experience. (p. 215)

This outcome for a person with a schizoid personality organization harks back to a person with a primitive personality organization engaging in compulsive and more extreme addictive behavior to reduce focusing on inner experience to escape from the emptiness (p. 214). In addition, according to Kernberg, "Other patients, in contrast, seem to succumb to this experience of emptiness and acquire what might be described as a mechanical style of life—going through the motions of daily activities with a deadening sense of unreality or a blurring of any subjective experience, so that they seem to merge, so to speak, with whatever immediate inanimate or human environment surrounds them" (p. 214). This attitude of detachment, isolation, and futility is particularly characteristic of the schizoid personality organization (Fairbairn 1952, p. 51).

COMPARATIVE ANALYSIS OF DRUGS AND ALCOHOL

The use of chemical substances, such as drugs and alcohol, is a means to *escape* from the subjective experience of emptiness. The effects of drugs and alcohol vary with the level of personality development and, most important, with the intrapsychic structure, as the relatively enduring part of the personality organization. According to Kernberg (1985A): "The psychoanalytic study of patients who attempt to escape their sense of emptiness by means of alcohol and drugs provides an additional illustration of the intrapsychic structural characteristics involved. The effects of drugs and alcohol vary, I think, according to the underlying intrapsychic structures of the individuals involved" (p. 222). The predominant nature of the pattern of consumer behavior is primarily determined by the intrapsychic structure of the personality organization. According to Kernberg, for chemical substances such as drugs and alcohol, "In general terms, the implication is that the psychological functions of alcohol or drugs are strongly influenced by the predominant nature of intrapsychic structuralized object relations" (p. 222).

The effects of drugs and alcohol vary with the intrapsychic structure, the level of personality development, and the particular personality organization. The narcissistic personality organization, in particular, is prone to addiction. In contrast to the addictive potential of the borderline personality organization at the primitive level of personality development, and in comparison to the depressive personality organization at the higher neurotic level of personality development, "The addictive potential is maximum, I think, for narcissistic personality structures, and the prognosis for treatment of addictive conditions of narcissistic personalities is much worse than is the case of the addictive borderline patients without narcissistic features, and of less regressed personality structures such as the depressive personality" (p. 222).

The predominant effect of alcohol and drugs in the narcissistic personality organization is to refuel the grandiose self: "In the case of narcissistic personalities, alcohol or drug intake may constitute a predominant mechanism to 'refuel' the pathological grandiose self and assure its omnipotence and protection against a potentially frustrating and hostile environment in which gratification and admiration are not forthcoming" (p. 222).

In the borderline personality organization, at the primitive level of personality development, alcohol and drugs activate a sense of wellbeing and goodness: "In contrast, for many borderline patients, drug intake activates a sense of well-being and goodness that activates the split-off 'all good' self and object images and permits the denial of 'all bad' internalized object relations, thus permitting an escape from intolerable guilt [I would say intolerable anxiety] or sense of internal persecution" (p. 222).

In the depressive personality organization, at the neurotic level of personality development, in comparison, the subjective sense of well-being brought on by alcohol and drugs stems from working through in fantasy an unconscious sense of guilt and a reunion with a lost, prohibiting, and now forgiving parental image:

> A patient with a depressive personality structure may experience, under the influence of alcohol, a subjective sense of well-being and elation which he interprets unconsciously as a reunion with a lost, prohibiting, and now forgiving parental image which had caused the unconscious sense of guilt and depression. The combination of elation and depression, of expansiveness and mourning, in depressive personalities under the influence of alcohol may illustrate the working through in fantasy of the sense of guilt, the need to repair the relation with the object, and the celebration of the re-encounter with it. (p. 222)

THE REGRESSIVE REFUSION OF ALL-GOOD SELF- AND OBJECT IMAGES

This section is a rare foray into an analysis of the psychotic level of personality development. The reaction to intolerable loss of a good object relation—the regressive psychotic fusion of all good self- and object images—is the result of a specific defect in the self: "In the psychoses, there is a severe defect of the differentiation between self and object images, and regressive refusion of self and object images occurs in the form of primitive merging fantasies, with the *concomitant blurring of the ego boundaries in the area of differentiation between self and non-self*" (Kernberg 1985A, p. 27). ("Primitive" here refers to the psychotic level of personality development and to a regressive psychotic fusion.)

To some extent, this defect in the self—the failure to differentiate the self from the object—characterizes the borderline personality organization at the primitive level of personality development, and therefore, to that extent there is a tendency to the regressive refusion of self- and object images as a reaction to loss in the borderline personality organization. The intensification of splitting, with reality testing maintained at the level of self differentiated from object, however, is the predominant reaction to loss in the borderline personality organization. Thus the outburst of compulsive or more extreme addictive behavior that restores the primitive defense of splitting, flipping up the all-good, positive introjects and identifications, is not a psychotic regression.

Excessive frustration causes the lack of differentiation of self and object in the formation of the intrapsychic structure of the personality: "From a clinical point of view, however, excessive frustration of early instinctual needs (especially oral) is probably the main cause of the lack of differentiation between self and objects, because *excessive frustration reinforces the normal disposition to regressive refusion of self and object images*, representing early merging fantasies between self and object in an attempt to retain or regain absolute gratification" (pp. 26–27). "Instinctual" here means inborn physiological dispositions and biological patterns of behavior related to early interpersonal relations, and "normal" should properly be *pathological* dispositions to regressive refusion of self- and object images. The attempt to retain or regain absolute gratification will be explored further after the regressive refusion of self and the object has been elaborated.

Kernberg elaborates on four factors that contribute to a tendency for regressive refusion of self- and object images for personality organizations at the psychotic level of personality development and, to some extent, for the borderline personality organization at the primitive level of personality development: "Such regressive refusion between self and object images may depend on: (i) lack of development of the apparatuses of primary autonomy [perception and memory]; (ii) constitutionally determined lack of anxiety tolerance (even minor frustrations are intolerable, and induce regressive fusion or merging processes); (iii) excessive frustration in reality; and (iv) consequent excessive development of aggression (or constitutionally determined excessive intensity of aggressive drives)" (p. 27). For the psychotic personality organizations and, to some extent, the borderline personality organization, excessive aggression results in a vicious circle: "*Vicious circles involving projection of aggression and reintrojection of aggressively determined object and self images* are probably a major factor in the development of both psychosis and borderline organization" (p. 27).

THE REGRESSIVE LURE OF IDENTIFICATION AT THE PRIMITIVE LEVEL OF PERSONALITY DEVELOPMENT

In interpersonal situations fraught with excessive frustration and aggression, the regressive refusion of self and object occurs at the psychotic level of personality development. In general, the regressive lure of identification is characteristic of personality organizations at the primitive level of personality development, with self differentiated from object, and affect modified and more diversified.

To recognize oneself as separate from the object is the interpersonal achievement in personality development that delineates the primitive from the psychotic range of the Personality Continuum. To achieve the higher neurotic level of personality development requires the successful integration of whole object relations. The person comes to accept another person and oneself as both good and bad and, therefore, a whole and more realistic person. To individuate—the successful outcome of the process of individuation, to achieve mature dependence, in Fairbairn's conception, growing up and becoming independent, as Kernberg (1977) put it—requires the successful integration of whole object relations. Therefore, in a person with a primitive personality organization, the progressive urge to separate from the object also contains the desire to grow up and become independent under ordinary functioning.

Fairbairn (1952) has characterized the failure to achieve the integration of whole object relations at the primitive level of personality development as a conflict between the progressive urge to separate from the object and the regressive lure of identification with the object:

> The anxiety attending separation manifests itself as a fear of isolation; and the anxiety attending identification manifests itself as a fear of being shut in, imprisoned or engulfed ("cribbed, cabined and confined"). These anxieties, it will be noticed, are essentially phobic anxieties. It may accordingly be inferred that it is to the conflict between the progressive urge towards separation from the object and the regressive lure of identification with the object that we must look for the explanation of *the phobic state*. (p. 43)

Although in this passage I believe that Fairbairn is confounding anxiety and fear—a frequent confusion in writing on affect, feelings, and emotions—the regressive lure of identification will be elaborated as a way to go deeper into the analysis of addiction at the primitive level of personality development.

Under extraordinary functioning, interpersonal situations fraught with severe anxiety, excessive frustration and aggression, or intolerable loss, object choice regresses to identification. To temporarily fall back on one's internal world of object relations represents the refinement of one of Freud's most fundamental insights on the regression to identification as a reaction to loss: "If one has lost an object or has been obliged to give it up, one often compensates oneself by identifying oneself with it and by setting it up once more in one's ego, so that here object-choice regresses, as it were, to identification" (Freud 1933, p. 63).

The regressive lure of identification at the primitive level of personality development represents an identification with the ideal object, "The image of the ideal object which represents the unharmed, all-loving, all-forgiving object" (Kernberg 1984A, p. 40). The ideal object, therefore, represents the primitively idealized all-good, all-loving and forgiving internalized image of the mother. This represents an intensification of splitting processes and not the psychotic regressive refusion of self and object (Kernberg 1985A, p. 27).

In Fairbairn's (1952) conception of the basic fault, the result is to regressively restore the relationship with the mother's breast: "Failure on the part of the mother to convince the child that she really loves him as a person renders it difficult for him to sustain an emotional relationship with her on a personal basis; and the result is that, in order to simplify the situation, he tends regressively to restore the relationship to its earlier and simpler form and revive his relationship to his mother's breast as a partial object" (p. 13). The lure of identification, then, is with the mother's breast, an internal object relation—the all-positive, early interpersonal relations of the infant nursing at the mother's breast, internalized through introjection and identification as the ultimate part-object.

Markedly Compulsive Behavior

According to Fairbairn (1952), "It is when [primary] identification persists at the expense of differentiation that a markedly compulsive element enters into the individual's attitude towards his objects. This is seen in the infatuations of schizoid individuals. It may also be observed in the almost uncontrollable impulse so commonly experienced by schizoid and depressive soldiers in wartime to return to their wives or their homes, when separated from them owing to military necessities" (p. 42). The individual with a schizoid personality organization, according to Fairbairn, is driven to resort to markedly compulsive behavior, "in an attempt to compensate by substitutive satisfactions for the failure of his emotional relationships with his outer objects" (p. 40). These substitutive satisfactions compensate for failures in interpersonal relationships and ultimately for the failure to achieve the higher neurotic and normal levels of personality development. Thus substitutive satisfactions represent internal object relations: "Fundamentally these substitutive satisfactions (e.g. masturbation and anal eroticism) all represent *relationships with internalized objects, to which the individual is compelled to turn in default of a satisfactory relationship with objects in the outer world*" (p. 40).

Substitutive satisfactions are manifested in compulsive, and more extreme addictive consumer behavior. Fairbairn's analysis has provided the developmental, interpersonal, and internal basis for this behavior. In general, the person with a primitive personality organization will compensate by substitutive satisfactions for a deficit in personality development. This is why the dependency of addiction is referred to as a crutch, holding up the person, who is starting at a deficit, by propping up the person's primitive defense of splitting against severe anxiety. For an addict, redosing is a desperate effort to restore the primitive defense of splitting, hence the term *fix*.

Bob Dylan captures this aspect of the restoration of splitting with alcohol in the lyrics to "I Shall Be Free" from *The Freewheelin' Bob Dylan* (1963) album:

> Well you ask me why I'm drunk alla time,
> It levels my head and eases my mind,
> I just walk along and stroll and sing,
> I see better days and I do better things.[6]

John Lennon (1971) perhaps put it most poignantly in the lyric from the song "Crippled Inside" on the *Imagine* album: "One thing you can't hide, is when you're crippled inside."

Such expressions of insight in the lyrics of songwriters and poets is essential for a deeper understanding of compulsive or more extreme addictive consumer behavior, because the individual does not have the capacity for genuine insight. This is expressed crisply by Sullivan (1956):

> Inquiring of the person about his compulsive rituals proves rather futile, for he cannot tell you anything about them. All that usually appears in the consciousness of the person who has a compulsive ritual is simply that he does it because he feels better when he does it; if he doesn't do it, then he gets nervous. Not doing it disturbs his mind and so on, and so he does it for peace of mind. (p. 248)

The Regressive Lure of Pure Affective States

Now let us go deeper into an analysis of the affect of addiction. The affect of addiction is the intense and overwhelmingly positive affect incorporated into the positive introject. The affect of addiction is the result of the regressive reactivation of the early infant's intense and overwhelmingly positive affective experiences at the mother's breast, before there was a boundary between self and object. That is why the gratification is absolute: There is no boundary between self and object. In general, for personality organizations in the primitive range of the Personality Continuum, the affect of addiction is the pure affect of the positive introject—the infant sated at the mother's breast, the tranquil quiet sense of well-being, what little good interpersonal experience the person has had in life, the intense and overwhelmingly positive affective state that goes with the positive introject, to wit, the Big Tit.

In the course of normal personality development, the integration of whole object relations neutralizes aggression, and affect becomes less intense and more modified and diversified. When splitting is excessive, this modification of affect does not occur: "This neutralization does not take place, or takes place very insufficiently; and thus an important energy source for ego growth fails" (Kernberg 1984A, p. 46).

In the primitive personality organization, as a result of the failure to integrate whole object relations, "the regressive pull of 'pure' affective states influences thought processes" (p. 51). Affect remains intense and overwhelming, and "the modification of affective dispositions available to the ego also indirectly fosters the emancipation of thought processes because the irradiating effect of earlier 'pure' affective states exerts a powerful regressive pull in the direction of primary process thinking, which decreases when modification of affect occurs" (p. 51).

In the primitive personality organization, there is a failure to emancipate thought processes from the pure affective states. The pure affective states exert a powerful regressive pull on the addict. This is the affect of addiction: The pure positive affect incorporated into the positive introject. This is the *high* of addiction. This is what the addict craves. This is the regressive lure of addiction. This is what the addict is looking for to restore the primitive defense of splitting.

THE INTERPERSONAL ORIGINS OF ADDICTIVE BEHAVIOR

We can now come full circle at the end of the intrapsychic structural analysis of addiction, to the interpersonal origins of addictive behavior. To trace the interpersonal origins of addictive behavior, it is fitting to return to the analysis of Michael Balint in his seminal essay "Early Developmental States of the Ego. Primary Object Love." According to Balint (1949), the interpersonal origins of addictive behavior can be traced back to early infantile experiences: "We asked ourselves *how many of these observable, monotonously recurring features of the analytical situation could be traced back to early infantile experiences, or more correctly how much of the early infantile mental processes can be inferred from these easily verifiable observations*" (Balint 1949, p. 268). These monotonously recurring patterns of adult behavior in the clinical situation represent infantile reactions: "Now it was but a step from here to surmise that our patients have brought these ever-recurring forms of reactions from their early infantile stages" (p. 269).

Balint's description of the pattern of behavior as "ever-recurring" is strikingly reminiscent of Sullivan's interpersonal definition of personality as the relatively enduring pattern of recurrent interpersonal situations that characterize a human life (Sullivan 1953, p. 111). The early interpersonal experiences of the infant are internalized in the intrapsychic structure of the personality organization. Balint (1949) refers to early infantile mental processes as being more correct than infantile experiences, because it is the intrapsychic structure of the personality organization that is relatively enduring. Balint concludes that infantile behavior in adults is determined by "precipitates of the earliest psychic experiences" (Balint 1949, p. 268). These psychic precipitates represent the intrapsychic structure of the personality, which, according to Balint, "*can be inferred from these easily verifiable observations*" (Balint 1949, p. 268).

Balint began "Early Developmental States of the Ego. Primary Object Love" with a statement of the principal method of psychoanalysis, which he described as tracing back to early infantile experience:

> A mental phenomenon observed in the present is explained by tracing it back to a previous one, and by demonstrating how far and by what external and internal influences the previous process was changed into the present one. This crab-like thinking must, however, come to a halt somewhere, i.e., where the previous earlier phenomenon, the original one, can no longer be observed but must be inferred from what can be observed. (p. 265)

In much the same way, when Freud described infants as greedy and insatiable, he did not observe the actual behavior of infants, but he drew inferences based on his observation of adult behavior in the clinical situation: "Why are infants so extravagant, greedy, insatiable, why does hostility appear unavoidably, whence the reproach [by adults] that the mother never fed them rightly, never treated them lovingly?" (Freud, quoted from Balint 1949, p. 267) Freud (1917C) said it this way: "These interpretations are arrived at on the basis of analytic examinations made by tracing from symptoms backwards" (p. 313).

Balint's process of tracing back infantile behavior in adults has an implication critical for economic theory: These behavior patterns already have a history, according to Balint (1949, p. 269), thereby remedying the consumers without a history of economic theory, in the admonition of Hirschman (1982, p. 79). A consumer with a history is a remarkable recommendation for the use of psychoanalytic object relations theory of the personality to explore the psychological foundations of consumer behavior.

TRACING BACK ADDICTION IN ADULTS TO EARLY INFANTILE BEHAVIOR

Addictive behavior represents a pattern of reactivated infantile behavior manifested in an adult. This is described by Balint (1949) in the following observation of behavior in the clinical situation: "An almost manic state broke out. The patients became overblissful; they wanted nothing but to experience again and again the satisfaction of these wishes" (Balint 1949, p. 268).[7] Further, according to Balint: "The patients felt super-healthy as long as they felt secure immediately on demand of the satisfaction of those extremely important wishes; at such times it was very difficult indeed to keep at the analytical work" (p. 268). The patient needed to feel secure in the immediate gratification, on demand, of these wishes. The shift to dissatisfaction for delay of the gratification was equally immediate: "At the first serious dissatisfaction for considerable delay of the gratification the whole structure of this enraptured blissfulness breaks down and abruptly the mood changes into the form described previously of despair, hatred and fears of retaliation" (p. 268).

The regressive reactivation of early infantile experiences and the return to earlier patterns of behavior in an adult are characterized as *primitive* by Balint: "It may be admitted that these phenomena repeat certain infantile situations, but why the most primitive ones?" (p. 269). Balint characterized this egoistic form of love as primitive:

> This primitive—egoistic—form of love works according to the principle: what is good for me is right for you, i.e. it does not recognize any difference between one's own interests and the interests of the object; it assumes as a matter of fact that the partner's desires are identical with one's own. Claims of the object

which go beyond this harmony are intolerable, and call forth anxiety or aggressiveness. (p. 270)

Anxiety and aggressiveness "are reactions to frustration in a similar way," according to Balint, reactivated infantile behavior (p. 269). Balint's touching description of the infant sated at the mother's breast, the "tranquil quiet sense of well-being," is, in actuality, a clinical observation of an adult displaying infantile behavior: "If the satisfaction arrives at the right moment, and with the right intensity, it causes reactions that are observable only with great difficulty because the experience of gratification happens so quietly. Properly this feeling of pleasure could be described as a *tranquil quiet sense of well-being*" (p. 269). Likewise, the stormy reaction to frustration also represents reactivated infantile behavior in an adult : "If, however, these wishes must remain unsatisfied, their gratification will be demanded very vehemently and an eventual frustration will call forth the most stormy reactions" (p. 269).

The primitive behavior of the adult is a reactivation of the stormy reaction to frustration in the (early) infant's relationship with the mother. Infantile behavior in an adult is primitive, and anxiety and aggressiveness are primitive reactions to intolerable frustration. In this primitive behavior manifested in an adult, Balint explicitly recognized the object-seeking behavior of the early infant, the cornerstone of British object relations theory: "*Without exception they are directed towards an object*," and "it is only the external world, the environment, that can satisfy them" (p. 269).

NOTES

1. For an important contribution in this area, see Benson (2000).
2. As recommended previously, see Ernst Kris (1952) for a brilliant application of object relations theory to art.
3. Refer to "Riff on Depression" in the previous chapter for an elaboration of the patterns of variation in depression with the level of personality development.
4. To say "pathological narcissism" seems redundant; narcissism is pathological, primitive, to be precise. I do not agree with Kernberg's use of the term '*normal narcissism*' to mean essentially self-esteem; narcissism is primitive, not normal, in a chronologically adult person.
5. Kernberg (1985A) sometimes uses the term "on a deeper level" when I would prefer to say at a "lower level" of personality development. I prefer to use the term "on a deeper level" to mean looking down from the vantage point

of a higher level of personality development. With the primitive personality organizations, everything is on the surface, which is not to say superficial.

6. See Dylan. 1985, p. 69.

7. Balint's surprising use of *bliss* is useful to economists in conceptualizing addictive behavior in an indifference-curve analysis: A bliss point is not optimal.

Chapter 15

Expanded Economic Analysis of Consumer Behavior

Broadening the behavioral foundations of the economic theory of the consumer to include the inconsistent pattern of behavior of the neurotic consumer, the chaotic alternating and contradictory, but rigidly patterned behavior of the compulsive and addictive consumer in the primitive range, and, to a lesser extent, the changing and capricious pattern of behavior of the truly irrational personality organizations in the psychotic range of the Personality Continuum has expanded the limits of applicability of economic theory. The methodological importance of the Personality Continuum is that it provides the integrative framework for the comparative analysis of personality organizations.

Compulsive and, in the more extreme case, addictive consumption behavior has been analyzed in excruciating detail using personality organizations in the primitive range of the Personality Continuum, in particular, the borderline and narcissistic personality organizations, respectively. This approach is crucial to a deeper understanding of compulsive and addictive behavior: It is the primitive level of personality development, not the substance or the activity, that determines the person's predisposition toward compulsive and addictive behavior.

Personality organizations at the primitive level of personality development are prone to compulsive and addictive behavior. This predilection of the personality organization, or personality tendency, is part of the package of the personality organization. The methodological importance of the personality organization is that it provides the organizational framework for a deeper understanding of human behavior and ultimately for a human understanding of consumer behavior. Further, since the defense of splitting has broken down, it is the underlying level of intrapsychic structural formation of the personality organization that primarily determines the nature of the compulsive and more extreme addictive consumer behavior. Thus it is the intrapsychic structure of the personality organization that is reflected in the structure of preferences.

MOTIVATION AND ADDICTION: THE ECONOMIC IMPLICATIONS

Compulsive and addictive consumption behavior has received increasing attention from economists. Scitovsky (1976) equated addiction with love, and Taylor (1988) and Solomon (1980) include eating and sleeping with addiction. This leads to a consideration of the theoretical contributions that have been made in economics to account for observable phenomena that do not fit the narrow postulate of rationality in the neoclassical theory of the consumer.

Addiction is a compelling caricature of consumption behavior—the insatiable greed and excessive dependency driving demand make it a seemingly ideal model of motivation for consumption behavior. For economists, it would legitimize the neoclassical model of consumption behavior because it seems to answer the essential question of motivation: *Why* does the consumer prefer one consumption bundle over another? The easy answer is because the consumer is addicted. On the one hand, this is the correct or the right answer, after all, as far as it goes; on the other hand, as economists are wont to say in their two-valued way, this is pure legerdemain and does not answer, but simply begs the question: Why is one person an addict and another not? We are back to the basic circularity: The consumer prefers what he likes and likes what he prefers—the consumer behaves as he behaves—a clear violation of the limits of applicability of economic theory.

The motivation for addictive behavior is deceptively simple, owing to the relatively simple structure of personality organizations at the primitive level of personality development. Addiction represents a clear-cut, qualitatively different pattern of consumer behavior in comparison to the stable and consistent pattern of behavior of the normal person and the inconsistent pattern of behavior common to personality organizations in the neurotic range of the Personality Continuum. The interpretation of a pattern of addictive behavior and an exploration of the particular personality organizations prone to addiction have been a central theme of this exploration of the psychological foundations of consumer behavior.

SPLITTING AND THE TWO-SELVES HYPOTHESIS

Kernberg's (1985A) contributions to an understanding of the borderline and narcissistic personality organizations have been analytically very useful in understanding compulsive and more extreme addictive consumer behavior, respectively. The lack of anxiety tolerance—the incapacity to tolerate marginal anxiety—is characteristic of personality organizations in the primitive range of the Personality Continuum. In a perverse sort of way, these personality organizations provide striking justification for the use of object relations theory as an integrative framework, the elucidation of one of the most cherished analytical notions of economics—marginal analysis. The marginal anxiety flips up the all-bad introjections and identifications that threaten to contaminate, spoil, or destroy the primitively idealized all-good object representation and the grandiose self. Splitting fails, severe anxiety proliferates, and additional symptom formation results in the form of compulsive and addictive behavior.

The primitive defense of splitting is central to the conception of the intrapsychic structural formation of the personality organizations in the primitive range of the Personality Continuum. It consists of the alternating activation of contradictory selves: "It was as if there were two selves, equally strong, completely separated from each other in their emotions although not in the patient's [person's] memory and alternating in his conscious experience. It was this successive activation of contradictory ego states which I would refer to as an example of splitting of the ego" (Kernberg 1984A, p. 23).

Kernberg's observation of the behavioral manifestations of splitting is a dead ringer for Schelling's (1980) observation, with regard to compulsive consumption behavior, that "people behave sometimes as if they had two selves" (p. 95). Winston (1980) observed the same phenomenon: "*Simultaneously* two sets of preferences order an individual's choices and they don't agree," and "the individual's preferences are not rigidly fixed over time; instead they flip-flop between two different preference states" (p. 303). Young (1961) has observed that preferences can be alternating using his technique of preference testing: "There is no way to force an animal [or human?] to show a preference. Either a preference develops, with repeated choices, or it does not develop. Weak preferences, strong preferences, alternating preferences, and no preferences at all have been observed" (p. 152).

This analysis confirms the view of Winston (1980): "This very simple non-constancy of tastes suggests that Becker's dichotomy of tastes as either 'constant' or 'irrational' is not helpful—that lots of analytically useful variety lies between those extremes" (p. 304). What this analysis clearly shows is that there is a broad range of behavior that lies between perfect rationality and the opposite extreme of complete irrationality, which would be represented by the psychotic range on the Personality Continuum. Contradictory preference behavior, however, should not be confused with preferences that change in response to the specific circumstances of the situation.

Winston's (1980) use of "constancy" is entirely consistent with "object constancy" of object relations theory, achieved with the integration of whole object relations. Some clarification of terminology is in order at this point. For the normal range of the Personality Continuum, preferences are stable and consistent. In the primitive range of the Personality Continuum, preferences are alternating and contradictory and can shift rapidly. Preferences cannot be considered stable in the primitive range of the Personality Continuum, yet the behavior is rigidly patterned. This is what I think Winston means by his characterization of preferences as stable-but-non-constant (p. 302). Winston has developed a mathematical model that is appropriate for the intrapsychic structural formation of personality organizations in the primitive range of the Personality Continuum and therefore for modeling compulsive or more extreme addictive consumer behavior.

As Sen (1977) has observed, "If you choose *x* and reject *y* on one occasion and then promptly proceed to do the exact opposite, you can prevent the revealed preference theorist from assigning a preference ordering to you, thereby restraining him from stamping a utility function on you which you must be seen as maximizing" (pp. 322–323). Thus, behavior that is characterized by the alternating activation of contradictory preferences cannot be explained by the economic theory of the consumer based on consistent preferences. Stigler and Becker's (1977) attempt to explain addictive behavior using neoclassical consumer theory represents an inappropriate use of the theory (pp. 77–81).

Since the postulate of rationality is violated in the chaotic alternating and contradictory, but rigidly patterned, behavior of a person with a primitive personality organization, can ordinal utility theory be useful for modeling? The answer is that ordinal utility theory can be modified to accommodate for compulsive and addictive consumer behavior, and this modification broadens the behavioral foundations of economic analysis and opens the way to the mathematical modeling and quantitative analysis of economics to other disciplines.

FUNDAMENT OF THE FORMS OF THE UTILITY FUNCTION ALONG THE PERSONALITY CONTINUUM

The interpretation of utility as both negative and positive is indicative of the separate inborn physiological capacity for positive and negative affective experience. This is an important contribution to ordinal utility theory. From this foundation, the intrapsychic structure of the personality organization is formed.

The intrapsychic structure of the personality organization is reflected in the structure of preferences; therefore, it can be used as the psychological foundation for the fundament of the utility function at each level of personality development. The fundament of the utility function at each level of personality development provides the prolegomena for a new panel of the Personality Continuum on the Form of the Utility Function.

The utility function is

$$U = F(P, N),$$

where N = negative introjections and identifications and P = positive introjections and identifications. For persons in the normal range of the Personality Continuum, preferences are stable and consistent: $P > N$, and P far outweighs N; $U > 0$.

For personality organizations in the neurotic range of the Personality Continuum, preferences are consistent under ordinary functioning and inconsistent under extraordinary functioning: $P > N$, $U > 0$. At the point of demarcation between the neurotic and primitive ranges of the Personality Continuum, $P = N$. As we move up the neurotic range, $P > N$ and varies continuously and increasingly within this range of the Personality Continuum.

For personality organizations in the primitive range of the Personality Continuum, preferences are alternating and contradictory as the result of the failure to achieve the integration of whole object relations. The compulsive and more extreme addictive behavior represents an effort to restore the defense of splitting when it breaks down. Personality organizations in the primitive range of the Personality Continuum are characterized by the preponderance of negative over positive introjections and identifications: $P < N$. For movements down the primitive range, $P < N$, varying continuously and increasingly. When $P < N$, $U < 0$ as the baseline level of ordinary functioning for the consumer in the primitive range of the Personality Continuum.

For personality organizations in the psychotic range of the Personality Continuum, preferences are changing and capricious, representing the collapse of the intrapsychic structure of the personality. $P < N$, and N far outweighs P; $U < 0$.

OBJECT RELATIONS THEORY, ORDINAL UTILITY THEORY, AND OPPONENT-PROCESS THEORY

A theoretical connection will be made between object relations theory and opponent-process theory, introduced by Richard L. Solomon and adapted to economic analysis by Lester D. Taylor (1988). Taylor (1986) and Saldanha and Lancry (1988) extended this approach to model consumer behavior dynamically.

Opponent-process theory takes over for ordinal utility theory to capture the oscillating pattern of compulsive and addictive consumer behavior triggered by marginal anxiety in primitive personality organizations already utilizing splitting as an active and powerful defense against intolerable anxiety. Splitting breaks down, activating the aggressive, all-bad, persecuting internal object relations, that is, the negative introjects, with self undifferentiated from the object, and affect intense and overwhelming.

The addict, from an object relations theory point of view, is flipping up the all-good side, the *a* process of opponent-process theory, accurately describing the pleasurable aspects of addiction. When splitting breaks down, the all-bad internal objects flip up, initiating the *b* process of opponent-process theory, and the urgent need for redosing occurs (see Figure 15.1).

The *a* and *b* processes oscillate in addiction as the all-good flips up with the high, then the negative opponent process catches up, and redosing occurs. This is especially clear in the case of addiction based on a chemical dependency. The oscillating opponent processes become damped and approach a baseline unless the dosage of the chemical substance is continually increased.

This analysis is related to the total utility curve and can be adapted to an analysis of addiction, as well as normal consumption behavior. For normal consumption behavior, the total and marginal utility curves of utility theory are appropriate for the analysis.

Figure 15.1
Opponent-Process Theory of Addiction

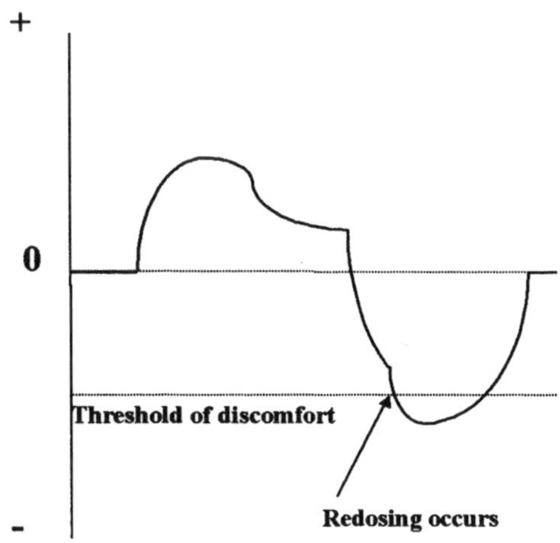

Total Utility And Marginal Utility

The total utility curve has a positive slope at lower consumption levels, $MU > 0$, and marginal utility is increasing, but at a decreasing rate of change (i.e., the second derivative is negative). The utility curve reaches a maximum when the marginal utility is zero, $MU = 0$, and marginal utility is negative for consumption beyond that point, $MU < 0$.

The slope of the total utility curve for a commodity is marginal utility, the additional utility for each additional unit of consumption of a commodity. The slope of the total utility curve reflects the principle of diminishing marginal utility. For each additional unit of consumption of a commodity, marginal utility decreases, that is, the additional utility for each additional unit of consumption decreases for the consumer (see Figure 15.2).

The Contributions of Opponent-Process Theory

Opponent-process theory describes the physiological patterns of consumer behavior. The link between object relations theory and opponent-process theory is evident with the oscillating pattern of addictive behavior. What is not so evident is the compatibility of opponent-process theory and ordinal utility theory, which is more evident with normal consumption behavior.

Figure 15.2
Total Utility Curve

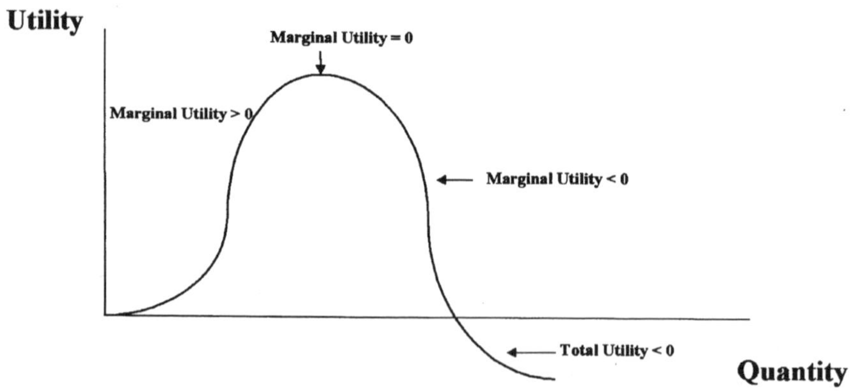

To elaborate on the link between opponent-process theory and ordinal utility theory, opponent-process theory deals serially with each bout of consumption, whereas the total utility curve is the result of consuming increasing quantities of one commodity. From the point of view of utility theory, the addict goes too far along the total utility curve, presumably past the point where the marginal utility—the slope of the total utility curve—is zero, and total utility is at a maximum for one commodity or consumption good, beyond to negative marginal utility and decreasing *total* level of utility, which goes to zero and thereafter becomes negative.

This is greed, satiation, and in Balint's clinical observation of infantile behavior in adults, an *overblissful* state, a state of enraptured blissfulness that breaks down abruptly with any delay of gratification (1949, p. 268). The addict exercises no self-control with regard to the particular consumption activity in a given situation, at one point in time. The more the addict has to consume, the more he or she does consume, and he or she always wants more. Then, the next day, the addict will get up and do it all over again, rigidly repeating the self-destructive pattern of behavior over and over again. Any self-control is external, to a large extent, such as market factors like price and income, to regulate the consumption behavior of an addict.

Twelve-step treatment programs, according to Hirschman (1992), are premised upon abstinence from those consumption activities over which the addict consciously acknowledges that he or she has no ability to control his or her behavior (e.g., drugs and alcohol). Abstinence is an attempt to maintain a boundary on the consumption behavior of the ad-

Figure 15.3
The New Opponent-Process Theory

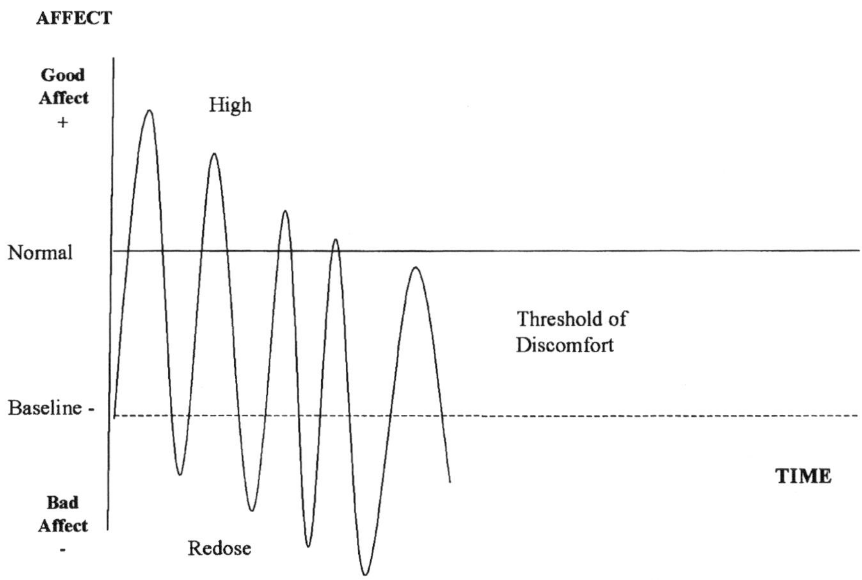

dict in the absence of self-control and in the face of self-destructiveness (Hirschman 1992).

While this case fits the movement along the total utility curve for one episode of consumption, it fails to capture the oscillating pattern of behavior that characterizes compulsive and addictive behavior. At this point, opponent-process theory becomes more useful for modeling these patterns of behavior (Taylor 1988). The link to the intrapsychic structure of the personality organization in the primitive range of the Personality Continuum leads to the defense of splitting into all-good and all-bad selves and objects and to the analysis of the marginal anxiety that breaks down splitting as an explanation for compulsive and addictive consumption behavior.

What is missing from opponent-process theory is the understanding that the addict starts at a *deficit*. The baseline for the addict is negative. Figure 15.3 presents the new opponent-process theory modified to capture the addict's deficit and the oscillations in consumption behavior over time.

Economic analysis and psychoanalysis, or more precisely, psychoanalytic object relations theory of the personality and neoclassical ordinal utility theory of the consumer, have been theoretically linked and tied tightly together in a sound methodological way. Opponent-process theory has now been theoretically linked to object relations theory and ordinal utility theory. This opens the way to the entire body of economic theory of the consumer to researchers from disciplines outside economics, and beyond the individual consumer to demand in the market, the market as part of the economy, and larger theoretical frameworks that will be explored later in this chapter in a section titled "Linking Theoretical Systems."

Myopic Consumption Behavior

Myopic consumption behavior means behavior without consideration for future consequences of one's current behavior. A *myopic consumer* does not have the capacity for concern for oneself or others and therefore has no concern for the consequences of compulsive or addictive behavior. There is no delay between the impulse and its immediate gratification. Impulses are crudely gratified. The need is to do *it* now. "I need *it* now."

Myopic consumption behavior is driven by severe anxiety. The primitive defense of splitting has failed to prevent the proliferation of severe anxiety. When splitting breaks down, severe anxiety is experienced as intolerable, and the punitive superego persecutes the person with severe anxiety, driven by the return of bad objects, against which all other defenses have broken down. The outbreak of compulsive or more extreme addictive consumption behavior is an effort to restore the primitive defense of splitting. Redosing restores the primitive defense of splitting.

The outbursts of compulsive or addictive consumption behavior represent the regression to a lower level of personality development and a return to earlier patterns of behavior. In the case of addiction, the motivation of the alcoholic for taking another drink, the head taking another hit of cannabis, the heroin addict taking another shot, the cigarette smoker, and so on, is to feel good again; precisely what that means depends on the level of personality development, in general, and the personality organization, in particular.

A Brief Note on the Rate of Time Preference

A person's time orientation, in terms of present versus future, as well as the past, has critical implications for the rate of time preference (see Maital 1982; Winston 1980; Strotz 1955–1956). In the primitive range of the Personality Continuum, personality organizations are characterized by a present orientation, and the rate of time preference is very high. In comparison, in the normal range of the Personality Continuum, a person has a future orientation, and the rate of time preference is far lower. The rate of time preference increases for movements down the neurotic range of the Personality Continuum.

HARVEY LEIBENSTEIN AND SELECTIVE RATIONALITY: RATIONAL AT THE BORDERLINE

Leibenstein's work on X-Efficiency theory of the firm in some ways has overshadowed his contributions to consumer behavior. The breadth of Leibenstein's views on economic man is contained in his classic *Beyond Economic Man* (1976), but his clearest conception of consumer behavior comes in his work on the demographic transition. The demographic transition accompanies economic development—the change in fertility patterns from a natural pattern of having as many children as biologically possible to a pattern of replacement fertility with planned families of two children, preferably a boy and a girl. I believe that Leibenstein's most mature statement of his overall conception of consumer behavior, especially his appreciation of social influences on consumption behavior, is contained in "The Economic Theory of Fertility Decline" (1975).

Leibenstein's theory of selective rationality is useful in understanding primitive consumption behavior. Selective rationality means that "one need not assume that *typical* behavior is 'rational' " (Leibenstein 1975, p. 3). A person's behavior can appear quite spontaneous as long as the start-stop points are determined by calculation: "It is sufficient that behavior at critical junctures be of a 'rational' type" (p. 3). Thus, according to Leibenstein, "Note that under these conditions *average* typical behavior appears to be nonrational, but marginal behavior is rational" (p. 3).

When typical behavior is nonrational, and rational behavior only occurs at the margins, this is clearly not the stable and consistent behavior of the normal consumer. At best, it is typical of the merely inconsistent behavior of the neurotic consumer, lacking stability, but striving for consistency. At worst, it characterizes the rigidly patterned, chaotic, alternating, and contradictory behavior of a person with a primitive personality organization—at worst because primitive personality organizations have achieved a higher level of reality testing than psychotic personality organizations. In the psychotic range of the Personality Continuum, the general pattern of human behavior is changing and capricious, and the pattern of consumer behavior is truly irrational.

LINKING THEORETICAL SYSTEMS

The integrative framework provided by the Personality Continuum opens the way to an exploration of economic development and population change, perhaps the largest theoretical framework in the social sciences. This theoretical linkage provides a major benefit to fields outside of economics.

Sustained economic growth results in change in the structure of the economic system. Structural change in the economic system refers to the shift in labor and output from the primary to the secondary and tertiary sectors of the economy, roughly corresponding to the movement from agriculture to manufacturing and into services. Economic growth and structural change lead to economic development (Kuznets 1966). The movement toward industrialization, urbanization, and large-scale corporate and bureaucratic organizations results in an industrial market economy and in the formation of the dual labor market.

Fertility Decline of the Demographic Transition and the Changing Pattern of Consumption Behavior

The consumption aspects of the successful achievement of upward social mobility result from changes in the entire pattern of consumption behavior to reflect the new higher social class and status. Successful upward social mobility, the change in the relative position in society, brings about changes across the entire pattern of consumption behavior to reflect the new higher social class. The social class is represented by the appropriate socially determined status-role consumption bundles (Kernberg 1972). This change in the pattern of consumption behavior entails an increase in expenditures for these status goods, especially services, as the market increasingly supplies what was previously provided by other members of the social system (Leibenstein 1975, pp. 6, 24).

The status-shift effects represent the shift in the pattern of consumption expenditures toward goods and services, or commodities, as defined in the new household production function approach. According to Leibenstein (1975), "If status expenditures become a significant portion of income, then a considerable squeeze on the proportion of the budget spent on ordinary goods takes place" (p. 6).

This is a manifestation of Engel's Law: As a family's income increases, the proportion allocated to ordinary consumption expenditures, necessities such as food, decreases, and that allocated to manufactured goods provided by the market and especially to services and new status expenditures increases. Engel's Law is a remarkably stable empirical phenomenon that can be applied to an individual, a nuclear family or extended household, a cross-sectional analysis of the class structure of society, a time-series analysis of the historical experience of one country over time in the process of economic growth and development, and an international comparison of income differentials between countries at different levels of economic development.

Where are these "other" members of the social system that had previously provided these services? The fertility decline of the demographic transition in the course of economic development is brought about by the need to limit family size in order to maintain the appropriate pattern of consumption behavior that reflects the new higher social class and status (Albanese 1988A). It is preferable to be above the relative income for the social class as a whole (Freedman 1963) and therefore to aspire to emulate families in higher social statuses for themselves or for their children (Leibenstein 1975).

Waves of Immigration to the United States

The structural change in the economic system in the United States at the end of the nineteenth and in the early part of the twentieth century was fueled by waves of immigration, largely from eastern and southern Europe, openly referred to as virtually unlimited supplies of cheap foreign labor, entering the secondary labor market. The children of the immigrants became the prime aspirants for the primary labor market. The motivation for upward social mobility among the children of the immigrants was magnified by their own experience with the insecurity and inferior social status of the secondary labor market of their own immigrant parents.

The waves of immigration resulted in the collision of cultures and initiated the process of adaptation and cultural change. The main social changes were the economic independence of the nuclear family, made possible by industrialization and urbanization, and the reduction in family size that resulted as a consequence. The increasing incidence of isolation and the overwhelming experience of loneliness resulted in the rise of intimacy as a predominant motivation in interpersonal behavior (Sullivan 1953, p. 262).

A primary-labor-market job was a prerequisite for marriage for the

American born generation children of the Italian immigrants. One thinks of the poignant portrayal of Doc, in William F. Whyte's *Street Corner Society* (1955), who never married because he was never able to hold a steady, stable job, ostensibly due to a physical handicap. Although he was a talented person, his skills did not fit those of the primary labor market in which he worked. He could not afford an appropriate apartment or house to raise a family; that is, he was not successful in obtaining a primary-labor-market job.

Since the first generation of American-born Italian women would not have routinely used contraception to plan families, marriage was usually followed shortly thereafter by children. These newly formed nuclear families were economically independent and had the responsibility of raising their children in the new higher social class and, further, fulfilling their aspirations to emulate higher statuses for their children, that is, giving their children everything they did not have when growing up. This put a considerable squeeze on the allocation of the family time and income; thus family size had to be limited, if not planned, to successfully maintain the pattern of consumption behavior representative of the new higher relative social class and status (Albanese 1988A).

Withdrawal of Status Respect and the Motivation of the Entrepreneur

An extension to the motivation of the entrepreneur can be explored here, drawing on the ideas of Everett E. Hagen in *On the Theory of Social Change: How Growth Begins* (1962). The entrepreneur is the engine of economic growth and, therefore, of structural change in the economic system. Hagen believed that immigrants to the United States experienced the withdrawal of status respect, and this magnified the economic motivation for upward social mobility for the immigrants and their children.

Hagen has provided a penetrating analysis of the internalization of the *status and role bundles* that represent social class:

> Like other values, the value one places on one's status becomes internalized, and one regards that status as a right. (In a nonstatic society, one's concept of status may be one of moving from position to position as one progresses in life.) For the inner satisfaction of the members of a society, as for social stability, it is essential that the status (the identity) of the members of each group in a society also be recognized by the other groups as appropriate and good. One cannot find satisfaction in one's adult pattern of behavior, including in this term

one's beliefs, if one does not also perceive that the groups whose opinion one values (one's "reference groups") approve of such behavior. If the members of a group, having learned a role and status in infancy and childhood—role and status which their forebears learned before them—and having learned also to value certain groups in society as reference groups, then find in adulthood that the members of their reference groups do not regard their role and status as worthy and proper, for example, disregard their beliefs and moral standards, the impossibility of believing (feeling) at the same time that their role and status are worthy and that the judgment of their reference groups is trustworthy creates tensions within them. They value both their position in life and the opinion of other social groups, but they cannot pursue the one and still have the other. (p. 186)

The internalized *socially determined status-role bundles* represent the status and various roles of the individual in his or her social system, as the relatively enduring pattern of recurrent interpersonal situations that characterize a human life, social class, as the relative position in society, and culture, as represented by a value system. This brings the analysis back to the fundamental position that the intrapsychic structure of the personality is manifested in the structure of the preferences and takes us beyond, to an elaboration of the specific status-appropriate roles that reflect the value system of the culture. It is at this point, perhaps, that we can fully appreciate Freud's (1933) understanding of the lofty position of a value system, the cultural contents of the protective superego, as "the vehicle of tradition and of all time-resisting judgments of value which have propagated themselves in this manner from generation to generation" (p. 67).

The implications for the analysis of consumer behavior are profound. Through this process of embedding the developing personality in the social system, the wider society, and the culture, psychoanalytic object relations theory relates the intrapsychic structure of the personality to the preference structure of the consumer. Further, relating the structure of preferences to the intrapsychic structure of the personality using object relations theory has transcended the overwhelmingly individual orientation of economic theory to provide a social foundation for the analysis of consumer behavior.

Chapter 16

Relentless Individual Pursuit of Self-Interest in America

I have been striving (or struggling, as the case may be) for a human understanding of consumer behavior. The nature of the individual pursuit of self-interest varies with the level of personality development. In the normal range of the Personality Continuum, the individual pursuit of self-interest is informed by a value system that transcends self-interest. In the neurotic range of the Personality Continuum, the individual pursuit of self-interest is done with the capacity for sympathy and within the moral system of society. In the primitive range of the Personality Continuum, the individual pursuit of self-interest is characterized as selfish. This is particularly the case with the narcissistic personality organization in the primitive range of the Personality Continuum, where the individual pursuit of individual self-interest is often ruthless, and the capacity to transcend the selfish pursuit of self-interest is an important positive prognostic indicator.

The historical misconception of Adam Smith's view of human nature and, therefore, the nature of economic man has now been rectified. Adam Smith's capacity for sympathy places a person at least at the neurotic level of personality development and would include a person at the higher normal level of personality development. The individual pursuit of self-interest stands at the center of the economic theory of the consumer. It is the invisible hand of Adam Smith driving the economy. The individual pursuit of self-interest, economic individualism, and individualism, in general, are fundamental to economic analysis as we know it in a capitalistic market economy. Individualism is at the cultural foundation of classical economics, a reflection of English society and Western culture.

The individual pursuit of self-interest has been taken to the extreme in the neoclassical theory of the consumer, based on the concept of consumer sovereignty. In much the same way, the individual pursuit of self-interest has been taken to an extreme in America. In American culture, self-reliance is highly valued, and the individual pursuit of self-interest is accepted as the norm. From a cross-cultural perspective, America represents an extreme variation in the high value placed on individual autonomy, self-reliance, and economic independence.

G.J. BARKER-BENFIELD AND THE RELENTLESS PURSUIT OF INDIVIDUAL SELF-INTEREST IN AMERICA

Economic individualism, rooted in the belief in individual autonomy, and the insistence on self-control and self-discipline of the Puritans, transplanted to America from England, went to an extreme. In his penetrating analysis of male attitudes toward women and sexuality in nineteenth-century America, *The Horrors of the Half-Known Life* (1976), G.J. Barker-Benfield argued persuasively that the Puritans represented only a fragment of English culture: "New England, and then American Culture generally, assumed a fragment of English culture for the whole" (p. 24). The cultural foundations of America, therefore, began with only a fragment of English culture and with only a slice of English society.

In America, the individual pursuit of self-interest is most often described as relentless. According to Barker-Benfield, this was the result of the unrelenting pressure created by an increasingly democratic society in America: "I suggest that white American men's experience of the increasingly democratic society was one of unrelenting pressure, and that their sexual beliefs and their treatment of women were shaped very largely by that pressure; beliefs and treatment affected child rearing in ways that perpetuated and reinforced the pressure" (p. xii). More to the point, Barker-Benfield located the source of the unrelenting pressure in the *vicissitudes of business* in America: "A pervasive theme in historical literature of the nineteenth century is the incessant pressure of vicissitudinous business" (p. 50).

Individualism, when taken to the extreme, is manifested in "a refusal to acknowledge any authoritative standard but one's own," according to Barker-Benfield (pp. 99–100). "The specter of children modeling their behavior on rebel parents by rebelling against them haunts American history" (p. 24). This contributes to the pragmatic nature of Americans and to the abruptness of adaptation and cultural change in America.

ALEXIS DE TOCQUEVILLE AND *DEMOCRACY IN AMERICA*

Alexis de Tocqueville created an enduring document of the individual pursuit of self-interest in volume 2 of *Democracy in America*, first published in the United States in 1838. In America, men had created an altogether individual existence:

> Intent on the one goal of making his fortune, the emigrant has finally created for himself an altogether individual existence. Family sentiments have come to fuse themselves into a vast egoism, and it is doubtful if in his wife and children he see anything else than a detached portion of himself. (Pierson 1938, pp. 243–244)

Thus, according to Barker-Benfield, "In Tocqueville's account, the demands of this struggle affected the attitude of the American male toward his wife and family." With the one goal of making their fortune in America, according to Tocqueville (1945), men explored the new country for purposes of profit:

> I have shown how the Americans are constantly driven to engage in commerce and industry. Their origin, their social condition, their political institutions, and even the region they inhabit urge them irresistibly in this direction. Their present condition, then, is that of an almost exclusively manufacturing and commercial association, placed in the midst of a new and boundless country, which their principal object is to explore for purposes of profit. This is the characteristic that most distinguishes the American people from all others at the present time. (pp. 247–248)

Tocqueville saw the attitude of complete insensibility and cold implacability toward Native Americans as a manifestation of the relentless pursuit of individual self-interest: "In the heart of this society, so policed, so prudish, so sententiously unreal and virtuous, one encounters a complete insensibility, a sort of cold and implacable egoism when it's a question of America indigenies. . . . This world belongs to us, add they.

. . . The true proprietors of this continent are those who know how to take advantage of its riches" (Tocqueville, quoted in Pierson 1938, p. 235).

In Tocqueville's view, it was a struggle to take advantage of the opportunity to exploit the vast resources in this boundless new country: "The American . . . was 'tenacious,' 'cold,' and 'pitiless' in his struggle against the soil and savage life" (Barker-Benfield 1976, p. 5). Further, "He struggles ceaselessly against it, despoils it daily of some of its attributes" (Tocqueville, quoted in Pierson 1938, p. 273).

Neurasthenia, or monomania, literally, working oneself into a state of nervous exhaustion, was a result of carrying the individual pursuit of self-interest too far and was a common malady diagnosed in nineteenth-century America (Tocqueville 1945, p. 146; Meyer 1980, p. 22; Barker-Benfield 1976, p. 99). In Tocqueville's view, "The constant strife between the inclination springing from the equality of condition and the means it supplies to satisfy them harasses and wearies the mind" (1945, p. 146). According to Barker-Benfield (1976), "Monomania was the appropriate form of derangement for a society preoccupied with self-making and individualism" (p. 99). Even Sullivan (1940) gave a diagnosis of neurasthenia: "weakness, debility, insomnia, vague to marked discomfort in the head, belly, or cardiac region" (p. 104). The consequences of the relentless individual pursuit of self-interest in twentieth-century America can be read in the titles of Thorstein Veblen's *The Theory of the Leisure Class* (1899), Staffan B. Linder's *The Harried Leisure Class* (1970), and Juliet B. Schor's *The Overworked American: The Unexpected Decline of Leisure* (1992).

ADAM SMITH'S VIEW OF THE DARK SIDE OF HUMAN NATURE

Adam Smith (1759) believed in individual competition, but he also believed that the competition should be fair:

> In the race for wealth, and honours, and preferments, he may run as hard as he can, and strain every nerve and every muscle, in order to outstrip all his competitors. But if he should justle, or throw down any of them, the indulgence of the spectators is entirely at an end. It is a violation of fair play, which they cannot admit of. This man is to them, in every respect, as good as he: they do not enter into that self-love, by which he prefers himself so much to this other, and cannot go along with the motive from which he hurt him. They readily, therefore, sympathize with the natural resentment of the injured, and the offender

> becomes the object of their hatred and indignation. He is sensible that he becomes so, and feels that those sentiments are ready to burst out from all sides against him. As the greater and more irreparable the evil that is done, the resentment of the sufferer runs naturally the higher: so does likewise the sympathetic indignation of the spectator. (pp. 162–163)

Death represents the irreparable evil: "Death is the greatest evil which one man can inflict on another, and excites the highest degree of resentment in those who are immediately connected with the slain. Murder, therefore, is the most atrocious of all crimes which affect individuals only, in the sight both of mankind and of the person who committed it" (p. 163).

Self-love is Adam Smith's perfectly apt term for the excessive self-reference that is characteristic of the narcissistic personality organization, and to "justle or throw down any" of his competitors represents the ruthless pursuit of self-interest that is particularly characteristic of the narcissistic personality organization (p. 162). In the end, the punishment for a person with a narcissistic personality organization, who ruthlessly pursues his own individual self-interest, stepping on anyone who gets in his way, is *remorse*. Adam Smith's ideas on remorse will provide the opportunity to explore the darkest side of human behavior.

Honor and the Ambitious Man

Adam Smith (1759) saw that what the ambitious man is really pursuing is *honor*, albeit an honor ill understood; hence the result is often dishonor:

> But, though they should be so lucky as to attain that wished-for greatness, they are always most miserably disappointed in the happiness which they expect to enjoy in it. It is not ease or pleasure, but always honour, of one kind or another, though frequently an honour very ill understood, that the ambitious man really pursues. But the honour of his exalted station appears, both in his eyes and in those of other people, polluted and defiled by the baseness of the means through which he rose to it. (p. 131)

For the ambitious man with a narcissistic personality organization, the "wished-for greatness" is a manifestation of the grandiose self, and the ruthless achievement of success is often dishonored by the "baseness of the means through which he rose to it."[1]

There is no escape from the dishonor, because memory persists, according to Smith:

> He invokes in vain the dark and dismal powers of forgetfulness and oblivion. He remembers himself what he has done, and the remembrance tells him that other people likewise remember it. Amidst all the gaudy pomp of the most ostentatious greatness; amidst the venal and vile adulation of the great and of the learned; amidst the more innocent, though more foolish, acclamations of the common people; amidst all the pride of conquest and the triumph of successful war, he is still secretly pursued by the avenging furies of shame and remorse; and, while glory seems to surround him on all sides, he himself, in his own imagination, sees black and foul infamy fast pursuing him, and every moment ready to overtake him from behind. (pp. 131–132)

The "avenging furies of shame and remorse . . . fast pursuing him and every moment ready to overtake him from behind," represent the punitive superego, persecuting the person with a primitive personality organization with severe anxiety. With brutal clarity, Smith captures the nature of the sentiment of remorse: "Such is the nature of the sentiment, which is properly called remorse; of all the sentiments which can enter the human breast the most dreadful. It is made up of shame from the sense of the impropriety of past conduct; of grief for the effects of it; of pity for those who suffer by it; and of the dread and terror of punishment from the consciousness of the justly-provoked resentment of all rational creatures" (p. 164).

Smith's use of the term *rational* is in perfect agreement with the conception of the rational economic man, mutatis mutandis, as a consistent consumer with the capacity for sympathy. Because of Smith's emphasis on fairness and justice, it is also in agreement with the more holistic conception of economic man, as the normal consumer.

Remorse, the most dreadful human sentiment, is made up of shame from past conduct, grief for the effects of it, pity for those who suffer by it, and the terror of punishment as a conscious experience. Remorse is not mere guilt over bad behavior for which the person can make reparations or amends. A person with a primitive personality organization, and a narcissistic personality organization in particular, does not have the capacity to experience guilt. The subjective experience of remorse is far worse, with its admixture of shame, grief, pity, and terror. The subjective experience of remorse is punishment for past conduct that represents "the greater and more irreparable evil that is done" to other people (p. 163). The subjective experience of remorse represents the persecution of the punitive superego by severe anxiety.

The punitive superego persecutes the person with a primitive personality organization with severe anxiety and thereby punishes the individual who does not have a prohibitive superego and the capacity to experience guilt. When the primitive defense of splitting breaks down, the intolerable experience of severe anxiety is sudden, like a blow on the head, and in Fairbairn's (1952) chilling observation, now familiar, but worth repeating; the person is "haunted by bad objects against the return of which all defenses have broken down, and from which there is no escape (except in death)" (p. 166). In Barker-Benfield's (1976) parallel observation, the specter haunting America history, children rebelling against their rebel parents, represents the return of bad objects, haunting the person with a primitive personality organization.

There is no escape into solitude for the person who has committed irreparable evil, according to Smith (1759), because solitude is still more dreadful than society:

> Everything seems hostile, and he would be glad to fly to some inhospitable desert, where he might never more behold the face of a human creature, nor read in the countenance of mankind the condemnation of his crimes. But solitude is still more dreadful than society. His own thoughts can present him with nothing but what is black, unfortunate, and disastrous, the melancholy forebodings of incomprehensible misery and ruin. The horror of solitude drives him back into society, and he comes again into the presence of mankind, astonished to appear before them loaded with shame and distracted with fear, in order to supplicate some little protection from the countenance of those very judges, who know he knows have already all unanimously condemned him. (p. 164)[2]

On the Higher Side of Life

To reinforce once again that Adam Smith (1759) had an exquisite understanding of human nature, in the very next paragraph that concludes the chapter, he elaborates on the higher side of human life:

> The opposite behaviour naturally inspires the opposite sentiment. The man who, not from frivolous fancy, but from proper motives, has performed a generous action, when he looks forward to those whom he served, feels himself to be the natural object of their love and gratitude, and, by sympathy with them, of the esteem and approbation of all mankind. And when he looks backward to the motive from which he acted, and surveys it in the light in which the indifferent spectator will survey it, he still continues to enter into it, and applauds himself by sympathy with the approbation of this supposed impartial judge. In both these points of view, his own conduct appears to him every way agreeable. His

mind, at the thought of it, is filled with cheerfulness, serenity, and composure. He is in friendship and harmony with all mankind, and looks upon his fellow-creatures with confidence, and benevolent satisfaction, secure that he has rendered himself worthy of their most favourable regards. In the combination of all these sentiments, consists the consciousness of merit, or of deserved reward. (p. 165)

HARRY STACK SULLIVAN ON COMPETITION, ENVY, AND THE MORBIDLY AMBITIOUS PERSON

The nature of competition varies with the level of personality development. In America, we value competition. The competitive way of life of a chronically juvenile person represents the arrest of development in the primitive range of the Personality Continuum. According to Sullivan (1953): "In what I call chronically juvenile people one sees a competitive way of life in which nearly everything that has real importance is part of a process of getting ahead of the other fellow. And if there is a malevolent transformation of personality, getting the other fellow down becomes the outstanding pattern in the integration of interpersonal relations. This is another of these instances of arrest of development" (p. 232).

Sullivan's conception of the *malevolent transformation* definitely fits into the primitive range of the Personality Continuum and represents a manifestation of splitting. Sullivan's motivation for formulating the concept of the malevolent transformation came out of his struggle with the concept of *evil*: "A great many years of preoccupation with this problem has eventuated in a theory which is calculated to get around the idea that man is essentially evil" (p. 213). Sullivan traces the origin of the malevolent transformation to the relatively enduring pattern of recurrent situations that characterized the early life of the child: "For a variety of reasons, many children have the experience that when they need tenderness, when they do that which once brought tender cooperation, they are not only denied tenderness, but they are treated in a fashion to provoke anxiety or even, in some cases, pain" (p. 214).

In the following elaboration of the malevolent transformation, Sullivan draws a clear distinction between situations that provoke anxiety and fear:

So one often learns costly ways of getting around anxiety-provoking and fear-provoking situations—costly in the sense that one never feels exceedingly good or worthy; and these ways of avoiding such situations are not greatly contributory to one's useful information and foresight about living. Thus there can occur this very serious distortion of what might be called the fundamental interpersonal attitude; and this distortion, this malevolence, as it is encountered in life, runs something like this: Once upon a time everything was lovely, but that was before I had to deal with people. (p. 216)

With such unfortunate early interpersonal experience, the child is forced to learn that he lives among enemies, according to Sullivan: "Under those circumstances, the developmental course changes to the point that the perceived need for tenderness brings a foresight of anxiety or pain. The child learns that, you see, that it is highly disadvantageous to show any need for tender cooperation from authoritative figures around him, in which case he shows something else; and that something else is the basic malevolent attitude, the attitude that one really lives among enemies" (p. 214). Finally, "There is literally the substitution of malevolent . . . behavior when there is a need for tenderness" (p. 202).

Malevolence is not only manifested in excessively aggressive behavior, but can also be manifested in "so-called timid children whose malevolence shows by their being so afraid to do anything that they just fail to do the things that are most urgently desired" (p. 213). Fairbairn (1952) described the little boy who would develop a schizoid personality organization in a similar way (p. 22) and concluded that the child feels that his love is bad because it appears destructive toward his loved objects (p. 25).

The striking behavioral manifestation of the malevolent transformation of personality is a pattern of competition that involves getting the other fellow down. The morbidly ambitious display a ruthless kind of behavior: "They are out to get the other fellow down, not because they have anything in particular against him or because they need any of his prestige marks—they intend to have much better prestige marks—but because he is in the way" (Sullivan 1956, p. 137). The ruthless pursuit of self-interest is characteristic of personality organizations at the primitive level of personality development, the narcissistic personality organization, in particular, especially when accompanied by clear antisocial tendencies, and in the more extreme case, the antisocial personality organization.

Narcissistic Vulnerability of the Grandiose Self

Failure and the refusal to compete are characteristic of the narcissistic personality organization and represent an expression of the vulnerability of the grandiose self:

A related issue is these patients' hypersensitivity to any "failure"; to them "failures" often mean not being able to be the first, the only one [unique, as in Sullivan's (1950) illusion of personal individuality], or the preferred one in a competitive situation. Inhibition of their competitiveness may be interpreted erroneously as an inhibition of oedipal rivalry, rather than stemming from narcissistic vulnerability of the grandiose self. It is often possible to help them become aware of the fact that they have to be winners of any competition or they will be unable to participate at all [i.e., the refusal to compete]; this is a frequent mechanism in school failures of borderline narcissistic adolescent patients. (Kernberg 1985A, p. 336)

Attitude toward Authority

The attitude toward authority is formed during childhood, according to Sullivan (1953): "It is from the second stage of personality development that a good deal of the foundations of one's attitude toward authoritative figures, superiors, and so on, is laid" (p. 216). It is during the stage of childhood that the malevolent transformation occurs: "Let me conclude by saying that the general conception of malevolence is of very considerable importance. It is perhaps the greatest disaster that happens in the childhood phase of personality development, because the kind of 'ugly'—as it often is called—attitude which it produces is a great handicap to the most profitable experience one could have in subsequent stages of development" (p. 216). With this understanding, Sullivan, I believe, has reached the heights of Fairbairn (1952) on the greatest disaster of childhood: "Failure on the part of the mother to convince the child that she really loves him as a person renders it difficult for him to sustain an emotional relationship with her on a personal basis" (p. 13).

Envy and Materialism

Envy was introduced as part of the basic character constellation of the narcissistic personality organization and was indicated as a cause of emptiness in a person with a narcissistic personality organization. Envy as a motivation for materialism is elaborated here.

Sullivan (1956) characterized the competitive way of life of a chronically juvenile individual clearly arrested at a primitive level of personality development as morbidly ambitious. He described such individuals as follows:

Now intensely competitive adults are people who continue to live at a relatively juvenile level—that is, who live as if they always have to prove that they are better than the other fellow. More specifically, the trait which is practically pathognomic for diagnosing a continued juvenile organization of interpersonal relations, or personality, is perverted or morbid ambition. The morbidly ambitious are extremely impatient, and sometimes horribly insecure under the impatience, about the speed at which they ascend to greater social position. (p. 137)

For the markedly envious person, material things come to have special meaning in interpersonal relationships: "And as a result the envious person comes to invest with importance all sorts of things which carry prestige or approval; he needs those things, he feels, to add to what he already has to demonstrate in the world, in order to be on an even footing with others" (p. 130). Hence the use of the term *prop* to mean material things that prop up one's insecurity. The narcissistic personality organization is particularly prone to envy and, therefore, to the material manifestations of envy to restore the primitive defense of splitting against severe anxiety. For personality organizations at the primitive level of personality development, an extreme manifestation of materialism is compulsive buying behavior.[3]

In a more general way, this represents what Duesenberry (1949) referred to as the "demonstration effect": "We can maintain then that the frequency and strength of impulses to increase expenditure depends on frequency of contact with goods superior to those habitually consumed. This effect need not depend at all on considerations of emulation or 'conspicuous consumption' " (pp. 27–28).

Duesenberry suggested self-observation as a way to experience the *relative deprivation* of the demonstration effect:

The best way to demonstrate that consumption expenditures can be forced up by contact with superior consumption goods is to ask the reader to consult his own experience. What kind of reaction is produced by looking at a friend's new car or looking at houses or apartments better than one's own? The response is likely to be a feeling of dissatisfaction with one's own house or car. If this feeling is produced often enough it will lead to action which eliminates it, that is, to increase expenditure. (p. 27)

Duesenberry found the source of this materialism in American culture: "In a fundamental sense the basic source of the drive toward higher consumption is to be found in the character of our culture. A rising standard of living is one of the major goals of our society" (p. 26).

The nature of the reaction to social comparison varies qualitatively with the level of personality development and the particular personality organization. The pursuit of material things becomes frantic as the person with a primitive personality organization tries to relieve intense envy: "As a result, the material trappings with which one frantically tries to relieve one's envy—and thereby magnifies it—grow apace" (Sullivan 1953, p. 135). A frantic pattern of behavior is characteristic of personality organizations in the primitive range of the Personality Continuum. The frantic pursuit of material things motivated by envy interferes with intimacy in interpersonal relationships:

> Because there is the unusually continuous insecurity, and the need for these irrational personalized props, such as Cadillac cars and one thing and another, the pursuit of satisfactions in interpersonal intimacies is apt to be poisoned and overcomplicated by efforts to remedy the insecurities. Thus while the tendency systems which would ordinarily result in the pursuit of satisfactions are not particularly distorted, the pursuit of satisfactions are always badly complicated by this property aspect of seeking security, which can, of course, reach rather fantastically revealing lengths. (Sullivan 1956, pp. 130–131)

Envy of the personal attributes of another person is related to envy of the props or personal attachments of another person:

> I define envy . . . as pertaining to personal attachments or attributes. It is a substitutive activity in which one contemplates the unfortunate results of someone else's having something that one does not have. And envy does not cease to be envy when it passes from objects to attributes of another human being, for envy may be an active realization that one is not good enough, compared with someone else. (Sullivan 1953, p. 348)

Thus it is the invidious comparison with another person that results in feelings of insecurity—severe anxiety—and the subjective experience of emptiness that has been explored in great depth with the narcissistic personality organization. A personal attribute of another person may include high intelligence, attractive good looks, physical gifts and athletic prowess, and body parts that constitute part-object relations, for example, the view of a woman by a promiscuous man with a narcissistic personality organization as a bundle of breasts, buttocks, cunt, and so on.

Sullivan (1956) believed that two aspects of American culture have had a disastrous effect on the evolution of the self of the envious person:

> The envious person's derogation of others naturally reflects the aspects of American culture that have been most disastrous to the evolution of an adequate self in these people. Here I refer to our singular dearth of good prescriptions for intimacy and accommodation to other people, coupled with our really staggering

success at doing things with our natural resources—both, I sometimes think, unparalleled thus far in history of man. (p. 134)

American culture has failed to prepare the individual for intimacy as he or she struggles ceaselessly at doing things with America's rich resources with staggering success in the relentless individual pursuit of self-interest. It is just this material manifestation of envy as a substitutive activity that Bob Dylan warned against in the song "Dear Landlord" on his soul-searching album *John Wesley Harding* (1968):

> And anyone can fill his life up
> With things he can see but he just cannot touch.

America, the Chronically Juvenile

Sullivan (1972) once speculated that cultures could be classified according to his heuristic stages of personality development. Sullivan saw America as being in the juvenile era of development: "If we now classify cultures on the basis of stages of personality growth—thereby attempting a genetic anthropology—the suggestion appears that, in several aspects at least, our offshoot of Western culture is an *early juvenile culture*" (p.158). Sullivan's speculation has clear implications for the economic motivation to achieve upward social mobility, to be a success in America, the most powerful economic motivation. According to Sullivan (1953), "Arrest in the juvenile era is not by any means an extraordinarily unusual developmental disorder among people in this culture and in these times" (p. 279).

Sullivan (1953) saw the flaw in American culture: "The degree to which the need for intimacy is satisfied . . . in the present-day American scene leaves much to be desired. The reason is not that the shift of interest toward the other sex in itself makes intimacy difficult, but that the cultural influences which are borne in upon each person include very little which prepares members of different sexes for a fully human, simple, personal relationship together" (p. 264). Sullivan, seeming somewhat cynical, I think, does see the significance of someone's sex life in a positive light: "In this culture the ultimate test of whether you can get on or not is whether you can do something satisfactory with your genitals or somebody else's genitals without undue anxiety and loss of self-esteem" (p. 294). This is the interpersonal achievement in personality development that demarcates the normal range of the Personality Continuum: Full integration of satisfying genital sexual relations into an interpersonal relationship by successfully resolving the oedipal situation. In Sullivan's view, the failure to achieve intimacy explains our preoccupation with sex in America: "Our culture is the least adequate in preparing one for meeting the eventualities of sexual maturity, which is another way of saying we are the most sex-ridden people on the face of the globe" (p. 289).

FORTUNATE INTERPERSONAL EXPERIENCE AND FAVORABLE CHANGE IN PERSONALITY: SULLIVAN'S THRESHOLD HYPOTHESIS

Sullivan (1953) was somewhat pessimistic about the prospects for favorable change in the personality organization of a chronologically adult person. He speaks of chance rather than hope: "The only chance that a person has then—except by an act of God—is through psychiatry. And how small that chance is has become more and more overwhelmingly apparent to me the longer I live" (p. 298).

Sullivan was optimistic about favorable change at the *threshold of each stage of personality development*: "It is in general true that, as one passes over one of these more-or-less determinable thresholds of a developmental era, everything that has gone before becomes reasonably open to influence" (p. 227). This is Sullivan's threshold hypothesis: The opportunity for favorable change in the personality organization, through fortunate interpersonal experience, arises at each developmental threshold.

> The changes which take place at the thresholds of the developmental eras, as outlined here, are far-reaching; they touch upon much of what has already been acquired as personality, often making it somewhat acutely inadequate, or at any rate not fully relevant for the sudden new expanding of the personal horizon. Thus the beginning phase of a developmental era may considerably affect those inappropriate aspects of personality which emerge from what the person has undergone up to then. (p. 228)

The threshold hypothesis holds for fortunate and unfortunate interpersonal experiences:

> I believe I have said earlier that it is at the developmental thresholds that the chance for notable favorable change tends to segregate itself. Although the structure of the self-system is such that its development in general is rather powerfully directed along the lines it has already taken, it is much more subject to

influence through new experience, either fortunate or unfortunate, at each of the developmental thresholds. The fact that the self-system can undergo distinct change early in each of the developmental stages is of very real significance. (p. 247)

For the chronologically adult person, fortunate interpersonal experience provides an opportunity for favorable change in the personality organization at any point in the human life cycle. The person is challenged once again with the same interpersonal achievement in personality development that earlier resulted in the arrest in personality development. Fortunate interpersonal experience at any point in life, therefore, provides an opportunity to achieve a higher level of personality development.

Sullivan's Orientation in Living and Moments of Illumination

Sullivan's (1953) concept of *orientation in living* provides a useful conception of the integrative aspects of normal personality development: "The degree to which one is adequately oriented in living is, I believe, a very much better way of indicating what we often have in mind when we speak about how 'well integrated' a person is, or what his 'character' is in the sense of good, bad, or indifferent" (pp. 243–244). Sullivan described these opportunities to improve one's orientation in living as *moments of illumination*: "These occur when, by extremely fortunate circumstance, one actually sees, to a considerable extent, a real situation that he had been selectively inattending to previously, so that he is really better oriented" (p. 362). This insight must be reached by the person: "This means that the patient must obtain new insight into himself, for otherwise the psychiatrist has no confirmation of his surmises and they are quite therapeutically useless" (Sullivan 1940, p. 97). Ultimately, Sullivan (1940) was optimistic that genuine insight would lead to favorable change in the personality organization, because "personality tends towards the state that we call mental health" (p. 97).

Genuine Insight and the Urge for Meaningful Change

It is worth repeating that genuine insight leads to an urge toward meaningful change in a positive way in the person with a normal personality organization. In comparison, the borderline personality organization, in the primitive range of the Personality Continuum, has available primary-process thinking: "Meaningful insight, in contrast to the simple availability of primary process material in conscious and preconscious mental life of borderline patients, refers to the combination of intellectual and emotional understanding of deeper sources of one's psychic experience, accompanied by concern for and an urge to change the pathological aspects of that experience" (Kernberg 1985A, p. 141).

In the case of a primitive personality organization, insight that comes too easily is questionable, because it does not result in a change in the individual's intrapsychic equilibrium (a use of the term *equilibrium* that should appeal to economists): "Insight which may come without any effort, is not accompanied by any change in the patient's intrapsychic equilibrium, and above all, is not accompanied by any concern on the patient's part for the pathological aspects of his behavior or experience, is questionable insight" (pp. 92–93).

For a person with a primitive personality organization, the paranoid transformation is the far more common unfortunate outcome, according to Sullivan (1953):

> But far more common than these fortunate illuminations is the onrushing of this paranoid transformation of personality—the transfer of blame—in which the person suddenly "sees it all." The beginning of this process comes literally as a sudden insight into some suspicion and comes with a blaze of horror. The suspicion may have hovered around before the sudden insight, and may have been marked by a little uncanniness; but with the insight, one has started living in a world in which not-me has become personified, very active, and very absorptive of one's weaknesses [Sullivan's use of single quotation marks]. (p. 362)

The transfer of blame is the essence of the paranoid transformation: "One is a victim, not of one's own defects, but of a devilish environment. One is not to blame; the environment is to blame" (Sullivan 1956, p. 146). But the paranoid transfer of blame is easily falsified, leaving the person subject to severe anxiety: "The person who has only transferred blame is always at the mercy of someone who is not taken in and who starts an inquiry. He is in the same position that all of us find ourselves in at times when we discover in the moment of saying something that is not so, or at least that we cannot prove it, which is quite an insecure situation to be in" (1956, p. 148).[4]

Optimism of American Object Relations Theory: Fortunate Interpersonal Experience

There is a fundamental optimism for the prospect of favorable change in the personality organization in American object relations theory. The optimism is based on the continuous internalization of interpersonal relationships throughout life. This is why fortunate interpersonal experience provides the person with the opportunity for favorable change in the personality organization. I have mentioned before Kernberg's case studies on individuals who achieved a higher level of personality development through fortunate interpersonal experience later in life in "Mature Love: Prerequisites and Characteristics" (1974 B), one of his three important articles on intimacy.

Sullivan's threshold hypothesis has illuminated our understanding of the fundamental interpersonal basis for change in the personality organization. Favorable change in a person's personality organization is the result of a fortunate change in the relatively enduring pattern of recurrent interpersonal situations that characterize a person's life.

Kernberg (1985A) has questioned the direction of causation in change in the personality organization between rapid changes in social stability and cultural values, on the one hand, and changes in interpersonal relations, on the other: "The question has been posed of whether contemporary social and cultural changes have affected patterns of object relations" (p. 223). He also weighs the contribution of rapid shifts in social stability and cultural values to the experience of emptiness and futility: "An important question has been raised in recent years regarding the relation between the subjective experience of futility and emptiness, on the one hand, and the rapid breakdown or shifts in social stability and cultural values, on the other" (p. 223). Kernberg concludes that rapid changes in social stability and cultural values do not cause changes in interpersonal relations and therefore do not bring about change in the personality organization: "On the basis of the analysis underlying what I have said so far, I do not think that changes in contemporary culture have effects on patterns of object relations, if we define object relations not simply in terms of actual interactions between a person and others, but in terms of the intrapsychic structures that govern such interactions, and in terms of the internal capacity to relate in depth with others" (p. 223).

What is important is that favorable or unfavorable change in the personality organization is based on fortunate or unfortunate change, respectively, in the relatively enduring pattern of recurrent interpersonal situations that characterize a person's life. In other words, a significant change in a person's interpersonal relationships, fortunate or unfortunate, is necessary for a change in the personality organization:

It seems to me that one has to make a distinction between the effects of social disorganization, of severe disruption of the family structure and of earliest child development (all of which have a definite impact on the development of the personality), and the effects of rapid cultural change reflected in changing social and sexual mores: these latter do not, I think, bring about chronic experiences of emptiness and futility, unless there exists severe pathology of internalized object relations which stems from infancy and early childhood. (p. 223)

Thus chronic experiences of emptiness and futility are not brought about by "rapid cultural change reflected in changing social and sexual mores." Further, according to Kernberg, the need and capacity for intimacy is not changed by changes in contemporary morality:

> By the same token, I do not think that changes in contemporary morality have changed the need and the capacity for intimacy in various forms. That is not to say that such changes in the patterns of intimacy could not occur over periods of several generations, if and when changes in cultural patterns affect family structure to such an extent that the earliest development in childhood would be influenced. (p. 223)

It is the relatively enduring intrapsychic structure of the personality organization that must be changed by fortunate or unfortunate interpersonal experience. Sullivan (1953) held similar ideas on durable and favorable change from interpersonal experience: "As I have said several times, there is a good deal of evidence to show that all the way down to the level of the amoeba there is actually favorable—that is, profitable—durable change from experience." "So I say that experience either *is* the useful durable change, or that it *brings about* the useful durable change in the function of the living organism" (p. 64).

The emphasis here, however, is on rapid changes in social stability and cultural values. When social instability and cultural change are *prolonged*, they may change the relatively enduring pattern of recurrent interpersonal situations that characterize a human life, and that may result in changes in the intrapsychic structure of the personality organization. A fundamental change in the personality organization, therefore, requires a relatively enduring change in interpersonal relationships.

NOTES

1. How can Bill Clinton, the former president of the United States, repair the damage he did on January 21, 1998, by wagging his finger at the television camera and lying with a straight face to the American people in a humiliating public display, "I did not have sex with that woman, Ms. Lewinsky"? In Clinton's final press release, shortly before leaving office on January 20, 2001, he

said, "I tried to walk a fine line between acting lawfully and testifying falsely, but now I recognize that I did not fully accomplish this goal and certain of my responses to questions about Ms. Lewinsky were false."

For a bit of historical perspective, I added this quotation in response to a reviewer's questioning of whether Clinton really did lie. To find the text of this press release, I walked from my study into the family room and picked up my copy of the *New York Times* of Saturday, January 20, 2001, inauguration day. I added this footnote on January 24, 2001, less than a week later. Only time will tell.

In the primitive range of the Personality Continuum, and for the narcissistic personality organization in particular, impulses are crudely gratified (e.g., a blow job for President Clinton by Monica Lewinsky in the pantry of the Oval Office, lurid details known from the Starr Report promulgated instantaneously on the Internet, or sex in a closet at a party for President Kennedy before him). At the moment of self-indulgence, such a man could not foresee the consequences that the crude gratification of his impulses would bring, and was myopic and willing to take the risk. There is no self-control, no delay of gratification, and no limit to the gratification. The unforeseen risk is that of dishonor. Bill Clinton dishonored the office of the president of the United States.

2. It is hard not to think of O.J. Simpson when I read this passage by Smith. To paraphrase, there is no escape into solitude for him, because he remembers himself what he has done, and his own thoughts haunt him for the irreparable evil that was done. He is haunted by the return of bad objects—the images of Nicole Brown and Ronald Goldman—against which all defenses have broken down, and from which there is no escape, except in death. He is secretly pursued by the avenging furies of shame and remorse, fast pursuing him and every moment ready to overtake him from behind, as the punitive superego persecutes him with severe anxiety until death.

3. For an application to marketing, see Belk (1985) on materialism.

4. Sullivan (1953) has commented on the way we sometimes fool ourselves: "Thus the most accessible aspects of the self-system in many late adolescents show such superficially incomprehensible falsifications in the person's view of himself that he is not apt to learn very much in this field unless somebody goes to a great deal of trouble to put him through educative experience" (p. 301).

Epilogue

PROBABILITY DISTRIBUTION OF THE PERSONALITY CONTINUUM

Speculation about the stage of personality development of America leads to a related question with respect to the Personality Continuum: What is the probability distribution over the Personality Continuum (Figure E.1)? What proportion of the chronologically adult population of the United States is distributed into the normal, neurotic, primitive, and psychotic ranges of the Personality Continuum? The probability distribution of the Personality Continuum is purely speculative at this point. What do you think? What are the implications if it is a normal distribution?

THE OPEN ROAD OF RESEARCH

It would not be fitting to reduce a book with integration as the prime directive to a concluding statement. I can only look down the open road of research. For me that is a validated technique for the classification of a person's personality organization along the Personality Continuum. I have proposed the template matching technique for personality classification using the California Adult Q Sort. The theoretical basis for the template matching technique was provided in Albanese (1990) and prom-

Figure E.1
The Probability Distribution of the Personality Continuum

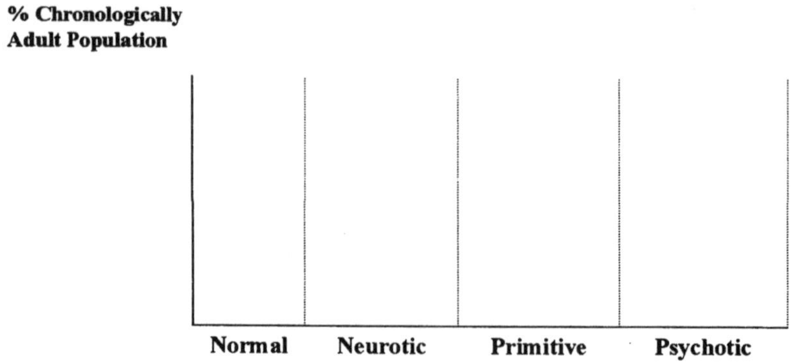

ising preliminary empirical results were reported in Albanese (1993). A validated technique for personality classification along the Personality Continuum would open the way to a wealth of information for the individual, the clinician, and the researcher.

A NEW BEGINNING

REFERENCES

Ainslie, George (1985). "Beyond Microeconomics: Conflict among Interests in a Multiple Self as a Determinant of Value." In Jon Elster, editor, *The Multiple Self.* Cambridge: Cambridge University Press, pp. 133–175.

Ainslie, George (1987). "Self-Reported Tactics of Impulse Control." *International Journal of the Addictions* 22, 2, pp. 167–179.

Albanese, Paul J. (1982). "Toward a Methodology for Investigating the Formation of Preferences." Ph.D. dissertation, Harvard University, March.

Albanese, Paul J. (1987). "The Nature of Preferences: An Exploration of the Relationship between Economics and Psychology." *Journal of Economic Psychology* 8, 1 (March), pp. 3–18.

Albanese, Paul J. (1988A). "The Changing Motivation for Having Children." In Shlomo Maital, editor, *Applied Behavioural Economics*. London: Wheatsheaf Books, pp. 255–268.

Albanese, Paul J. (1988B). "The Formation and Change of Fertility Preferences." *Journal of Behavioral Economics* 17, 1 (Spring), pp. 35–55.

Albanese, Paul J., editor (1988C). *Psychological Foundations of Economic Behavior*. New York: Praeger.

Albanese, Paul J., editor (1988D). "Symposium on Preference Formation." *Journal of Behavioral Economics* 17, 1 (Spring).

Albanese, Paul J. (1989). "The Paradox of Personality in Marketing: A New

Approach to the Problem." In Paul Bloom, et al., editors, *Enhancing Knowledge Development in Marketing*. Chicago, IL: American Marketing Association, pp. 245–249.

Albanese, Paul J. (1990). "Personality, Consumer Behavior, and Marketing Research: A New Theoretical and Empirical Approach." In Elizabeth C. Hirschman, editor, *Research in Consumer Behavior*, vol. 4. Greenwich: JAI Press, pp. 1–50.

Albanese, Paul J. (1991). "Behavioral Economics, Psychological Economics, and Socioeconomics: Object Relations Theory at the Crossroads." In Roger Frantz, Harinder Singh, and James Gerber, editors, *Handbook of Behavioral Economics*, vol. 2A, *Behavioral Environments*. Greenwich: JAI Press, pp. 19–34.

Albanese, Paul J. (1993). "Personality and Consumer Behavior: An Operational Approach." *European Journal of Marketing* 27, 8, pp. 28–37.

American Psychiatric Association (1980). *Diagnostic and Statistical Manual of Mental Disorders* (DSM-III). 3rd ed. Washington, DC: American Psychiatric Association.

American Psychiatric Association (1994). *Diagnostic and Statistical Manual of Mental Disorders* (DSM-IV). 4th ed. Washington, DC: American Psychiatric Association.

Bagozzi, Richard P. (1992). "The Self-Regulation of Attitudes, Intentions, and Behavior." *Social Psychology Quarterly* 55, pp. 178–204.

Balint, Michael (1932). "Character Analysis and the New Beginning." In *Primary Love and Psycho-analytic Technique*. New York: Da Capo Press, 1986, pp. 159–173.

Balint, Michael (1936). "Eros and Aphrodite." In *Primary Love and Psycho-analytic Technique*. New York: Da Capo Press, 1986, pp. 73–89.

Balint, Michael (1937A). "Early Developmental States of the Ego. Primary Object Love." *Imago* 23, pp. 270–288 (in German). Published in English in 1949, *International Journal of Psycho-analysis* 30, pp. 265–273. In *Primary Love and Psycho-analytic Technique*. New York: Da Capo Press, 1986, pp. 90–108.

Balint, Michael (1937B). "Frühe Entwicklungsstadien des Ichs Primäre Objektliebe." *Imago* 23, pp. 270–288.

Balint, Michael (1947). "On Genital Love." In *Primary Love and Psycho-analytic Technique*. New York: Da Capo Press, 1986, pp. 128–140.

Balint, Michael (1949). "Early Developmental States of the Ego. Primary Object Love." *International Journal of Psycho-analysis* 30, pp. 265–273. Reprinted in Michael Balint (1986). *Primary Love and Psycho-analytic Technique*. New York: Da Capo Press, pp. 90–108.

Balint, Michael (1951). "On Love and Hate." In *Primary Love and Psycho-analytic Technique*. New York: Da Capo Press, 1986, pp. 141–158.

Balint, Michael (1959). *Thrills and Regressions*. New York: International Universities Press.

Balint, Michael (1979). *The Basic Fault: Therapeutic Aspects of Regression.* New York: Brunner-Mazel.

Balint, Michael (1986). *Primary Love and Psycho-analytic Technique.* New York: Da Capo Press. (Reprint of original edition published in 1953 by Liveright Publishing.)

Barker-Benfield, G.J. (1976). *The Horrors of the Half-Known Life: Male Attitudes toward Women and Sexuality in Nineteenth-Century America.* New York: Harper & Row.

Baumol, William J. (1972). *Economic Theory and Operations Analysis.* 3rd ed. Englewood Cliffs, NJ: Prentice-Hall.

Bearden, William O., F. Kelley Shuptrine, and Jesse E. Teel (1991). "Self-Monitoring: Relationships to Different Advertising Appeals." In Mary C. Gilly, et al., editors, *Enhancing Knowledge Development in Marketing.* Chicago, IL: American Marketing Association, pp. 204–209.

Becker, Gary S. (1965). "A Theory of the Allocation of Time." *Economic Journal* 75, 299 (September), pp. 493–517. Reprinted in Gary S. Becker, *The Economic Approach to Human Behavior.* Chicago: University of Chicago Press, 1976, pp. 89–114.

Becker, Gary S. (1981). *A Treatise on the Family.* Cambridge, MA: Harvard University Press.

Becker, Gary S., and Robert T. Michael (1973). "On the New Theory of Consumer Behavior." *Swedish Journal of Economics* 75, 4 (December), pp. 378–396.

Beebe-Center, J.G. (1932). *The Psychology of Pleasantness and Unpleasantness.* Princeton, NJ: Van Nostrand.

Belk, Russell W. (1975). "Situational Variables and Consumer Behavior." *Journal of Consumer Research* 2 (December), pp. 157–164.

Belk, Russell W. (1985). "Materialism: Trait Aspects of Living in the Material World." *Journal of Consumer Research* 12 (December), pp. 265–280.

Belk, Russell W. (1988). "Possessions and the Extended Self." *Journal of Consumer Research* 15 (September), pp. 139–168.

Benson, April Lane, editor (2000). *I Shop, Therefore I Am: Compulsive Buying and the Search for Self.* Northvale, NJ: Jason Aronson.

Blackwell, Roger G., Paul W. Miniard, and James F. Engel (2001). *Consumer Behavior.* 9th ed. Orlando, FL: Harcourt College Publishers.

Blake, William (1996). "Proverbs of Hell." In Michael Mason, editor, *Selected Poetry.* New York: Oxford University Press, pp. 76–78.

Bly, Robert (1990). *Iron John: A Book about Men.* Reading, MA: Addison-Wesley.

Bowles, Samuel, and Herbert Gintis (1976). *Schooling in Capitalist America: Educational Reform and the Contradictions of Economic Life.* New York: Basic Books.

Buss, Arnold H. (1989). "Personality as Traits." *American Psychologist* 44, 11 (November), pp. 1378–1388.

Chasseguet-Smirgel, Janine (1974). "Perversion, Idealization, and Sublimation." *International Journal of Psycho-analysis* 55, pp. 349–357.

Chasseguet-Smirgel, Janine (1975). *l'Idéal du Moi. Essai sur la Maladie d'Idéalité*. Paris: Tchou.

Choca, James P., Luke A. Shanley, and Eric Van Denburg (1992). *Interpretative Guide to the Millon Clinical Multiaxial Inventory*. Washington, DC: American Psychological Association.

Chodorow, Nancy (1978). *The Reproduction of Mothering: Psychoanalysis and the Sociology of Gender*. Berkeley: University of California Press.

Coleman, James S. (1984). "Introducing Social Structure into Economic Analysis." *American Economic Review* 74, 2 (May), pp. 84–88.

Corbitt, E.M. (1994). "Narcissism from the Perspective of the Five-Factor Model." In P.T. Costa and T.A. Widiger, editors, *Personality Disorders and the Five-Factor Model of Personality*. Washington, DC: American Psychological Association, pp. 199–204.

Costa, P.T. and R.R. McCrae (1992). "Normal Personality Assessment in Clinical Practice: The NEO Personality Inventory," *Psychological Assessment* 4, 1, pp. 5–13.

Costa, P.T., and T.A. Widiger, editors (1994). *Personality Disorders and the Five-Factor Model of Personality*. Washington, DC: American Psychological Association.

Craig, Robert J., editor (1993). *The Millon Clinical Multiaxial Inventory: A Clinical Research Information Synthesis*. Hillsdale, NJ: Lawrence Erlbaum.

Deshpande, Rohit, Wayne D. Hoyer, and Naveen Donthu (1986). "The Intensity of Ethnic Affiliation: A Study of the Sociology of Hispanic Consumption." *Journal of Consumer Research* 13 (September), pp. 214–219.

Dichter, Ernest (1960). *The Strategy of Desire*. Garden City, NY: Doubleday.

Dichter, Ernest (1971). *Motivating Human Behavior*. New York: McGraw-Hill.

Digman, J.M. (1990). "Personality Structure: Emergence of the Five-Factor Model." *Annual Review of Psychology* 41, pp. 417–440.

Duesenberry, James S. (1949). *Income, Saving, and the Theory of Consumer Behavior*. Cambridge, MA: Harvard University Press.

Dylan, Bob (1985). *Lyrics, 1962–1985*. New York: Alfred A. Knopf.

Easterlin, Richard A. (1969). "Towards a Socioeconomic Theory of Fertility: A Survey of Recent Research on Economic Factors in American Fertility." In S.J. Behrman, L. Corsa, Jr., and R. Freedman, editors, *Fertility and Family Planning: A World View*. Ann Arbor: University of Michigan Press, pp. 127–156.

Easterlin, Richard A., Robert A. Pollak, and Michael L. Wachter (1980). "Toward a More General Economic Model of Fertility Determination: Endogenous Preferences and Natural Fertility." In Richard A. Easterlin, editor, *Population and Economic Change in Developing Countries*. Chicago: University of Chicago Press, pp. 81–150.

Edgeworth, Francis Y. (1967). *Mathematical Psychics: An Essay on the Application of Mathematics to the Moral Sciences*. New York: A.M. Kelley.

Elster, Jon, editor (1985). *The Multiple Self*. Cambridge: Cambridge University Press.

Emerson, Ralph Waldo (1968). "Self-Reliance." In Brooks Atkinson, editor, *The Selected Writings of Ralph Waldo Emerson*. New York: Modern Library, pp. 145–169.

Erikson, Erik H. (1950). *Childhood Society*. 2nd ed. New York: W.W. Norton.

Etzioni, Amitai (1985). "Opening the Preferences: A Socio-economic Research Agenda." *Journal of Behavioral Economics* 14 (Winter), pp. 183–206.

Evans, Franklin B. (1959). "Psychological and Objective Factors in the Prediction of Brand Choice." *Journal of Business* 32 (October), pp. 340–369.

Faber, Ronald J., and Thomas C. O'Guinn (1988). "Compulsive Consumption and Credit Abuse." *Journal of Consumer Policy* 11, 1, pp. 97–109.

Faber, Ronald J., Thomas C. O'Guinn, and Raymond Krych (1987). "Compulsive Consumption." In Melanie Wallendorf and Paul Anderson, editors, *Advances in Consumer Research* 14. Provo, UT: Association for Consumer Research, pp. 132–135.

Fairbairn, W.R.D. (1941). "A Revised Psychopathology of the Psychoses and Psychoneuroses." *International Journal of Psycho-analysis*, 22, pp. 250–279. Reprinted in W.R.D. Fairbairn (1952). *Psychoanalytic Studies of the Personality*. London: Routledge & Kegan Paul, pp. 28–38.

Fairbairn, W.R.D. (1944). "Endopsychic Structure Considered in Terms of Object Relationships." *International Journal of Psycho-analysis*, 25, pp. 70–93. Reprinted in W.R.D. Fairbairn (1952). *Psychoanalytic Studies of the Personality*. London: Routledge & Kegan Paul, pp. 82–136.

Fairbairn, W.R.D. (1952). *Psychoanalytic Studies of the Personality*. London: Routledge & Kegan Paul.

Fairbairn, W.R.D. (1954). "Observations on the Nature of Hysterical States." *British Journal of Medical Psychology* 27, 3, pp. 105–125.

Fairbairn, W.R.D. (1955). "Observations in Defence of the Object-Relations Theory of the Personality." *British Journal of Medical Psychology* 28, pp. 144–156.

Fairbairn, W.R.D. (1963). Synopsis of an Object—Relations of the Personality." *International Journal of Psycho-analysis* 44, 2, pp. 224–225.

Fishbein, Martin (1963). "An Investigation of the Relationship between Beliefs about an Object and the Attitude toward That Object." *Human Relations* 16, pp. 233–239.

Foxall, Gordon R. (1983). *Consumer Choice*. London: Macmillan.

Foxall, Gordon R, and Ronald E. Goldsmith (1989). "Personality and Consumer Research: Another Look." *Journal of Marketing Research* 30, 2, pp. 111–125.

Frank, Robert H. (1985). *Choosing the Right Pond*. New York: Oxford University Press.

Frank, Robert H., Thomas Gilovich, and Dennis T. Regan (1993). "Does Studying Economics Inhibit Cooperation?" *Journal of Economic Perspectives* 7, 2 (Spring), pp. 159–172.

Franz, Marie-Louise von (1981). *Puer Aeternus*. 2nd ed. Santa Monica, CA: Sigo Press.

Freedman, Deborah (1963). "The Relation of Social Status to Fertility." *American Economic Review* 53 (June), pp. 414–426.

Freud, Anna (1966). *The Ego and the Mechanisms of Defense*, Rev. ed. (based on 1937 Translation). New York: International Universities Press.

Freud, Sigmund (1900). *The Interpretation of Dreams*. In James Strachey, editor, *The Standard Edition of the Complete Psychological Works of Sigmund Freud*, vol. 4. London: Hogarth Press, 1953.

Freud, Sigmund (1915A). "Repression." In James Strachey, editor, *The Standard Edition of the Complete Psychological Works of Sigmund Freud*, vol. 14. London: Hogarth Press, 1957, pp. 146–158.

Freud, Sigmund (1915B). "The Unconscious." In James Strachey, editor, *The Standard Edition of the Complete Psychological Works of Sigmund Freud*, vol. 14. London: Hogarth Press, 1957, pp. 159–215.

Freud, Sigmund (1917A). "Mourning and Melancholia." In James Strachey, editor, *The Standard Edition of the Complete Psychological Works of Sigmund Freud*, vol. 14. London: Hogarth Press, 1957, pp. 243–258.

Freud, Sigmund (1917B). "Resistance and Repression." In James Strachey, editor, *The Standard Edition of the Complete Psychological Works of Sigmund Freud*, vol. 16. London: Hogarth Press, 1963, pp. 286–302.

Freud, Sigmund (1917C). "The Sexual Life of Human Beings." In James Strachey, editor, *The Standard Edition of the Complete Psychological Works of Sigmund Freud*, vol. 16. London: Hogarth Press, 1963, pp. 303–319.

Freud, Sigmund (1923). *The Ego and the Id*. In James Strachey, editor, *The Standard Edition of the Complete Psychological Works of Sigmund Freud*, vol. 19. London: Hogarth Press, 1961, pp. 12–66.

Freud, Sigmund (1933). "The Dissection of the Psychical Personality." *New Introductory Lectures on Psycho-analysis*. In James Strachey, editor, *The Standard Edition of the Complete Psychological Works of Sigmund Freud*, vol. 22. London: Hogarth Press, 1964, pp. 57–80.

Geertz, Clifford (1973). *The Interpretation of Cultures*. New York: Basic Books.

Geertz, Clifford (1980). "Blurred Genres: The Refiguration of Social Thought." *American Scholar*, 49, 2, pp. 165–179.

Georgescu-Roegen, Nicholas (1954). "Choice, Expectations, and Measurability." *Quarterly Journal of Economics* 69, 4 (November), pp. 503–534.

Gilligan, Carol (1982). *In a Different Voice: Psychological Theory and Women's Development*. Cambridge, MA: Harvard University Press.

Goethals, George W. (1973). "Symbiosis and the Life Cycle." *British Journal of Medical Psychology* 46, 1, pp. 91–96.

Goethals, George W. (1976). "The Evolution of Sexual and Genital Intimacy: A Comparison of the Views of Erik H. Erikson and Harry Stack Sullivan." *Journal of the American Academy of Psychoanalysis* 4, 4, pp. 529–44.

Goethals, George W. (1980). Instructions to a student.

Grinspoon, Lester (1971). *Marihuana Reconsidered.* Cambridge, MA: Harvard University Press.

Guntrip, Harry (1973). *Psychoanalytic Theory, Therapy and the Self: A Basic Guide to the Human Personality in Freud, Erikson, Klein, Sullivan, Fairbairn, Hartmann, Jacobson, and Winnicott.* New York: Basic Books.

Hagen, Everett E. (1962). *On the Theory of Social Change: How Economic Growth Begins.* Cambridge, MA: Massachusetts Institute of Technology.

Haire, Mason (1950). "Projective Techniques in Marketing Research." *Journal of Marketing* 14, 5 (April), pp. 649–656.

Hall, Calvin S., and Gardner Lindzey (1957). *Theories of Personality.* 1st ed. New York: John Wiley & Sons.

Hall, Calvin S., and Gardner Lindzey (1970). *Theories of Personality.* 2nd ed. New York: John Wiley & Sons.

Hall, Calvin S., and Gardner Lindzey (1978). *Theories of Personality.* 3rd ed. New York: John Wiley & Sons.

Hall, Stephen S. (1999). "Fear Itself." *New York Times Magazine*, February 28. p. 42.

Hicks, John R. (1934). "A Reconsideration of the Theory of Value." *Economica* n.s., 1 (February), pp. 52–76.

Hicks, John R. (1946). *Value and Capital: An Inquiry into Some Fundamental Principles of Economic Theory.* Oxford: Clarendon Press.

Hirschman, Albert O. (1982). *Shifting Involvements: Private Interest and Public Action.* Princeton: Princeton University Press.

Hirschman, Elizabeth C., editor (1989). *Interpretive Consumer Research.* Provo, UT: Association for Consumer Research.

Hirschman, Elizabeth C. (1991). "Secular Morality and the Dark Side of Consumer Behavior: How Semiotics Saved My Life." In Rebecca H. Holman and Michael R. Solomon, editors, *Advances in Consumer Research* 18. Provo: UT: Association for Consumer Research, pp. 1–4.

Hirschman, Elizabeth C. (1992). "Recovering from Drug Addiction: A Phenomenological Account." In John F. Sherry and Brian Sternthal, editors, *Advances in Consumer Research* 19. Provo, UT: Association for Consumer Research, pp. 541–549.

Hirschman, Elizabeth C., and Morris B. Holbrook (1982). "Hedonic Consumption: Emerging Concepts, Methods, and Propositions." *Journal of Marketing* 46 (Summer), pp. 92–101.

Hobbes, Thomas (1950). *Leviathan.* New York: E.P. Dutton.

Holbrook, Morris B. (1988). "The Psychoanalytic Interpretation of Consumer

Behavior: I Am an Animal." In Elizabeth C. Hirschman and Jagdish N. Sheth, editors, *Research in Consumer Behavior*, vol. 3. Greenwich, CT: JAI Press, pp. 149–178.

Holbrook, Morris B. (1992). "Patterns, Personalities, and Complex Relationships in the Effects of Self on Mundane Consumption: These are 495 of My Most and Least Favorite Things." In John F. Sherry and Brian Sternthal, editors, *Advances in Consumer Research* 19, Provo, UT: Association for Consumer Research, pp. 417–423.

Holbrook, Morris B. (1995). *Consumer Research: Introspective Essays on the Study of Consumption*. Thousand Oaks, CA: Sage Publications.

Holbrook, Morris B., and Elizabeth C. Hirschman (1982). "The Experiential Aspects of Consumption: Consumer Fantasies, Feelings, and Fun." *Journal of Consumer Research* 9 (September), pp. 132–140.

Jacobson, Edith (1964). *The Self and the Object World*. New York: International Universities Press.

Jacoby, Jacob (1969). "Personality and Consumer Behavior: How *Not* to Find Relationships." In *Purdue Papers in Consumer Psychology*, no. 102. Lafayette, IN: Purdue University, pp. 1–13.

James, William (1884). "What Is Emotion?" *Mind* 9, pp. 188–205.

Jung, Carl G. (1924). *Psychological Types; or, The Psychology of Individuation*. London: Kegan Paul, Trench, Trubner & Co.

Kapteyn, Arie, and T. Wansbeek (1982). "Empirical Evidence on Preference Formation." *Journal of Economic Psychology* 2, pp. 137–54.

Kassarjian, Harold H. (1971). "Personality and Consumer Behavior: A Review." *Journal of Marketing Research* 8 (November), pp. 409–418.

Kassarjian, Harold H., and M.J. Sheffet (1975). "Personality and Consumer Behavior: One More Time." In E.M. Mazze, editor, *Combined Proceedings*. Chicago: American Marketing Association, pp. 197–201.

Kassarjian, Harold H., and M.J. Sheffet (1981). "Personality and Consumer Behavior: An Update." In Harold H. Kassarjian and Thomas S. Robertson, editors, *Perspectives in Consumer Behavior*. 3rd ed. Englewood Cliffs, NJ: Prentice-Hall, pp. 160–180.

Kassarjian, Harold H., and M.J. Sheffet (1991). "Personality and Consumer Behavior: An Update." In Harold H. Kassarjian and Thomas S. Robertson, editors, *Perspectives in Consumer Behavior*, 4th ed. Englewood Cliffs, NJ: Prentice-Hall, pp. 281–303.

Kernberg, Otto F. (1966). "Structural Derivatives of Object Relationships." *International Journal of Psycho-analysis* 47, pp. 236–253. Reprinted in Otto F. Kernberg (1984). *Object-Relations Theory and Clinical Psychoanalysis*. New York: Jason Aronson, pp. 19–54.

Kernberg, Otto F. (1967). "Borderline Personality Organization." *Journal of the American Psychoanalytic Association*, 15, 3 (July), pp. 641–685. Reprinted in Otto F. Kernberg (1985). *Borderline Conditions and Pathological Narcissism*. New York: Jason Aronson, pp. 3–48.

Kernberg, Otto F. (1968). "The Treatment of Patients with Borderline Personality Organization." *International Journal of Psycho-analysis*, 49, pp. 600–619. Reprinted in Otto F. Kernberg (1985). *Borderline Conditions and Pathological Narcissism.* New York: Jason Aronson, pp. 69–110.

Kernberg, Otto F. (1970). "Factors in the Psychoanalytic Treatment of Narcissistic Personalities." *Journal of the American Psychoanalytic Association*, 18, 1 (January), pp. 51–85. Reprinted in Otto F. Kernberg (1985). *Borderline Conditions and Pathological Narcissism.* New York: Jason Aronson, pp. 227–262.

Kernberg, Otto F. (1971). "Prognostic Considerations Regarding Borderline Personality Organization." *Journal of the American Psychoanalytic Association*, 19, 4 (October), pp. 595–635. Reprinted in Otto F. Kernberg (1985). *Borderline Conditions and Pathological Narcissism.* New York: Jason Aronson, pp. 111–152.

Kernberg, Otto F. (1972). "Early Ego Integration and Object Relations." *Annals of the New York Academy of Sciences*, 193, pp. 233–247.

Kernberg, Otto F. (1974A). "Barriers to Falling and Remaining in Love." *Journal of the American Psychoanalytic Association* 22, pp. 486–511. Reprinted in Otto F. Kernberg (1984). *Object-Relations Theory and Clinical Psychoanalysis*. New York: Jason Aronson, pp. 185–213.

Kernberg, Otto F. (1974B). "Mature Love: Prerequisites and Characteristics." *Journal of the American Psychoanalytic Association* 22, pp. 743–768. Reprinted in Otto F. Kernberg (1984). *Object-Relations Theory and Clinical Psychoanalysis*. New York: Jason Aronson, pp. 215–239.

Kernberg, Otto F. (1974C). "Further Contributions to the Treatment of Narcissistic Personalities." *The International Journal of Psycho-analysis*, 55, pp. 215–240. Reprinted in Otto F. Kernberg (1985). *Borderline Conditions and Pathological Narcissism.* New York: Jason Aronson, pp. 263–314.

Kernberg, Otto F. (1977). "Boundaries and Structure in Love Relations." *Journal of the American Psychoanalytic Association* 25, pp. 81–114. Reprinted in Otto F. Kernberg (1985). *Internal World and External Reality: Object Relations Theory Applied.* New York: Jason Aronson, pp. 277–305.

Kernberg, Otto F. (1978). "Leadership and Organizational Functioning: Organizational Regression." *International Journal of Group Psychotherapy* 28, pp. 3–25.

Kernberg, Otto F. (1979). "Regression in Organizational Leadership." *Psychiatry* 42 (February), pp. 24–39.

Kernberg, Otto F. (1984A). *Object-Relations Theory and Clinical Psychoanalysis*. New York: Jason Aronson.

Kernberg, Otto F. (1984B). *Severe Personality Disorders: Psychotherapeutic Strategies*. New Haven: Yale University Press.

Kernberg, Otto F. (1985A). *Borderline Conditions and Pathological Narcissism.* New York: Jason Aronson.

Kernberg, Otto F. (1985B). *Internal World and External Reality: Object Relations Theory Applied.* New York: Jason Aronson.

Kets de Vries, F.R. Manfred, and Danny Miller (1984). *The Neurotic Organization.* San Francisco: Jossey-Bass.

Kets de Vries, F.R. Manfred, and Danny Miller (1988). "Personality, Culture, and Organization: A Conceptual Framework." In Paul J. Albanese, editor, *Psychological Foundations of Economic Behavior*. New York: Praeger, pp. 81–100.

Keynes, John Maynard (1936). *The General Theory of Employment, Interest, and Money*. New York: Harcourt, Brace, & World.

Kris, Ernst (1952). *Psychoanalytic Explorations in Art*. New York: International Universities Press.

Kuznets, Simon (1966). *Modern Economic Growth*. New Haven: Yale University Press.

Lasch, Christopher (1978). *The Culture of Narcissism: American Life in an Age of Diminishing Expectations*. New York: W.W. Norton.

Lastovicka, John L., and Erich M. Joachimsthaler (1988). "Improving the Detection of Personality—Behavior Relationships in Consumer Research." *Journal of Consumer Research* 14 (March), pp. 583–587.

Lazarus, Richard S. (1991). "Cognition and Motivation in Emotion." *American Psychologist* 46, 4 (April), pp. 352–367.

Leibenstein, Harvey (1975). "The Economic Theory of Fertility Decline." *Quarterly Journal of Economics* 89, 1 (February), pp. 1–31.

Leibenstein, Harvey (1976). *Beyond Economic Man: A New Foundation for Microeconomics*. Cambridge, MA: Harvard University Press.

Lennon, John W. (1971). *Imagine*. EMI Records.

Levitt, Theodore (1960). "Marketing Myopia." *Harvard Business Review* 38 (July–August), pp. 45–56.

Levy, Sidney J. (1992). "Constructing Consumer Behavior: A Grand Template." In John F. Sherry and Brian Sternthal, editors, *Advances in Consumer Research* 19. Provo, UT: Association for Consumer Research, pp. 1–6.

Maital, Shlomo (1982). *Minds, Markets, and Money: Psychological Foundations of Economic Behavior*. New York: Basic Books.

Marshall, Alfred (1920). *Principles of Economics*, 8th ed. London: Macmillan.

Marwell, Gerald, and Ruth E. Ames (1981). "Economists Free Ride, Does Anyone Else?" *Journal of Public Economics* 16, pp. 295–310.

McCrae, R.R., and O.R. John (1992). "An Introduction to the Five-Factor Model and Its Applications," *Journal of Personality*, 60, pp. 175–215.

Meyer, Donald B. (1980). *The Positive Thinkers: Religion as Pop Psychology from Mary Baker Eddy to Oral Roberts*. New York: Pantheon Books.

Millon, Theodore (1981). *Disorders of Personality: DSM-III: Axis II*. New York: John Wiley & Sons.

Miniard, Paul W., and Joel B. Cohen (1979). "Isolating Attitudinal and Normative Influences in Behavioral Intentions Models." *Journal of Marketing Research* 16 (February), pp. 102–110.

Miniard, Paul W., and Joel B. Cohen (1981). "An Examination of the Fishbein-Ajzen Behavioral-Intentions Model's Concepts and Measures." *Journal of Experimental Social Psychology* 17, 3 (May), pp. 309–339.

Miniard, Paul W., and Joel B. Cohen (1983). "Modeling Personal and Normative Influences on Behavior." *Journal of Consumer Research* 10 (September), pp. 169–180.

Mowen, John C. (2000). *The 3M Model of Motivation and Personality: Theory and Empirical Applications to Consumer Behavior*. Boston: Kluwer Academic Publishers.

Nakanishi, Masao (1972). "Personality and Consumer Behavior: Extensions." In M. Venkatesan, editor, *Proceedings 3rd Conference*. College Park, MD: Association for Consumer Research, pp. 61–65.

O'Guinn, Thomas C., and Ronald J. Faber (1989). "Compulsive Buying: A Phenomenological Exploration." *Journal of Consumer Research* 16, 2 (September), pp. 147–157.

Parsons, Talcott (1964). "The Superego and the Theory of Social Systems." In *Social Structure and Personality*. London: Free Press, pp. 17–33.

Perry, Helen Swick (1982). *Psychiatrist of America: The Life of Harry Stack Sullivan*. Cambridge, MA: Belknap Press of Harvard University Press.

Pierson, George Wilson (1938). *Tocqueville and Beaumont in America*. New York: Oxford University Press.

Piore, Michael J. (1979). *Birds of Passage: Migrant Labor and Industrial Societies*. New York: Cambridge University Press.

Pollak, Robert A., and Michael L. Wachter (1975). "The Relevance of the Household Production Function and Its Implications for the Allocation of Time." *Journal of Political Economy* 83, 2 (April), pp. 255–278.

Rapaport, David (1957). "Cognitive Structures." In *Contemporary Approaches to Cognition: A Symposium Held at the University of Colorado*. Cambridge, MA: Harvard University Press, pp. 157–200.

Rapaport, David, and Merton M. Gill (1959). "The Points of View and Assumptions of Metapsychology." *International Journal of Psycho-Analysis* 40, pp. 153–62.

Rapaport, David, Merton M. Gill, and Roy Schafer (1968). *Diagnostic Psychological Testing*, Rev. ed. New York: International Universities Press.

Rogers, Martha, and Christine A. Seiler (1994). "The Answer Is No: A National Survey of Advertising Industry Practitioners and Their Clients about Whether They Use Subliminal Advertising." *Journal of Advertising Research* 34, 2 (March/April), pp. 36–45.

Rogers, Martha, and Kirk H. Smith (1993). "Public Perceptions of Subliminal Advertising: Why Practitioners Shouldn't Ignore This Issue." *Journal of Advertising Research* 33, 2 (March/April), pp. 10–18.

Rook, Dennis W. (1987). "The Buying Impulse." *Journal of Consumer Research* 14 (September), pp. 189–199.

Saldanha, Fernando B., and Pierre-Jean Lancry (1988). "A Psychological Opponent Processes Theory of Consumption." In Shlomo Maital, editor, *Applied Behavioural Economics*, vol. I. London: Wheatsheaf Books, pp. 114–133.

Samuelson, Paul A. (1947). *Foundations of Economic Analysis*. Cambridge, MA: Harvard University Press.

Schelling, Thomas C. (1980). "The Intimate Contest for Self-Command." *Public Interest* 60, pp. 94–118.

Schelling, Thomas C. (1984). "Self-Command in Practice, in Policy, and in a Theory of Rational Choice." *American Economic Review* 74, pp. 1–11.

Schumpeter, Joseph A. (1934). *The Theory of Economic Development*. Cambridge, MA: Harvard University Press.

Schumpeter, Joseph A. (1954). *History of Economic Analysis*. New York: Oxford University Press.

Scitovsky, Tibor (1976). *The Joyless Economy: An Inquiry into Human Satisfaction and Consumer Dissatisfaction*. New York: Oxford University Press.

Sen, Amartya K. (1977). "Rational Fools: A Critique of the Behavioral Foundations of Economic Theory." *Philosophy and Public Affairs* 6, pp. 317–344.

Shapiro, David (1965). *Neurotic Styles*. New York: Basic Books.

Smith, Adam (1759). *The Theory of Moral Sentiments*. Indianapolis: Liberty Fund, 1976.

Smith, Adam (1776). *An Inquiry into the Nature and Causes of the Wealth of Nations*. New York: Modern Library, 1937.

Smith, Kirk H., and Martha Rogers (1994). "Effectiveness of Subliminal Messages in Television Commercials: Two Experiments." *Journal of Applied Psychology* 79, 6, pp. 866–874.

Solomon, Richard L. (1980). "The Opponent-Process Theory of Acquired Motivation: The Costs of Pleasure and the Benefits of Pain." *American Psychologist* 35, 8 (August), pp. 691–712.

Solomon, Richard L. (1988). "How the Opponent Process Theory of Acquired Motivation Came into Economics." In Paul J. Albanese, editor, *Psychological Foundations of Economic Behavior*. New York: Praeger, pp. 31–34.

Solomon, Richard L., and John D. Corbit (1974). "An Opponent-Process Theory of Motivation: I. Temporal Dynamics Affect." *Psychological Review* 81, 2, pp. 119–345.

Stigler, George J., and Gary S. Becker (1977). "De Gustibus Non Est Disputandum." *American Economic Review* 67, 2 (March), pp. 76–90.

Strotz, R.H. (1955–1956). "Myopia and Inconsistency in Dynamic Utility Maximization." *Review of Economic Studies* 23, 62, pp. 165–180.

Sullivan, Harry Stack (1940). *Conceptions of Modern Psychiatry*. New York: W.W. Norton.

Sullivan, Harry Stack (1950). "The Illusion of Personal Individuality." *Psychiatry* 13, pp. 317–332. Reprinted in Harry Stack Sullivan (1964). *The Fusion of Psychiatry and Social Science*. New York: W.W. Norton, pp. 198–228.

Sullivan, Harry Stack (1953). *The Interpersonal Theory of Psychiatry*. New York: W.W. Norton.

Sullivan, Harry Stack (1956). *Clinical Studies in Psychiatry*. New York: W.W. Norton.

Sullivan, Harry Stack (1964). *The Fusion of Psychiatry and Social Science*. New York: W.W. Norton.

Sullivan, Harry Stack (1972). *Personal Psychopathology: Early Formulations*. New York: W.W. Norton.

Sweezy, Alan R. (1934). "The Interpretation of Subjective Value Theory in the Writings of the Austrian Economists." *Review of Economic Studies* 1, 3, pp. 176–185.

Taylor, Lester D. (1986). "Opponent Processes and the Dynamics of Consumption." In Alan J. MacFadyen and Heather W. MacFadyen, editors, *Economic Psychology: Intersections in Theory and Application*. Amsterdam: North-Holland, pp. 135–161.

Taylor, Lester D. (1988). "A Model of Consumption and Demand Based on Psychological Opponent Processes." In Paul J. Albanese, editor, *Psychological Foundations of Economic Behavior*. New York: Praeger, pp. 35–57.

Tocqueville, Alexis de (1945). *Democracy in America*, Vol. 2. New York: Alfred A. Knopf.

Trull, T.J., and R.R. McCrae (1994). "A Five-Factor Perspective on Personality Disorder Research." In P.T. Costa and T.A. Widiger, editors, *Personality Disorders and the Five-Factor Model of Personality*. Washington, DC: American Psychological Association, pp. 59–72.

Vaillant, George E. (1977). *Adaptation to Life*. Boston: Little, Brown & Company.

Watts, Alan (1961). *Psychotherapy, East and West*. New York: Pantheon House.

Watts, Alan (1970). *Nature, Man, and Woman*. New York: Vintage Books.

Webster, Frederick E., Jr. (1988). *Rediscovering the Marketing Concept*. Cambridge, MA: Marketing Science Institute, Report 88–100.

Weizsäcker, Carl Christian von (1971). "Notes on Endogenous Change of Tastes." *Journal of Economic Theory* 3, 4, pp. 345–372.

Wells, William D., and A.D. Beard (1973). "Personality and Consumer Behavior." In S. Ward and Thomas S. Robertson, editors, *Consumer Behavior*. Englewood Cliffs, NJ: Prentice-Hall, pp. 141–191.

Wells, William D., and Leonard A. Lo Sciuto (1966). "Direct Observation of

Purchasing Behavior." *Journal of Marketing Research* 3 (August), pp. 227–233.

Whalen, Paul J., Scott L. Rauch, Nancy L. Etcoff, Sean C. McInerney, Michael B. Lee, and Michael A. Jenike (1998). "Masked Presentations of Emotional Facial Expressions Modulate Amygdala Activity without Explicit Knowledge." *Journal of Neuroscience* 18, 1 (January), pp. 411–418.

White, Timothy (1994). *The Nearest Far Away Place: Brian Wilson, the Beach Boys, and the Southern California Experience*. New York: Henry Holt & Company.

Whyte, William F. (1955). *Street Corner Society: The Social Structure of an Italian Slum*, 2nd ed. Chicago: University of Chicago Press.

Widiger, Thomas A., and Allen J. Francis (1994). "Toward a Dimensional Model for the Personality Disorders." In Paul T. Costa and Thomas A. Widiger, editors, *Personality Disorders and the Five-Factor Model of Personality*. Washington, DC: American Psychological Association, pp. 19–39.

Wiggins, J.S., and A.L. Pincus (1992). "Personality: Structure and Assessment." *Annual Review of Psychology* 43, pp. 473–504.

Winnicott, D.W. (1953). "Transitional Objects and Transitional Phenomena: A Study of the First Not-Me Possession." *International Journal of Psychoanalysis* 34, 2, pp. 89–97.

Winnicott, Donald W. (1955). "The Depressive Position in Normal Emotional Development." *British Journal of Medical Psychology* 28, pp. 89–100.

Winnicott, D.W. (1963). "The Development of the Capacity for Concern." *Bulletin of the Menninger Clinic* 27, pp. 167–176. Reprinted in D.W. Winnicott (1965). *The Maturational Processes and the Facilitating Environment: Studies in the Theory of Emotional Development*. New York: International Universities Press, 1965, pp. 73–82.

Winnicott, Donald W. (1965). *The Maturational Processes and the Facilitating Environment: Studies in the Theory of Emotional Development*. New York: International Universities Press.

Winston, Gordon C. (1980). "Addiction and Backsliding: A Theory of Compulsive Consumption." *Journal of Economic Behavior and Organization* 1, pp. 295–324.

Young, Paul T. (1961). *Motivation and Emotion: A Survey of Human and Animal Activity*. New York: John Wiley & Sons.

Zajonc, Robert B. (1980). "Feeling and Thinking: Preferences Need No Inferences." *American Psychologist* 35, 2, pp. 151–175.

Zaleznik, Abraham (1988). "Decisions, Coalitions, and the Economy of the Self." In Paul J. Albanese, editor, *Psychological Foundations of Economic Behavior*. New York: Praeger, pp. 101–142.

Zanot, Eric J., J. David Pincus, and E. Joseph Lamp (1983). "Public Perception of Subliminal Advertising." *Journal of Advertising* 12, 1 (November), pp. 39–45.

INDEX

About the Author

PAUL J. ALBANESE is Assistant Professor of Marketing at Kent State University. An economist by training, he has spent the past 20 years researching personality and consumer behavior.